P9-DGU-954

Quiltmaking by Hand

Simple Stitches, Exquisite Quilts

Jinny Beyer

BP
Breckling Press

Library of Congress Cataloging-in-Publication Data

Beyer, Jinny.
Quiltmaking by hand : simple stitches, exquisite quilts / Jinny Beyer.— 1st ed.
p. cm.
Includes bibliographical references and index.
ISBN 0-9721218-2-X
1. Patchwork—Patterns. 2. Quilting—Patterns. 3. Patchwork quilts.
I. Title.
TT835.B443 2003
746.46—dc22

2003015827

Acknowledgments

My thanks to all those who helped make this book possible, my editor, Anne Knudsen, art director, Kim Bartko, photographers Sharon Hoogstraten and Steve Tuttle, and illustrator Kandy Petersen. Thanks to Morna McEver Golletz of *The Professional Quilter.* Morna attended one of my classes and learned how I use a small hole-punch to indicate on my templates the exact spot where seam allowances cross. She suggested the idea of a set of master-templates with pre-punched holes. Many design drafts and prototypes later, I created *Jinny Beyer Perfect Piecer,* featured on page 56.

Thanks to Jill Amos Gibbons who not only allowed her quilt to be used in the book, but also helped with proofreading, and to several others for lending their quilts and for the moral support they gave me: Carole Nicholas, Paola Novara, my niece Tanis Rovner, and my daughter and son-in-law, Kiran and Rob Wardwell.

Special thanks to my husband, John, who, once again, had to undergo added chaos during the final stages of completing the project.

This book was set in Walbaum Book and Didot by Bartko Design, Inc.
Editorial direction by Anne Knudsen
Art direction, cover and interior design by Kim Bartko, Bartko Design, Inc.
Photography by Sharon Hoogstraten
All quilt photographs, other than quilts in environments and details on pages 117, 160, and 163 (*Columbia*), by Steve Tuttle
Technical drawings by Kandy Petersen
Pattern writing by Jinny Beyer and Helen J. Gregory

All antique quilts and vintage sewing notions, including pincushions, thimbles, and chatelaines, are from the collection of Jinny Beyer. All antique needlework calligraphy and the illustrations on pages 18, 22, and 25 were originally published in *La Mode Illustrée*, issues dated from 1871 to 1876.

Published by Breckling Press
283 Michigan, Elmhurst
IL 60126 USA

Printed and bound in Canada
International Standard Book Number: 0-9721-2182-X

Dedication

To the memory of my mother, Pauline Kahle, who taught me to sew when I was a small child and passed her enthusiasm for learning, her perseverance, and her creative spark on to me, my sisters, her grandchildren and great-grandchildren.

You gain Knowledge from lessons in books.
You gain Wisdom from the lessons of life.

Pauline Kahle, *9 January,* 2002

Contents

Introduction: What Was Old Is New Again *1*

Chapter 1

The Fabric Stash and Other Quilting Essentials *6*

Chapter 2

A Primer on Pattern Drafting *30*

Chapter 3

Preparing to Sew *48*

Chapter 4

Piecing Basics: Running Stitch, Squares, and Rectangles *62*

Chapter 5

Beyond the Basics: Bias Edges, Angles, and Points *84*

"Then you thread a needle and settle comfortably in your chair. The needle runs easily back and forth through soft cloth while nerves relax and useless worries fade away. Smoothing out a finished block, you have a pleasant sense of achievement. You are making a thing of beauty that generations to come will prize."

Rose Wilder Lane,
The Woman's Day Book of American Needlework, 1964

Chapter 6

Piecing Mastery: Setting-In Angles and Piecing Curves *106*

Chapter 7

Enriching Patchwork Designs with Border Prints *126*

Chapter 8

Borders for Quilts *142*

Chapter 9

Preparing to Quilt *158*

Chapter 10

Quilting and Finishing *180*

Ten Hand-Pieced Quilts *198*

Templates *244*

Bibliography *259*

Index *260*

Windows. *Designed, hand-pieced, and hand-quilted by Jinny Beyer, 2002*

What Was Old Is New Again

"[This quilt] is an outburst of joy . . . At the sight of it, every face brightens. How can . . . mere pieces of cloth sewed together have this power to lift the human spirit? No one can explain this; it is the mystery of art."

Rose Wilder Lane,
The Woman's Day Book of American Needlework, 1963

IT IS A WONDER TO MANY OF US THAT WOMEN OF PAST GENERATIONS had the time to hand stitch the beautiful heirloom quilts that have survived to this day. Considering the endless list of household tasks that fell to their lot–fetching water, growing vegetables, canning and preserving foods, gathering eggs, making, mending, and washing clothes–it is truly amazing women found time to sew patchwork projects. Yet sew them they did, often in evening hours by candlelight and always by hand. The sewing basket rested next to the chair and in "found" moments here and there throughout the day, a few stitches would be taken. Those quiet, restful moments accumulated until the quilt top was complete.

The making of my quilt *Windows,* featured on the cover of this book, took me back to those days long gone when women made patchwork in found moments. *Windows* was made in the aftermath of the terrible events that rocked the world on September 11, 2001. My husband John and I were to leave on a two-week vacation to Italy that day. Looking out the window early that bright, sunny morning, I imagined viewing Italian arches and cathedral floors that would inspire a new quilt design. Others looked out windows that day as well . . . windows of airplanes, windows of the World Trade Center, windows of emergency vehicles. We all watched the windows of our televisions, stunned and dazed.

In those first few days after the attacks, the world was filled with visions of smoke and ash. Yet amid the rubble, flags danced defiantly, showing through the grays that were ever present in our minds. As events spiraled, we delayed our plans to visit Italy. Even so, I was compelled to begin my quilt. Studying a floor plan of St. Mark's Cathedral in Venice, I selected one of the designs as the inspiration for the central circle and began sorting fabrics. I selected faded reds, whites, and blues tinged with smoke and ash. But I also chose occasional vibrant reds, colors that represent our strength, courage, and spirit. As the drone of fighter planes broke the silence up above, I cut pieces and sewed. To me, it was therapy, a brief respite from the world outside. As I pieced patches together, I visualized looking down from the Windows on the World restaurant at the Statue of Liberty standing proudly below. The star in the center and the flags and statues around the outermost circle represent Liberty's crown.

My goal in making *Windows* was to have at least one piece for each victim of the attacks. The fabric in the very center is a tribute for a friend who was in the plane that crashed into the Pentagon. The quilt contains 4,777 pieces and is hand pieced and hand quilted. The last stitch was taken on October 5, 2002.

Piecing in Found Moments

People are often in awe when they learn that I stitch all of my quilts by hand. Since the quilts I make tend to be very large, they wonder how I can possibly have enough time to get it all done and maintain a busy schedule of designing, teaching, and writing. I reply that I don't have time to stitch by machine! To sew by machine requires having a block of time set aside. It means getting out the sewing machine, setting it up, filling the bobbin, finding a new needle, setting up the ironing board, and on and on. Machine quilting, after all, is not a very portable activity. Sewing by machine also means that you most likely won't sit and sew while keeping your husband company as he watches the Super Bowl. For one, he probably wouldn't stand for the noise! When I am at home, I never have the blocks of free time that it takes to piece by machine. If I do, I usually prefer to spend that time in the garden. I always have a quilt set up on a quilting frame and, when I do find I have any extra time, I will sit and hand quilt. I keep a headset by the phone and, if I receive a phone call that is going to take quite a bit of time, I put on the headset and either quilt, or do some hand stitching.

Almost all of my piecing is done on-the-go, when I am out of the house. You would be amazed at how much sewing you can get done in found moments throughout the day. I sew in doctor's offices, in the car, on trains, on airplanes, in airports, and in traffic jams. When my children were small, I sewed at their sporting events. Several years ago there were long lines at the gas station. I would have lost my sanity if I hadn't had some stitching to do while I sat and waited. I always have a little bag of stitching to carry with me wherever I go. I advise you to do the same, because you never know when you might have a little bit of time to take a few stitches, and you will be amazed at how much you can get done in those found moments when you would otherwise be doing nothing at all. Like me, you will come to cherish the times when you can quietly stitch–and your final quilt will have so many more memories attached to it because of where you were when you pulled out your little bag of sewing.

The whole secret to piecing on-the-go is to have the pieces you need for a complete block cut out, organized, and at the ready. I sort the pieces and arrange them into blocks or units in the way they will be sewn and pin each group together. I put them in a zip-lock plastic bag. That way, I can just pull out one of the pinned groups and start stitching. I keep these little bags, along with my sewing supplies, in a larger plastic bag, but all of this fits in my purse or tote bag. When I have a found moment, I take out my little baggie of pieces, slip on a thimble, thread a needle, and stitch.

Columbia. *Designed, hand-pieced, and hand-quilted by Jinny Beyer, 2003*

Starflower. *Designed by Jinny Beyer. Hand-pieced and hand-quilted by Paola Novara, 2002*

Beginning Hand Piecing

Many new quilters will look at a quilt and feel it is just too difficult to tackle. Two of the quilt projects in this book, *Columbia* and *Starflower*, are ones that I designed specifically for beginning hand-piecing classes. I deliberately presented these as "Mystery Quilts"–the quilt is completed block by block and students do not know how the final quilt will look until the last block is done. During each class a new technique is taught, and students are sent home to complete some sewing using that particular technique. We begin with simple seams and progress to joining different numbers of points, sewing curves, and setting in pieces. At the next to last class we bring all the disparate pieces together and see how they join in the final quilt design. At the last class we have great fun seeing all of the different combinations and how beautiful all the quilt tops are. Everyone is always amazed and pleased with what they have done. Many students have told me that if they had seen the quilt project first they would have never signed up for the class. They would have thought it would be too difficult for them.

The information in this book is presented in a manner very similar to my Mystery Quilt classes, with each chapter building on skills learned in the pre-

*Detail from **Windows**.*
See full quilt on cover

vious one. You will quickly progress from sewing a simple running stitch to working with triangles, diamonds, and curved pieces. Every step is photographed in amazing detail, so that you can see and learn precise yet comfortable hand movements. You will have plenty of practice to master each new skill before you move on to the next. At the end of the book, there are ten quilt patterns, each focused on particular techniques. There is even a *Mariners' Compass,* a pattern that many experienced quilters are in awe of. You will find that by using the techniques described in *Quiltmaking by Hand,* even *Mariners' Compass* is within your quiltmaking ability. Similarly, the quilt on the cover of this book, *Windows,* often strikes viewers as difficult to sew. Yet if there is any difficulty at all, it has nothing to do with the stitching technique. Rather, it lies in the number and arrangement of pieces in the quilt and the perseverance it takes to sew them all together. You will see as you read through the chapters that follow that once you master the basic running stitch and a few other simple techniques, you will have the skills to sew pieces together to make any quilt you wish.

You will find as you sew that your stitching style may differ from mine. Just remember that there are no rules. Quilting is what you want it to be. Practice, find a rhythm that is comfortable, and then begin a project. Cut out enough pieces at one time for a little bag full patches and then enjoy those "found" moments as you quietly stitch, reflect, and create your own special quilt.

CLOPEDIA
LEWORK

The Fabric Stash

And Other Quilting Essentials

"A basket of patchwork held its place upon a low stool (bankje) beside the chair, also to be snatched up at odd intervals."

The Social History of Flatbush, quoted in Marie D. Webster, *Quilts: Their Story and How to Make Them*, 1915

Over the centuries, sterling silver thimbles, scissors, elegant chatelaines, and other unique needlework tools have been finely crafted for the needlewoman. These items were admired, coveted, given as gifts, and lovingly used and cherished. Yet, for the most part, generations of quilters made do with minimal supplies and created perfectly pieced quilts that have lasted a hundred years or more. All it took was a needle and thread, a thimble, a pair of sharp scissors, cardboard or stiff paper for making templates, batting or other stuffings, and, of course, fabric.

Fabric, Glorious Fabric

For hundreds of years, quilters made the most of the materials they had on hand and caring for those materials was part of a daily routine. Fabrics, often scarce, were chosen then handled with the utmost care. Nothing was wasted, and every last scrap made its way into the scrap basket. Many of those eventually found a spot in a quilt.

Today, many quilters will tell you that they had "collected" fabrics long before they began to quilt. A love of beautiful prints and colors lures many of us to simply amass as many as we can. One day while in a quilt shop I overheard one woman say to another, "I just love this fabric, but I promised myself

I wouldn't purchase any more until I used up some of what I already have." Her friend commented back, "Maybe I've missed something. Are we supposed to *use* it?"

Since making a quilt by hand takes time and care, it is important that all the materials that go into it should be of the best possible quality. This is particularly important when choosing fabrics. Traditional patchwork is made with 100 percent cotton, "apparel weight" fabric. (*Apparel weight* is the fabric industry's description of the type of cloth that typical blouses or men's shirts are made from.) Today, quilt stores almost exclusively stock 100 percent cotton fabrics.

Quick Tip

My advice to any new quilter is to start building a fabric stash. For instance, instead of buying five yards of a print that you don't think you can live without, purchase 20 quarter-yard pieces of different fabrics and start building your own spectrum of colors.

When I began quilting in the early 1970s, there was not a wide variety of cotton prints to choose from. Most 100 percent cottons were either solid colors or small-scale, multi-colored calicos. Today there are thousands of prints available, all in a rainbow of colors and produced by some fine manufacturers. I have been designing fabric for RJR Fabrics since 1984 and have been very pleased with the standard of excellence that this company maintains. There are also many other fabric manufacturing companies, among them Hoffman California Fabrics, Moda, and Benartex, who produce quality fabric for quilters. Quilt shop owners today recognize the time and effort that goes into quilting and make every effort to stock only the best fabrics. Yet it is impossible for any one shop to stock all that is available. In fact, part of the fun of quiltmaking is visiting different shops and finding hundreds of new fabrics in each one! You can feel secure purchasing fabrics from an established quilt shop, which typically offers a better quality of fabric that will needle better, wash better, hold color better, and stand the test of time.

"Many of the scrap quilts . . . are very pretty when made from gay pieces—carefully blended—of the various shades of a single color. The stars in the design . . . are made of a great variety of different patterns of pink calico, yet the blending is so good that the effect is greatly heightened by the multiplicity of shades."

Marie D. Webster,
Quilts: Their Story & How to Make Them, 1915

Fabrics of All Colors

Greeted by hundreds of fabrics in an array of colors in the quilt shop, in addition to a possible stash at home, many quilters become overwhelmed when it comes to selecting colors for a project. When I first began quilting, I worked with fabrics and colors instinctively. But as I began teaching, students wanted to know how I selected colors and fabrics to go into a quilt. During the ensuing years my color system evolved. Simple and fun to work with, my system is based on four basic principles. First, whatever colors you select, make sure you have several shades of those colors. Second, always have a color that is darker

Day Lilies. *See full quilt in pattern section*

Orange/purple

Red/dull peach

Khaki/gray

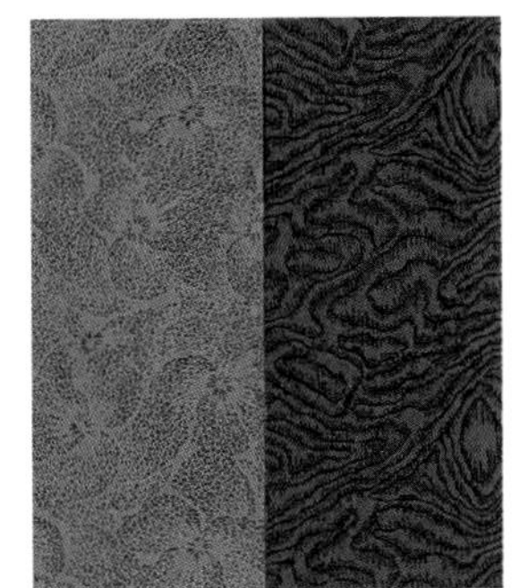

Grayed purple/brown

than the general range of colors you are working with (the *deep dark*). Third, always have a color that is a brighter shade of one of the colors you are working with (the *accent*). Finally, make sure to have some neutral colors such as brown, gray, taupe, or khaki.

All these conditions can be met if you follow this simple process. Whatever colors you choose, select other colors to add to them that will allow you to *shade* those colors together. Think of a rainbow, where you never can tell where one color ends and the other begins. What you see is a smooth blending of colors. That is what you want to achieve when you create a palette of colors for a quilt–a smooth, subtle blending of all the colors where they shade from one color to the next. This will not only give you several shades of the colors you have selected, but will also force you to add other colors that allow you to blend those original colors together.

How do you go about shading colors together? There are many different ways. You can go darker and darker with each of the colors until you can join them through black; you can go lighter and lighter with the colors until you can join them through lights; or you can blend through medium tones. If you practice and work at this simple concept, you will find that in the end you have an exciting color scheme that automatically includes the essential ingredients of a successful palette–several shades of the colors, neutrals, the deep dark, and the accent.

I believe that any colors look good together. It is not the colors you choose, but what you put *with* them that makes the difference. In class, I have my students select two colors that they would never ever use together. Very often, these pairings are chosen–orange and purple, red and dull peach, khaki and gray, grayed purple and brown.

I gather all of those colors together and ask how many people would select any of these as the basis for a quilt. Most people think these colors do not look good together. At this time, I open out my quilt, *Day Lilies*, shown in the pattern section, and I explain that every one of those colors is in the quilt. Regard-

Three ways to shade from yellow to periwinkle

Portable Palette by Jinny Beyer

THE PORTABLE PALETTE is a tool I designed for selecting colors for quilts. It contains a swatch of each of the 150 colors in RJR Fabrics' *Jinny Beyer Color Palette* fabric collection. I use this tool for the selection of all of my colors for quilts. The prints are all tonal, which allows for easy shading. The swatches can be moved around, and different color swatches can be arranged so that they shade together in a wide range of possibilities. Once you have created a color palette by pulling out all the swatches similar to the colors you want to include in your quilt, simply check your fabric stash to find the colors in your palette. You can then take the Portable Palette shopping with you to fill in where necessary from your local quilt store. The illustrations here show different ways that the same two colors can be shaded together. Just pick up the Palette, choose two colors, and shade away!

less of the individual colors, it is the fabrics added to them, allowing all the colors to shade together smoothly, that make for a pleasing palette.

I like to use many different fabrics in my quilts. But some people want to use only a few and want to know how to select the ones that will look the best. One good way to develop a color palette is to select a multi-colored "theme" print that you like, identify all the colors within the print, and then shade those colors together. This will automatically show you which colors you need to add to make your palette complete. However, I advise against trying to find fabrics that exactly match the theme print. I believe that the more shades of colors you select, the better. So, even if you are going to limit the number of fabrics that will be used, why repeat a color when you already have it in the theme fabric? Instead of trying to exactly match a color to the print, find a color that is a little darker, a little brighter, a little lighter, or a little duller than each of the colors in the print. Make sure that one of the fabrics is the deep dark and another the accent.

"Opinions vary much as to the age when a little girl may safely be instructed in sewing; and each mother will be guided in this matter by the nature of her own child, some little ones being sufficiently advanced to commence at three years of age."

Cassell's Household Guide to Every Department of Practical Life, Volume IV, circa 1875

Selecting Fabrics

You've selected a palette of colors. What next? Remember that your palette is simply a guide. When I select colors for a new quilt, this does not mean I will use those exact fabrics; it means that I need fabrics that contain each of those colors. Now is the time to go to your fabric stash and find all the prints you have that will blend with the palette. Try to select a good balance in the scale and type of print. Choose large-, medium-, and small-scale prints as well as ones with different types of designs–florals, plaids, checks, or geometrics. Decorative border-print fabrics add a unique touch to a quilt design, and I incorporate at least one of these into each of my quilts. (Chapter Seven explains how to work with border prints). Try to have a good balance between tonal and multi-colored prints. If you are still missing some of the colors that are in your shaded palette, then fill in the gaps from your local quilt shop.

Snow Birds. *Designed, hand-pieced, and hand-quilted by Jinny Beyer, 1999. This quilt contains all 150 colors in the Jinny Beyer Color Palette.*

My color system depends upon having a wide variety of colors from which to choose, either from your own stash or from a nearby quilt shop that stocks a wide range of printed fabrics. Several years ago I realized that anyone doing embroidery, cross stitch, needlepoint, or crewel work had access to threads and yarns in a wide range of colors. These were standard colors and always available. Looking around at the fabrics then available to quilters, I realized that there were gaps in the range of color choices–and as long as those gaps existed, my color system would not work.

It was at that time that I approached RJR Fabrics and suggested that quilters needed a palette that would always be available to them. RJR agreed. The collection we created together now contains 150 fabrics in colors that span the spectrum. These are available to quilters, just as standard colors of thread are available to people doing other needle arts. Of course, I would like the palette to contain 500 or more colors, but it is impossible for a company to manufacture and retain that kind of inventory. Therefore, as I design more fabrics, I make sure that the colors in my collections are different from the colors in the palette, allowing me to add new hues and tones to my collection.

Preparing and Caring for Fabrics

Whether you are making a simple nine-patch quilt from fewer than twenty fabrics or a dazzling charm quilt from hundreds of different scraps, a little extra care and attention before you begin will help the quiltmaking process run smoothly. Today's quilters have the good fortune to work with a variety of quality fabrics designed especially for quiltmaking. The range of colors, patterns, and textures available is astounding. Yet as more fabrics are incorporated into quilts, we need to feel confident that the quilts we make today will stand the test of time. Before you even begin to sew a line of stitches, a few simple preparatory steps will help your quilt come together smoothly and quickly. They will also increase the pleasure you take in quiltmaking. The first step is careful pre-washing of fabrics to ensure that colors will stay true no matter how many different patches are incorporated into a quilt.

Because quilts by their nature combine a variety of different colors, quilters have long been concerned with two problems associated with their use–*bleeding* of color from one fabric to another when it is wet or washed; and *crocking* of color that rubs off of one fabric onto adjacent fabrics.

Bleeding

There are few sights as devastating to a new quilter as the bleeding of dark colors onto lighter blocks when a quilt gets wet. Yet with proper care and attention to fabrics before quiltmaking begins, this problem is easily avoided.

Ironically, bleeding of color has been a greater issue for today's quilters working with quality, contemporary fabrics than it was even a generation ago. During the 1970s new environmental codes put restrictions on the amount of formaldehyde permissible in the fabric-dyeing process. Formaldehyde is a chemical agent that acts as a binder and aids in colorfastness when a type of printing called *pigment printing* is done. The amounts used in pre-1970s fabrics to limit the problem of bleeding are now illegal. Newer methods are constantly being developed to serve the same purpose as formaldehyde. But to solve the problem, many manufacturers, including RJR Fabrics, the company I design for, have changed to a printing process called *fiber-reactive dyeing*, where the dye stuff permeates the yarn instead of just sitting on top of it. This type of dyeing is more expensive, but it is also produces a more colorfast cloth. Unfortunately, it is very difficult for a consumer to tell whether or not the fabric purchased has been printed with pigment or fiber-reactive dyes.

Any dark- or bright-colored fabric contains a certain amount of residual dye that will come from the fabric when it is washed. The darker or brighter the color, the more inclined the fabric is to bleed. Also, the hotter the water used in washing, the more those dyes will run. After all, we've all seen what happens when a red sweatshirt or towel is accidentally mixed in with the white wash instead of being washed separately in cold water.

Washing Fabrics for the First Time

When fabric is sold in a store, it comes on large bolts. Because the manufacturer doubles the fabric before rolling it onto a standard-sized bolt, there is a soft fold line down the center of every yard. A shop owner is often perplexed when a disappointed customer returns with a piece of washed fabric that has a distinct crease where the fabric had been folded. Along the crease, the color looks washed out. The shop owner may not have received any other complaints and inspection of the remainder of the fabric on the bolt will show only the manufacturer's soft double-fold, with no faded color. Here is what likely happened. Quite simply, the customer neglected to unfold the fabric before putting it into the washer. As the fabric agitated during the washing, color rubbed off along the soft fold line, changing it into a more distinct crease and fading the color. Always unfold fabric before washing it or you may see the same problem.

Washing "in cold water" should give us a clue on how to prepare quilting fabrics. I have heard of quilters who have washed a piece of dark or bright fabric a dozen times in hot water and still complain that they see dye in the rinse water. They end up washing the life out of the fabric and then say that it looks faded and dull. The fact is that *any* cotton fabric washed in hot water 12 times or more is going to look somewhat faded. Rather than wash a fabric in hot water to get as much color as possible to come out, the simplest answer is to wash all dark or intense colors in cold water to prevent as much bleeding as possible.

Unfortunate as it may be, color will continue to run out of some fabrics despite the most careful of cold-water washings. When this happens, the question to ask is not, "How do I keep the color from running?" Rather, ask "Will the color that runs from this fabric *contaminate* other fabrics?" Once you have prewashed bright- or dark-colored fabrics separately in cold water, wash them again, but this time add some small pieces of the lighter fabrics that will be in the quilt. If the lighter pieces do not pick up any of the color from the darker ones, it is safe to use them in the quilt with the darker fabrics. The secret is not to keep washing the fabric in hot water until no color runs (because this will surely fade it), but to wash carefully in *cold* water and to be certain that light-colored fabrics remain uncontaminated by the darker fabric dyes.

The type of detergent used to wash fabrics can also play a major role in how colorfast the fabrics remain. A detergent containing phosphates can contribute to the bleeding of colors. I have conducted experiments in which I have taken one piece of fabric and washed it with a detergent with phosphates and then taken another piece of the same fabric and washed it with a *phosphate-free* detergent. The difference is clearly evident if you look at the wash water as it drains from the machine. There is also a considerable difference in the appearance of the two fabrics after they have dried. The fabric washed with phosphate looks faded, while the other looks as it did before washing.

Often quilters ask if soaking fabrics in vinegar or salt will help retard bleeding. The answer–provided by a quality control expert at a major US print plant–is that while salt will help to make the dye stay on the fabric, excessively large quantities are required. It takes approximately four to five ounces of salt per gallon of water, a quantity that would probably do considerable damage to the washing machine. However, if the fabric were immersed in a large kettle to soak, then rinsed, and put back in the machine, the salt treatment would probably help to retard bleeding. Far simpler and just as effective, my expert recommended putting all fabrics through a cold water rinse first and then washing them with phosphate-free detergent.

One last but important caution when washing fabric: Do not let excess water stay in fabric for any length of time. I use the washing machine as a vessel in which to wash my quilts and fabrics, but I do not let them stay in there for long. I allow the machine to agitate gently for a few minutes, then I run the spin cycle *only* until all excess water is spun out. If there are any fabrics that are likely to bleed, this process helps prevent it, since they will not stay excessively wet long enough to bleed onto adjacent fabrics. After fabrics are washed I like to either hang them to dry or put them in the dryer on a permanent-press cycle. I never put quilts in the dryer, but rather spread towels out on a large surface and lay them out flat to dry.

Crocking

Another problem associated with fabric dyes is known as *crocking*. This problem is more prevalent with fabrics that have been pigment-dyed than with those that are treated with fiber-reactive dyes. As explained above, however, it is very difficult to tell how fabrics are dyed, so you need to take certain precautions. Have you ever pressed a finished block and found to your dismay that color from one fabric patch suddenly bleeds onto an adjacent fabric while you are ironing? The common assumption is that the fabric got damp from the steam in the iron and the colors ran because of the wetness. The correct explanation, however, is that some fabric dyes are composed of a latex material, very similar to a latex house paint. These are pigment dyes. The dye sits on top of the fabric. An iron that is too hot can actually melt the dye, causing it to transfer onto adjacent fabrics. To avoid this problem, always use a permanent press setting on the iron when pressing 100 percent cotton printed fabrics.

Crocking can also occur whenever fabrics printed with certain dyes are rubbed together, such as in the washing or drying process. Large pieces of fabric tend to twist together when washed or dried. If they are left like this and put in the dryer and then forgotten, it is possible that where the multiple creases in the fabric rub together, some crocking may occur. To avoid this, make sure that all folds and twists are out of the fabric before putting it into the washer or dryer. When drying, after about five minutes, check the fabric to make sure that it has not twisted. It may be necessary to pull it out of the dryer, shake any folds out, and put it back in.

Olde Worlde Star. *Designed, hand-pieced, and hand-quilted by Jinny Beyer, 1994*

Quilts of Many Colors!

THIS DETAILED EXPLANATION of how to wash and care for fabrics has not been meant to discourage you from using multiple fabrics in your quilts, but rather serves to make you aware of the properties of fabric and potential problems that can occur. If you purchase your fabrics from a reputable quilt store and wash, dry, and store them with care, they will reward you by carrying their true colors into your quilts. Like you, one reason I was drawn to quiltmaking was the seemingly endless array of irresistible fabrics—and I use as many of them as possible in my quilts. *Olde World Star,* shown here, for example, contains more than 60 different fabrics. They range in color from off-white to peaches and bright reds, greens, and blacks. When planning the colors, I selected the border print first and then found colors that were in the border print and shaded them all together. From there, I found all the fabrics I could that contained those colors. Each star has a different configuration of fabrics. There are many places in the quilt where a very dark fabric is next to a very light one, but I washed the fabrics carefully in cold water and have since washed the quilt (in cold water as well) and have had no problems.

Shrinkage

Some people ask if they even need to pre-wash their fabrics at all. If the benefits of removing excess dyes are not enough to persuade you, keep in mind that even good quality quilting fabrics may have a small amount of shrinkage when washed. Part of this has to do with the fact that when the fabric is "finished" in the plant, there is a certain amount of stretching that takes place. When the fabric is washed, this "stretch" may relax a little. In quality fabrics, however, shrinkage is minimal and should not really affect the quilt. One of the best precautions you can take is always to buy quality fabrics, such as those sold in specialty quilt stores. As long as I know the fabric is from a quality manufacturer, I am more inclined to recommend pre-washing to soften the fabric and make it easier to needle than to avoid shrinkage.

Seven Simple Steps to Prepare Fabrics

To begin your quilt on the right footing, make sure you follow these simple guidelines when preparing your fabrics for quiltmaking. You'll find that taking these extra steps will save you time, energy, and frustration as you proceed to make your quilt. Once it is finished, you can be completely confident that neither shrinkage nor transfer of colors will occur when the quilt is laundered.

1. Unfold all newly purchased fabrics and sort by color.
2. Soak dark- and bright- colored fabrics individually in cold water for at least half an hour to set the dyes.
3. Wash dark-, bright-, and light-colored fabrics separately with a phosphate-free detergent in a short, cold-water cycle.
4. For bright- or dark-colored fabrics, watch the wash and rinse waters to see how much color comes out.
5. If there is a lot of color in the water, wash the fabrics again in cold water, along with some samples of the light-colored fabrics that you plan to use in the quilt. Chances are, the second cold-water wash will produce no bleeding. If there is bleeding but it has not contaminated the other fabrics, it is safe to use those fabrics together. If the light-colored fabrics have changed color, then I recommend not using the fabrics together.
6. Tumble fabrics almost dry, then remove from the dryer and press with an iron on a permanent-press setting. To avoid wrinkling, do not put more than six yards (meters) of fabric in the dryer at one time.
7. Precut samples, kit pieces, or small scraps should not be machine washed or machine dried. Being careful not to over-handle, separate these pieces into piles of same-colored patches, and preshrink them by soaking in cold water. If color bleeds, repeat until the water runs clear. Place patches on toweling or white paper towels to dry.

"The first thing is to provide a work-box properly fitted up with every requisite . . . large enough to hold six reels of sewing cotton . . . a needle-book, containing a page for needles of each sized needle, not omitting darning and worsted needles. A pin-cushion, an emery-cushion, bodkins, thimble, a stiletto, a little yard-measure, and two pairs of scissors, one being of medium size, and one pair for button-holes."

Cassell's Household Guide to Every Department of Practical Life, Volume IV, circa 1875

A Quilter's Basket

Today, there are all kinds of gadgets and special tools available for the quilter to add to the modern-day work basket. Many of these are very useful or beautiful to have but, for the most part you, too, can get by with the simplest of supplies. Here is a summary of the materials I use for cutting, piecing, and quilting by hand.

Thread

There are many types of thread available for hand piecing and quilting. Quilters each have their own preferences. You will have to find the thread you like the best. I use a different thread for piecing than for quilting, and I always use 100 percent cotton thread for both. It is best to use the same fiber content in thread as in the fabric you are using. I favor 100 percent cotton fabric, therefore 100 percent cotton thread is also my preference.

There are three other reasons why I choose 100 percent cotton thread over polyester or cotton/polyester blend for both piecing and quilting. First, cotton thread does not stretch and thus allows a smoother result. A thread of a polyester-cotton blend tends to be elastic. It stretches as it is being pulled taut and then when the quilt is removed from the frame, the thread relaxes, causing puckers. The puckering can be particularly bad when a lot of quilting, such as stippling, is done. Second, I prefer all-cotton thread because it knots less readily than polyester or polyester blends. And, third, a synthetic thread that is not the same fiber content as the fabric may over time have a tendency to actually cut through the fabric, causing small slits. This actually happened to me and I had to take all the quilting out, replace the split pieces, and begin again with an all-cotton thread.

Thread for Piecing

For hand piecing I prefer a thread slightly thicker than the standard 50-weight sewing thread, but not as thick as quilting thread. For years I have been using Conso Heavy Duty thread, at 40 weight. It comes in a variety of colors on two-ounce, 1,200 yard spools, making it one of the greatest bargains in sewing! Most other thread comes with

200 to 300 yards on a spool and to purchase 1200 yards would cost more than twice as much as a tube of Conso.

The color of thread to use for hand piecing depends on what you are sewing. I mostly use only five spools of different colored Conso thread—black, burgundy, navy, medium brown, and light tan. These colors pretty much serve me for whatever I am sewing. When sewing a dark piece to a light one, use thread of the darker color or close to it. The stitches are more apt to show when using a light-colored thread. For instance, if I am sewing a dark blue piece to a yellow one, I'll use navy. The medium brown serves as a neutral color for a variety of different colors. I only use my light tan thread when sewing two light colored fabrics together. Never use a thread that is lighter in color than either of the two pieces you are sewing, or the stitches will likely show.

Thread for Quilting

One hundred percent cotton quilting thread, which is thicker than standard sewing thread, is available from a variety of manufacturers and in a wide range of colors. YLI makes an excellent product, which I mostly use, but there are many other manufacturers, among them J & P Coats, Guterman, and Mettler, who also make excellent quality 100 percent cotton quilting thread. A thread made specifically for quilting has a waxed finish and is more "wiry" than regular thread. It produces a nice quilting stitch. I find this thread a little too thick for hand piecing, however.

The color of thread to use for quilting is a matter of personal preference. Expert opinion on the matter, too, has changed over the years. My first quilt, made in 1972, was made from very dark-colored fabrics in shades of reds and blues with a solid navy set between the blocks. I wanted to use a navy thread because I was afraid my stitches would be too big and I didn't want them to show. To my surprise, I discovered that dark-colored quilting thread was nowhere to be found. The only colors available were white and ecru. One shop owner even advised me that no one ever used colored thread for quilting. Further, if I were to enter the quilt in a contest, judges would disqualify it if the thread was anything but white or ecru. At the time I thought to myself that if I ever judged a quilt contest, I would certainly never mark anyone down for using a colored thread! I went out and bought some 100 percent cotton standard navy blue sewing thread and some beeswax and waxed the thread myself.

Today, quilters use all sorts of colors for quilting. There are even variegated threads available. Some quilters choose a thread to match the backing of the quilt, while others match the color to the front. Another determining factor may be how much or how little you want your stitches to show. Remember, too, that there is absolutely nothing wrong with using more than one color of thread in the same quilt.

"Wadding, as sold in the shops, is carded cotton wool; bleached, unbleached, slate-coloured, and black, cut into sheets of various sizes, and sold by the gross; but it is also manufactured in lengths of 12 yards for quilting . . . The French name for Wadding is Ouate, which was that originally given to the downy tufts found in the pods of the plant called Apocynum, imported from Egypt and Asia Minor. To make Wadding, a lap or fleece, prepared by the carding machine, is applied to tissue paper by means of a coat of size, which is made by boiling the cuttings of hareskins, and adding alum to the gelatinous solutions. When two laps of cotton are glued with their faces together, they form the most downy kind of Wadding."

S. F. A Caulfield and Blanche C. Saward,
The Dictionary of Needlework, 1882

Batting

Batting (wadding) is the filler that is sandwiched between the quilt top and back. It can be made of cotton, cotton/polyester blend, polyester, silk, or wool. It also comes in a variety of thicknesses or *lofts*. My preference is for a fairly thin, 100 percent cotton batting. Thin battings make quilting go faster, are smoother to quilt through, and make it easier to achieve small, even quilting stitches. I prefer cotton battings because the amount of *bearding* that occurs is minimal. Bearding is the migration of fibers to the surface or backing of the quilt. Fibers gradually force their way through the fabric and cause a fuzz on the surface. All-cotton batting tends to produce less bearding than those made with other fibers. One of my favorite battings is manufactured by Quilters' Dream Cotton. This batting is produced in four different weights. I like the two thinnest weights the best. Many other manufacturers, among them Stearns and Foster, Hobbs, and Fairfield, also produce fine quality cotton batting.

Template Essentials

Templates are the pattern pieces that are used for cutting the shapes for patchwork out of fabric. There is a wide range of different types of material available for making templates, but my preference is 12″ × 18″ (30 cm × 45 cm) slightly opaque, non-gridded vinyl plastic sheets that do not curl and are easy to cut with scissors. There are two reasons why I prefer an opaque plastic for making templates. A perfectly clear plastic material is easy to misplace and difficult to see around when placed on the fabric. I like to have a slightly frosted plastic. This allows me to easily see the template, but also to see the design of the fabric through the plastic in case I want to center some motif from the fabric within the template. Template plastic is available from quilt shops.

If you are anxious to begin a project and don't have any template plastic on hand, cardboard, sandpaper, x-ray film, and plastic lids, among other materials, have all been used by quilters for making templates. I have at one time or other used all of these, so if you don't have what you think is the perfect

Jinny Beyer Perfect Piecer. See page 56

product, be resourceful. Many tablets of paper have lost their cardboard backs when I have become desperate for some template material.

An exacto knife, Olfa Touch Knife, or rotary cutter are all useful for scoring template plastic when making templates. These help to get perfectly straight lines. (See Making Templates on page 51).

A 1⁄16″ (0.2 cm) hole punch, available from specialty manufacturers (Fiskers makes one, for example), is a useful tool for making holes in template plastic in order to mark places where seam allowances intersect. The *Jinny Beyer Perfect Piecer*, a tool created to accompany *Quiltmaking by Hand*, accomplishes the same task in seconds (see page 56 for an explanation).

Rulers

A wide variety of rulers is available and it is sometimes difficult to know what type is best to have. The main consideration is to make sure that the markings on the rulers are accurate. I prefer see-through rulers that have at least 1⁄4″ increments marked all the way across. I have a 1″ × 6″ (2.5 cm × 15 cm) and a 3″ × 18″ (7.5 cm × 45 cm) and that is all I really need. A 90°/45° right-angle triangle is also very useful for mitering corners and drafting patterns. Some wider rulers have various angles marked on them and these can take the place of a right-angle triangle.

Pencils, Pens, Chalk, and Other Markers

A red or black permanent marker is good for making notations on template plastic. A good quality ballpoint pen is useful for marking around templates onto fabric. Please note that this is *only* done when the templates include the seam allowance and you are working without a sewing line. When cutting the pieces out, cut just inside the pen line so the mark is not on the fabric piece. If you use a sewing line, *never mark it with a ballpoint pen.* (See page 57.) A white or yellow Sanford Verithin pencil is also a good fabric marker.

Clover makes a triangle-shaped tailor's chalk that is excellent for marking fabric. It has a nice, sharp edge on all three sides. I use it for marking around templates, for marking lines when cutting bias binding, and for marking quilting designs. When the edges become a bit dull, the chalk can be sharpened with an emery board or blade from an old pair of scissors. Clover also makes a tailor's chalk in the form of a pencil.

Masking tape is useful for marking straight seams when hand quilting. I like to have both 1⁄4″ (0.75 cm) and 1″ (2.5 cm) masking tape on hand. Marking quilting designs is explained in detail in Chapter Nine. Whatever you select to use for marking, test the marker on a piece of the fabric that you will be using to make sure it will wash out. For marking quilting designs, in addition to using a piece of tailor's chalk or a chalk pencil, I sometimes use a hard leaded pencil or a sharp sliver of soap.

It is important to add a note of caution. I do not recommend water-soluble pens for marking quilting designs. Supposedly the marks made by these pens will disappear when the fabric is spritzed with water or washed. I have seen several disasters concerning these pens, where several years later the mark reappears as a brown line. The water may seem to dissolve the color of the pen temporarily, but the chemical is still in the fabric and can be affected by soap, light, or a variety of other factors that allow it to show up again later.

Scissors and Thread Cutters

A good, sharp pair of dressmaker shears is invaluable for cutting out the pieces for a quilt. Nothing is more frustrating than a pair of scissors that does not make a nice, clean cut. There are many excellent brands available and it is best to find the pair that is most comfortable in your hand. The ones I use are made by Clover and have a 4½″ (11.5 cm) blade. The indentations in the handle are almost formfitting to my fingers. The thumb fits comfortably into the smaller hole and the other four fingers fit into the larger hole. These scissors can cut through four layers of fabric as if it were butter.

In addition to dressmaker shears, a good quality pair of small scissors is necessary for both piecing and quilting. The pair I use is German, made by Dovo, and folds down to fit into a small leather case. The blades are sharp enough to cut fabric with precision and are great for snipping threads. They were expensive, but worth the investment. I have had mine for more than ten years and they are still as sharp as the day I bought them. Since I do so much sewing when I am out of the house, my little folding scissors are perfect. They add very little bulk to a small sewing bag and, since the tips are folded away when not in use, there are no points to cut into my bag or sewing.

Airport security regulations since the events of September 11, 2001, have banned scissors from all passenger planes. For someone like me who sews on the plane all the time, this restriction was a big worry. Fortunately, however, I found that there are several non-threatening thread cutters on the market today. Some have even been designed since September 11 for the specific purpose of cutting threads while sewing on an airplane. These thread cutters are usually in the form of a small disk with indentations around it. At each indentation is a small cutting surface. The thread is pulled through one of these grooves and is cleanly cut. Clover makes an inexpensive brass cutter that has a hole in one end. A ribbon can be threaded through this hole so it can be worn around the neck. This keeps it from slipping to the floor or between cushions. There are several decorative sterling silver and even gold thread cutters. These can be worn on a chain around the neck and, as well as being functional, are quite a conversation piece. My thread cutter, thimble cage, and thimble, designed and made by Tommie Jane Lane, are shown here.

La Chatelaine

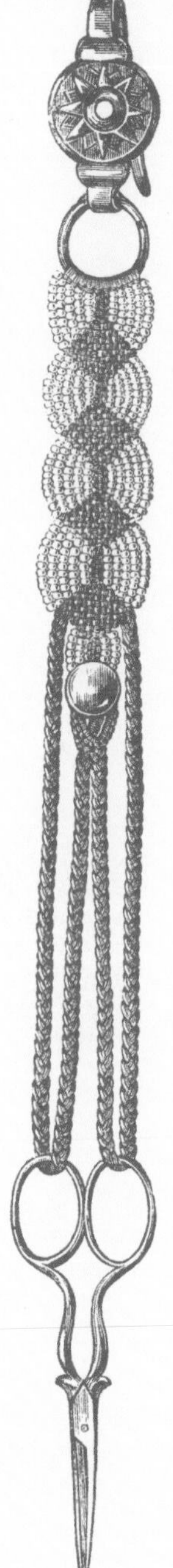

In medieval times, the mistress of the castle was known by the French word, *chatelaine*. She was in charge of the keys to the keep and other important areas of the castle. So as not to be misplaced, these keys hung from chains attached to her belt or from a decorative waist ornament. As times passed, items other than keys were attached to the chains for safe keeping. Eventually the word *chatelaine* was used, not so much for the mistress, but for any waist-hung appendage that contained various items that the woman would use. These items included any number of sewing necessities.

During the 1800s, as fashion often dictates, there was a revival of interest in the chatelaine and many decorative ones were devised. A woman would purchase the clasp with chains and then select items that matched the design and add them according to her needs. *The Englishwoman's Domestic Magazine* published a detailed article about chatelaines in 1873. (The article was quoted at length in Cummings and Taunton's wonderful, illustrated book *Chatelaines: Utility to Glorious Extravagance,* 1994.)

The writer of the article talks about the "new fashion" for chatelaines and how she searched for one for a friend who always wanted to be up on the latest styles.

> " . . . partly on her account and partly because I dearly love pretty things, I have been looking out for chatelaines in all directions. I should be sorry to be obliged to disclose the number of inoffensive shop-keepers I have tormented in this search, . . . That I am now able to cry 'Eureka' is not owing to . . . perseverance, but simply to chance . . . "

The author states that by chance one day she passed a shop, Mr. Walter Thornhills, No. 144.

> "On first entering the eye is caught by a quantity of chatelaines of every conceivable variety as well as fittings or appendages for the chatelaines. These are made to match each style of chatelaine in oxidized steel, silver, parcel, gilt, electro-plate, and in plain and chased gold and silver, and the following list will give some idea of the numerous necessaire of the modern chatelaine . . ."

Almost 100 items are mentioned, such as pen holders, pencil-cases, whistles, and more. But most important for our purposes are the sewing items that could be purchased and added to such a chatelaine:

> " . . . eggs fitted with pins, needles, thimble, reels and yard measure; barrels fitted in same manner, pails for pins, thimble and yard measure, . . . *etui* fitted with scissors, needles, reels, yard measure, thimble . . . pincushions, thimble cases . . ."

Of course, chatelaines were not only in the domain of women. In nineteenth century France, gentlemen of high fashion were not to be outdone by the ladies of the time. Henri René d'Allemagne, in his 1928 tome, *Les Accessoires du Costume et du Mobilier,* describes chatelaines.

> *"Les grandes breloques suspendues aux chatélaines faisaient beaucoup de bruit en s'entrechequant et c'etait lá une marque de grand distinction: Voyez entrer un elegant, dit Mercier dans ses Tableaux de Paris. Il faut d'abord que ses breloques, par un joli frémissement announcent son arrivée. On produisait ce bruit en se dandidant d'une certain façon."*

> "The big keys suspended on chatelaines clanged together noisily as the bearer came near, and this was a mark of great distinction: See how the gentleman of fashion prepares his grand entrance, says Mercier in his *Pictures of Paris.* First, it is of the utmost importance that his jangling keys announce his arrival.That is the sign of a true dandy."

Now, once again we are seeing a resurgence of interest in fine-quality sewing tools that can be both functional and decorative. Over the years, I have collected several chatelaines and display them in my sewing room. Are these items essential for creating hand-made quilts? Not at all. Do we enjoy using one of them to create our heirloom quilts? I know that I do.

ENCYCLOPEDIA
OF
NEEDLEWORK
BY
TH. DE DILLMONT

"The original Pin was a thorn. Sharpened fish and other bones were also in use before the modern metal Pin was manufactured. The date of the latter in England is doubtful, possibly the thirteenth century."

S. F. A Caulfield and Blanche C. Saward,
The Dictionary of Needlework, 1882

Needles and Pins

Needles come in a variety of styles. *Sharps* or *Betweens* are most commonly used for patchwork. Sharps are long and slender, while Betweens tend to be short and stubby. Sizes are indicated by numbers; the higher the number the smaller the needle, with size 12 being the smallest. The sizes of needles are not consistent from manufacturer to manufacturer. One company's number 10 might be the same size as another company's number 9, so you will want to experiment with a brand you like and then find the needle within that brand that you like the best. The size of the eye of a needle also varies from manufacturer to manufacturer. My favorite needles, in Betweens size 10 and 11, are packaged and sold through Jinny Beyer Studio. Other fine needles are available from Clover, John James, Hemming, and Colonial to name but a few.

Quilters tend to use either sharps or Betweens for hand piecing and Betweens for hand quilting. I use Betweens size 10 or 11 for both. I like a short but sturdy needle that is not too thick, and this size works best for me.

Frequently, when I am teaching hand-piecing classes, students will complain that they cannot seem to get the hang of my stitching technique. The moment I see them stitch, I know what the problem is. Most often, they are trying to sew with a dagger of a needle! While it may be easier to thread a larger needle, it is much more difficult to get a large needle to glide with ease through the fabric. Working with small needles is apt to be a little awkward at first and it will take some time to get used to it. I suggest purchasing a package of needles that has a range of sizes. Begin working with the smallest needle that you feel comfortable with and gradually work down to a Betweens size 10 or 11. If you need help threading, use a needle threader or ask your son or daughter to thread a few needles for you!

The only time I use a different needle than a Betweens size 10 or 11 is when I am basting the layers of a quilt together. Then I want a long, sturdy needle, such as a darner.

There are many different types of pins available. My preference is 1¼″ to 1½″ (3 cm to 4 cm) long silk pins with glass heads, which I use for all my quilting needs. Silk pins glide smoothly through the fabric and the glass heads make them easy to see.

Nimble Thimbles

PROBABLY THE THIMBLE was invented eons ago when early civilizations discovered that layers of bark or leather sewn together would create warmth and that pieces could be stitched with a needle made of bone and thread of strong grass, narrow strips of leather, or other materials. When the ruins of Pompeii, buried by lava in the volcanic eruption of 79 A.D., were discovered in the 1700s, thimbles were amongst the wealth of items discovered. Initially, thimbles were strictly utilitarian, but eventually decorative bands were added. Thimbles made of gold and silver and studded with stones are now coveted and cherished by collectors. Many of these thimbles made of precious metals have holes worn in them from repeated use.

I have been collecting thimbles for several years and I love to use antique thimbles when I sew. My favorites are made of brass or other common metals, with a slightly rounded rim for quilting. I like a special type of thimble, commonly known as a Dorcas thimble (shown here), for hand piecing. The Dorcas thimble is made with a core of hardened steel sandwiched in between two layers of sterling silver. This construction makes the thimble extremely durable. A seamtress can stitch for years with one of these thimbles without wearing holes in it. While this type of thimble had been made for several years, Charles Horner received the first patent for it in England in 1884. Even earlier, Henry Griffith also produced a similar thimble which he named Dreema, after his niece.

Thimbles

As a child I never used a thimble while sewing. In fact, as an adult, I pieced my first quilt top without using a thimble. Learning to do the actual quilting stitch, however, is another story. The first time the eye end of the needle went through my finger, I immediately purchased a thimble. Since then, wearing a thimble has become almost second nature to me. Sometimes I don't even realize that I have it on. I once lost my favorite thimble and two weeks later found it in the freezer! I hadn't realized I was wearing it, and it must have fallen off when I was preparing dinner.

I have used a variety of different thimbles over the years. Until recently, I used one type of thimble for piecing and another for quilting. Since I use different hand positions when piecing and quilting, thimbles affect my fingers in different ways. Some thimbles have a rolled edge around the bottom and others are fairly flat along the bottom edge. The rolled edge digs into an adjacent finger while hand piecing, so I use a thimble with a straight rim. However, when quilting, the straight rim cuts into my thimble finger, so I prefer one with a rolled edge. Now, when hand quilting I wear a thimble on the middle finger of both hands. I am ambidextrous and quilt about the same with either hand.

"And that I'll prove upon thee,
Though thy little finger be armed in a Thimble."

—*The Taming of the Shrew,*
WILLIAM SHAKESPEARE

"THIMBLE.—An appliance fitted as a guard to the top of the right-hand middle finger, and for the purpose of pressing a needle through any material to be sewn. The name is derived from the Scotch Thummel, from Thumb-bell, a bell-shaped shield, originally worn on the thumb; . . . The Dutch have the credit of the invention; . . .They are made in gold, silver, plated steel, brass, celluloid, bone, ebony, ivory, steel, brass-topped, &c., and are pitted with little cells to receive the blunt end of the needle . . . In England Thimbles are made by means of moulds, and then of a stamping and punching machine. In the fourteenth century our Thimbles were made of leather . . . Thimbles were called Fingerlings so long as they were made of leather; and when in the fourteenth century, they were superseded by metal, the name Thimble was adopted."

S. F. A CAULFIELD AND BLANCHE C. SAWARD,
The Dictionary of Needlework, 1882

Even so, when I am quilting in certain directions, I usually prefer one hand or the other. Since I quilt on a stationary frame, I am constantly switching between my right and left hand to quilt in the direction that is most comfortable. Having two thimbles already in place saves the time it takes to switch one thimble back and forth.

I have collected antique thimbles for years and am always looking for ones that I can actually use. I like common brass thimbles with a rounded edge for quilting. However, the eye end of the needle will eventually wear holes in this type of thimble–you will find that you tend to wear holes in exactly the same places. When the eye of your needle suddenly breaks off, check your thimble for holes, because it usually means that the needle has become caught in a hole which forces the tip of the eye to snap.

A few contemporary silversmiths make sterling silver thimbles. They usually provide a variety of sizes and styles, including open-top versions that allow for air circulation and also accommodate long fingernails. I use one of these types, designed by Tommie Jane Lane, for quilting and often for

"Your ladies and pale visag'd maids,
Like amazons, come tripping after drums;
Their thimbles into armed gauntlets change,
Their needles into lances."

—*King John,*
WILLIAM SHAKESPEARE

hand piecing. The rim she makes on her thimbles seems to be a comfortable midpoint between too straight and too round, so I can use it for both piecing and quilting. Many of these handmade thimbles are beautiful and become a piece of jewelry as well as a useful tool.

It may take you a while to find the perfect thimble for you. Whether it is antique, new, silver, brass, ornamental or even leather, one day you will know that this is the one!

Quilting Spoon or Finger Protector

There are several products available to help produce even stitches as well as protect the fingers of the hand underneath the quilting frame or hoop. TJ's Quick Quilter and Aunt Becky's Finger Protector are two such products. Some thimbles are also manufactured for the same purpose and have a disk or lip across the end of the thimble. These devices are used to catch the needle on the underneath side of the quilt and guide it to the top of the quilt during the quilting process. To find out more about how I use these devices, see Chapter Ten.

"To make a quilting frame, order from a lumber yard or sawmill four strips of hard pine 1 inch thick, 3 inches wide, and 6½ feet long. These could not cost more than twenty-five cents. Tack a piece of muslin along the edge of each strip. Buy four clamps for a dime at a hardware store, or have them made by a blacksmith, and you have a cheap set of frames that will last a lifetime."

Sidney Morse,
Household Discoveries, 1908

Quilting Frame or Hoop

The type of frame described in *Household Discoveries* was perhaps used over and over in poorer households. Sometimes, rather than use clamps, the poles were simply tied together, or a nail might be hammered in to hold them in place. The set of poles was then balanced on chairs or on simple sawhorses. Many women could sit around such a frame and quilt at one time. As the quilting was completed along the edge, the clamps, nails, or twine would be removed. The finished portion would be rolled under, and the quilting would continue. When the quilting was finished for the day, the frame could be picked up and leaned against the wall. Sometimes, a pulley device was made that would pull the frame to the ceiling when it was not in use. Some frames were more elaborate and would contain a wooden or metal ratchet on one of the poles that was used to tighten the quilt in the frame.

Whatever is used, some type of quilting frame or hoop is essential for getting fine, even stitches during the quilting process. To achieve the smoothest quilting stitches, a piece should be stretched fairly taut in a frame or hoop. As the stitches are made, the quilter gives a slight tug on the thread, thus causing the stitches to become tight and look smooth and even. Use of a frame controls the tension so that the stitches are neither pulled too tight nor allowed to be too loose.

I use a floor-standing frame that is similar in style to the old Stearns and Foster pattern from the 1930s. This pattern is still available from the Stearns and Foster company. I prefer this type of a frame over a smaller hoop as I can quilt twice as fast. There is no need to constantly change the position of the quilt in the hoop, long lines of quilting can be done much more efficiently, and you don't have the bulk of the quilt to contend with as you do when using a hoop.

Portable Piecing Kit

As I mentioned in the Introduction, I do almost all of my hand stitching when I am out of the house. This means that I have to have a little sewing kit ready to go. My kit includes my folding scissors, a couple of needles (I keep some extras in my purse, too, nestled just alongside the zipper in the coin pocket), and one or two spools of Conso thread, depending on what I am sewing. I use one end of the spool as a pin cushion for the needles and the three or four pins I bring along. (Some quilters advise against putting pins into the spool of thread, since the points might split the thread, but I haven't had a problem and the thread makes a perfect mini pincushion.)

The spool is also a handy thimble holder. The hole through the center of the tube is just the right size to wedge a thimble. Better still, especially when sewing in a car or on the train, I slip the points of my scissors through the hole in the spool. I automatically rest my scissors there to avoid losing them in my lap or between cushions. On a rough road or in stop-and-start traffic, the points are well protected. If I am traveling by plane, I have to remember to remove my scissors from the bag.

I usually wear the thimble around my neck in a "thimble cage." I also hang my thread cutter and even a small needle holder from the cage. That way, I have my modern day version of the Victorian chatelaine with me at all times. It is functional, keeps the thimble secure when I'm not sewing, and also makes a pretty piece of jewelry.

Along with my cut pieces, these basic supplies are all I need. I always try to have more sewing with me than I will probably get done. My biggest fear is running out of something to sew!

World in Their Hands. *Designed, hand-pieced, and hand-quilted by Jinny Beyer, 2002. This "guest book" signature quilt is in honor of the wedding of my daughter Kiran to Rob Wardwell*

A Primer on Pattern Drafting

"Ninety nine percent of all pieced quilts represent the working out of geometrical designs, often so intricate that their effective handling reflects most creditably on the supposedly non-mathematical sex."

Ruth E. Finley, *Old Patchwork Quilts and the Women Who Made Them*, 1929

Passed down from generation to generation or shared among friends, quilt patterns have traveled through time and around the world. It is hard to say whether quilters are first inspired by the pattern to make a quilt, or whether the growing mound of scraps in their baskets call to them to find a design and begin stitching. While many older quilts were made from scraps, fabric was often purchased to add to those scraps for a specific quilt. For me, ideas for a new quilt sometimes come from beautiful pieces of fabrics or from color images I see. At other times, I develop a design before even considering a palette of colors or looking through my fabrics.

Patterns, Patterns, Patterns

In addition to the many time-tested traditional patterns that have been handed down to us from earlier generations of quilters, there are also thousands of new patterns available today. Not only do hundreds of designers publish their own quilt patterns, but books, magazines, and Web sites all offer patterns, many of which are free. All cater to different tastes and skill levels or offer different techniques. The ten patterns in *Quiltmaking by Hand*, for instance, have been specifically selected for the beginning hand piecer.

Center of **Starflower.** See full quilt in pattern section

While the wealth of patterns available is astounding and most come with complete and clear directions, I strongly believe that all quilters should gain a basic understanding of how to create their own patterns. If you are able to draft your own patterns, there is no need for compromise when choosing a design for a new quilt. You can spend a lot of time and energy seeking out exactly the right pattern, only to find once you have started piecing your blocks that there are aspects of the design that do not appeal to you. You can also spend a lot of money on books, just to get the one pattern you like. Even if you are lucky enough to find a design that is perfect for the quilt you have in mind, there is no guarantee that the blocks or borders are the size you want them to be. Being able to draft your own patterns in whatever size you choose is one of the most important elements of patchwork. It allows you the freedom to make your quilts exactly the way you want them to be.

This chapter explains how easy pattern drafting can be; you will learn how to resize existing patterns or draft any pattern of your choice, either in a traditional way with pencil and paper or in seconds on the computer. Technology makes the task of pattern drafting incredibly simple–you'll soon learn how to create patterns on the computer in a snap.

"She would use the patterns her mother and her grandmother used, and her great-grandmother before her, as these patterns have descended down through the ages, and very often their meanings have been passed on."

Beatrice Scott,
The Craft of Quilting, 1935

Basics of Pattern Drafting

The words *geometry* and *drafting* scare a lot of people. For many, they bring back memories of falling behind in math class at school or dreaded algebraic formulas and geometric theorems. Yet all we are doing when we create patchwork quilts is working with simple geometric designs. In past centuries, even children without the benefit of schooling had no trouble in figuring out how shapes should go together. The fact is that drafting patchwork designs is very easy and does not require math skills. All you need is a simple understanding of how the designs are structured. Then, with the help of paper, pencil, ruler, compass, and a 45° right-angle triangle, you can draw any geometric pattern you please.

Underlying Grid

Almost all of the geometric designs we use in patchwork have a basic *underlying grid* that acts as an invisible guide to drafting the design. Most designs we work with are based on grids made up of a certain number of equal-size squares, as explained below. *The secret to drafting any design is to learn to*

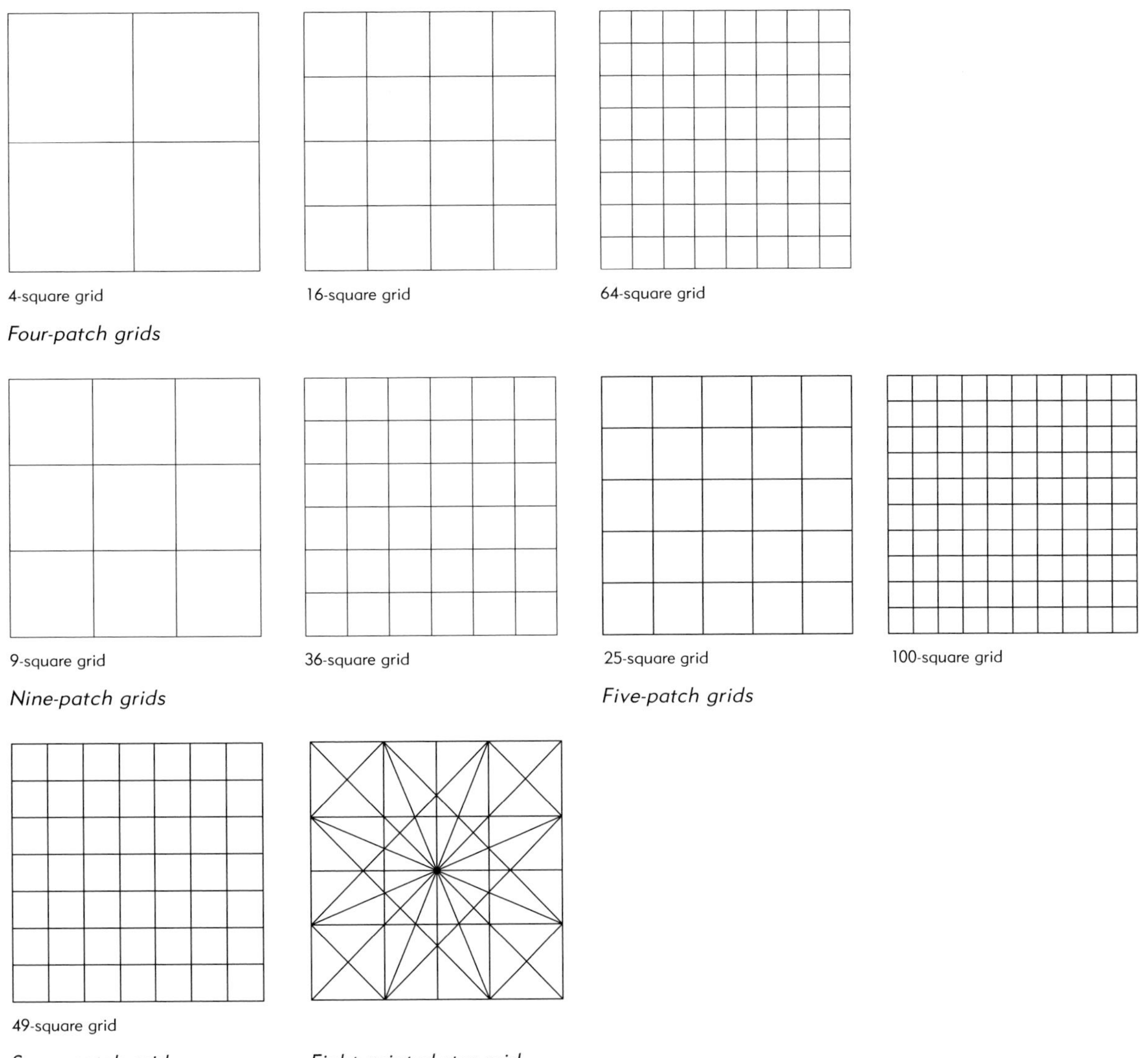

Four-patch grids

Nine-patch grids

Five-patch grids

Seven-patch grid

Eight-pointed star grid

recognize: first, which grid is needed to draft the design, and, second, how to get that grid onto a piece of paper.

Four-Patch Grid. The four-patch grid is based on dividing a square into a two by two (four square), four by four (16 square), or eight by eight (64 square) layout.

Nine-Patch Grid. The nine-patch grid is based on dividing a square into a three by three (nine square) or six by six (36 square) layout.

Five-Patch Grid. The five-patch grid is based on dividing a square into a five by five (25 square) or ten by ten (100 square) layout.

Seven-Patch Grid. The seven-patch grid is based on dividing a square into a seven by seven (49 square) layout.

Eight-Pointed Star Grid. All the grids we've seen so far simply divide a square into a certain number of smaller, equal-sized squares. The eight-pointed star grid is different. It is based on 16 spokes radiating at equal angles from the center of the square to the edges.

Drawing a Perfect Square

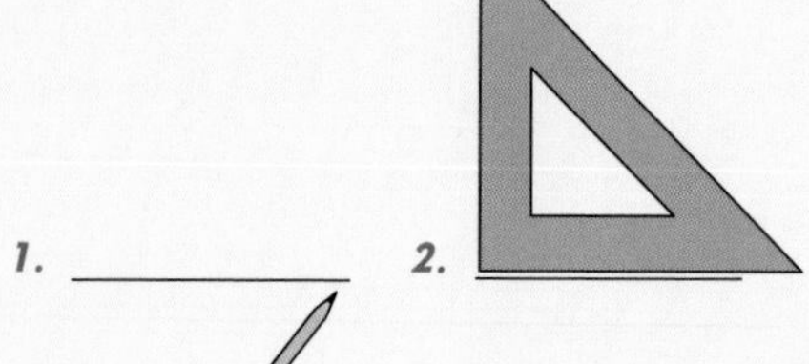

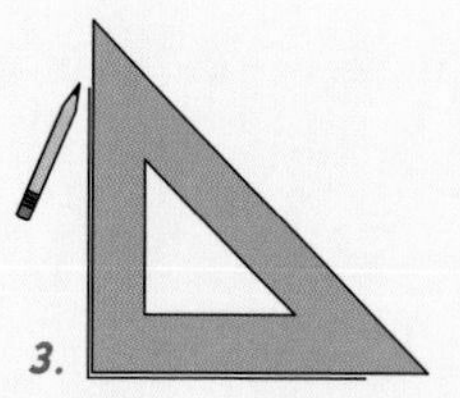

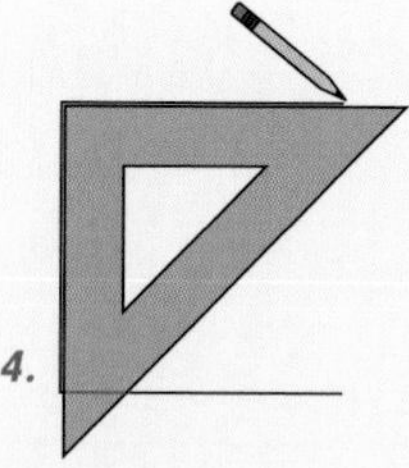

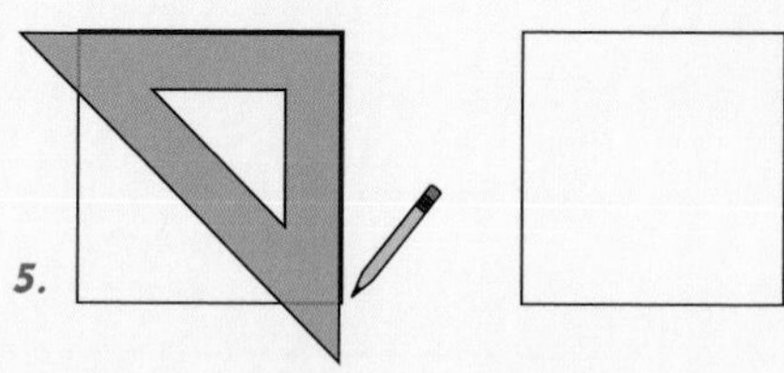

FOLLOW THESE SIMPLE GUIDELINES for making a perfect square.

1. Begin by drawing a horizontal line the length of the size of the finished square.
2. Place a large 45° right-angle triangle along the line with one side exactly on the line and the right angle of the triangle at one of the endpoints of the line.
3. Draw a line perpendicular to the first line that is exactly the same length.
4. Turn the triangle so it is along the newly drawn line, with the right angle stopping at the exact endpoint of the new line. Draw a third line the same length as the first two.
5. Turn the triangle one last time with the right angle at the end of the new line and draw the final segment of the square.

Other Grids

While most geometric designs use one of these basic grids, some patterns require even further divisions, and some require grids with different divisions altogether, such as 11 by 11 squares. Though not as prevalent in patchwork, patterns based upon a hexagon or a pentagon have their own basic grids as well.

Recognizing the Underlying Grid

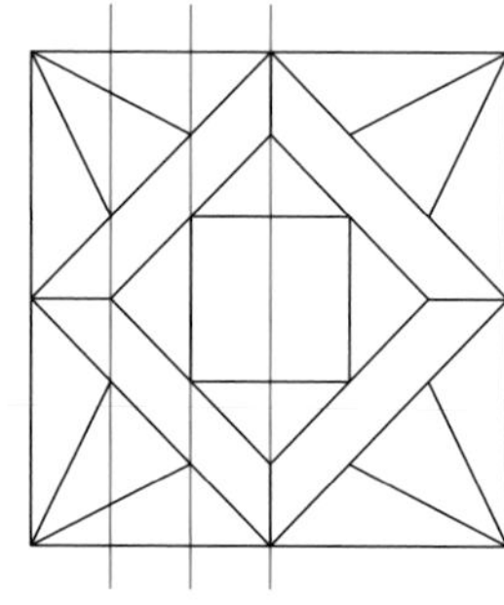

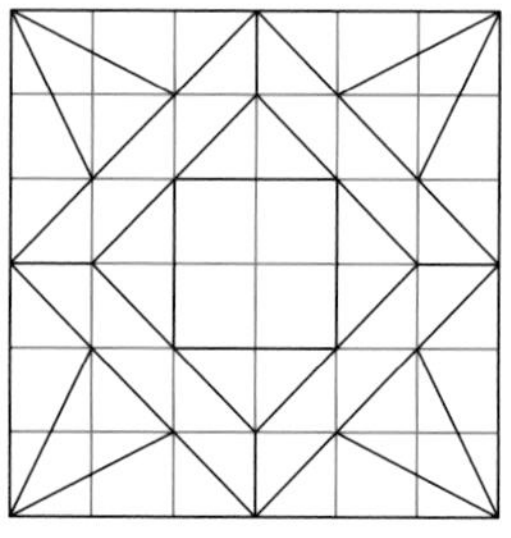

Place ruler over design to determine grid

By far the majority of traditional quilt patterns are based on four-patch and nine-patch grids, perhaps because these were considered the easiest of all to draft. But, as we shall see, there are many beautiful patterns based on the other basic grids as well, and they are just as easy to draft as a simple four-patch.

It is important to note that you will not necessarily *see* the grid in the pattern. In fact many designs based on a grid of squares have no squares at all in the design. The easiest way to recognize the grid needed to draft a pattern is to place a piece of tracing paper over the design. Then, using a small ruler or other straight edge, find some obvious points around the edge of the block that you can connect with straight lines to a parallel side of the block. These points could be edges of squares or the points of a star. Continue working your ruler across the block until you see how many equal divisions there are. This will then tell you how many squares you need in your grid to draft that particular design.

Here, we see several designs and the underlying grids on which they are based. With practice you will eventually be able to "see" the grid without the aid of a straight-edge.

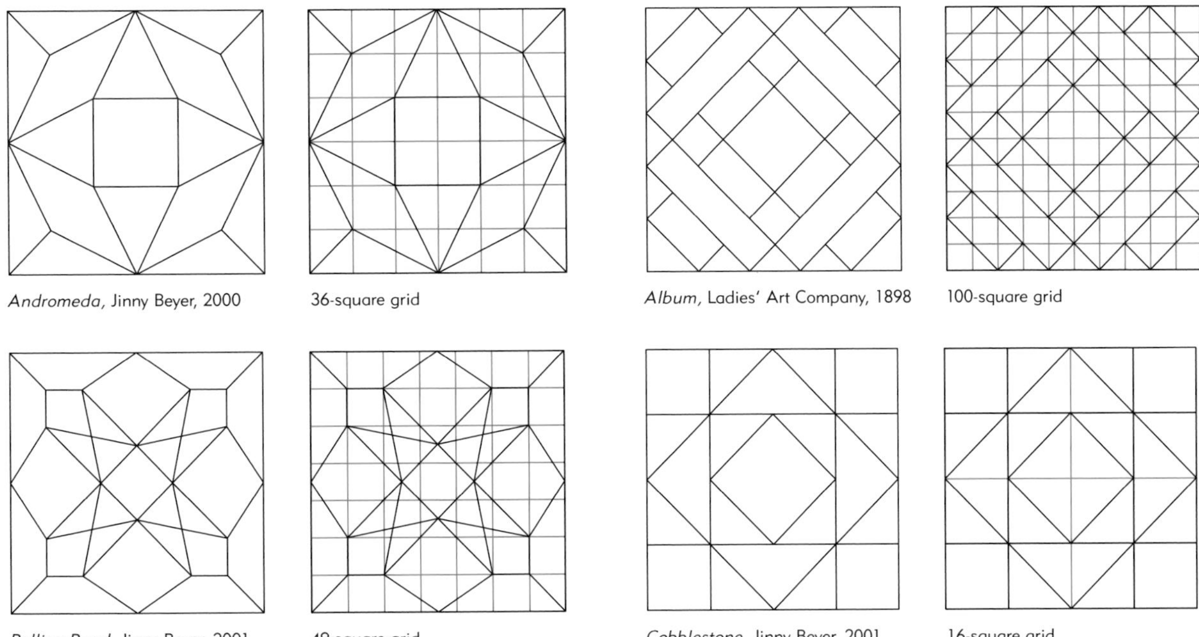

Andromeda, Jinny Beyer, 2000 | 36-square grid | Album, Ladies' Art Company, 1898 | 100-square grid

Rolling Road, Jinny Beyer, 2001 | 49-square grid | Cobblestone, Jinny Beyer, 2001 | 16-square grid

Find the grid behind these simple designs

Recognizing the Underlying Grid

Designs based on the eight-pointed star grid can be a little tricky because not all such patterns contain a star with eight points. Moreover, many designs that do contain stars with eight points are not based on this grid–the stars may be made, for instance, from parallelograms instead of diamonds. Look at the basic eight-pointed star grid again. Some people mistakenly think that certain eight-pointed star designs are based on one of the four-patch grids, because you can see that the block is broken down into four large squares (see drawing on left, below). Others think it is based on a nine-patch grid because they see three divisions–from the corner to the points of the star, and between the star points (see center drawing). But the similarity stops there. If you look across the top edge of the grid, you will see four divisions, but those divisions are *not* equal. Likewise it is not a nine-patch grid, because the middle division (the distance between the points of the star) is wider than the other two. Furthermore, notice that the distance between the points of the star is equal to the diagonal division across the corner and, in fact, the combination of the middle divisions and the diagonal produces a perfect octagon (see drawing on right).

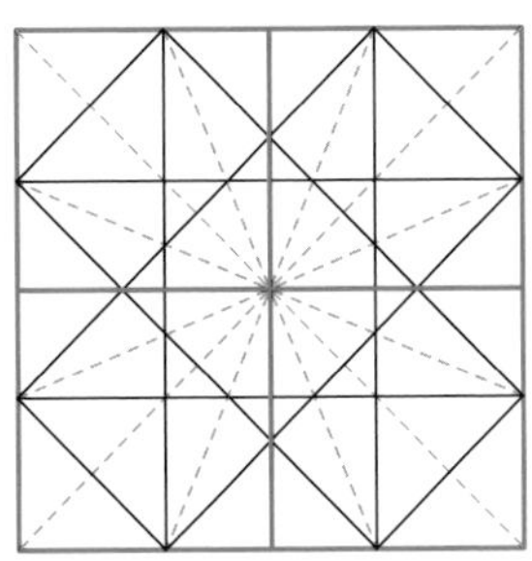

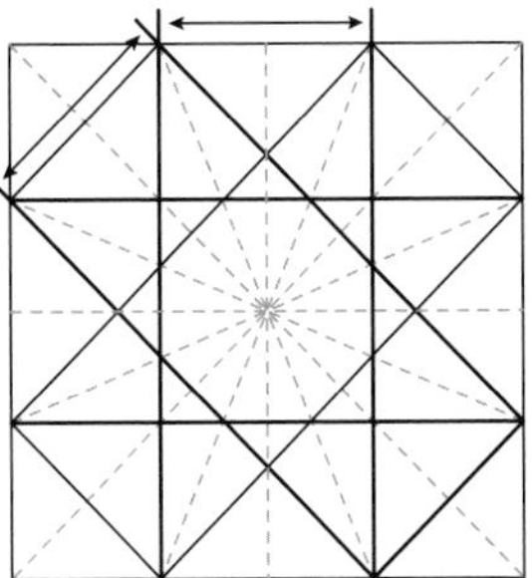

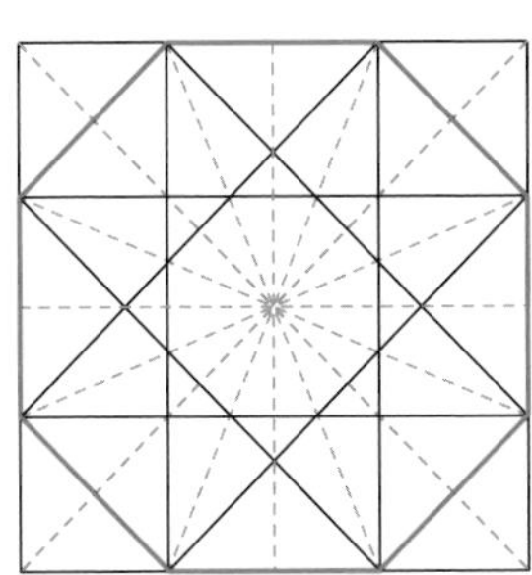

Eight-pointed star grid

Asking the following questions might help you to recognize whether or not a design falls into the eight-pointed star grid.

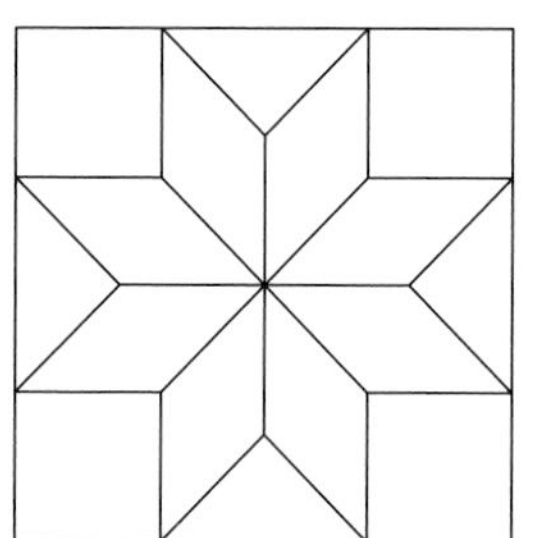
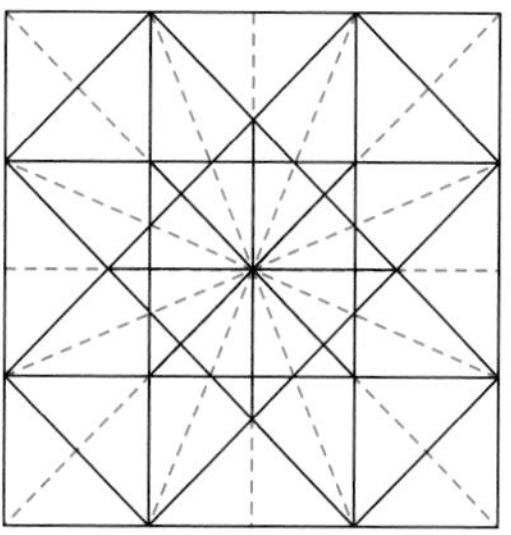

Eight-Pointed Star, Ladies' Home Journal, 1898

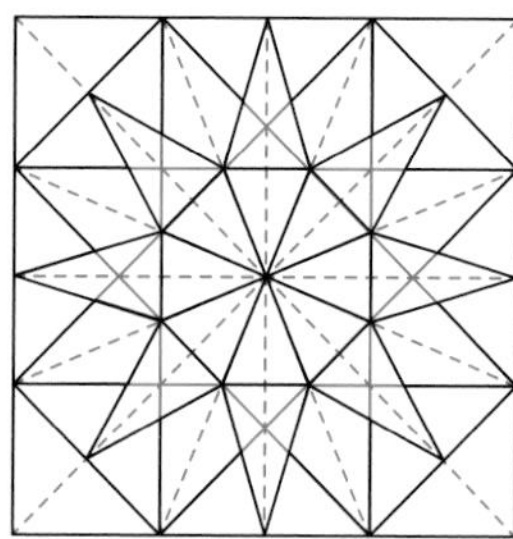

Atlantic Jewel, Jinny Beyer, 1984

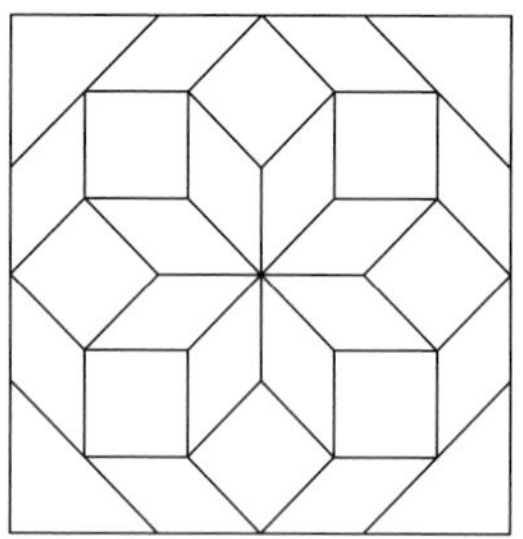
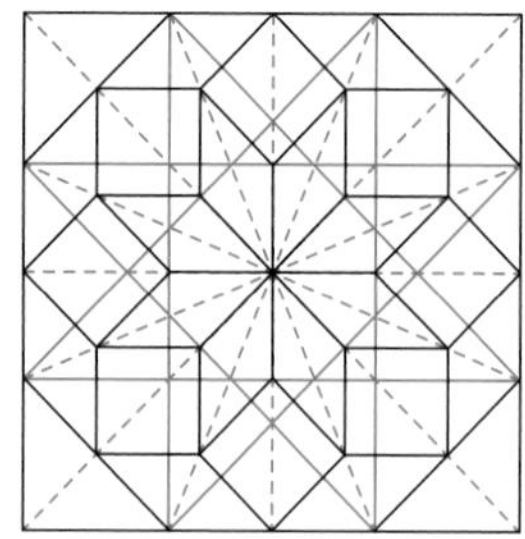

Rolling Star, Ladies' Art Company, 1898

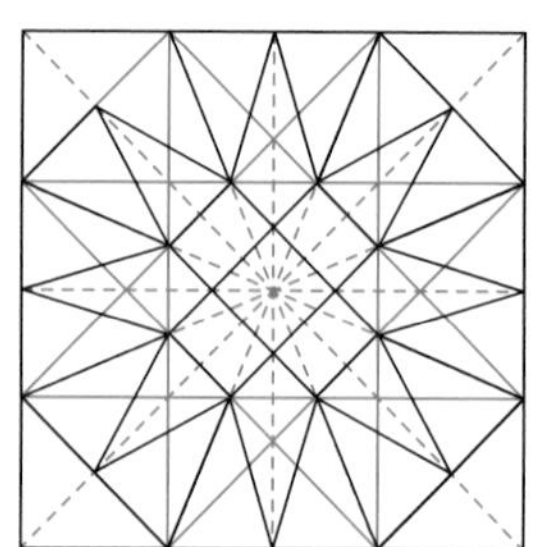

Star of North Carolina, Ladies' Art Company, 1922

Grids beneath eight-pointed stars

Eight-Pointed Star Designs

1. Is the middle division equal to the diagonal across the corner?
2. Are there any true octagons in the design?
3. Are there any perfect 45° degree diamonds?

A few eight-pointed star designs are shown here, with the basic grids underneath. The only way to really learn to recognize a design's underlying grid is to practice. The designs shown on pages 37 to 38 are based on one of the grids discussed above. Get out a piece of tracing paper and a straight edge and see if you can determine which grid is required to draft each of the designs. Test yourself and then turn to pages 46 to 47 for the key.

Creating Grids of Squares

Once you have selected a design and have figured out what grid is needed to draft it, it's time to draw the grid. Grids can be made in a variety of ways. If your design is a size that is in equal inches (centimeters), you can use ordinary graph paper that is already divided into inch (centimeter) segments. Many times, however, you'll find you need the design to fit in an odd-sized space. It would be difficult, for instance, to draft a 10¾″ grid onto graph paper divided into equal segments.

One of the easiest methods is to begin by drawing an accurate square the size that you want for your finished design. You can then create the grid by simply folding the paper. Fold it in half two ways to make a four-square grid, in half and half again for a 16-square grid, in thirds for a nine-square grid, and so

Practice Sheet 1 *(See key on page 46)*

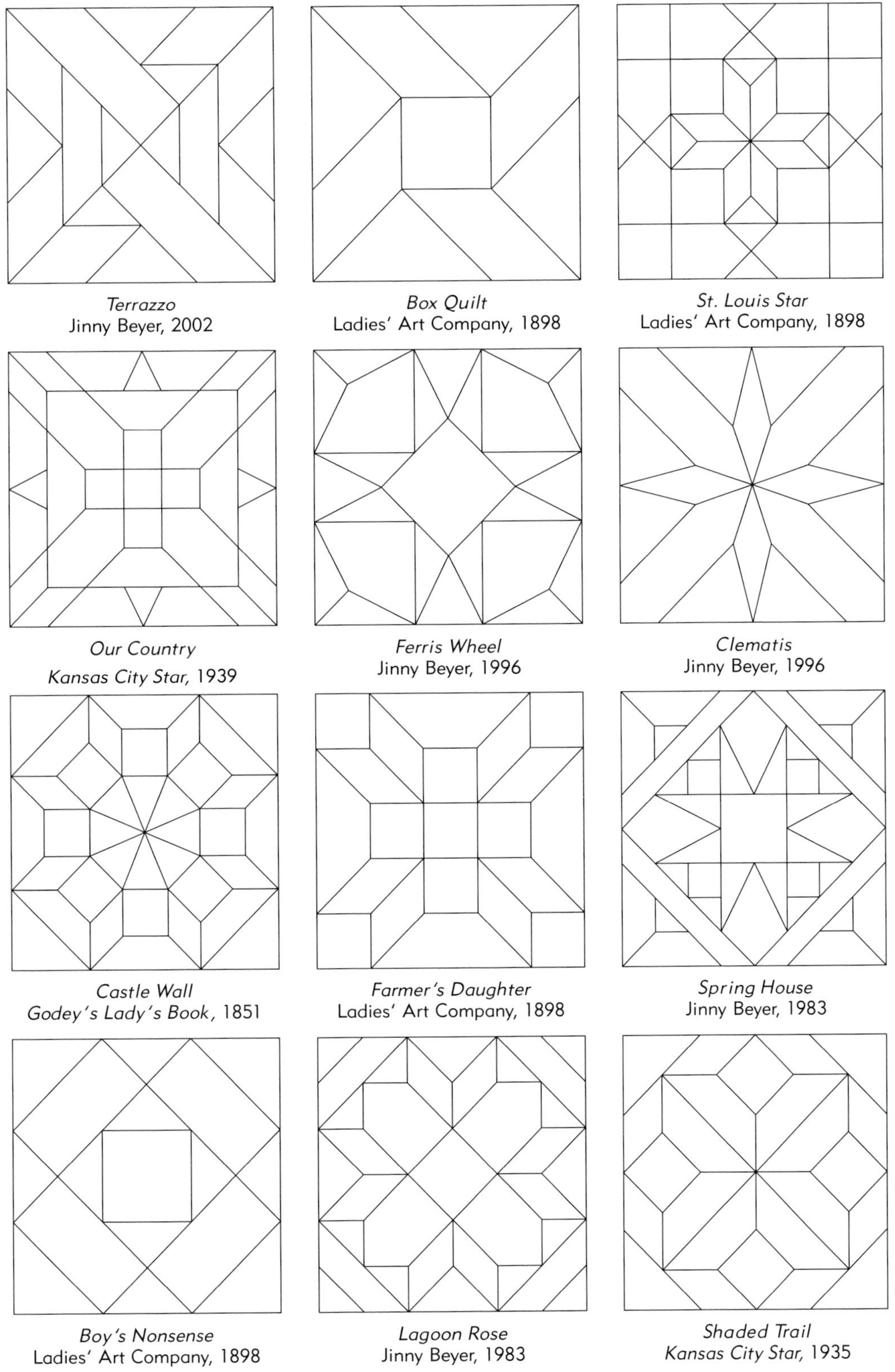

Terrazzo
Jinny Beyer, 2002

Box Quilt
Ladies' Art Company, 1898

St. Louis Star
Ladies' Art Company, 1898

Our Country
Kansas City Star, 1939

Ferris Wheel
Jinny Beyer, 1996

Clematis
Jinny Beyer, 1996

Castle Wall
Godey's Lady's Book, 1851

Farmer's Daughter
Ladies' Art Company, 1898

Spring House
Jinny Beyer, 1983

Boy's Nonsense
Ladies' Art Company, 1898

Lagoon Rose
Jinny Beyer, 1983

Shaded Trail
Kansas City Star, 1935

Practice Sheet 2 *(See key on page 47)*

Lead Glass
Jinny Beyer, 1988

Quasar
Jinny Beyer, 2000

Patchwork Design
The Ladies' Friend, 1866

King David's Crown
The Romance of the Patchwork Quilt in America, 1935

Light House Tower
Jinny Beyer, 1981

The Disk
Ladies' Art Company, 1898

Symphony
Jinny Beyer, 2002

Palm Leaf
Ladies' Art Company, 1922

Key West Beauty
Ladies' Art Company, 1928

All Kinds
Ladies' Art Company, 1898

Rolling Road
Jinny Beyer, 2001

Lisbon Lattice
Jinny Beyer, 2002

Step 1. *Draw a square*

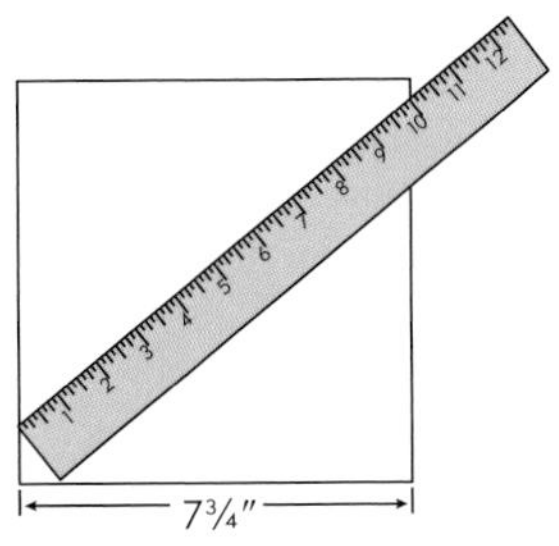

Step 2. *Place zero mark on left and 10″ mark on parallel side*

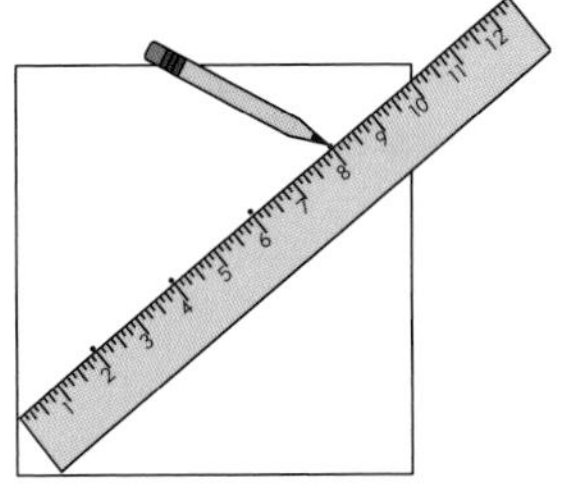

Step 3. *Make a mark every 2″, dividing square into five*

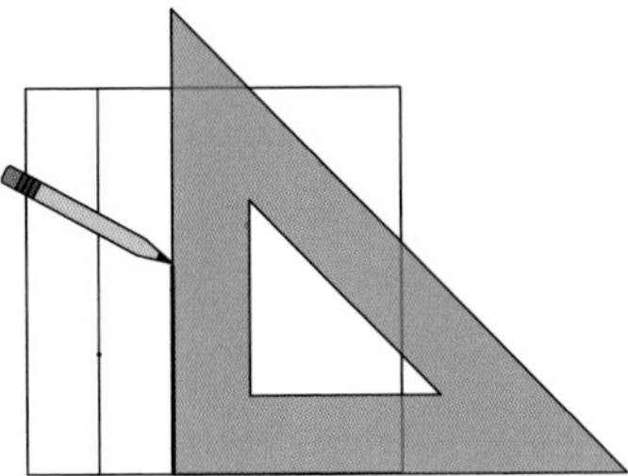

Step 4. *Position triangle and draw lines*

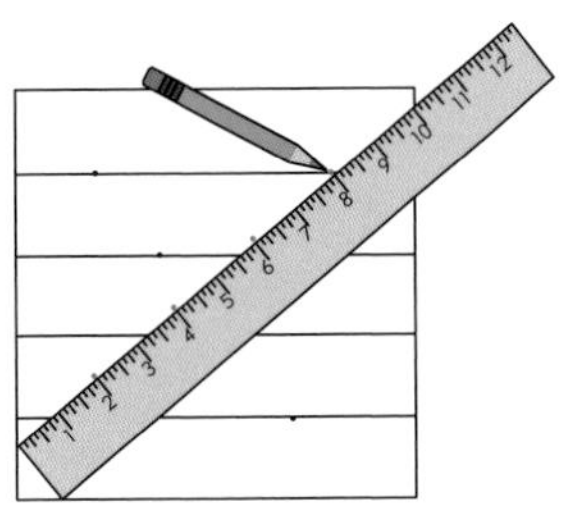

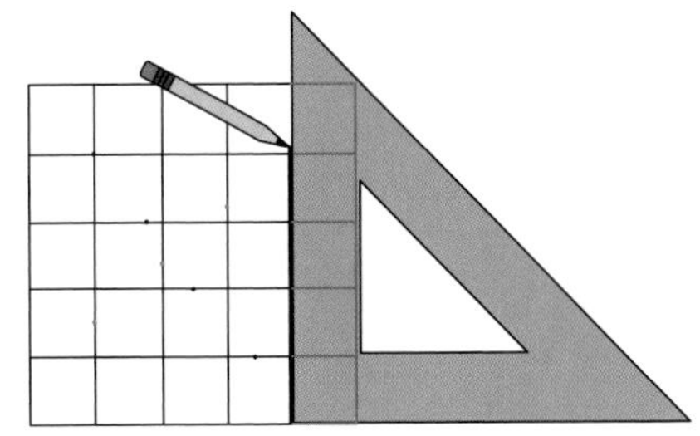

Step 5. *Draw lines in other direction*

on. Keep in mind, though, that paper folding is not always perfectly accurate. Moreover, while there are ways to make them by paper folding, five-patch and seven-patch grids are difficult to achieve.

Besides paper folding, there is another very easy way to create a grid of any number of squares and on any size piece of paper. All you need is a ruler that is *longer* than the square you want to divide (a ruler with both inches and metrics is good) and a right-angle 45° triangle.

For illustration purposes, let's say that the design you want to draft is based on a 25-square grid and you want to draft it in a 7¾″ size. First, you will need to divide the square into five equal divisions in both directions in order to get the grid. If you do the math, you will realize that each division must measure 1.55″. This is tough to measure on a ruler–unless you use your ruler a little differently than usual. Here's how.

1. Draw an accurate 7¾″ square on a piece of paper (see page 34).
2. Begin dividing the square into five equal divisions. If the paper were 10″ square it would be very easy to divide by five because each division would be every 2″ and, using the ruler, you would simply make a mark across the square at 2″ intervals. But wait, all you have to do is *pretend* that your 7¾″ square is 10″. To do this, place zero on your ruler somewhere along the left side of the square. Then angle the ruler so that the 10″ mark falls somewhere on the opposite *parallel* side of the square.

A Little Extra Help . . .

MANY OF TODAY'S QUILTERS have a computer that they use for e-mail or word processing. Very few, however, take advantage of their computers to draft patterns for quilts. The same basic knowledge required to draft patterns with pencil and paper applies to computer-aided drafting, too. The difference is that the computer allows you to draw out your designs much faster and with assured accuracy. Further, after you have drawn the design once, you need never draw it again. The pattern can be saved and later resized for use on future projects.

Any good graphics program will work for drafting patterns. Some of the better ones are Canvas, Adobe Illustrator, and Corel Draw. I use Canvas, but all drawing programs have similar features and work in pretty much the same way.

GRIDS IN A SNAP!

Creating a grid on the computer is a lot easier than doing it with pencil and paper and can take less than a minute. Most computer graphics programs will have an option to "turn on" or "view" a grid. When this feature is on, the background of the page will display a grid that, in the default mode, is usually in 1/2" increments. In addition to displaying the grid, there is also a feature that allows you to "snap to grid." What this means is that any line you draw will automatically align with the grid. You can specify at what interval you want the line to snap to the grid. I usually set the snap-to-grid function to 1/8". What this means is that when I begin drawing a line, as long as I am within 1/8" from the place where I want the line to begin, that line will automatically snap to that spot. Consequently, you can be a little sloppy with your mouse and not worry because you will always have perfectly straight lines.

There are two methods I use to create a grid. First, if you don't actually want to see the grid in the finished design, it is not necessary to draw it. With the "display grid" feature (or similar features in other programs) turned on, you already have the grid in the background! Simply draw a box around the portion of grid to get the number of boxes you need. For instance, if I am making a block that needs a 36-square grid, I will draw a box that measures 3" × 3". Within that box, the dotted lines of the grid will automatically show six divisions at 1/2" increments. Never mind that my finished design is going to be 8 1/2" square. I will draw it at 3" and, when I have finished drawing all the lines for the pattern, I will "group" the lines into a single object and then resize it to the dimensions of my pattern. Likewise, if the design is based on a 25-square grid, I will draw a box that is 2 1/2" × 2 1/2". For a 49 square grid, the box will be 3 1/2" × 3 1/2", and so on. With a little practice, you'll soon be making grids in a snap.

QUICK TIP

In Canvas, if you hold the shift key down while drawing a box, the box will always remain a perfect square. (The same holds true if you are drawing a circle.) If you hold the shift key down while drawing a straight line, the line will either be perfectly straight, or will go at a perfect 45° angle. Other drawing programs offer similar features—check your help index.

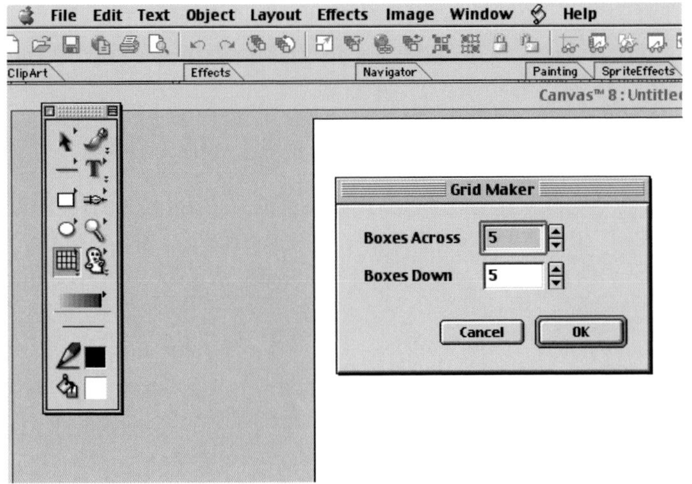

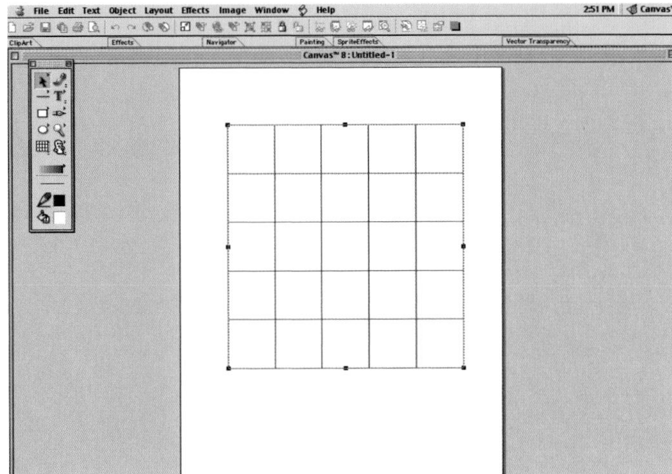

Using the "grid-maker" feature in the graphics program Canvas

Redrafting on the Computer

3. Now make a mark every 2″ along the edge of the ruler and you will see that–from left to right–the square is divided into five equal divisions, each of them exactly 1.55″ wide.
4. Using a right-angle 45° triangle, align the bottom of the triangle along the bottom edge of the square. Move the triangle until the perpendicular side hits the first dot and then draw a straight line. Continue moving the triangle to each dot until all lines are drawn.
5. Now you need the lines going the other direction, so turn the paper one quarter turn and repeat the process again. You must make a *new* set of dots. So as not to get the dots confused, it is helpful to use a different colored pencil for this step.

This same process can be used for dividing any size square into any number of divisions. All that is needed is a ruler *longer* than the width of the square. Find a number on the ruler, greater than the width of the square, which can be easily divided by the number of divisions you are trying to achieve. Place zero on the left side of the square and angle the ruler until that number falls on the parallel side on the right side of the square, then simply mark off the increments. Because a metric ruler has smaller divisions, sometimes it is easier to use the metric side of the ruler and sometimes the inch side.

The second way to create a grid is to use the "grid-maker" feature included with most graphics programs, including Canvas (again, check your help pages). When the dialog box for that tool is opened, you can specify how many blocks across and how many blocks down you want. So, for a 25-square grid, specify five squares across and five squares down. Then, go to the drawing page and drag with the tool while holding the shift key. The result will be a perfect square with the grid inside. This can be resized to any dimensions.

"To sit down with paper and pencil and try to figure out how to cut a square of cloth into eight diamonds which, when joined together, will form a perfectly matched star of a definitely desired size, is a task that the modern girl just out of college may well hesitate to undertake. But great-great-grandmother did not waste time bothering her head over any such problem. Many years before the kindergarten was dreamed of, she employed one of its elementary practices, with the aid of scrap bag and scissors. Diamond patches are the most ingenious of the results she achieved."

Ruth E. Finley, *Old Patchwork Quilts and the Women Who Made Them*, 1929

Creating an Eight-Pointed Star Grid

The eight-pointed star grid is created differently from the square grids described above. This grid is based on spokes radiating at equal angles from the center of the square out to the edges. Every other spoke is marked with A and B points, as shown here. Then those points are connected (A to A, B to B, and A to B) to get the grid. The lines created form the basis of the eight-pointed star grid. This is the easiest way to create the underlying grid.

1. Draw a square and divide it diagonally from corner to corner.
2. Using a right-angle 45° degree triangle, line it up with the center of the square and draw a line dividing the square in half from top to bottom.
3. Turn the square and repeat, dividing it in half the other direction.
4. Place a compass point at each of the four corners and open the compass out so the pencil reaches the *center* of the block. Draw a quarter circle. The points where the quarter circles touch the *edges* of the square are the A/B points.
5. Mark the A/B points and connect A points to A points and B point to B points to create radiating lines.
6. Connect the A/B points to get the basic star grid.

Eight-Pointed Stars, Fast and Easy

Drafting the eight-pointed star grid on the computer is very quick and easy.

1. Turn on the "display grid" and the "snap to grid" functions (check the help pages in your graphics program to find out how to turn these on).
2. Draw a square of average size that will snap to the grid. (I usually make one about 6″.)
3. Divide the square diagonally from corner to corner.
4. At this point I use the star tool in Canvas. (Other programs have similar features–check your help pages.) I specify that I want "spokes" instead of points and set the number at "16."
5. Next, going back to the drawing, place the cursor at the center of the block and, by holding down the option key (on a Mac) or alt key (on a PC), draw from the center of the block outwards, and there you have 16 spokes radiating outwards at the perfect angles. Mark the A/B points.

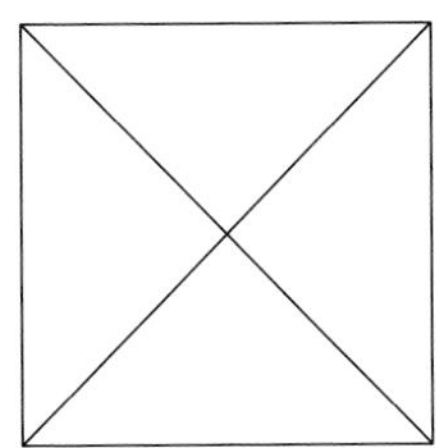

Step 1. Divide square diagonally from corner to corner

Step 2. Divide square in half from top to bottom

Step 3. Turn square and repeat

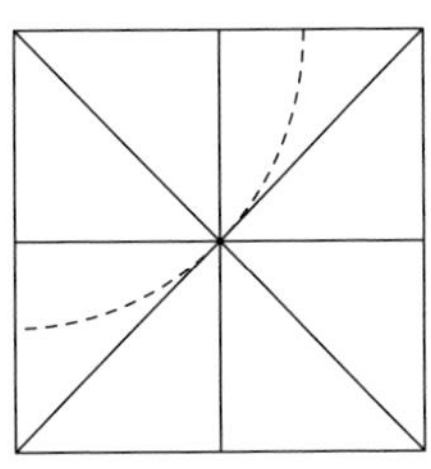

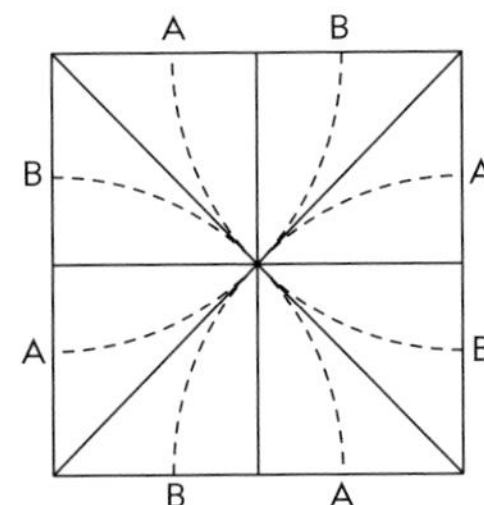

Step 4. Draw a quarter circle

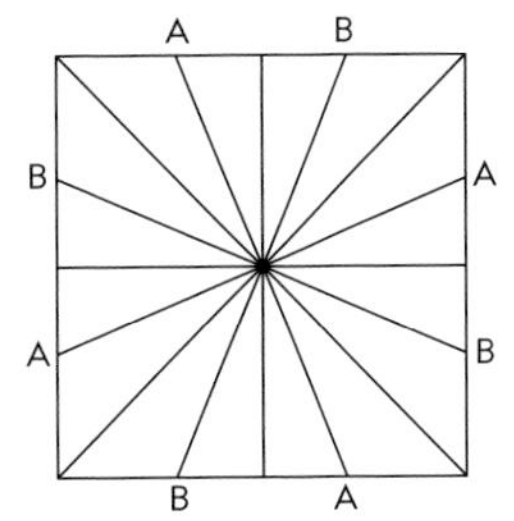

Step 5. Connect A to A and B to B

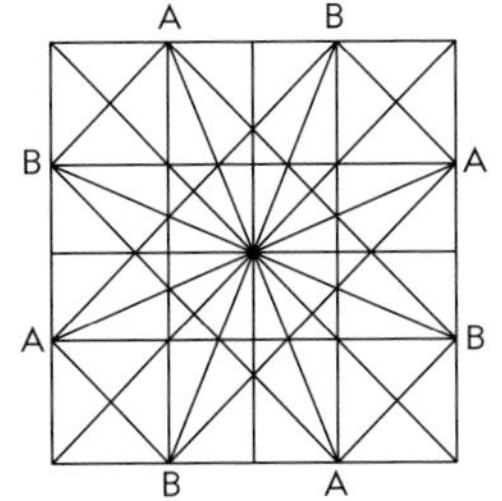

Step 6. Connect A/B points to get basic star grid

Creating an Eight-Pointed Star Grid

6. Now, turn *off* the "snap to grid" function (because these A/B points do not fall on the grid) and connect the A/B points as was explained in drafting the grid on paper.

Drafting the Pattern

Once you have determined the necessary grid for the design and drafted the grid in the correct size, you are ready to draw the pattern. Place a piece of tracing paper over the grid and secure it with tape. Then draw the outside of the square, so that if your paper slips, you can line it up again. It is easiest to see what you are drawing if you use one color pen or pencil for drawing the grid and a different color for drawing the pattern.

Sometimes, looking at the entire pattern can be a little overwhelming. I advise people to look at the part of the design that they can readily see. Perhaps it is a center square or a corner square. Draw the portion that you see first, and you will soon find that the rest of the design just falls into place. Try to look at any long lines that may extend from one side of the square to another part. Determine which portion of the grid is used for these lines and draw the entire line instead of just small sections of it.

Computer Time Savers

Drafting the design on the computer is much quicker than doing it with pencil and paper, but the concept is exactly the same. Here are a few hints for saving time by avoiding unnecessary work or repetition.

Patchwork Ingenuity

Antique ***Lone Star****, circa 1850*

"The arranging of patterns to make a good and well-balanced design calls for much ingenuity. . . . A few designs carefully arranged are much more effective than a mass of different ones showing no forethought."

Beatrice Scott,
The Craft of Quilting, 1935

Early writers who talked about patchwork patterns were often amazed by the complexity of designs achieved by women with little or no schooling in geometry or rudimentary mathematics. Girls with no formal education were nonetheless able to draft their own patterns, create their own color schemes, and sew often complex geometric shapes with absolute accuracy. As quilt historian Ruth E. Finley comments, "Ninety-nine percent of all pieced quilts represent the working out of geometrical designs, often so intricate that their effective handling reflects most creditably on the supposedly non-mathematical sex."

Ms. Finley goes on to describe a method of cutting that involved folding the fabric to create the desired pieces. While this is not a method I would recommend since it can lead to inaccuracies, it does provide insight into the work-a-day attitude of our grandmothers and great-grandmothers toward their needlework—"A piece of cloth carefully folded, a pair of scissors, a snip or two, and the trick was done!"

Quite simply, Ms. Finley explained how the quilter could take a square of fabric and quickly cut eight same-size diamonds, with no waste whatsoever. Here is how she describes and illustrates the process:

> "Take a square of cloth (Figure 1) and fold it successively into Figures 2 and 3. Fold Figure 3 diagonally, producing Figure 4. Now, using A as a fulcrum, fold C over to the line A—B, producing Figure 5. Next fold A up to meet C, as shown in Figure 6. Then, using the top fold to guide your scissors, cut along C—E. Unfold and to obtain eight diamonds cut to center along the shorter creases. You will have eight diamond patches precisely alike, as shown in Figure 7."
>
> Ruth E. Finley, *Old Patchwork Quilts and the Women Who Made Them*, 1929

- On the computer, there is no need to take pains to draw a square the exact size of your finished design. Rather, it is better to draw a square the size that will fit the grid of the design you are drafting. Follow the grid lines to draw the various elements of the design and resize it later.
- If there are several portions of the design that are exactly the same, such as several squares, it is only necessary to draw that square once, using the square tool. Then, holding down the option key on the Mac or the alt key on the PC, drag a new copy of the object. This is often quicker than drawing each object individually.
- Once the design is drawn it can be resized to the exact measurements needed for your design. To do this, select all of the lines or objects that make up the design and group them together. After the objects are grouped, go into "group specs" (or similar feature in your graphics program) and resize the block to whatever proportions you need for your design. This block can then be saved. If you need it in a different size in the future, all you need to do is open the block, go into "group specs" again, and punch in the numbers of whatever size you need.

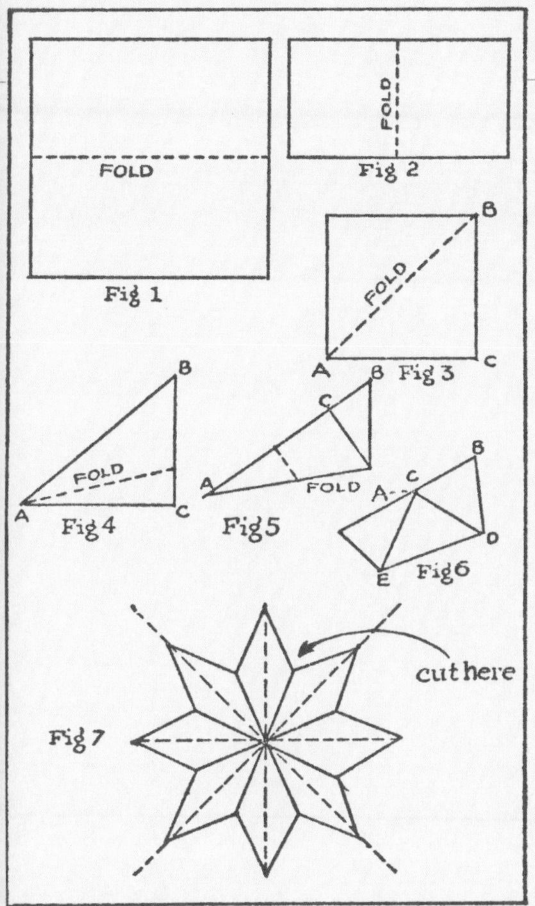

"The great object of all instruction . . . is to strengthen the mind, and form the character. Even needlework, humble as the employment may appear, may be made conducive to this end. When it is intelligently taught, the mind is employed as well as the fingers; powers of calculation are drawn out, habits of neatness acquired, and the taste and judgement cultivated in a way which eminently fits women for the higher branches of service, . . . credit to themselves, and comfort to their employers."

Cassell's Household Guide to Every Department of Practical Life, Volume IV, circa 1875

While I firmly believe that using accurate templates is the best way to cut fabrics for quiltmaking, the folding method Ms. Finley describes is very similar to a paper folding system that I have used for drafting patterns. If very thin paper is used and extreme care taken in the folding, this is a quick way to draft an eight-pointed star in any size. Rather than cut the paper apart as Ms. Finley suggests, simply unfold it and you will have all the lines needed for the templates.

- Computer graphics programs have a "layer" feature which is essentially like using layers of tracing paper. Particularly with eight-pointed star designs, I like the grid to be on one layer and the actual block on another. I change the color of the grid from black to red and then I use black to draw the actual design.

The sheets of designs shown on the next two pages are the same as the "test" on page 37 to 38. But now the grid is showing under the designs. Study the blocks to see how the grids are used for creating other geometric patterns.

Freedom to Create

The next time you pick up a quilt book or magazine, look at some of the block designs and see if you can figure out the underlying grid. With practice, you will be amazed at how easy it is to find the grid needed for a design, create the grid, and then draw the design following the grid lines. You will find that the knowledge of how to draft your own patterns will allow you the freedom to create any pattern you desire.

Key to Practice Sheet 1 (See practice sheet on page 37)

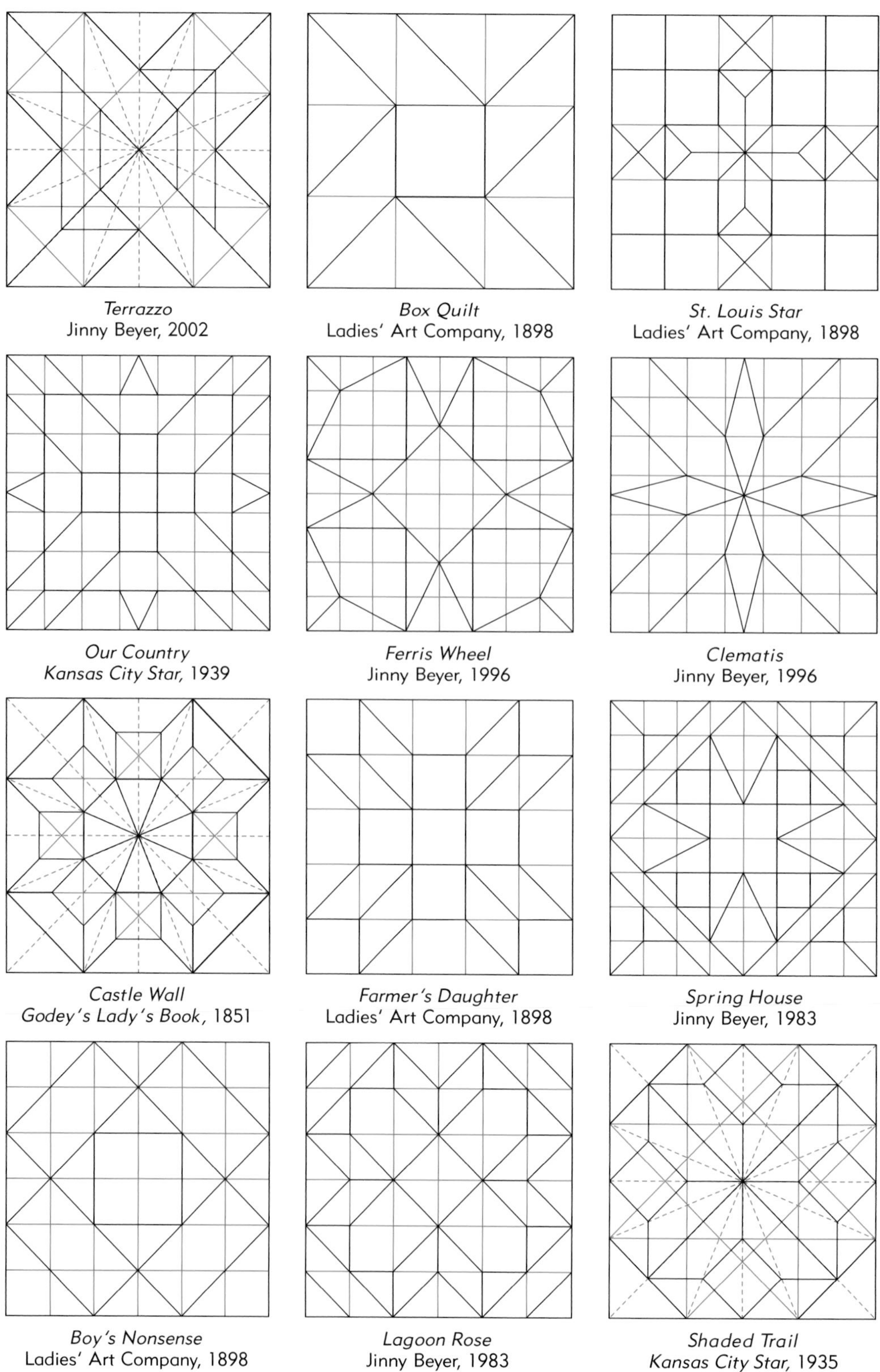

Terrazzo
Jinny Beyer, 2002

Box Quilt
Ladies' Art Company, 1898

St. Louis Star
Ladies' Art Company, 1898

Our Country
Kansas City Star, 1939

Ferris Wheel
Jinny Beyer, 1996

Clematis
Jinny Beyer, 1996

Castle Wall
Godey's Lady's Book, 1851

Farmer's Daughter
Ladies' Art Company, 1898

Spring House
Jinny Beyer, 1983

Boy's Nonsense
Ladies' Art Company, 1898

Lagoon Rose
Jinny Beyer, 1983

Shaded Trail
Kansas City Star, 1935

Key to Practice Sheet 2 *(See practice sheet on page 38)*

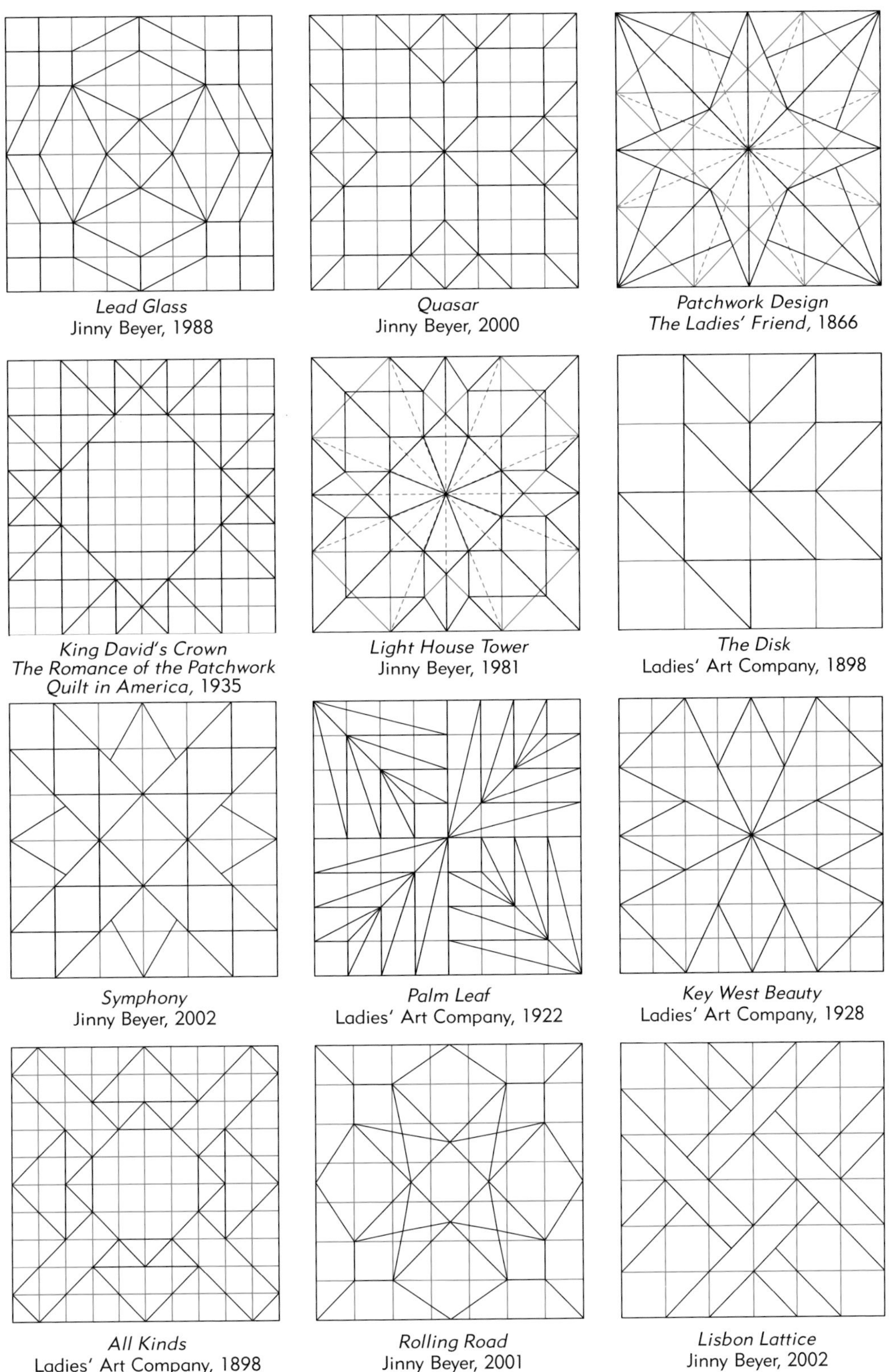

Lead Glass
Jinny Beyer, 1988

Quasar
Jinny Beyer, 2000

Patchwork Design
The Ladies' Friend, 1866

King David's Crown
The Romance of the Patchwork Quilt in America, 1935

Light House Tower
Jinny Beyer, 1981

The Disk
Ladies' Art Company, 1898

Symphony
Jinny Beyer, 2002

Palm Leaf
Ladies' Art Company, 1922

Key West Beauty
Ladies' Art Company, 1928

All Kinds
Ladies' Art Company, 1898

Rolling Road
Jinny Beyer, 2001

Lisbon Lattice
Jinny Beyer, 2002

Hexagon Star charm quilt, circa 1875. Maker unknown

Preparing to Sew

"We hear so much about this 'jazz age' being hard on the nerves. Quilt-making is the ideal prescription for high-tension nerves. It is soothing and there is no exercise can equal that of really creating something with the hands. And later the product of these hands may be handed down as treasured heirlooms."

CARRIE A. HALL AND ROSE G. KRETSINGER,
The Romance of the Patchwork Quilt in America, 1935

NOW THAT YOU HAVE DECIDED UPON A PATTERN AND either drafted it yourself or secured it from another source, gathered all of your supplies, and selected a palette of colors in fabrics of your choice, you are almost ready to begin stitching. But there are a few more preparatory steps to take. You must decide on the placement of each fabric within the design, make the pattern pieces, cut the fabric, and determine the order in which you will sew the pieces.

Fabric Placement

One of the most important–and most enjoyable–elements of quilt design is determining the placement of dark, medium, and light values within the pattern. I do all of my quilt designing on paper or on the computer in black and white. Only after finalizing the value placement in the various elements of the design will I go to my fabrics. When working on a design that is made up of repetitions of an individual block, the first step is to make a series of line drawings of the block. Then, using a black marker, I color several of them, placing light, medium, and dark values in different places on each one. When finished, I photocopy them several times, cut them apart, and sort them into piles, with all the blocks shaded the same way in their own stack. Then I paste blocks shaded the

Designing on a Computer

WHEN WORKING WITH a graphics program on the computer, the task of deciding value placement in a quilt design is so much quicker than shading, photocopying, and cutting out blocks to paste together. For instance, in Canvas begin by drawing the design as was explained on pages 43 to 45. Using the "fill" tool (or similar function in your graphics program), fill the various portions of the design with dark, medium, and light values. Next, group all objects in the design, then go into "object specs" and resize the block to 1" or 1½." Set the "snap to grid" function and drag the block to one corner of the page until it snaps to the grid. Holding down the option (Mac) or alt (PC) key, drag a new copy of the block to the right and just beside the first one. Now hold the command key (or control key on a PC) down and type "d." In Canvas, this is the shortcut for duplicating a block. (Check your help index for a similar feature.) Another block will miraculously appear beside the last one. Continue pressing command "d" until you have as many blocks as you want in the row. Now press command and type "a" (select all), which selects all of the blocks on the page. Hold the option key down and drag a new copy of the entire row down to just below the first row. Now continue to type command "d" and the row will continue to be duplicated until you have as many rows as you want. Within seconds you can see what multiple blocks of your shaded design will look like.

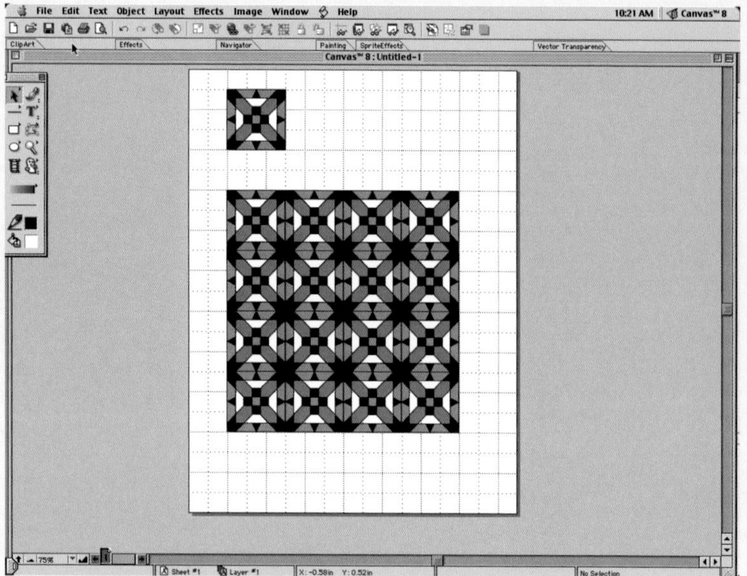

Designing on a computer

***Day Lilies.** See full quilt in pattern section*

same together. This helps me to determine which layout I prefer. It is only after I am satisfied with the value differences within the design that I sort the fabrics by colors and values and then determine which prints will go in what part of the design.

Some of my quilts, such as *Day Lilies*, shown in the pattern section, have subtle values of shading within the block rather than strong contrasts. Here again, this is all done first in black and white. In *Day Lilies*, each flower is made up of six smaller pieced units. Each of those units is identical in terms of the placement of light and dark. In the design stage, working in black and white, I shaded that unit light to dark in a couple of different ways, photocopied those, and then determined which placement I liked best. It was only after I was satisfied with the shading arrangement that I began sorting my fabrics into color groups and then by light and dark within the color groups.

"After the pattern and material are decided, the problem of cutting out our quilt is next. This is conceded to be the least interesting and most tedious part of quilt making; however, it is certainly not a step that can be hurried as blocks must be cut exact. There is no alternative to this."

Ruby Short McKim,
101 Patchwork Patterns, 1931

Making Templates

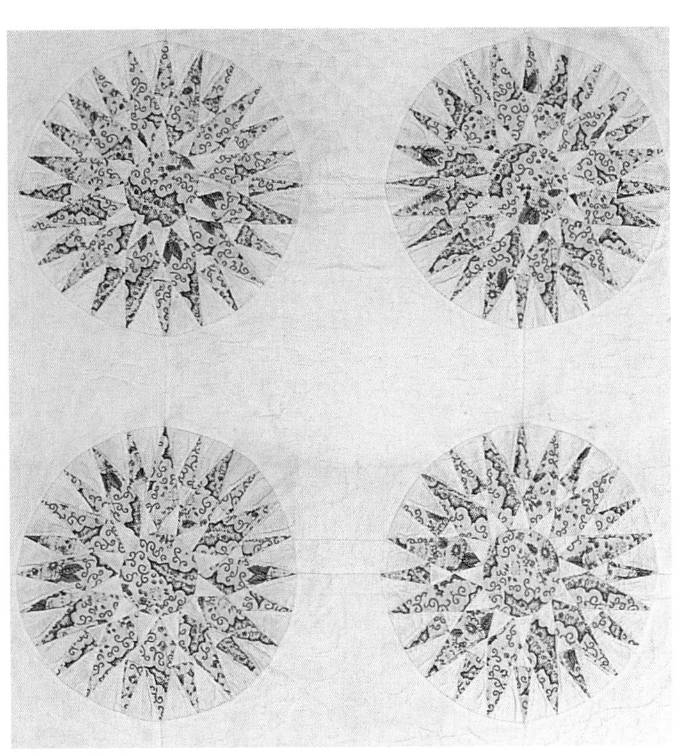

*Antique **Mariners' Compass**, circa 1840. Maker unknown*

Probably the most important of any of the steps involved in making a quilt is to ensure that the fabric pieces are cut with accuracy. Too often, in our hurry to begin sewing, we overlook the simple but critical fact that if pieces are not cut accurately, they will not sew together accurately either. Careful cutting means that pieces will fit together precisely, with a minimum of mistakes or unmatched corners or points. Most of the patterns in *Quiltmaking by Hand* are made from shapes such as squares, rectangles, diamonds, or triangles that are easy to cut. Others, like *Compass Rose* or *Day Lilies* are more challenging and require you to work with oddly shaped templates or with curved edges. No matter how complex the shape, accurate cutting will make the sewing go faster, smoother, and trouble free. In my experience, the most reliable method of cutting fabric with the precision needed for hand piecing is to use accurate templates and a sharp pair of scissors. The first step is making templates.

Templates are the pattern pieces that are used to cut out the shapes in a quilt design. Unlike dress patterns made from tissue paper that is pinned to fabric and cut around, quilting templates should be made from a sturdy material with firm edges, such as plastic or stiff cardboard. In a quilt, many pieces are typically cut from the same pattern piece; if the material used for the templates is not sturdy, the edges soon wear down, and the accuracy of the template is lost.

My favorite template material is rigid semi-transparent plastic. This comes in sheets that are approximately 11″ × 17″ (28 cm × 43 cm) and is available from most quilt stores. Plastic template material is also available with grid lines marked on one side as an aid to measurement. I prefer the plain, semi-transparent kind because the grid lines are often not compatible to the design of the pattern, and the grids make it more difficult to see the fabric design through

Rotary Cutter or Scissors?

In recent years, rotary cutting equipment has become increasingly popular. With a circular blade, a rubber cutting mat, and a hard-edged ruler, it is possible to slice through three or four layers of fabric at the same time, cutting multiple same-shape pieces at once. Typically, the fabric is cut into long strips, then into smaller shapes such as squares or triangles. Rotary cutting works best when you are cutting same-shape pieces from a relatively small number of fabrics of which you have a lot of yardage. Rotary cutting is designed for simple geometric shapes; it is difficult to cut curved and odd-shaped pieces with accuracy.

The patches in the quilts our grandmothers made were cut the old-fashioned way—with accurate templates and a sharp pair of scissors. I still prefer this method. Many of my quilts are made from scores of different fabrics and small pieces left over from other projects rather than from new yardage fresh off the bolt. By hand cutting, I can work just as easily with precious scraps of favorite fabrics as I can from newly purchased yardage. I can also easily incorporate curved pieces or oddly-shaped templates into my designs. Best of all, hand cutting allows me the flexibility to change my mind once my quilt begins to take shape—I'm not limited to the hundreds of tiny squares or triangles that may have been pre-cut from a particular fabric I no longer feel is right for the quilt.

For these reasons, *Quiltmaking by Hand* deals with the traditional method of cutting. Even so, the ten patterns at the end of the book do include some help on rotary cutting. If you are working with simple shapes and your preference is to rotary cut, there are a variety of good books available on the topic that also explain how to adapt a traditional pattern to this type of cutting.

the template. If you prefer to make templates from "found" materials, try old x-ray film, plastic lids, or even plastic bacon wrappers!

Most commercial quilting patterns and books provide patterns for template pieces like the ones at the back of this book. Usually these have ¼″ (0.75 cm) seam allowances added around all sides of each piece. The sewing line is often indicated by a dashed line and the cutting line is a solid line. The transparent template material can be placed directly over these patterns and copied onto the plastic. If you have drafted your own pattern, the same process is used, but you will need to add your own ¼″ (0.75 cm) seam allowance around all sides of each piece. To prepare your templates:

1. Place the template plastic directly over the pattern in the book, the pattern leaflet, or your drafted design and trace each piece onto the plastic. I like to place a short ruler along the line, then mark along the edge of the ruler to get a clean, straight line.
2. Trace any identification marks and grain lines. Use a permanent marker to record all identification letters and lines that appear on each pattern piece, as well as the size and name of the block and the number of pieces

needed. If you have drafted your own pattern, use a ruler with ¼″ (0.75 cm) lines marked to add an exact seam allowance around all sides of each piece. Place the ruler along the sewing line with ¼″ (0.75 cm) extending beyond that line. Mark along the edge of the ruler. This will allow for the ¼″ (0.75 cm) seam allowance.

3. Using a sharp pair of scissors, cut around the template piece on the solid cutting line. Do not use your good fabric scissors for cutting templates as the plastic causes them to blunt quickly. Alternately, place a ruler along the cutting line and score the plastic with an exacto knife or rotary cutter.
4. Double check your templates against the pattern for accuracy.

To Mark a Sewing Line or Not to Mark a Sewing Line?

When you have a drawing of a pattern to use for a quilt, you cannot just cut fabric for those pieces and expect them to join together accurately. Extra fabric must be allowed for the seam allowance. For this reason, a seam allowance of ¼″ (0.75 cm) is commonly added to each pattern piece. There are basically two methods. The first is to add the ¼″ (0.75 cm) directly to the template, in which case the marked line is the cutting line. You then simply "eyeball" the sewing line or, if a guide is needed, mark another line along which you will sew. The second method is to cut the template the size of the *finished* piece. Draw around each piece and use that pencil line as your sewing line. Cut each piece approximately ¼″ (0.75 cm) from the line.

Of these two methods, I far prefer the first, mainly because it takes much less time. I have to admit that I am extremely biased in that I *always* add the ¼″ (0.75 cm) to the template and eyeball the seam allowance. But even 70 years ago there was a difference of opinion in the literature as to which method was best. Ruby Short McKim was non-committal:

> "It is a matter of preference again whether your master cardboards be the cutting or sewing size. Some like to cut on the pencil line and gauge their seams back from this. Others prefer to cut a seam out from lines which are penciled onto the wrong side of the cloth, then sew back on these lines . . . "
>
> Ruby Short McKim,
> *101 Patchwork Patterns*, 1931

In the following two quotes we see conflicting opinions. In the first, Ms. Miall agrees with me, and in the second Hall and Kretsinger take the opposite point of view.

> "Have an absolutely accurate paper pattern and cut every patch from this. To make sure that exactly uniform quarter-inch turnings are allowed on each patchedge, it is best to allow these when making the pattern, so that the patches are cut to its exact size."
>
> Agnes M. Miall,
> *Patchwork Old and New*, 1937

> "Cut the pattern of a good grade of paper, without allowing any seams, then lay the pattern on 'pressboard' and cut them out actual size. This will insure a perfect pattern that will not curl up or tear and one that will last forever . . . Lay the pressboard pattern on the wrong side of the material and mark around it with a well sharpened pencil. When cutting, allow for all seams and sew in the pencil mark, which will insure a perfect match."
>
> Carrie A. Hall and Rose G. Kretsinger, *The Romance of the Patchwork Quilt in America*, 1935

Let me get on my soap box for a moment and explain why I prefer to add the exact ¼″ (0.75 cm) to the template. As noted in the above quotes, during the 1930s, some quilting books began to suggest that quilters need a sewing line in order to ensure accuracy when stitching two pieces of fabric together. Earlier writings on hand piecing make no mention of such lines, assuming that quilters who have cut an accurate fabric patch from an accurate template are able to eyeball a standard seam allowance used for stitching. Somehow, however, the notion that a sewing line aids accuracy took hold during the quiltmaking revival of the early 1970s and remains strong today. My research leads me to believe that this practice altered the way piecing had been done for centuries, needlessly increasing the time and effort it takes to complete a quilt by hand. Furthermore, the extra time it takes to mark a sewing line on every piece of fabric and the extra effort involved in checking and double-checking that you are staying on that line when sewing may have discouraged a lot of people from hand piecing. One reason so many people prefer machine work is that they can cut more than one piece at a time! I have found, for example, that it takes me at least three times longer to cut the pieces and sew with a line on each piece as it takes me to sew without the line.

When our grandmothers and great grandmothers hand stitched pieces together for a quilt, they made a simple template from cardboard. The template already included a standard seam allowance, typically ¼″ (0.75 cm). They held the template securely onto the fabric and then traced around the template to cut out their fabric pieces. They discovered that with a sharp pair of scissors they could stack the fabric up to four deep, pin those layers together and cut as many as four of the same piece at one time. Once the pieces were cut, they would simply line up the cut edges of two pieces, pin them together, and begin stitching. From an early age, they learned to eyeball the seam allowance. This is the method I have always used and still use today. My classroom experience tells me that new quilters have no difficulty at all in doing the same–by the time their first few blocks are complete, they are as proficient as I am in eyeballing a ¼″ (0.75 cm) seam allowance.

If you are still not convinced, compare my method with the laborious process of working with a sewing line. Here, the template is made the size of the *finished* piece (without seam allowance). It is then carefully placed on a single layer of fabric, allowing at least ½″ (1.5 cm) between each piece for seam allow-

Adding a Seam Allowance on the Computer

ADDING A ¼″ SEAM ALLOWANCE when working with a good graphics program is very easy. Canvas has a special tool called the "parallel line tool;" other programs offer similar tools that work in the same way (check the help pages in your graphics program). To add ¼″ around shapes, this is what I do.

1. Draw the design and size it to the dimensions for the block.
2. With the "polygon" tool (other programs have similar functions, usually accessed from the main toolbar through the line tool), click *clockwise* around the shape to create an "object."
3. With the object selected, go to the parallel line tool. The dialog box will have you enter specifications, as follows:
   - Under "total lines" enter "2"
   - Under "orientation" enter "outside"
   - For "spacing", enter ".25"
   - If you want the sewing line to appear as a dashed line, select the bottom of the two lines, then go to "dash," just to the left of the lines. Select the size of the dashes you want.
4. Click "apply" and your shape will change with a ¼″ parallel line around the outside.

ances. A piece of chalk or a pencil is used to mark the sewing line. Finally, each piece is *individually* cut, with a more-or-less accurate ¼″ (0.75 cm) seam allowance. Since there are hundreds of pieces in a full-size quilt, this takes time. Consider the amount of fabric that is wasted in between each cut piece! The sewing line also causes problems during stitching. Since the seam allowance is never quite exact, it takes quite a bit of time to line up any two pieces that will be stitched together. First, you must put a pin through the corner of one of the pieces at the point where two seam allowances cross. Next, the pin goes into the same point on the second fabric piece. Care must be taken to ensure that the sewing lines on both pieces line up exactly, requiring several more pins to keep them in place. You will soon find that you are constantly turning the pieces over to make sure that your pins exit in exactly the right spot on the sewing lines! The same thing happens when you begin to sew–every couple of stitches you must keep turning over to the back to check that you are staying on the line.

There are still more reasons why I do not like marking a sewing line. Since this method requires that seams allowances are cut arbitrarily outside the stitching line, the seams, once stitched, often end up more than ¼″ (0.75 cm) wide. Unless you carefully trim each seam after stitching, you will encounter extra thickness of fabric when quilting the finished top. Furthermore, if the wrong kind of marker is used, such as a hard pencil or a pen, those marks may show through to the right side of the fabric, especially once the quilt is washed.

Proponents of the sewing line method argue that they have a hard time sewing a straight seam and having the line gives them the security of knowing that their pieces will be accurate. There are ways to still have a sewing line yet also benefit from an accurate ¼″ (0.75 cm) seam allowance. You will be able to

The Jinny Beyer Perfect Piecer

A TOOL CREATED SPECIFICALLY to accompany *Quiltmaking by Hand* allows you to mark the point where seam allowances cross without having to use a hole punch on every template you create. *Jinny Beyer Perfect Piecer,* the tiara shaped template shown here, includes the common angles used in patchwork. Holes are pre-punched in this master template at the precise points where the seam allowances will cross. Once you have cut your fabrics, simply line up the correct angle of the Perfect Piecer to the angle of your fabric pieces, then mark a dot through the holes.

Marking the seam allowance with a ruler

cut out more than one piece at a time, pin the pieces together more rapidly, and have a speedier sewing stitch.

First, I want to emphasize again that, with practice, you will eventually be able to eyeball a 1/4" (0.75) seam allowance. In the meantime, there are two methods I recommend that give you a sewing guide. Both of them involve only marking the guidelines on the piece that will be *facing* you as you sew. Since the pieces are cut with exact 1/4" (0.75 cm) allowances and the cut edges will be lined up evenly, only the piece facing you when stitching needs to be marked, thus saving time. This marking should be done when you are ready to sew, not ahead of time, because you may not be sure which piece will be on top and it is not necessary to take the extra time to mark *all* pieces.

The first method involves marking with a ruler. Many see-through rulers are available today that have 1/4" (0.75 cm) lines marked. Place a small 6" (15 cm) ruler such as this along the edge of the fabric piece and using a pencil, tailor's chalk, or other washable marking device, mark the 1/4" (0.75 cm) as shown.

The second method involves using a 1/16" (0.2 cm) hole punch. (Alternatively, use *Jinny Beyer Perfect Piecer* described above.) Carefully put small holes at the intersections of the seam allowances on each template piece. After lining up the edges and pinning two of the pieces together, place the template on the fabric piece that will be facing you as you sew and, using a mechanical chalk pencil or other pencil with a sharp point, mark small dots through the holes. If you need more of a guideline than dots only at the corners, put additional dots along the seam line marked on the template. You can then sew "dot to dot." This method will save a lot of time, as you do not have to mark the seam line on each piece, but only on the piece facing you as you sew.

I have asked beginning quilters to experiment by stitching pieces together using both methods of adding a seam allowance to the pieces. Even if they take the extra time to mark dots on the pieces facing them, they have found that the method of marking every seam on all pieces and then arbitrarily cutting the seam allowance takes them up to four times longer–with no increase in accuracy!

"Several patches can usually be cut at once by folding the material or piling up several layers of different stuffs. The pattern should be pinned on securely through them all, so that no slipping during cutting is possible."

Agnes M. Miall,
Patchwork Old and New, 1937

Cutting Fabric Pieces

For me, cutting out the pieces is a bit tedious. I would rather get to the stitching! Therefore to speed up the process I will cut more than one piece at a time. You can safely cut two pieces at a time and, with a good sharp pair of scissors, up to four pieces can be cut. If you cut four, I recommend pinning the fabric layers together to avoid slipping. I actually find that it is more difficult to cut a single piece, because the fabric is so flimsy. Two to four pieces creates more body and is easier to cut. The only time I cut single pieces is if I only need one piece for my pattern or if, for special effects, I am centering some motif from the fabric in the middle of the template.

With templates in hand that already include a ¼″ (0.75 cm) seam allowance, you are ready to begin cutting. First, make sure that you have all the templates you need for your blocks. If you are using just a few fabrics, organize them so that all the fabrics that require Template A are together, all those that require Template B are together, and so on. (If you are making a scrap-look quilt, however, that uses multiple fabrics or fabric scraps, sorting them in this way may take you more time than it saves!)

There are a variety of markers suitable for transferring a template's shape onto fabric. For light-colored fabric, many people use a pencil. For dark or light prints, tailor's chalk works well. Many people are shocked to learn that I use a good-quality ballpoint pen to mark around templates, but let me clarify my method. My templates *always* include a seam allowance. After marking around the template, I cut the fabric just within the marked line, so the pen line is actually cut away from each piece. I like to use a pen because its mark is visible on most fabrics and the pen glides easily, without tugging at or distorting the fabric. *Never* use a ballpoint pen to mark the *sewing* line. The pen mark would remain on the fabric, might not wash out, and could stain the quilt.

Since I often center motifs within a piece and need to see the right side of the fabric, I place the template right side *up* on the front of the fabric for marking. Another reason why I prefer to mark on the right side is that on many fab-

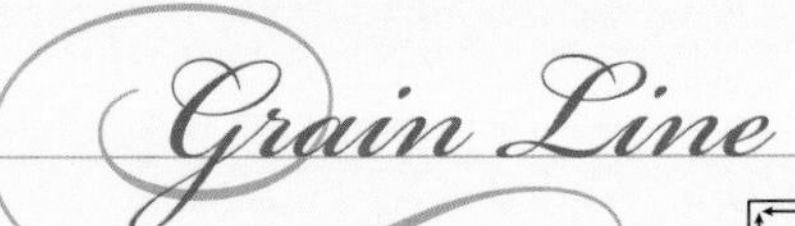

Grain Line

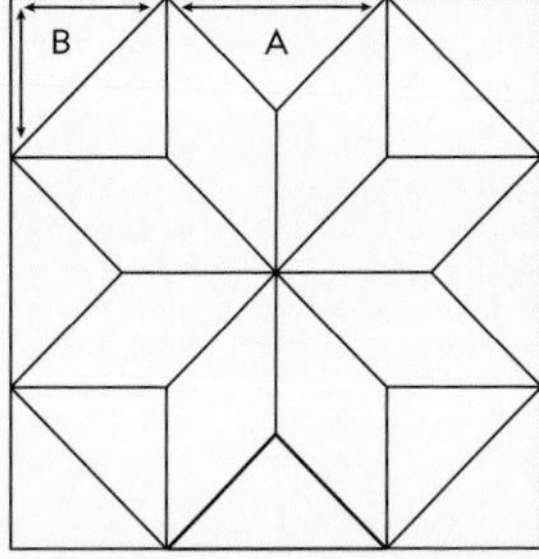

Crosswise or lengthwise grain at outer edge of block

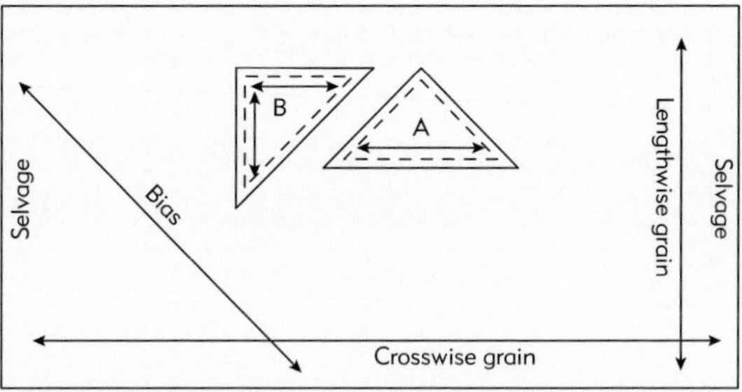

Cutting on crosswise or lengthwise grain

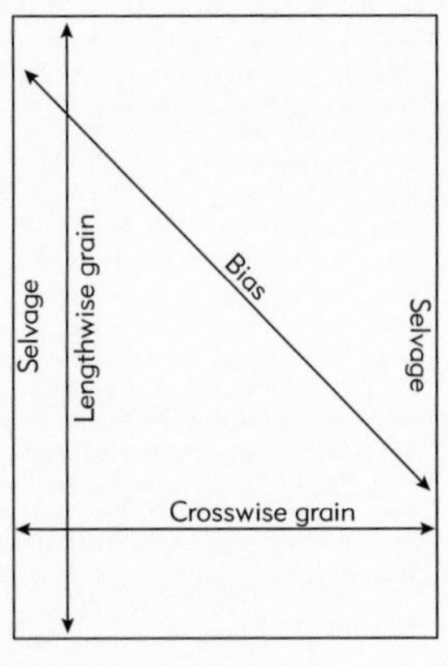

Grain line

It is important to be aware of the grain line of a fabric before beginning to cut. The *lengthwise* grain runs parallel to the selvage. The *crosswise* grain is perpendicular to the selvage, and the *bias* runs diagonal to the selvage. The lengthwise grain has the least amount of stretch, the crosswise grain has some stretch, and the bias is the most stretchy.

Most patterns have an arrow that indicates the direction in which the grain line should run. Wherever possible, place the arrow along the lengthwise or crosswise grain of the fabric. In general, when making a patchwork block, try not to have any bias edges that fall on the *outside* edge of the block. Whenever possible cut the pieces so that the lengthwise or crosswise grain falls along the outer edges of the block or unit, as shown here. This will help to prevent distortion of the block and will make it easier to sew to adjacent blocks or fabrics.

Note that even though the two triangles marked A and B are the same size and will use the same template, they are cut differently in

rics the design is not so prominent on the reverse and is hard to see. If you would rather mark on the wrong side of the fabric, however, place the template right side *down* to mark around it.

"Cloth should be smooth to cut, so iron any wrinkled material before laying on the patterns . . . Inaccuracies in cutting are as fatal in their way in this operation as in the so-called 'major operations'! And 'lastly' cut economically; a thrifty cutter has mighty few scraps left after her patterns have been laid on to the best advantage."

Ruby Short McKim,
101 Patchwork Patterns, 1931

Other Cutting Tips

- Make sure that the fabric is well pressed before cutting. After cutting do not press the pieces, as it might distort the shapes.
- A good sharp pair of scissors will save time and make the job much easier.

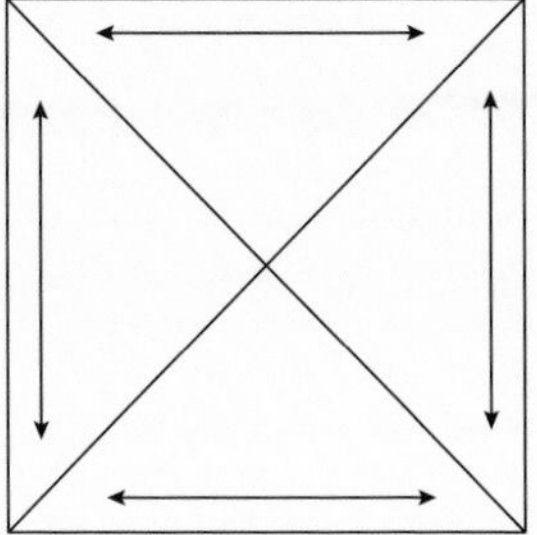

Cutting triangles

Cutting diamonds and sharp points

order for the lengthwise or crosswise grain to fall on the outside edges of the block.

When piecing a square composed of four triangles, the triangles should be cut with all the inner edges along the bias and the outer ones along the straight of the fabric.

When cutting diamonds, where the grain line goes depends on the size of the diamond. For stability and to eliminate distortion of the pieces, I tend to cut thinner diamonds with the straight of grain up the middle and wider diamonds with two edges on the straight of grain. For instance, for diamonds that are 45° degree angles or less, I like the grain to go up the middle of the piece. For 60° degree diamonds, I place the straight grain on two of the edges. When rotary cutting diamonds, however, the grain will almost always go on two of the sides.

Cutting fabric for *Mariners' Compass* or other blocks with sharp points is different. For the most part those shapes should be cut with the grain going up the middle of the piece.

"True bias and edges cut with the weave are imperative for right triangle sides, and on equi-angular triangles one side must be with the weave. Squares and oblongs must be with the weave of course . . . The center threads in the rays of the 'Rising Sun' run directly from center base to apex."

RUBY SHORT MCKIM,
101 Patchwork Patterns, 1931

- The selvage, which is thickly woven, runs on either edge of the full width of fabric. Do not incorporate this edge in any of your cut pieces. It is very difficult to stitch through, and often the design of the fabric does not go all the way to the selvage.
- If you are cutting several pieces from the same template and the same piece of fabric, save time by using "common" lines for two adjacent pieces. That way one cut can take care of two lines.
- Sometimes the marked line will be more visible on the reverse side of the fabric than on the front.
- Double check your pattern to see if there are any "reversed" or "mirrored" pieces. If the pattern calls for mirrored pieces, fold the fabric with wrong sides together and cut two pieces at a time, and you will automatically have one piece with its reverse. On the other hand, if you have any "directional" pieces, such as parallelograms, that do not have a reversed version, you must be careful to make sure all pieces are cut the same. The parallelograms in *Box Quilt* all go in the same direction and therefore must be cut from the same side of the fabric. The parallelograms in *St. Louis*

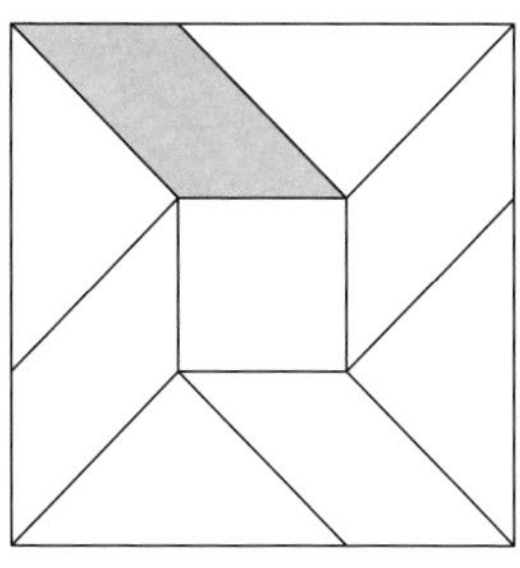

Box Quilt

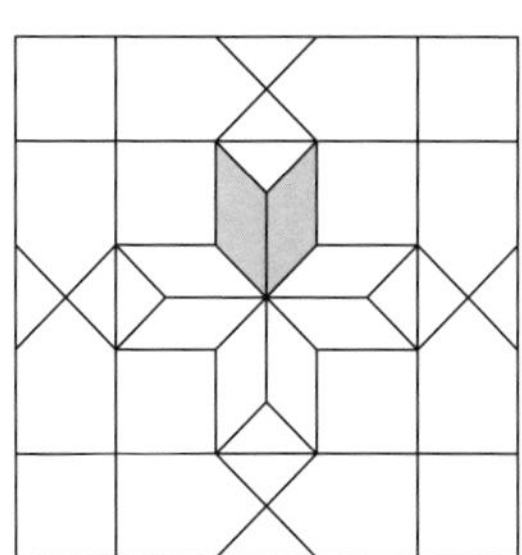

St. Louis Star

Star are mirrored, so the fabric can be folded with wrong sides together, and two pieces can be cut at the same time (one right-side-up and one mirrored).

- Don't cut out all of your pieces at once. You may find after you sew a couple of blocks that you want to alter some of the fabrics or add some additional colors. Cut enough that you have some sewing to pick up in odd moments, but after all the cut pieces are sewn, spread them out and see if you are happy with the balance of color and pattern in the fabrics you have selected. If not, add some more fabrics.
- Once the pieces are cut, keep track of the individual pieces by putting like pieces in a zip-lock bag. Or lay out individual blocks and put each block in a separate bag. This will make it easier to have sewing "on-the-go."

Assembling Pieces

In preparation for sewing it is important to know the order in which you will put the pieces together to form the unit or block. The hand piecing patterns included in *Quiltmaking by Hand* will provide more help with this, as does Chapter Four, Piecing Basics. For now, keep in mind that it is important to try to have straight line seams wherever possible. For instance, when sewing four squares together, you would sew two squares and then two more and join these two sets with one straight seam.

Sew two sets of squares

Join with straight seam

When assembling blocks, keep in mind these basic rules: Combine smaller pieces to make larger units, join larger units into rows or sections, and join sections to complete blocks. If you follow these rules, you should be able to build most blocks using only straight seams. Setting-in pieces at an angle should only be done when necessary. Sewing in this manner makes even very complex looking designs easy to construct with all straight seams and no setting-in of pieces. The *Mariners' Compass* block in *Columbia* shown opposite appears to be quite complex, but a closer look shows that almost all the sewing on both of this blocks can be done with straight lines.

When sewing quilts with an all-over design such as *Tumbling Blocks*, I still like to break the sewing down into workable units (see page 114) and I then wait to sew these together until all of the units are complete. Doing so gives the flexibility of adjusting colors and fabrics along the way. After several units are complete, I arrange them on the floor or a design wall and stand back and study them. Sometimes I decide there needs to be more darks or a spark of something bright. So I will make some units that contain the missing elements. There is no need to discard any units, because in the final layout of the design, the units are spread out and interspersed and a happy balance can be reached. This is the technique used in *Shamrock* and *Boxed Blocks*. Each quilter made stacks of diamond units, occasionally adding other colors, but did not arrange the units or sew any together until they were all complete.

"The child must be taught that the seam is not finished unless it be flattened down . . . An old toothbrush handle forms an excellent "flattener," and the unpleasant sound of scratching with the finger-nail, or the thimble, is avoided."

Cassell's Household Guide to Every Department of Practical Life, Volume IV, circa 1875

Pressing

Since I am usually sewing "on-the-go" at various places when I have a free moment, I do not normally have access to an iron. When sewing small seams together for a block, I finger press each seam after it is complete by running my thumb and index finger along the finished seam. When joining seams, I finger press one seam one direction and the other seam the opposite direction. I never press seams open.

When the block is complete, I fold a large fluffy towel and place it on the ironing board. Then I put the block right side up on this towel and press from the top, using a permanent press setting on the iron. I find it is easier to just let the seams go where they want to, instead of trying to force them to go in a particular direction, which sometimes causes bulk at the intersections. The only exception is when I am joining a very light colored fabric to a dark one. In that case, I press the seams toward the darker fabric so that the dark fabric doesn't show through the light one.

For borders, the seams are all pressed to one side or the other. But first it is best to "set" the seam. Do this by pressing along the stitched line, with the right sides of the fabric pieces still together. Then open out the piece and press the seam to one side. The decision as to which side is based on where the quilting stitches are going to be. When quilting "in the ditch" (see page 161) or close to the seam, you definitely want to quilt on the side without the seam.

Columbia. *Sections with straight sewing. See full quilt in pattern section*

Shamrock. *Diamond units. See full quilt in pattern section*

Roses, *circa 1850. Maker unknown. The entire quilt top is made up of tiny squares and rectangles, intricately designed and hand-pieced*

Chapter 4

Piecing Basics

Running Stitch, Squares, and Rectangles

"Piecing a quilt top is not such a formidable task. Really a knowledge of plain sewing, accuracy and neatness are all that are required . . ."

Ruby Short McKim,
101 Patchwork Patterns, 1931

A review of antiquarian needlework books yields very little information on the precise sewing stitch that has been used for patchwork for hundreds of years. Extraordinarily beautiful steel engravings show the stitches and how the thread is to go, but there is very little description of how to hold your hands, where the thimble should be, or even on what side of the work the various fingers are positioned. The running stitch used for hand piecing is elegantly described as "plain sewing," the simplest of stitches. Yet there is virtually no guidance on how it is achieved. The fact of the matter is that, in years gone by, as Ruby Short McKim so aptly reminds us, the running stitch required no explanation at all. A skill passed down from mothers to very young daughters, everyone already knew how to do it!

Since piecing has become far less intuitive as time has passed, the simple guidelines in this chapter will help you quickly master the technique of creating neat and tidy lines of running stitch. You will learn how to sew simple shapes. You will also join together four right-angled pieces–squares or rectangles–achieving perfect, crisp points where the angles meet. *Golden Rectangle*, shown in the pattern section, is among the easiest quilts to make and is an excellent project to practice basic hand-piecing skills. Or perhaps you would like to make a start on one of the beginning-piecing quilts designed for this book, such as *Columbia* or *Starflower*. You will learn all the techniques needed to sew the first portion of one of these quilts and, in so doing, gain good skills with the practice.

Hand Piecing with Ease and Speed

As with any other task, there are simple techniques that can help you quicken the pace and lead to perfect results every time. The simple steps that follow will help you quickly master the running stitch used to piece one patch of fabric to another.

When sewing a dark piece to a light one, use thread of the darker color or close to it. The stitches are more apt to show when using a light-colored thread. Never use a thread that is lighter in color than either of the two pieces you are sewing, or the stitches will show.

Threading the Needle

It does not seem that there could be much of a discussion about the simple task of threading a needle, but in fact there are certain considerations to keep in mind. I have observed many people as they thread a needle and find that there are a variety of different ways of doing so. Some people hold the needle steady and move the thread to the needle with the other hand; others hold the thread steady and bring the needle to the thread. From what I have observed, it seems that the hand that is doing the moving tends to be the dominant hand. Usually the needle is held vertically and the thread passes through the eye horizontally. However, some people hold the thread vertically and bring the needle, which is horizontal, down to the thread.

I am ambidextrous in most things I do, and even though I am more comfortable hand stitching with my right hand, I consider myself left-handed. When threading a needle I hold the needle steady in my right hand and push the thread through the eye with my left. You will find it much easier to thread the needle if one hand steadies the other. I hold the needle between the thumb and index finger of my right hand and the thread between the thumb and index finger of my left hand. Then I steady my hands by bringing the three remaining fingers of my left hand over the fingers of my right hand. If you are right handed, you might want to try the opposite–holding the needle in your left hand and bringing the thread to the eye of the needle with your right.

Cut the thread approximately 18″ (45 cm) long–any longer and it is apt to knot and break from the wear of constantly being pulled through the fabric. Hold the thread taut as you pull it from the spool. Then, with very sharp scissors or a cutter, make a clean cut at an angle. If the thread is cut blunt across, it is more difficult to put through the eye of the needle. Thread is twisted in a specific direction and has a *nap*. It is always wound onto the spool with the nap going the same way. The edge that is cut from the spool is the one that should be inserted into the eye of the needle. Because of the nap and the way the thread is twisted, the other end tends to split and ravel, making it difficult to insert into the needle and causing knotting and twisting while sewing.

Cut thread at angle

Through the Needle's Eye

"Except for tacking, your thread should never be more than from 18 to 20 inches long . . . thread your needle with the end next to the reel when you cut it; as the other end is apt to split, and unravel, when twisted from left to right, as is generally done, to facilitate threading. The cotton should always be cut as breaking weakens it."

Therese de Dillmont,
Encyclopedia of Needlework, 1884

The Dictionary of Needlework, compiled in 1882, describes and illustrates two needle threaders:

"*Needle-threader.*—A small appliance, made for the use of persons of imperfect sight. It is usually made of ivory. The top portion above the handle is flat, on which a small metal plate is fixed, through which a hole is pierced; a corresponding hole being in the ivory, of larger size, the needle is passed through it, the eye fitting exactly over that in the plate, so that the thread passes through the three holes at once. Other kinds may be had; such, for instance, as that illustrated. . . . A is the hole through which the thread is to be passed, and so through the eye of the needle,

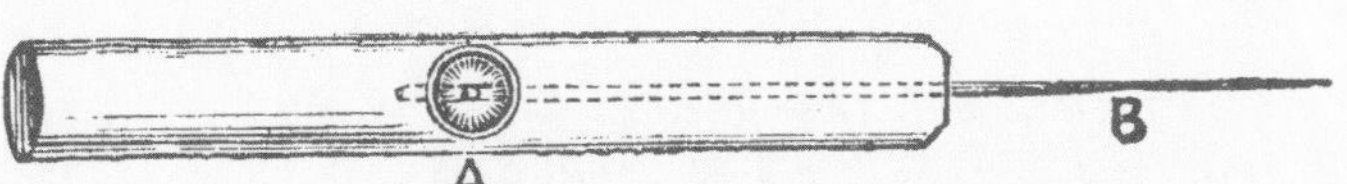

which is to be placed with the eye exactly even with it; B is the pointed end of the needle. The central hole is cup-shaped, sloping towards the middle, and so directing the thread into the small opening, which would be unseen to failing sight."

From the description of these two threaders, it would seem more difficult to thread the needle *with* the threader than without it! If eyesight is failing, what sort of guidelines allow the eye of the needle to stop and be turned at just the right spot?

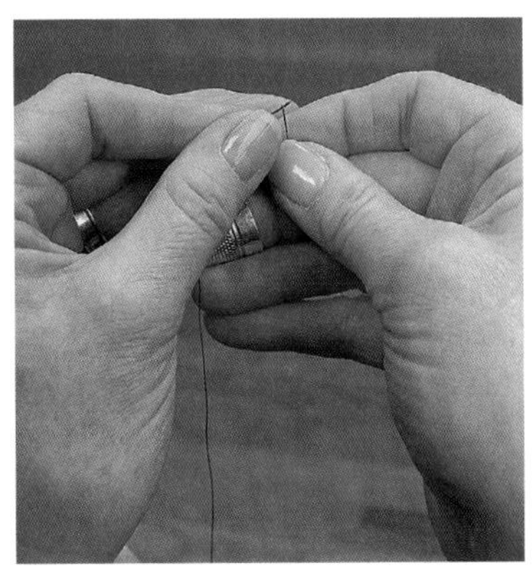

Position of hands threading needle

Depending on the size of the eye of the needle and the thickness of the thread, it can be difficult to get the thread through the eye. This is particularly true with the small Betweens needles that I like to use when hand piecing. There are several techniques that you can try to make the process easier. In addition to making sure that the thread is cut at an angle, try moistening it slightly and then pinching it between your fingers to flatten it. Send it through the eye with the flat edge vertical. This makes the thread more or less the same shape as the eye of the needle. Also, hold the thread very close (about ½" or 1.5 cm) from the end. This seems to lend support and keeps it from falling limp. You might also find it easier to see the eye of the needle if you hold it up against a white background. Moistening the actual eye of the needle may also facilitate threading.

The orientation of the eye of the needle can also make a difference. During the manufacturing process, the eye is punched out with a sharp tool. This means it is easier to thread the needle if the thread is going the same direction

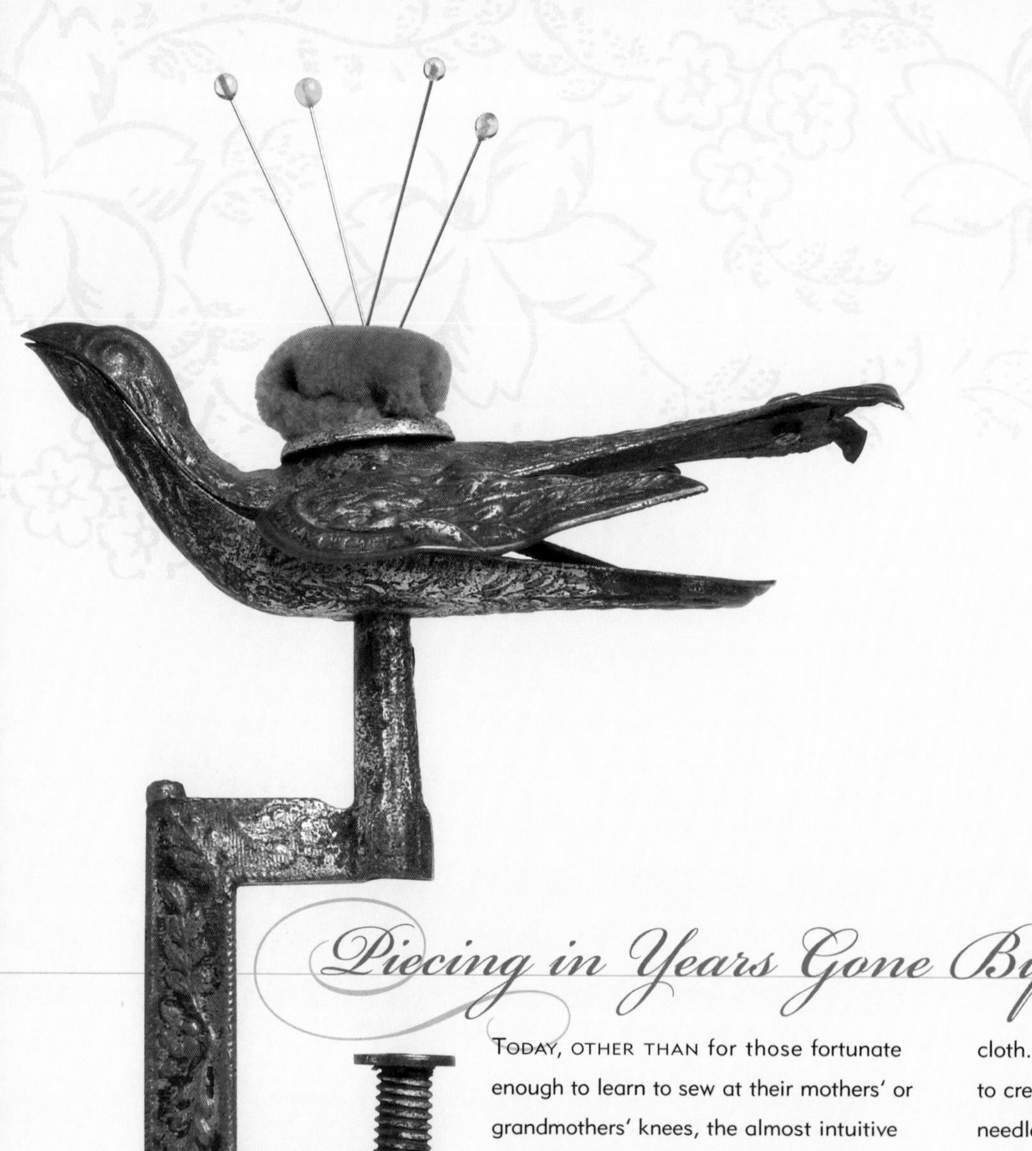

Piecing in Years Gone By

Today, other than for those fortunate enough to learn to sew at their mothers' or grandmothers' knees, the almost intuitive sense of how to stitch shared by past generations is all but lost. A complete novice who wants to learn the specifics that separate untidy stitches from a perfect row of running stitch would be hard pressed to find detailed information, whether it be on how to make a knot, how to position the needle, or how to take the stitch. We can, however, glean some good advice from various sources. Most experienced quilters agree that the single most important requirement for sewing neatly and evenly is to maintain a tension in the cloth. Yet while hoops or frames are used to create tension when doing embroidery, needlepoint, crewel work, and hand quilting, no such tool exists for those piecing together a quilt top. Even so, a slight tension on the work is critical for sewing the straight running stitch required in patchwork.

There are good and not-so-good ways to maintain tension. Often, early sewers would pin their work to the clothing on their knees, leaving both hands free to do the stitching. Writers like Therese de Dillmont, however, decried this method:

"Before describing the different kinds of stitches, a word should be said as to the

"Ah, my dear, you've not been lonely," said Grandma, ". . . You've been playing with my old fashioned sewing bird, I see. Many a year this pretty little beak has held Grandma's long seams and hems while she sewed them . . . the first time she ever helped me," she added softly, "was with my wedding dress."

Jane Eayre Fryer,
The Mary Frances Sewing Book for Girls, 1913

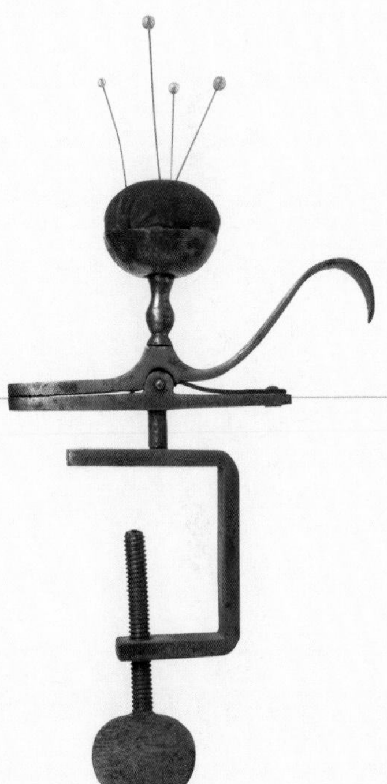

position of the body and hands when at work. Long experience has convinced me that no kind of needlework necessitates a stooping or cramped attitude. To avoid this, see that your chair and table suit each other in height, and hold your work so that you hardly need to bend your head at all. Never pin your work to your knee, it obliges you to stoop over it in a way that is both tiring and ungraceful."

Therese de Dillmont,
Encyclopedia of Needlework, 1884

To avoid an ungraceful posture while sewing, a variety of weighted pincushions or clamps were devised, dating to the mid 1800s. Used mainly for sewing longer seams, the clamps usually incorporated one or two pincushions and often had a movable clasp, similar to a clothespin. Sewing birds were the most elaborate of these types of devices, with the clasp being the bird's beak. The sewer would secure the clamp to the table, then either put the cloth between the bird's beak or pin it to the cushion. This would then serve as a "third hand." With one end of the work held securely by a clamp or pincushion, the sewer would use one hand to hold the opposite end and create tension. The other hand would hold the needle and stitch in and out quickly and with ease. In this way, the proper tension could be maintained, allowing for lines of stitching that were not only even but that went very rapidly.

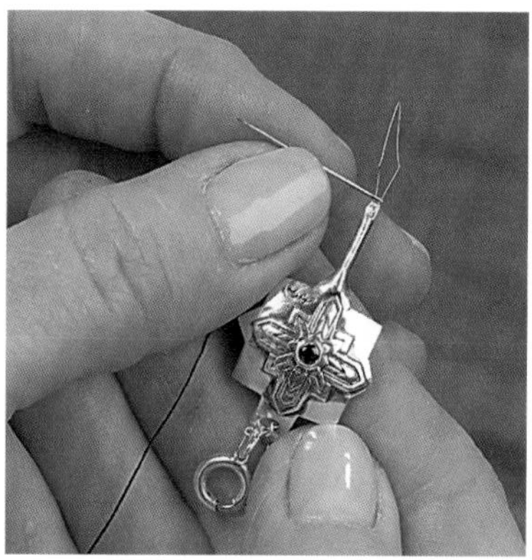

Push wire through eye of needle

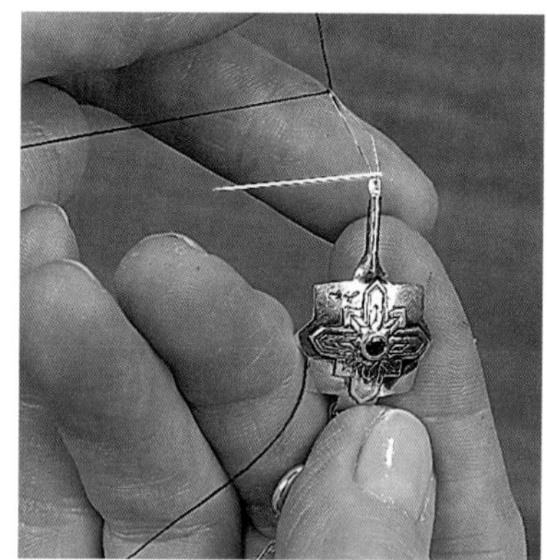

Insert thread through wire

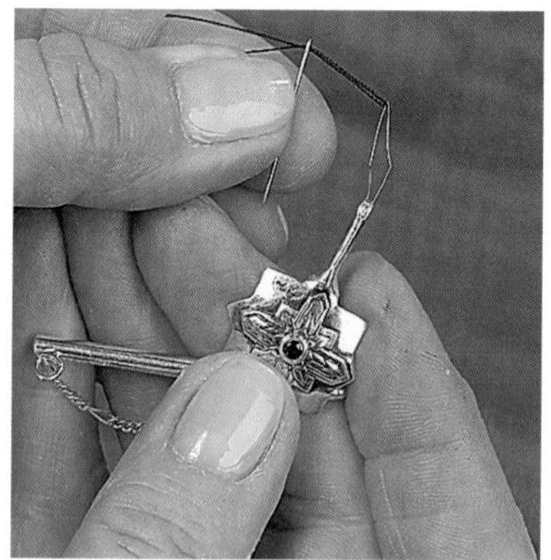

Pull thread through

as the tool did when punching the eye. Of course, it would be impossible for us to know which side of the needle this is, but if you are having unusual difficulty getting the thread through the eye, gently twist the needle so that the opposite side of the eye is facing you. You may have better luck!

If you are still having difficulty, try using a needle threader. A variety of different types are available. Most have a thin but stiff double-looped wire that is easier to fit through the eye of the needle than limp thread. Once the wire goes through the eye, the thread is inserted through the wire loop and as the wire is pulled out of the eye, it brings the thread as well.

"I know how to knot my thread; I'll show you, after I get this needle threaded—now!

1. *I wind the thread around the tip of the first finger of my left hand.*
2. *I press it with my thumb and roll the thread downward to the tip end of my finger—so!*
3. *Then I bring the second finger over the thread on the thumb*
4. *Then draw the thread tight with the right hand as I hold it."*

JANE EAYRE FRYER,
The Mary Frances Sewing Book for Girls, 1913

The Beginning Knot

There are many ways to make a knot in the thread as one prepares to begin stitching. The two most common methods are described here. Some quilters do not make a knot in their thread at all, preferring a series of backstitches to secure the thread in place. If this is what you are most comfortable with, you should do the same. One of the nicest things about hand stitching is that there are no hard and fast rules.

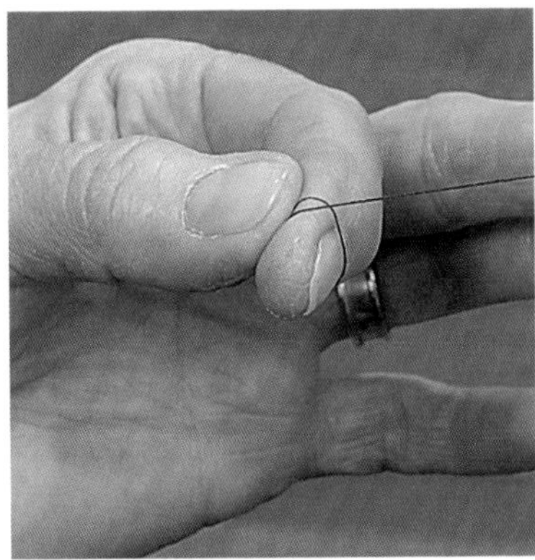

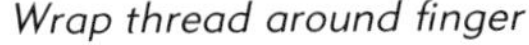

Wrap thread around finger

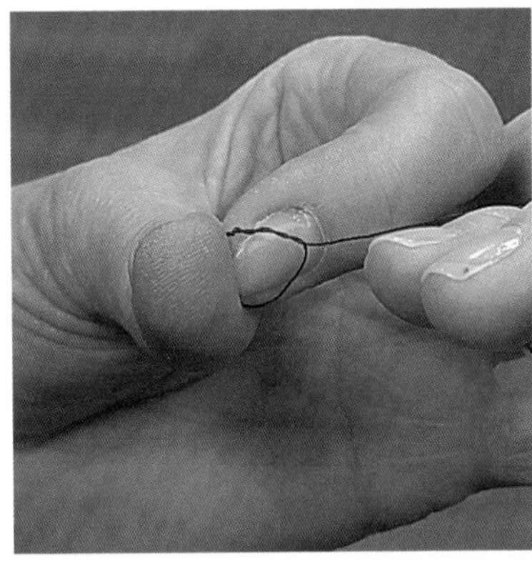

Twist thread off finger

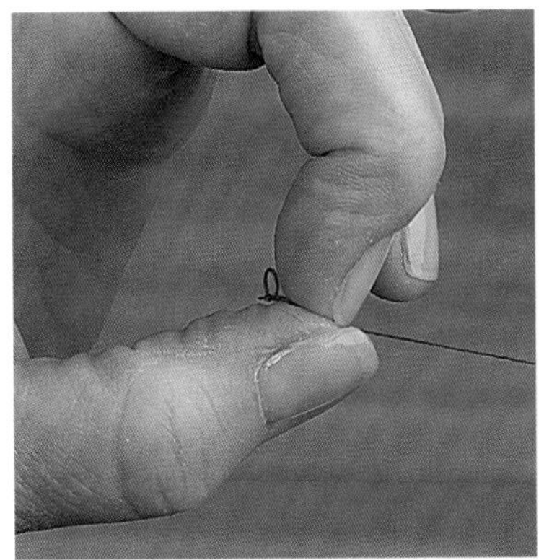

Pull knot

The Beginning Knot

The knot I make is the one I have been using forever. I have no memory of learning it, but I'm sure my mother must have shown me. I have been shown other knots, but this one is second nature to me. The knot is made by following these simple steps.

1. Hold the end of the thread to be knotted between the index finger and thumb of the hand making the knot. Keep tension on the thread by pulling with the other hand. Maintaining this tension, twist the thread around the index finger one time, so that you are now holding a circle of thread between the thumb and index finger.
2. Gently roll and push this circle of thread off the index finger with your thumb, allowing the thread to twist as it moves.
3. As the thread comes off the index finger, quickly move your middle finger over and right above the twisted portion, securing the thread between the nail of the middle finger and the thumb. With the opposite hand, pull the thread through, allowing the twisted portion at the end of the thread to knot as it meets the resistance between the index finger and thumb.

The second type of knot is often called a *tailor's knot.* Many people prefer this knot, but I find it takes at least twice as long as making the previously described knot.

1. Hold the threaded needle between the index finger and thumb of one hand, and with the opposite hand, wrap the tail end of the thread around the tip of the needle several times. Move the thumb and index finger of the hand holding the needle towards the tip of the needle just above the wrapped portion.
2. Keep the thumb and index finger firmly on the needle and the thread as you pull this twisted part past the needle and on down to the end of the thread. The result is a small knot.

Position of the hands when a weighted cushion is used

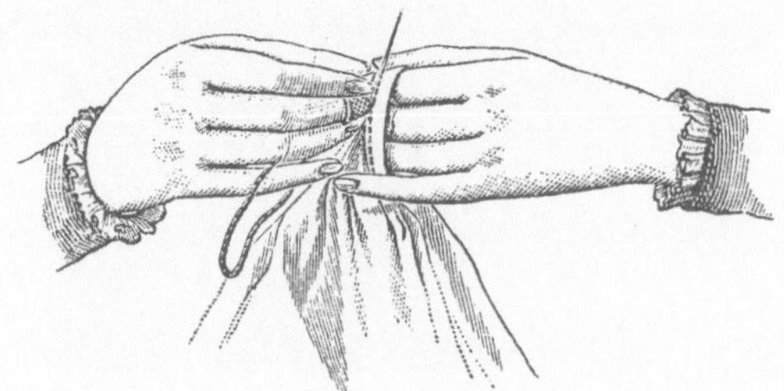

Position of the hands without cushion

The Simplest Stitch

THE RUNNING STITCH HAS been described as the simplest of all stitchery. Yet our quilting forebears have provided little instruction on how it is accomplished. Here is a tasting of their best advice.

"This is the simplest and easiest of all and the first to teach to children. Pass the needle in and out of the material, at regular intervals, in a horizontal direction, taking up three or four threads at a time. If the stuff allow, several stitches may be taken on the needle at once, before the thread is drawn out. Running-stitch is used for plain seams, for joining light materials, and making gathers."

S. F. A. CAULFIELD AND BLANCHE C. SAWARD, *The Dictionary of Needlework,* 1882

"I always recommend hand-sewing the tiny seams in fine running stitch with an occasional backstitch for greater strength. Keep the turnings an even quarter-inch everywhere or the uniformity of the patches will suffer and the pattern not fit together so well."

AGNES M. MIALL, *Patchwork Old and New,* 1937

Therese de Dillmont provides perhaps the most helpful information of all, complete with early illustrations:

"The stuff, fastened to a cushion must be held with the left hand, which should neither rest on the table, nor on the cushion, the needle must be held between the thumb and forefinger of the right hand and the middle finger, protected by the thimble, pushes the needle far enough through the stuff, for the thumb and forefinger of the right to be able to take hold of it and draw it out; the thread will then lie between the fourth and fifth fingers in the form of a loop, which must be gradually tightened to avoid its knotting.

"When the work cannot be fastened to a cushion, it must not be rolled over the forefinger of the left hand, but should merely be held between the thumb and forefinger and allowed to fall easily over the other fingers. Should the stuff need to be slightly stretched, draw it between the fourth and fifth fingers, this will prevent it from getting puckered or dragged."

THERESE DE DILLMONT, *Encyclopedia of Needlework,* 1884

Joining Two Pieces—The Running Stitch

When sewing a running stitch, I hold my hands differently than either Ms. Dillmont or Ms. Miall recommends. The technique I use is so natural to me that I don't even know when or how I learned to do it. My mother, Pauline Kahle, taught her four daughters all kinds of skills from a very early age. I was knitting at five, sewing doll clothes by age six, and making my own clothes by age ten. In seventh grade, all the boys took shop while the girls were taught home economics, which was boring because I already knew how to do everything that was taught. One project was a dirndl skirt. There were no sewing machines and the entire skirt was made by hand. The project required two rows of stitching around the top to use for gathering the skirt to fit the waistband. I remember using a running stitch, then hand-gathering those rows of stitching and pulling the gathers up to fit the waistband. As the needle went in and out I would use the index finger of my right hand to actually pull or gather the stitches onto the needle. This is something I had probably done over and over when sewing doll clothes or other projects; but the dirndl skirt stands out in my memory. The technique I used way back then to gather the fabric onto my needle when sewing those long seams is the same process I use today for the running stitch when hand piecing quilts.

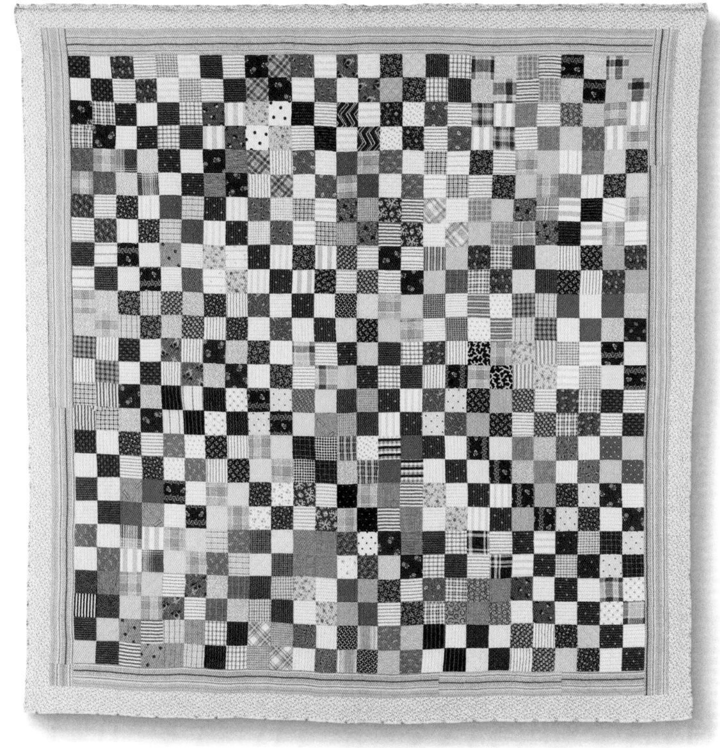

***Four Patch**, circa 1890. Maker unknown*

I have since discovered that there many different ways to sew a simple running stitch. It was not until a few years ago that I realized my method differed from that of other quilters. In fact, it caused a little bit of a stir at a quilt guild meeting. Stitching on a project while listening to the speaker, I suddenly realized that almost everyone in the room was staring at me. When I asked what the matter was, someone blurted out, "You are sewing so fast!" Since then, whenever I stitch among other quilters, people marvel at the speed at which I sew. Some even suggest that I hand stitch faster than most people sew by machine! Curious, I have watched how other people sew and have been surprised to observe that few quilters use the same piecing technique that I use. Yet, I do often hear comments like "That is the way my grandmother sewed." I have observed, too, that many Japanese quilters use a technique that is very similar to mine.

While the rest of this section will describe the way that I sew a running stitch, keep in mind that there are many different ways of completing this simple task. You should always choose the method that is most comfortable and most natural to you. With practice, you will increase your speed and the neatness of your stitches. Everyone sews a little differently and my hope is that by learning about my method, you will pick up some techniques and ideas to help you turn your simple stitches into perfect quilts.

Making the First Seam

The stitch described here is the one I use for hand piecing. All I can say is that if you master this technique, you too may have friends marvel that you are stitching as fast as a sewing machine! To learn the basic stitch, I recommend you practice with squares of fabric cut the same size, with exact ¼″ (0.75 cm) seam allowance added. Template F from *Starflower*, provided in the template section, would be a good one to use for cutting out the practice squares. Cut out a few from light fabric and a few from dark fabric. I have found that it is easier on the eyes if you have the lighter colored fabric facing you when you sew, although this is not always possible.

Pinning

When piecing two patches of fabric together, I begin by lining up the cut edges and pinning them in place. The pins should be placed at a right angle to the edge being stitched, with the point of the pin coming out right at the seam allowance.

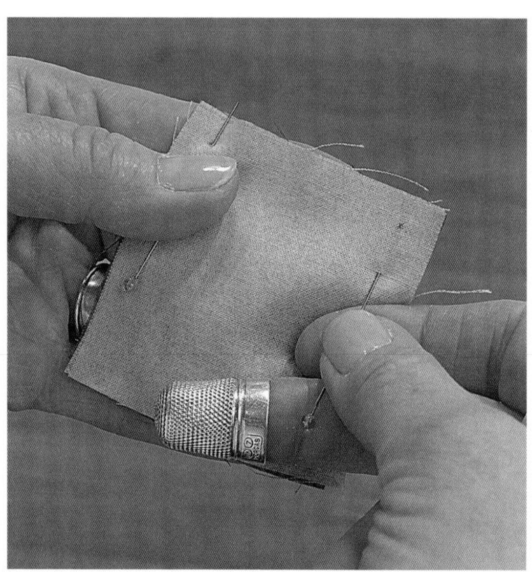

Position of pins

After the pieces are pinned into place, I "eyeball" a ¼″ (0.75 cm) seam allowance. (My reasons for eyeballing the seam allowance rather than marking it on the fabric are explained in detail on pages 53 to 57). If you are uncomfortable with the no-sewing line method and need guides for sewing with an accurate ¼″ (0.75 cm) seam allowance, mark the piece facing you at this time according to the directions on page 56.

I recommend that all beginning hand piecers carefully pin the patches together. However, when I am sewing small shapes together, I rarely use pins, except at the joining of seams. Instead, I use a method that I call *finger pinning*. While learning the basic stitch you should pin the pieces so they do not slip, but at the same time practice holding the fabric in the finger-pinning position. Not only will this help in maintaining the correct tension while stitching, but you may find that eventually you are able to hold the pieces secure enough to do without pins when sewing small pieces together. My method of finger pinning is as follows.

1. Begin by placing the fourth and fifth fingers on the front of the fabric pieces.

Step 1

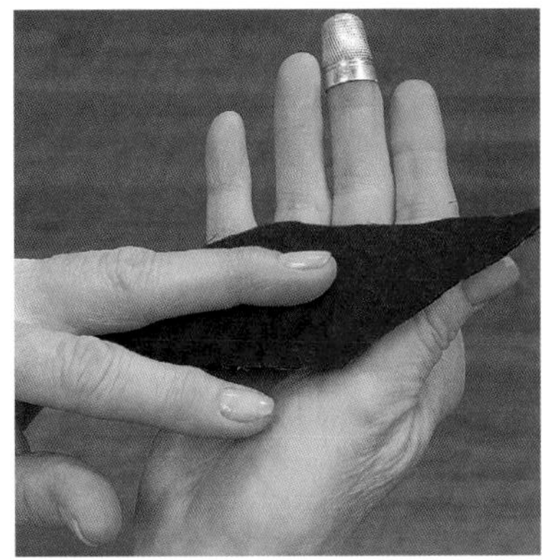
Step 2

Step 3

2. Place the middle finger on the back side of the pieces with it nestled right next to the fourth finger, holding the fabric in between.
3. Bring the thumb and index finger over to the edges of the pieces to be sewn.

Finger Positions

While sewing, the needle is held with the thumb more or less pushing the middle part of the needle in one direction (towards the back of the work). The index finger and middle finger (which has the thimble) are pulling the tip and eye ends of the needle towards the front of the work. Imagine taking the needle and trying to snap it in two by pushing the middle of the needle with the thumb and pulling back on the tip and eye with the index and third fingers. That is the same position I use when holding the needle for sewing. This pushing with the thumb and pulling with the middle finger and index finger causes a great deal of stress on the needle. This is one reason why I like to use a short, sturdy needle such as a Between size 10 or 11, otherwise I am constantly snapping my needles in two. Even so, my needle will sometimes bend to the extent that I need to discard it and get a new one. The photograph here shows, without fabric, how the needle is held in the fingers.

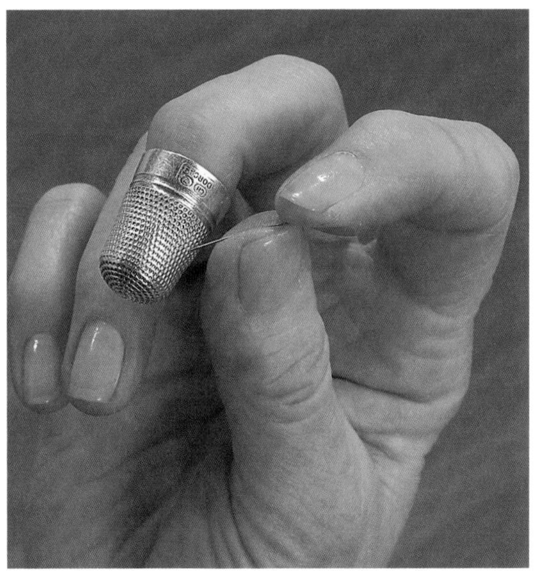
Position of needle and fingers without fabric

As mentioned earlier, a slight tension on the fabric while sewing produces neater stitches and allows for quicker sewing. That tension can be achieved by holding the fabric with both hands with the index fingers at the back of the work and the thumbs at the front of the work as shown. The entire time I am sewing, the index fingers are never more than about ⅛″ (0.4 cm) apart from each other. My two hands are pulled slightly apart to allow for tension in the pieces being sewn. The tricky part is getting the needle and thimble finger into position.

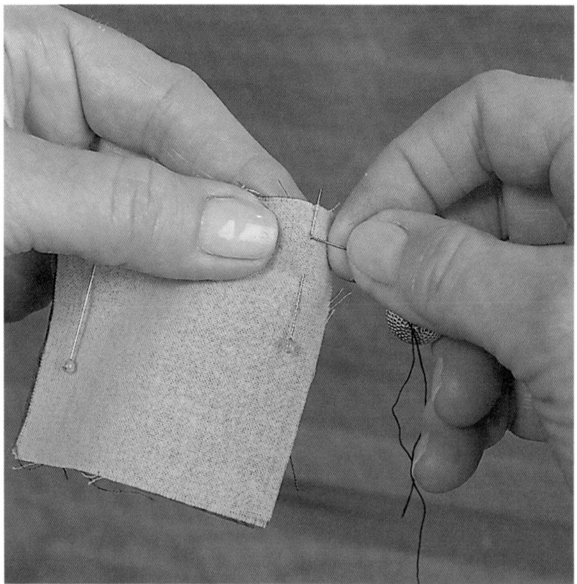

Position of hand when first inserting the needle

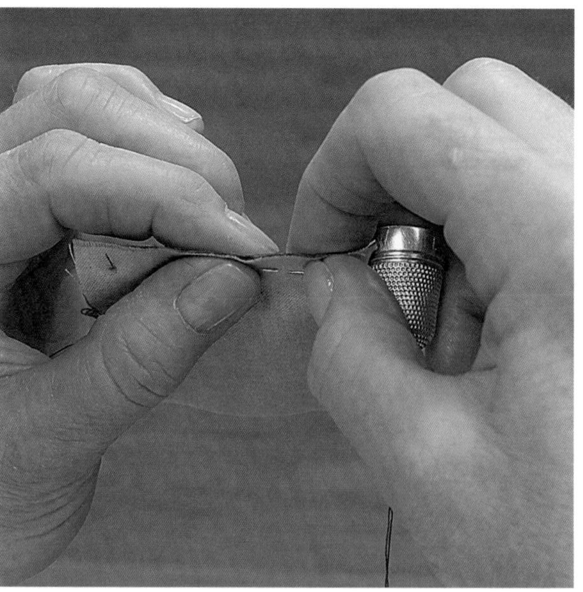

Position of fingers while sewing

Begin Sewing

To begin sewing I start with the needle held between the index finger and thumb at the *front* of the pieces being sewn, as shown. As soon as the needle goes into the cloth, the index finger immediately goes to the back of the work. The thimble finger (middle finger) remains on the front side at the eye end of the needle, with the eye resting against the side of the thimble.

Develop a Rhythm

Once the needle is into the cloth, nothing moves on my right hand except the index finger and thumb. The right elbow is pretty much anchored to the side of the waist, holding the hand steady. The needle does not move at all. The index finger and thumb of the left hand are holding the cloth and pulling slightly to the left to create tension and, at the same time, moving the cloth up and down, allowing the needle to go in and out of the fabric. As the needle goes in and out, the right index finger is actually *gathering* the cloth onto the needle. Up to 15 stitches at a time can be gathered onto the needle in this way before drawing the thread through.

A little more explanation is needed as to how this gathering occurs:

1. As the left index finger and thumb pull the fabric down, the needle comes out at the front side of the cloth.
2. Then, as the left hand pulls the fabric up, the needle goes to the back of the cloth. At this time the index finger on the right hand lets go of holding the pieces long enough to reach out and grab a little of the fabric and pull it onto the needle. Then that finger immediately goes back to maintaining its hold and the tension on the cloth.

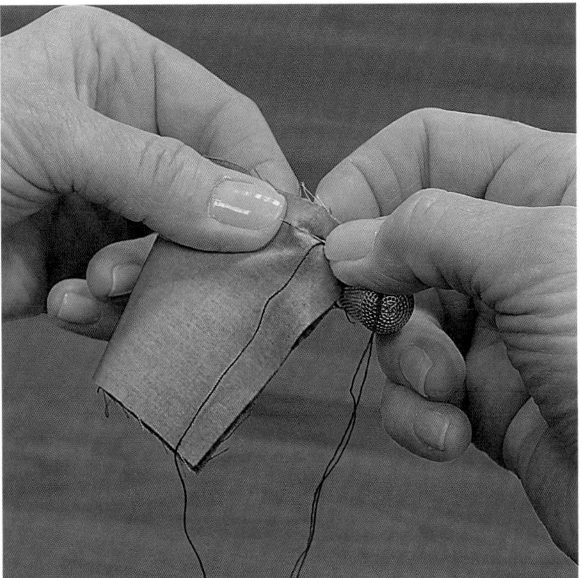

Step 1. *Left hand down, needle up*

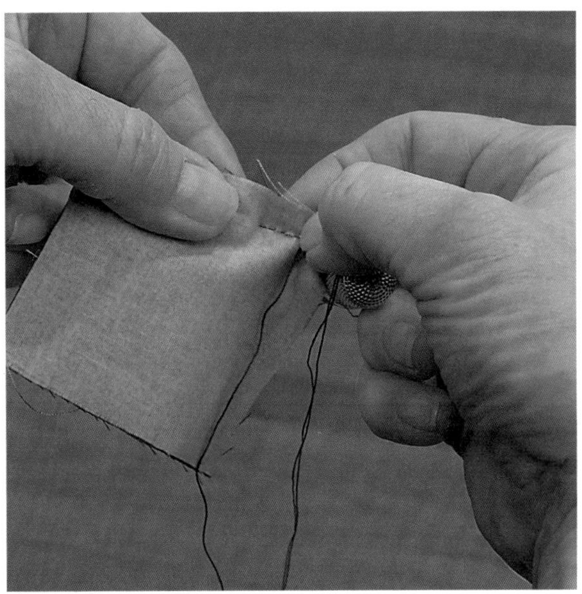

Step 2. *Left hand up, needle down, finger reaches and gathers*

DEVELOP A RHYTHM

3. The left hand continues to go up and down and the right index finger continues to reach and gather. The right thumb now and then inches a little forward along the needle, helping to pull the fabric onto the needle. A rhythm develops–left hand down, needle comes to the front; left hand up, needle goes to the back, reach and gather with right index finger. Fabric down, fabric up, reach and gather; down, up, reach and gather; down, up, reach and gather, and so on.

The entire time, care must be taken to ensure that the index fingers on the two hands are no more that about ⅛″ (0.4 cm) apart and that they are gently pulling away from each other to create tension. When there is more than ⅛″ (0.4 cm) space between the two index fingers, it is difficult to do the down–up–reach–gather motions and to create the proper tension. As soon as the tension is relaxed, there is slack in the cloth and the seam starts to get crooked. Tension must be maintained to create a straight seam and even stitches.

When the needle is full of stitches, the thimble finger on the right hand pushes the needle through the cloth and the thread is drawn out. Before putting the needle in again, I reach along the stitches just sewn with the index finger and thumb of my left hand and gently finger press the seam, so as to alleviate any gathers that might cause puckering.

Backstitch

To give more stability to the seam, each time I pull the thread through, I take a small backstitch before continuing the stitching. The backstitch is made by inserting the needle back about 1/16″ (0.2 cm) from where the thread last came out. Once this backstitch is taken, the running stitch is continued.

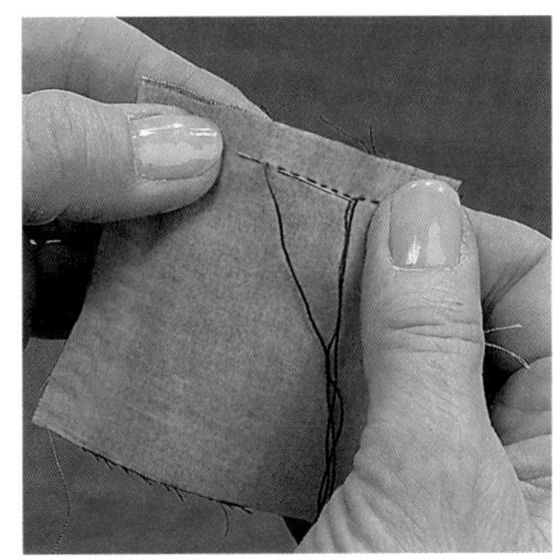

Backstitch

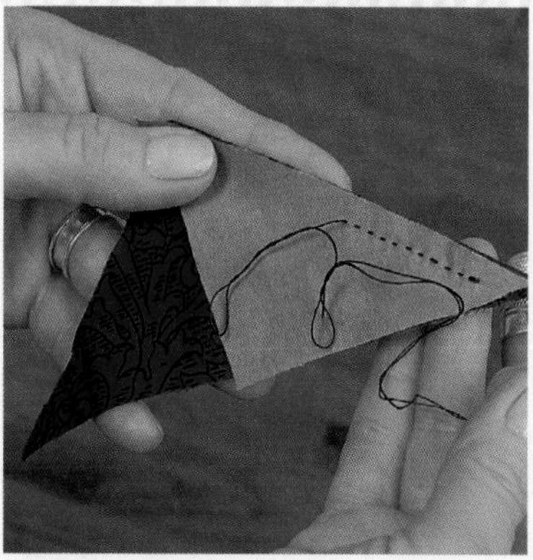
Twisted thread

Pull thread down needle

Pull needle up to untwist thread

Untwisting Thread

SOMETIMES WHILE SEWING, the thread will begin to twist, which can lead to unwanted knots. When this occurs, hold the end of the thread that was passed through the needle, then slide the needle down the thread all the way to the sewing. Let go of the end of the thread and slowly pull the needle back up. As the needle comes up, the thread will untwist.

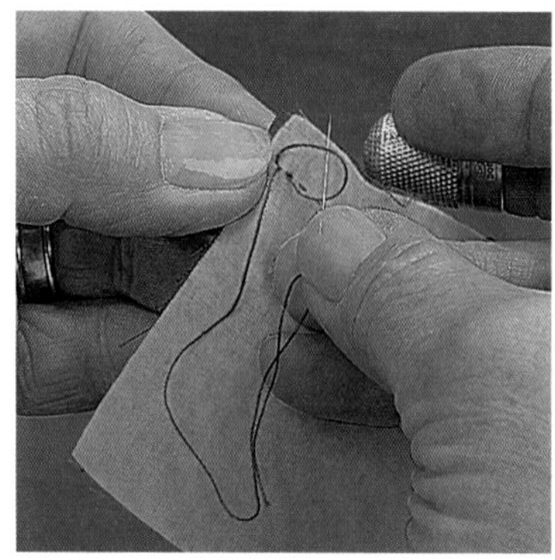
Ending knot

The Ending Knot

When finishing off the end of a row of stitches, a very simple loop knot can be used to secure the thread. Take a small backstitch and pull the thread almost all the way through until there is a small loop remaining. Then insert the needle through the loop and pull the thread the rest of the way. Clip the thread off about 1⁄16″ (0.2 cm) from the knot.

Practice Makes Perfect

Ultimately, the size of the stitches should be no larger than an 1⁄8″ (0.4 cm). It may take some practice to achieve stitches of that size. To get the rhythm of making the stitches, my advice is to practice the down–up–reach–gather technique over and over on some scrap cloth without a knot in the thread. Concentrate first on getting the technique down, even if the seams are not straight and the stitches are very large. Once you are comfortable with the technique, then gradually try making the stitches smaller and the seam line straight.

When using the down–up–reach–gather technique, the tip of the needle slightly grazes the pad of the left index finger. When I do a lot of stitching a slight callous develops on that finger.

Alternate Method

There is an alternate method of sewing a running stitch that I have observed. It is similar to the technique described by Therese de Dillmont (see page 70), which recommended the use of a weighted cushion or sewing clamp to hold the cloth taut. Instead of such a device, the hand is used to anchor the pieces against the knee. While this method maintains a good tension so that the stitches are neat and the seams straight, I find it to be a much slower process than the technique described above. Furthermore, you run a much greater risk of actually catching a piece of your clothing in the stitches!

When using this alternate method, the pieces are held in the left hand with the index finger in the back and the thumb in the front. The index finger is slightly forward towards the right hand; during the sewing process it is right beneath the tip of the needle. This hand moves the cloth up and down helping the needle to go in and out. The right hand holds the needle with the index finger and thumb at about the center of the needle. The middle finger with thimble rests at the eye end of the needle and pushes the needle through as the stitches are taken. The right hand rests on the knee on top of the pieces being sewn and helps to maintain tension. This is very similar to the illustration showing the position of the hands in *Encylopedia of Needlework*, shown on page 70.

Quick Tip

Resist the urge to press your work after completing each seam or even each block. Too much pressing distorts bias edges, spoiling the shape of your finished block. Since I sew "on-the-go" during free moments, I simply finger press the seam once it is sewn. For more tips on pressing, see page 61.

Joining Four Pieces with Right Angles

Once you have mastered the running stitch and are adept at stitching two pieces together, it is time to practice sewing pairs together. A very important rule to remember when hand piecing is to *never* sew seams down into the line of stitching. Always leave the seams free. This will help to create a more secure joining of the seams to the next piece and, eventually, when sewing several points together, will help to create neat, sharp points that come together perfectly. The following steps can be used any time two pieces that have been sewn together are to be joined to a second pair.

Sewing any pieces where four right angles join together, such as four squares, is done in two simple stages. First, sew the two pieces together in pairs. Next, sew the pairs together with one straight seam, making tight stitches at the seams and making sure to leave the seam allowances free. Practice by cutting two light and two dark squares from Template F from *Starflower* in the template section. The squares can be sewn together with points meeting perfectly if you follow these steps.

*The techniques learned in this chapter were used for a large part of my quilt, **Windows.** In addition to the simple running stitch used throughout, the pieced borders contain many places where four points come together at right angles, as shown here.*

Step 1. *Lay out squares on table*

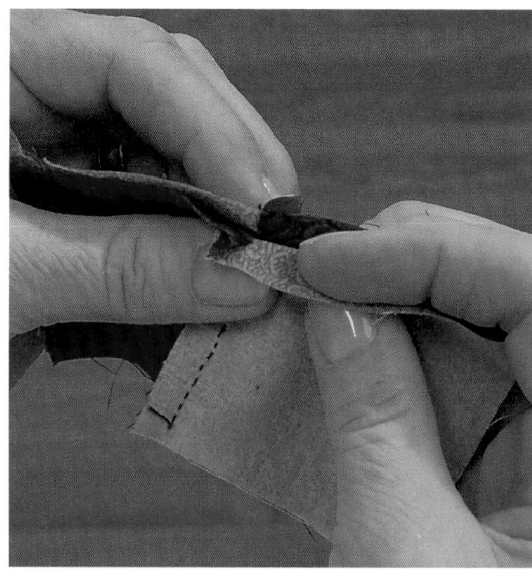

Step 2. *Line up seams*

Step 3. *Pin*

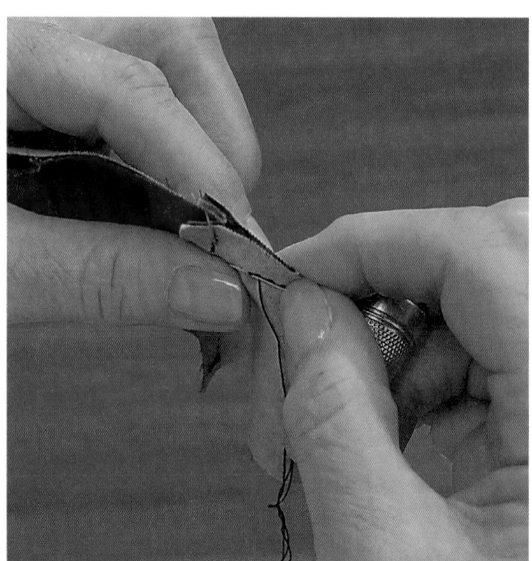

Step 4. *Pull seam allowance to left*

Joining Four Pieces with Right Angles

1. Lay the squares out into the two pairs, then sew each of the light squares to a dark one.
2. Place the two sets of squares next to each other with right sides facing. Finger-press one seam in one direction and the other seam in the opposite direction. This creates a ridge where the two seams can butt next to each other, helping to keep them in place.
3. Put a pin directly through this ridge, bringing the point out ¼″ (0.75 cm) from the edge, exactly at the seam allowance.
4. Begin stitching, aiming at the place where the pin has come up at the seam allowance. As you approach the seam, carefully pull the pin out and make

Step 5. *Push needle beyond ridge . . .* *. . . snap needle off ridge*

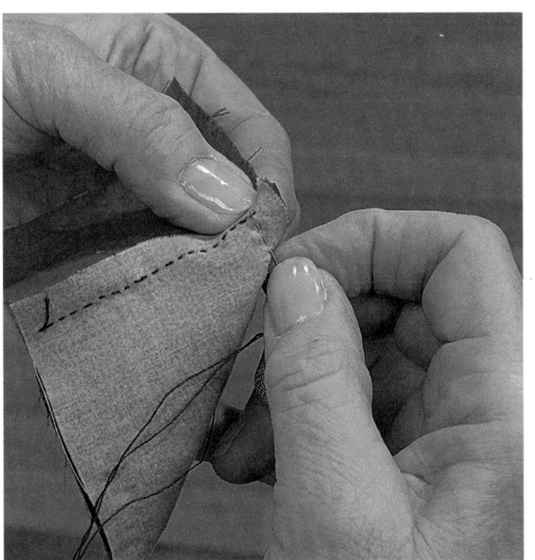

Step 6. *Bring needle up at base of seam*

Step 7. *Push thumbnail next to seam*

sure that the two seams are still butted next to each other, then pull all of the seam allowances gently to the left. This creates a bulky ridge that you can easily feel.

5. Put the needle in to take a stitch. When the tip is at the back of the work, push the needle beyond the ridge created by the seam. Gently pull it back until the tip of the needle snaps off the ridge to the base of the seam line.
6. Bring the tip of the needle up through to the front of the work, right at the base of the seam, and draw the thread out. Take a small backstitch, repeating the push–pull back–snap off ridge process.
7. Let go of the seams and push your thumbnail next to the base of the seam.

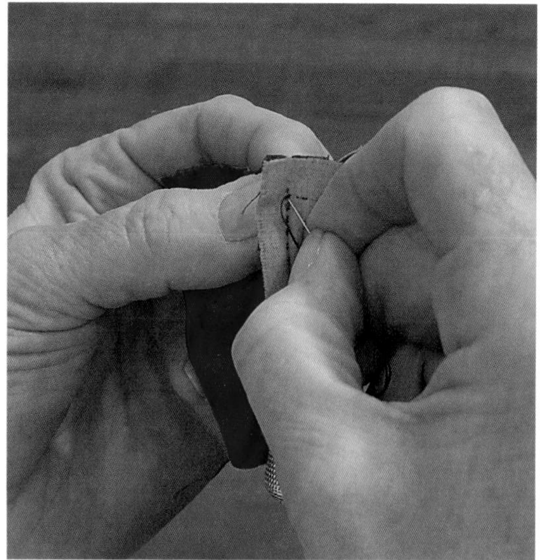

Step 8. *Insert needle at right of seam*

Step 9. *Bring the needle up on top of the thumbnail*

Step 10. *Nestle needle next to ridge*

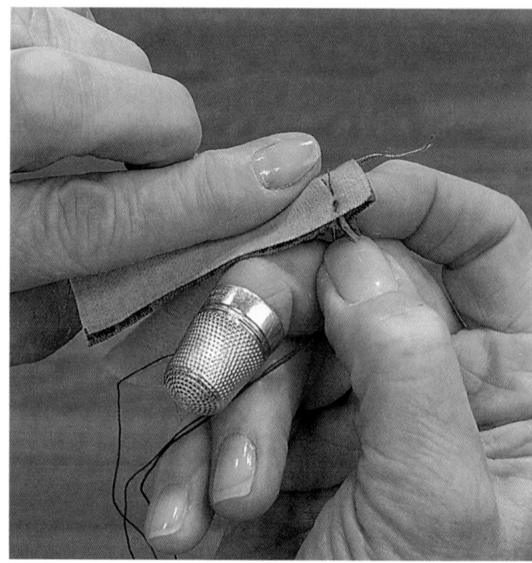

Step 11. *Check the back*

Joining Four Pieces with Right Angles

continued

8. Put the needle on the right side of the seam, at the same spot where the thread last came out, at the end of the row of stitches as shown.
9. Insert the needle directly through the base of the seam facing you, bringing it to the left side of the seam, right on top of your thumbnail. Make sure the seam on the back side is free. The needle will not go into this seam on the back, only the base of the seam facing you.
10. Now, gently pull the seams on the top and bottom to the *right*. Push the thumbnail of your left hand directly next to the ridge created by this seam, then nestle the tip of the needle right next to the seam and your thumbnail

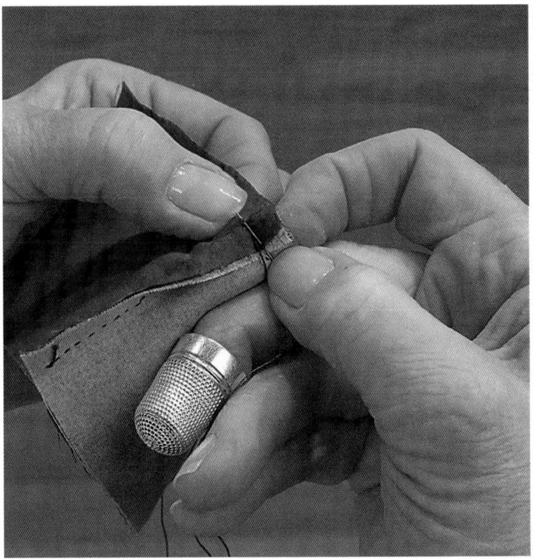

Step 12. Bring needle back up and continue sewing

Step 13. Complete

and go straight down. You are not going into the seam at all, just very tightly next to it.

11. Flip the work to the back to make sure the needle has come out next to the seam.
12. Bring the needle back up to make a small stitch and continue the running stitch to the end of the piece.
13. Open out the pieces to see how sharp this makes the points.

This method of working the needle through the seam allowance and not sewing the seam down to the row of stitches is the secret of creating sharp points and making secure intersections, no matter how many pieces are being joined. With practice it will become second nature, and you will be pleased with the sharp points you achieve.

QUICK TIP

The key to getting points to match when hand piecing is to take tight backstitches at the joining of pieces and to never sew the seam allowances down; always leave them free.

Joining Two Stitched Pieces to a Third Piece

To practice the technique of sewing two pieces joined with a seam to another fabric, cut two squares from Template B from *Starflower* and one rectangle cut from Practice Template (both templates are in the template section at the back of the book). Make sure you cut the pieces exactly with the ¼″ (0.75 cm) seam allowance included. Sew the two squares together, as above, and lay them out with the rectangle as shown. Then, follow these steps.

1. With right sides together, match up and, if desired, pin the sewn squares to the rectangle along one of the long edges. Be sure to line up the raw edges perfectly. Depending on what you are sewing, sometimes the seam will be

Lay out two sewn squares and a rectangle

Steps 1 and 2. *Pin sewn squares to rectangle, bringing tip out exactly at seam allowance*

Step 3. *Pull seam allowances to left to create bulky ridge*

Step 4. *Push needle beyond ridge, draw it back, then let it snap off ridge*

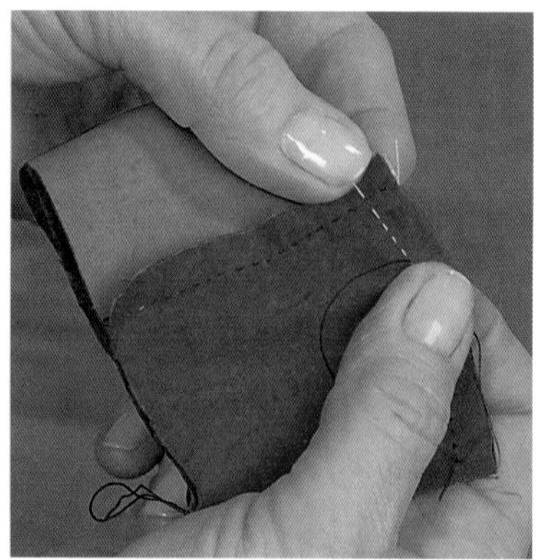

Step 5. *Bring needle up at base of seam line, then push through to other side*

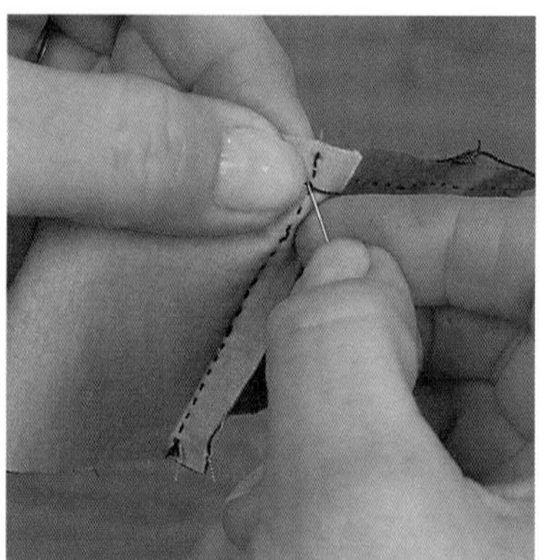

With seam allowance to right, push needle straight down, tightly next to seam

Joining Two Stitched Pieces to a Third Piece

facing you and at other times it will be in the back. In either case, the technique for joining the completed pair to a new piece of fabric is the same.

2. Insert a pin right along the seam line of the two squares, so it is running at right angles to the edges to be sewn. Bring the point of the pin out so that it is exactly at the seam allowance.
3. Begin sewing at the edge of the piece, taking a fine running stitch. As you approach the seam, pull the seam allowance gently to the left. This creates a bulky ridge that you can easily feel.
4. At the last stitch before the seam, insert needle so that the tip exits at the back of the work. Push the needle beyond the ridge created by the seam that is pulled to the left.
5. Gently pull the needle back until its tip "snaps" off the ridge, then insert and bring it up at the front, just at the base of the seam line. Remove the pin. (See also photographs for steps 4 and 5 on pages 78 and 79)
6. Pull the thread through, then take a small backstitch, repeating the push-pull back–snap off ridge process. Note that you have not sewn into the seam allowance; it is still free.

Step 8. At back, needle exits right at seam line

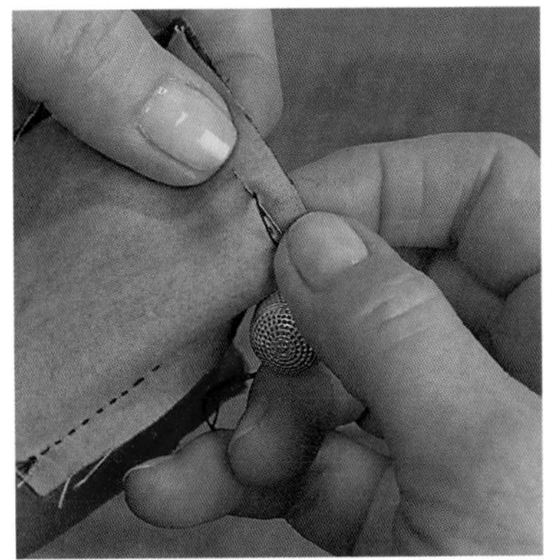

Step 9. Bring tip of needle back up and continue with running stitch

Complete

Joining Two Stitched Pieces to a Third Piece

continued

7. Let go of the seam so that it is more or less standing straight up, facing you. Push your left thumbnail against the base of the seam, pushing gently against it. From the right side, insert the needle directly through the base of the seam, bringing it to the left side, right on top of your thumbnail. Draw the needle through and pull the thread up. (See steps 8 and 9 on page 80.)
8. Now, gently pull the seam allowance to the right. Push the thumbnail of your left hand directly next to the ridge created by this seam. Nestle the tip of the needle right next to the seam and your thumbnail and go straight down. You are not going into the seam at all, just very tightly next to it.
9. Bring the tip of the needle back up to make a small stitch then continue the running stitch to the end of the piece. Open the seam to see the finished points.

Beginning a New Hand-Pieced Quilt

With the mastery of sewing a simple running stitch and joining three or four points together, you are ready to begin your first pattern block. One of my favorite antique quilts is shown here. The pattern is simply a set of staggered rectangles. You don't have to join any more than two pieces to one other piece. Besides the simple running stitch, the only techniques involved are sewing the rows of rectangles together and eventually joining four large squares of the sewn rectangles. Many beautiful quilts composed of only squares and rectangles have also been made through the centuries, including the stunning example on page 62.

As an alternate first project, you may want to begin the first steps of one of the beginning-piecing projects designed for this book, *Columbia* or *Starflower*, shown in the pattern section. By now you have learned all the techniques you need for the first steps of these two quilts. Complete directions for making each quilt are provided.

Antique quilt with rectangles, circa 1890. Maker unknown

Antique ***Flying Geese****, circa 1800.*
Maker unknown

Beyond the Basics

Bias Edges, Angles, and Points

"The advantages of making patchwork, besides the useful purposes it is put [to] . . . are its moral effects. Leisure must either be filled up by expensive amusements, 'mischief,' or by listless idleness, unless some harmless useful occupation is substituted. Patchwork is, moreover, useful as an encourager of perfection in plain work, because it must be very neatly sewn . . . So patchwork often plays a noble part, while needlework is encouraged and brought to perfection, and idle time is advantageously occupied."

Cassell's Household Guide to Every Department of Practical Life, Volume II, circa 1875

WITH A LITTLE PRACTICE YOU SHOULD SOON become adept at the piecing techniques described in the previous chapter–sewing squares and rectangles together so that four corners meet in nice sharp points. Most quilt patterns, of course, contain other shapes than those with easy-to-match right angles. You will often need to sew together pieces where the angles do not match. You will also need to sew along bias edges, where the fabric is a little more difficult to manipulate and can easily stretch out of shape. This chapter invites you to practice working with bias edges and odd angles and, finally, leads you to master the piecing techniques of joining three, six, and eight points. While these skills allow you to create quite complex quilt patterns, the basic sewing techniques you need are very much the same as those you mastered in the previous chapter. The process is no more difficult and no less exact.

Sewing Bias Edges

When sewing with squares and rectangles, as in the previous chapter, the pieces are cut in such a way that all sides lie on the straight or cross grain of the fabric. There are no bias edges to contend with. When working with shapes

How would you line up these diamonds for piecing?

Incorrect alignment

After sewing

other than squares or rectangles, however, some edges of the shape must end up being cut on the bias. Depending on the pattern, you will often need to sew a bias edge to a straight edge. There will also be times when it is necessary to sew two bias edges together.

As explained in Chapter Three, when cutting out the pieces for a block, it is important to try and have the straight or crosswise grain of the fabric fall along the outer edges of the block. This helps avoid any distortion when blocks are sewn to each other. There are times, however, when it is not possible for this to happen, and bias edges may fall along the outside edges of pieced units. In these cases, extreme care must be taken to ensure that the bias portions of the block do not become distorted.

First and foremost, handle pieces with bias edges gently and as infrequently as possible. If you have a bias edge falling on the outside portion of a unit or block, do not press that section until the bias edge is joined to another piece. Pressing bias raw edges can distort and stretch the piece, making it difficult to sew these units accurately to the adjacent pieces.

When sewing individual pieces with bias edges, it is very important to carefully pin these pieces together, making sure you have pins at the points where the seam allowances cross on the two pieces. If the bias edge has stretched, ease in the fullness by pinning until it is the same length as the piece to which it is sewn.

Quick Tip

If you are not able to accurately eyeball the places on the two pieces where the seam allowances cross, then punch small holes in your template at these intersections (as explained on page 56). Place the template on the wrong side of the pieces being sewn and mark dots through the holes. Alternatively, mark the dots using *Jinny Beyer Perfect Piecer,* a simple tool designed to accompany this book. It is described on page 56.

Sewing Unmatched Angles

When sewing two squares of the same size together, one square is simply placed on top of the other. Their sides and corners all match up. The same is true when sewing rectangles or even more complex shapes like hexagons together–the straight edges and corner angles are all exactly the same. But there are many times when you will be sewing pieces together where the angle on one is different than the angle on the other. In order to ensure an accurate seam, it is important to know how to line these pieces up correctly.

Pins exit exactly where seam allowances cross

Correct alignment

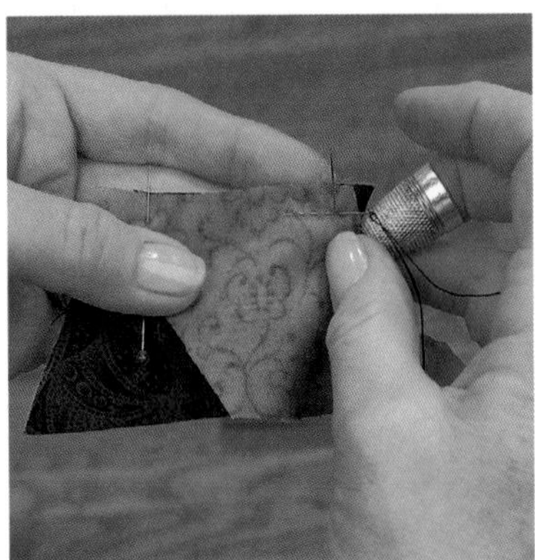

Sew seam

After sewing

Lining Up Angles

Many people get into trouble when sewing patches together where the angles on the pieces do not match, because they fail to line up the pieces correctly. When sewing pieces where there are different angles in shapes, and two unmatched angles come together, care must be taken to pin the pieces together at the places where the seam allowances cross on each piece. To illustrate, look what happens when four 60° diamonds are joined together to form a larger diamond.

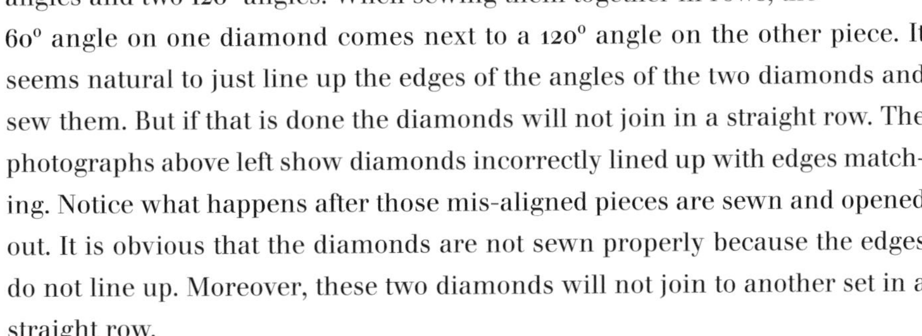

The easiest way to sew these four pieces together is first to join two diamonds, join the other pair, then finally sew the two "rows" together with one straight seam. Each diamond shape has two 60° angles and two 120° angles. When sewing them together in rows, the 60° angle on one diamond comes next to a 120° angle on the other piece. It seems natural to just line up the edges of the angles of the two diamonds and sew them. But if that is done the diamonds will not join in a straight row. The photographs above left show diamonds incorrectly lined up with edges matching. Notice what happens after those mis-aligned pieces are sewn and opened out. It is obvious that the diamonds are not sewn properly because the edges do not line up. Moreover, these two diamonds will not join to another set in a straight row.

In order to sew these diamonds together accurately, it is necessary to line up the places where the seam allowances cross on each piece. For inexperienced quilters, this is where it is helpful to mark a dot on both the front and the back pieces where the seam allowances will cross (see page 56). When lining up for stitching, make sure that the dots on the two pieces exactly line up by inserting a pin directly through the two dots on each of the pieces. When this is done, the 60° angle from one diamond will extend beyond the 120° angle on the other piece at each of the two ends, as shown here.

With the pins in place, stitch the seam line. When you open out the pieces, you will see that the edges of the diamonds are lined up in a neat row. Next, the rows of diamonds will be sewn with one straight seam, as explained in the next section.

Joining Rows of Diamonds

Step 1. *Align rows of diamonds, making sure points where seam allowances cross form X*

Step 2. *Exit pin exactly where seam allowances cross*

Step 3. *Approach seam and pull seam allowances to left*

Step 4. *Backstitch and push needle beyond ridge*

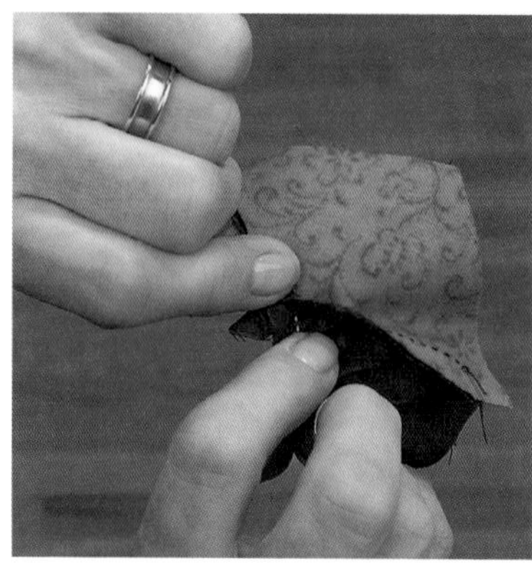

Step 5. *Let tip of needle bounce off ridge*

Bring needle to front of work. . .

Step 6. *Insert needle through base of seam*

Step 7. *Insert needle directly next to seam and take small stitch. . .*

. . . then continue sewing

Step 8. *Open out and finger press*

Many quilt patterns have pieces with unmatched angles that must be lined up in this way. With practice, these will soon become apparent and you will be able to eyeball the placement of the pieces. However, until you are able to do this, I again recommend marking with dots the places where the seam allowances cross the angles. Make sure that the dots are exactly lined up where the two pieces should join before stitching the pieces together.

Joining Rows of Diamonds or Other Pieces with Unmatched Angles

Many quilt designs are constructed by sewing together rows of pieces that have unmatched angles. Diamonds are a perfect example. Look at the quilts *Shamrock* and *Boxed Blocks*, shown in full in the pattern section. Units for these quilts are made by joining rows of diamonds, which then form larger diamond sections–four diamonds in each unit for *Shamrock* and nine diamonds in rows of three diamonds each for *Boxed Blocks*. Getting the four points of adjoining diamonds to meet where these rows come together requires a slightly different technique than joining four squares or rectangles. Let's see how this is done by continuing the example begun above, sewing four diamonds together. First, sew the two rows of diamonds, as described above, then follow these steps.

1. With right sides together, line up two rows. At the point where four diamonds come together, finger press the seam on the back piece to the right; finger press the seam on the top piece to the left. As you put the rows next to each other, gently pull the seam allowances apart and make sure that the points where the seam allowances come together on the front and back rows form an X. Make sure, too, that the seams are butted right up next to each other.
2. From the front, carefully insert a pin below the X and bring the point to the back, beyond the bulk of the seam. Then, gently pull the pin back until it "snaps" off the seams, right at the base of the X. Bring it to the front of the piece.
3. Begin stitching towards the place where the pin has come up at the bulk of the seams. As you approach the seam, gently pull both seam allowances to the left.
4. Stitch right up to the base of the seam and remove the pin. Take a tight backstitch and, when the tip of the needle is at the back of the work, push the needle beyond the ridge created by the bulk of the seam allowance.
5. Gently pull the tip of the needle back until it bounces off the ridge, then bring it to the front of the work right at the seam line.
6. Bring the bottom seam allowance to the right and let the top one stand up. Push your left thumbnail right next to the base of the top seam. Insert the needle directly through the base of that seam from right to left and bring the tip out right on top of your left thumbnail.

Shamrock. *See full quilt in the pattern section*

7. Bring both seams to the right and push against this with your thumbnail. Go straight down to the back of the piece with the needle directly next to the seam. Bring the tip back up in a small stitch and continue sewing.
8. Open out the piece and finger press the seams. If you are working with units such as this in a quilt, because of the bias edges on the diamonds, it is not advisable to iron these pieces until they are joined to other units.

"Occasionally modern patchwork is made by machine. But such short seams are rather fiddling work done in this way and to my mind much of its charm lies in its restful handwork opportunities."

Agnes M. Miall,
Patchwork Old and New, 1937

Columbia. *See full quilt in pattern section*

Flying Geese. *See full quilt in pattern section*

Joining Three Points

There are many exquisite quilt designs that have places where three points must come together. Two examples in this book are *Columbia* and *Flying Geese*, details of which are shown here. The technique is exactly the same for all examples. Let's look at how it is done for a simple *Flying Geese* unit.

When sewing three points together by hand, it is important to get a nice, sharp point without any gaps in the piece that is in the middle of the other two. Begin by laying out the three pieces to be sewn together. In the case of a *Flying Geese* unit, the large triangle will be in the center, with the long side at the bottom. Two smaller triangles will be above and on either side, as shown opposite.

It is important that the pieces are cut with the straight or cross grain on the *long* side of the large triangle and on the two *short* sides of the small triangles. This means that the pieces will be joined with a bias edge sewn to another bias edge. If you need a guide for the sewing line, mark dots or a line on the wrong side of the two small triangles. Follow the instructions on page 56.

When stitching these three pieces together, stitch the small triangle on the right to the larger one. Begin on the lower right and stitch *towards* the right-angle point of the larger triangle. Then, without breaking the thread, pick up the other piece and continue stitching to the lower left corner of the larger triangle. Follow these steps.

1. Pick up the small triangle on the right and, with right sides together, place it on top of the large triangle. You will notice that the sharp 45° points of each piece on the lower right corner are the same. Carefully match these up. Also, line up the bias edges going

Lay out pieces

Step 1. *Place pin . . .*

. . . making sure smaller triangle extends beyond larger triangle

Step 2. *Sew to point where seam allowances would cross . . .*

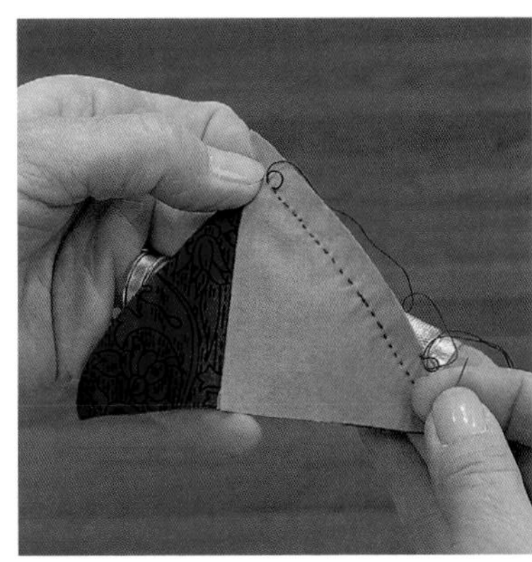

. . . and take small backstitch

Step 3. *Open out and fingerpress seams to right*

up the side and the straight edges across the bottom. Since the top of the large triangle is a 90° angle, and the point of the smaller triangle that joins to it is a 45° angle, these angles will not match. This is where it is important to see that the places where the seam allowances cross on each piece are exactly lined up. Secure these two angles with a pin and make sure that the tip of the pin comes out right at the dot that marks the point where the seam allowances cross. If you turn the piece to the back, you will see where the 45° angle of the smaller triangle extends beyond the 90° angle of the larger triangle.

2. Turn the piece to the front again. Starting at the outside edge and sewing towards the center of the large triangle, sew just to the point where the seam allowances cross. Remove the pin and take a small backstitch, bringing the needle up exactly at that crossing point. Do not break the thread.
3. Open out the two pieces and, with the seam at the back, gently finger press the seam towards the right. By doing this you will be able to feel a ridge with your left thumbnail. Try clicking your nail off of that ridge to get the feel of it.
4. Place the next small triangle directly on top of the large one, again aligning the 45° angles at the lower left and matching the points where the seam

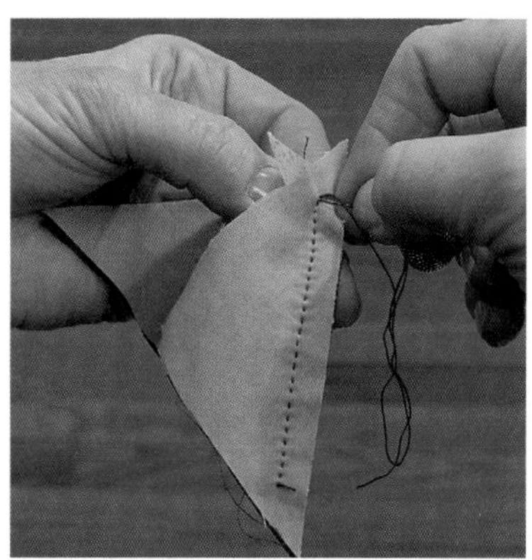

Step 5. Bring needle through last stitch

Exit on top of thumbnail

Step 7. Complete

allowances cross. Push your thumb directly against the ridge created by the bulk of the seams.

5. Carefully bring the needle directly through the end of the last stitch, through the base of the seam allowance, and right on top of your thumbnail.
6. Pull the needle all the way through, then nestle the point next to the ridge. Go straight down to the back of the work, right next to the ridge and your thumbnail. Immediately bring the tip up in a small stitch and continue sewing.
7. Knot the thread at the end and cut it. Open out and check to make sure that the point in the middle of the large triangle is securely bounded by the pieces on either side. If this point is not neat and sharp at this stage, it will not be neat and sharp when it is joined to other sections of the quilt. There should be ¼″ (0.75 cm) seam allowance above the point.

QUICK TIP

When sewing rows of triangles together, as in a border, don't break the thread, but just keep going up the side of one triangle and down the next, joining the three points zig-zag fashion.

Joining a Three-Point Unit to Another Piece

Many times, such as with strips of *Flying Geese* units (see quilt in pattern section), you'll come up against a new challenge–a piece where three points meet must be stitched to a piece with no seams. Here, again, it is very important to have a sharp point at the places where the fabrics come together. Follow these steps.

1. To achieve a nice point, first finger press the seams on the piece with three points away from the point. Place this piece on top of the other fabric, lining up the cut edges. With the seams arranged in this manner, you will be able to feel with your fingers the thickness of the seams and then the sudden void where the point is. Take a pin and insert it below the point, into the back of the work, extending it well beyond the point. Gently pull the pin back until it snaps off the bulk of the seams and bring it to the front of the work so that the pin comes out right at the point.

Lay out pieces

Step 1. *Place pin*

Step 2. *Pull seam allowances to left to create ridge. . .*

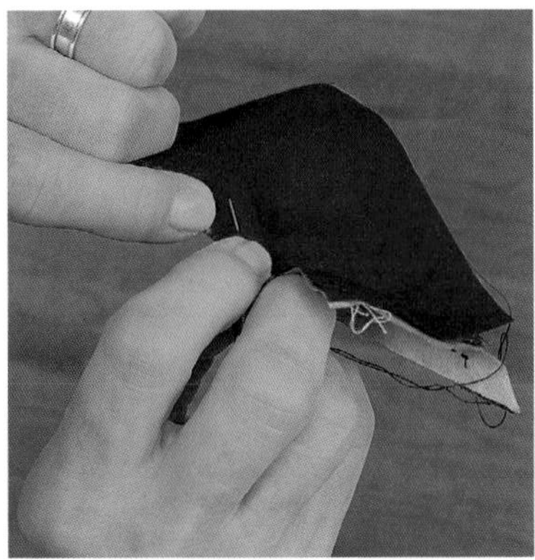
Step 3. *Push needle beyond ridge . . .*

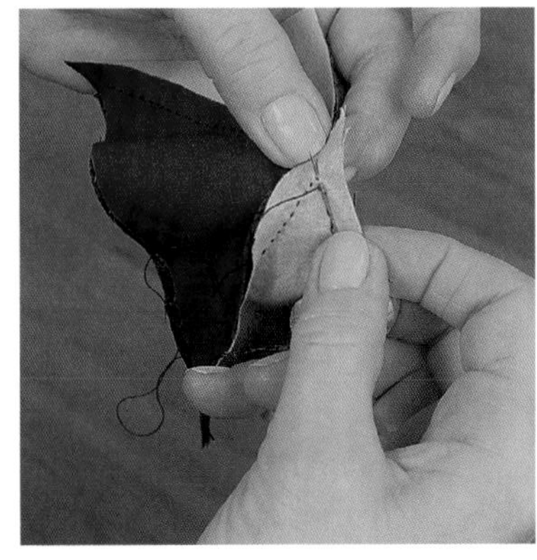
. . . then snap needle off ridge and come up at base of seam

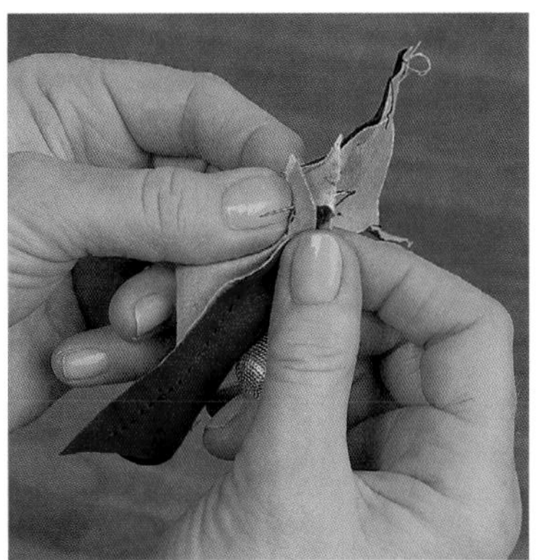
Step 4. *Bring needle through base of seam, exiting on top of thumbnail*

Joining a Three-Point Unit

2. Begin sewing towards the point, aiming at the exact place where the pin exits. As you approach the seams, pull all of the seam allowances gently to the left. This creates a bulky ridge that you can easily feel.
3. Put the needle in to take a stitch. With the tip at the back of the work, push the needle beyond the ridge created by the seam and then gently pull it back until the tip of the needle snaps off the ridge and comes out just at the base of the seam line. Take a small backstitch and repeat the process.
4. Carefully remove the pin and bring the seam allowances up. Press the thumbnail of your left hand against the base of the seams and insert the needle from the right of the seam directly through the base. Bring it through to the left, exiting on top of your thumbnail.
5. Now, gently pull the seam allowances to the *right.* Push the thumbnail of your left hand directly next to the ridge created by this seam. Nestle the tip of the needle right next to the seam and your thumbnail and go straight down. You are not going into the seam at all, just very tightly next to it. As soon as the tip of the needle goes down next to the ridge, bring it back up to make a small stitch and continue the running stitch to the end of the piece.
6. Knot the thread at the end and cut it. Open out the piece and finger press the seams away from the point.

Step 5. *Seam allowances to right, nestle needle next to seam*

Step 6. *Complete*

This same process will be used whether the pieces with the point are on the front or the back of the work. If, for example, I am sewing a border of pieced triangles to another piece of fabric, I insert a pin at each and every point in the manner described above. This is the only way to ensure that the points will not be cut off.

Joining Pairs of Three-Point Units

When joining two *Flying Geese* units, the process is exactly the same as explained above, with one exception. Now there will be a seam to contend with at the beginning and end of the units. To join pairs of three-point units, lay out the pieces, then use this simple technique.

1. Begin by pinning the two units together with the three points on top.
2. Finger press the seam on the right hand side of the back piece to the right. This creates that same ridge described earlier. Nestle the thumbnail tightly next to that ridge, right at the point where the seam allowances cross. Now insert the needle from the back of the work, making sure it is at the exact point where the seam allowances cross on that back piece. Bring the needle from the back, through the seam, and exit right on top of the thumbnail.
3. Pull the thread up, then nestle the needle next to the ridge and between the ridge and thumbnail and go straight down. Bring the needle back up, taking a small stitch, and continue sewing towards the point in the center.
4. Sew the center points as explained in the previous stitching sequence, and continue to the left side. As you approach the end, bring the seam on the back of the work to the left, once again creating that ridge. Just short of the seam, insert the needle, go beyond the ridge, and then gently pull back on the needle until it snaps off the ridge. Bring the needle up at the base of the ridge. Take a backstitch and repeat the process.
5. Knot the thread and cut it off. Do not sew the seams down. Leave them free.

Joining Pairs of Three-Point Units

Lay out pieces

Step 1. Pin together pair of units

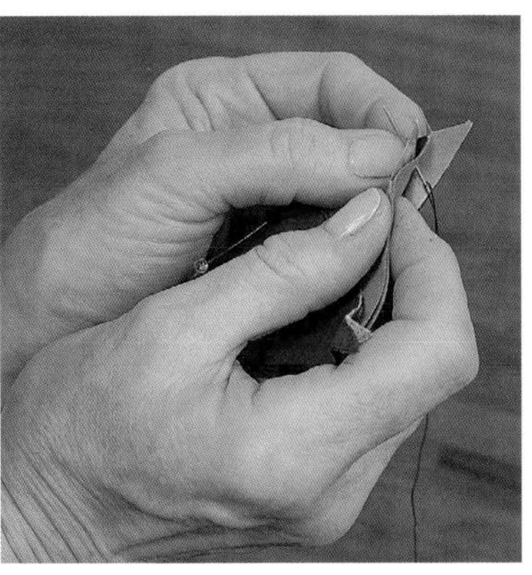

Step 2. Insert needle from back and exit on top of thumbnail

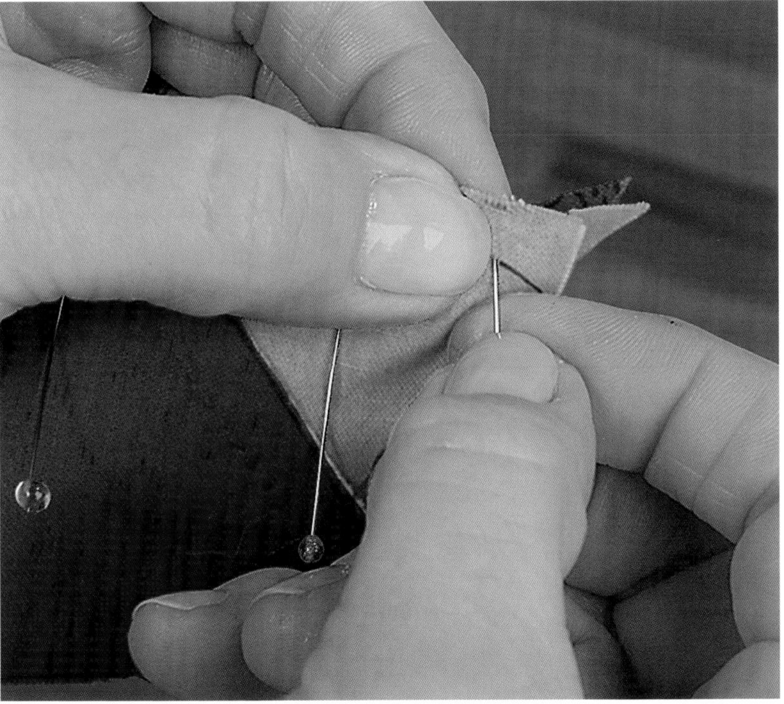

Step 3. Nestle needle next to ridge, then go straight down . . .

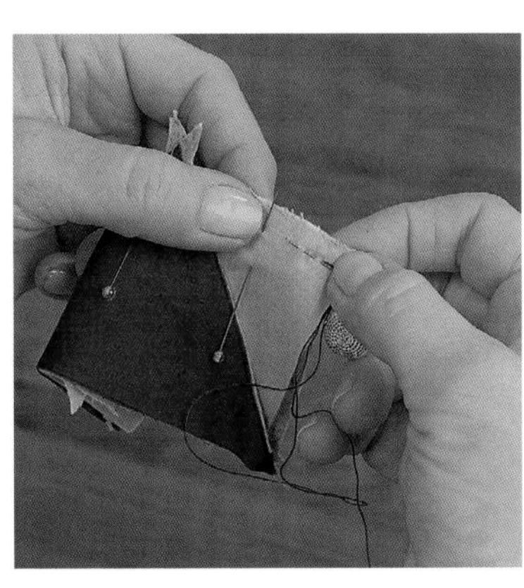

. . . bring tip up and continue sewing

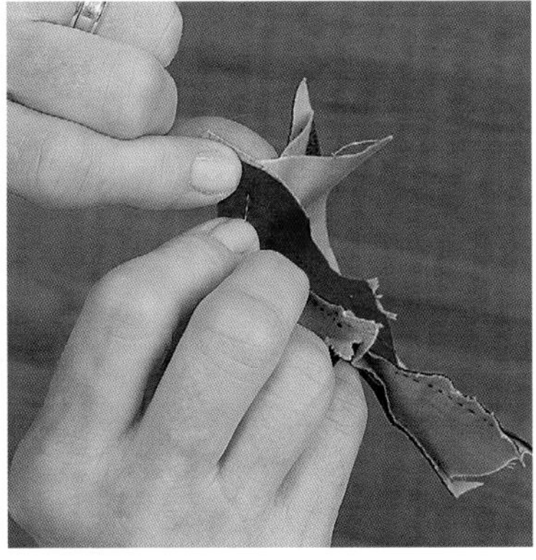

Step 4. Seam allowances to left, insert needle and snap off ridge . . .

. . . bring needle up at base of ridge

Step 5. Complete

"Even a thirty-secondth of an inch if added to several diamonds on one side of a big Lone Star diamond, and the same number less several times on an adjacent point, will throw the plan awry. Seams must be even. Quilt piecing is a most precise craft where a few tiny inaccuracies add quickly into a total of ugly stretch or puckers."

Ruby Short McKim,
101 Patchwork Patterns, 1931

Joining Multiple Points

Many quilt patterns contain places where multiple pieces come together at a single point. The previous two chapters discuss joining two, three, and four points, but six and eight points are also very common in patchwork design. *Windows*, *Shamrock*, *Columbia*, and *Day Lilies*, for instance, all contain places where six or eight points come together. Occasionally patterns are encountered where even more points come together at a single spot. I find that it is quite easy to accurately join up to eight points, and even up to 12 can be sewn if extreme care is taken. Beyond that, there is so much bulk with the seam allowances that it is difficult to get a nice, sharp point.

Charm quilt with equilateral triangles, circa 1880. Maker unknown

Joining Six Points

Six points come together in stars, triangles, and many other elements of patchwork design. The technique for achieving sharp points for any six-point project is exactly the same. When sewing six points together, you must first sew just three pieces together in the exact same way described earlier for joining three points. Sew from the outside to the center of the first two pieces. Without breaking the thread, pick up the third piece and sew from the center to the outside. Repeat the same process for a second set of three points. Finally, make one straight seam to join the two halves together.

Let's look at the process in more detail. Here, six 60° diamonds will be sewn into a six-pointed star. Begin by laying out the pieces for the star on a table. Separate them into the two halves. This is important so that you will pick up and sew the pieces in the correct order.

Lay out pieces

***Step 1.** Line up edges and pin in place*

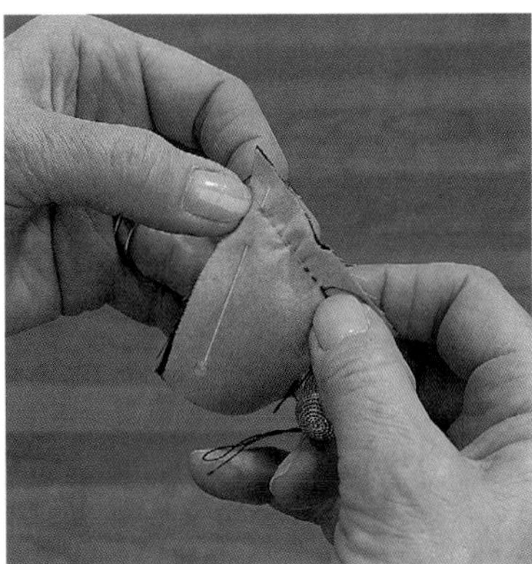

***Step 2.** Sew from outside to center*

***Step 3.** Position third diamond*

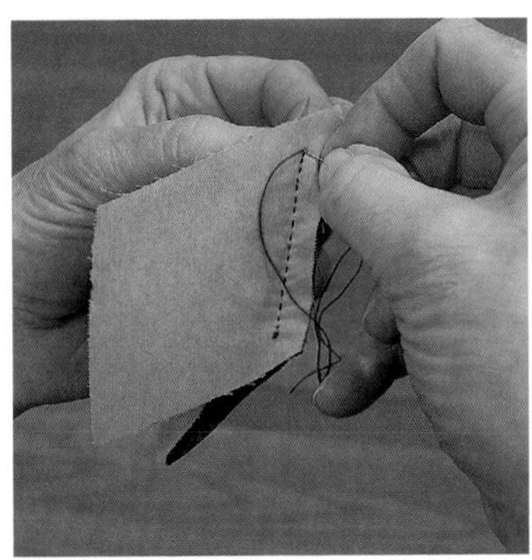

***Step 4.** Insert needle from back . . .*

. . . and bring out on top of thumbnail

Joining Six Points

1. Pick up the piece on the right hand side of one of the halves and place it on top of the piece in the middle. Mark dots where the seam allowances cross, then line up the edges and pin the pieces together. Bring the point of the pin out right at the dot as shown.
2. Begin sewing from the outside towards what will be the center of the star. When you reach the pin, bring the needle up right at its exit point. Remove the pin and take a backstitch, once again coming up right at the dot. Do not cut the thread.
3. Open the pieces and finger press the seam to the right. Lay the third diamond on the top of the middle diamond and pin in place. Nestle your thumb right next to the ridge created by the seam and push tightly against it.
4. Now go to the back to the place where the thread came out at the end of the row of stitches. Insert the needle right into the same place and bring it out right on top of your thumbnail.
5. Bring the needle up, then nestle it right next to the ridge and go straight down to the back. Without pulling the thread through, bring the tip of the needle back up and continue stitching to the dot where the seam allowances cross on the top piece.

Quick Tip

When sewing diamonds, the stitching must begin and end at the dots where seam allowances cross. The reason is that later—to complete the background of the star—another diamond will be *set in*, using a technique explained in the next chapter. Note that these diamonds are identical to those sewn in the earlier example where unmatched angles were joined (see page 86). For the six-pointed *star*, the 60° angles line up perfectly. For the *rows,* where the sharp angles do not meet, unmatched angles are sewn together, thus the pieces are lined up differently.

Step 5. *Re-insert needle . . .*

. . . and bring tip back up and stitch.

Step 6. *Open out, note tip extending*

Step 8. *Position two halves together*

Step 9. *Insert pin and exit at point*

Pin edges of two halves together

Joining Six Points *continued*

6. Open out the pieces and make sure that the point of the middle diamond is sharp and secure, and there is ¼″ (0.75 cm) of fabric above the point.
7. Sew the other three diamonds in the same manner so that you now have two halves. Check to make sure that the point in the middle of each half is securely bounded by the pieces on either side. If this point is not neat and sharp at this stage, it will not be neat and sharp when the two halves are sewn together.
8. Sew the two halves together with one straight seam, taking care that all points come together neatly and securely. Begin by finger pressing the seams on the two halves away from the point. Place the two halves together with right sides facing each other, taking great care to ensure that the tips of the points of the center piece in each half meet exactly. You will be able to feel with your fingers the thickness of the seams and then the sudden void where the point is.
9. Take a pin and insert it from the front about ¼″ (0.75 cm) below the point into the back, extending it well beyond the point. Gently pull the pin back until it snaps off of the bulk of the seams and bring it to the front again so that the tip of the pin comes out right at the point of the piece facing you. (This is the spot where the seam allowances cross.) Pin the edges of the

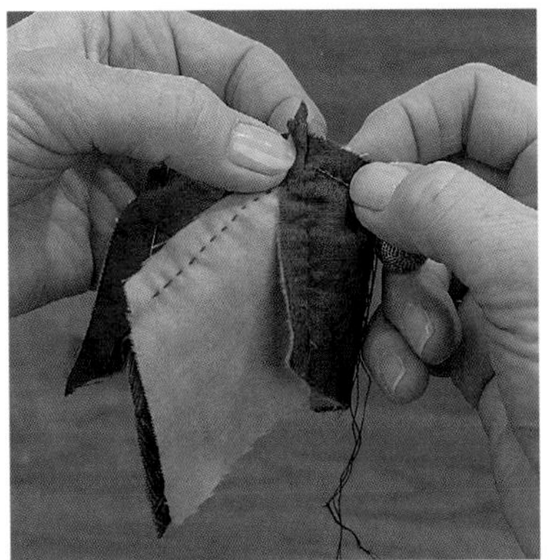

Step 10. *Sew from pin toward point*

Step 11. *Push needle beyond ridge*

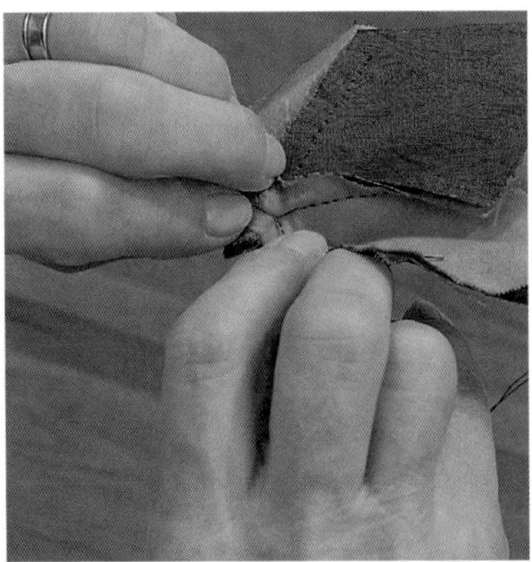

then pull needle back and snap off ridge

Backstitch

Step 12. *Push thumbnail against seams*

Bring needle out above thumbnail

two halves together as well, with the tips of the pins coming out right at the place where the seam allowances cross.

10. Begin sewing from the pin towards the point. As you approach the seams, pull the seam allowances gently to the left. This creates a bulky ridge that you can easily feel. Without disturbing the placement of the two halves, gently remove the pin.
11. Put the needle in to take a stitch. When the tip is at the back of the work, push the needle beyond the ridge created by the seams and then gently pull it back until the tip snaps off the ridge and comes out just at the base of the seam line. Take a small backstitch and repeat the process.
12. Push your left thumbnail firmly against the seams and insert the needle directly through the base of the seams from the right side, bringing it through to the left, just above your thumbnail.
13. Now, gently pull the seam allowances to the *right.* To ensure a nice, tight joining of the points, the thumbnail of your left hand should still be pushing directly next to the bulk of the seams. Nestle the tip of the needle right next to the seam and your thumbnail and go straight down. You are not going into the seam at all, just very tightly next to it. As soon as the tip of the needle goes down next to the ridge, bring it back up to make a small stitch and continue the running stitch to the end of the piece.

Step 13. *Seam allowances to right, nestle needle next to seam*

Make small stitch and continue sewing

Step 14. *Completed piece*

Joining Six Points *continued*

14. Open out the pieces and check to make sure that all six diamonds meet at the center in sharp points.

Joining Eight Points

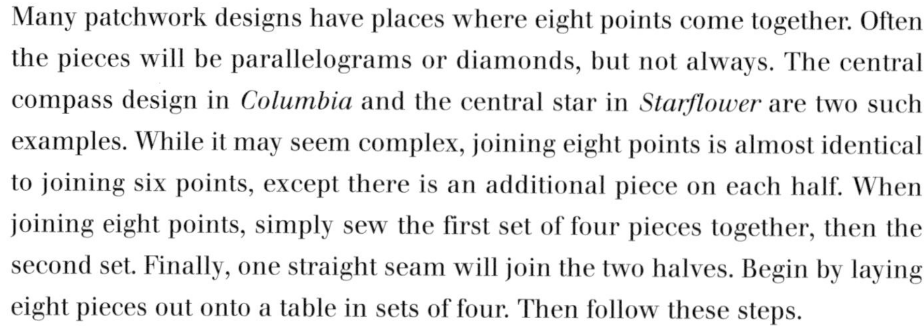

Many patchwork designs have places where eight points come together. Often the pieces will be parallelograms or diamonds, but not always. The central compass design in *Columbia* and the central star in *Starflower* are two such examples. While it may seem complex, joining eight points is almost identical to joining six points, except there is an additional piece on each half. When joining eight points, simply sew the first set of four pieces together, then the second set. Finally, one straight seam will join the two halves. Begin by laying eight pieces out onto a table in sets of four. Then follow these steps.

Columbia. *See full quilt in pattern section*

Starflower. *See full quilt in pattern section*

1. Pick up the piece on the far right of one of the halves and, with right sides together, place it on top of the second piece. Mark the place on the point where the two seam allowances cross (see page 56) and secure the two pieces together with a pin. The point of the pin should come out right at the mark indicating seam allowances. Starting at the outside edge where the seam allowances cross and sewing towards the center, sew to the pin and take a small backstitch. Do not break the thread.
2. Take the pin out, open up the two pieces, and gently finger press the seam towards the right. You should be able to feel the ridge from the seam allowance with the thumbnail of your left hand.
3. With right sides together, place the third piece on top of the second. Push the thumbnail right next to that ridge.
4. Carefully bring the needle from the right directly through the end of the last stitch and through the base of the seam allowance so that it comes out on top of your thumbnail.
5. Nestle the needle next to the seam allowances between the ridge and your thumbnail and go straight down. If you check the back, you will see that the needle will come out right at the end of the seam line.

Lay out pieces

Joining Eight Points

Step 1. Pin at point where seam allowances cross

Starting at outside, sew to pin and take small backstitch

Step 2. Open out and finger press

Step 3. Position third piece; push thumbnail next to ridge

Step 4. Bring needle through end of last stitch made . . .

. . . then go through base of seam allowance and up on top of thumbnail

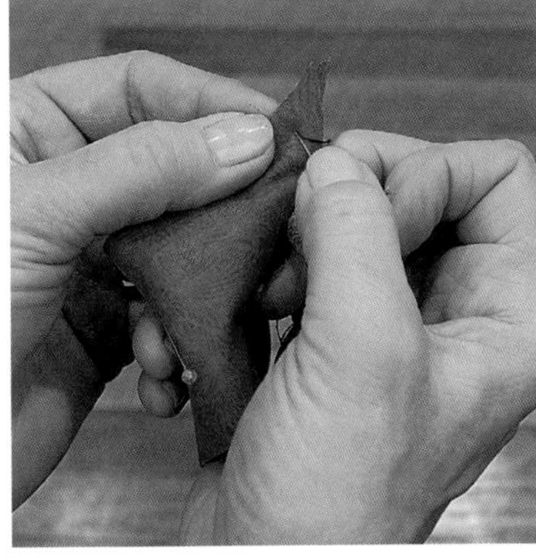

Step 5. Nestle needle next to seam allowances and go straight down

On back, needle comes out right at end of seam line

Step 6. *Bring needle up and continue sewing to end. Cut thread*

Step 7. *Check that middle piece is securely bounded on either side*

Step 8. *Position fourth piece*

Step 9. *Push thumbnail against base of ridge*

Bring needle all the way from back of first piece . . .

. . . through bases of the three points, and out through fourth piece on top of thumbnail

6. Bring the needle up in a small stitch and continue sewing to the end. Cut the thread.
7. Check to make sure that the point on the piece in the middle is securely bounded by the two pieces on either side. If this point is not neat and sharp at this stage, you will not have sharp points when all eight are joined.
8. The fourth piece is added next. This piece will be sewn from the center point out. With right sides of the three sewn pieces facing you, finger press the seams towards the right. Pin the fourth piece on top of the third one, again making sure that the tip of the pin comes out at the intersection where the two seam allowances cross. This will be the stopping point for the stitches.
9. Push the thumbnail of your left hand directly next to the base of the ridge created by the seam allowances at the points. Using a new thread, bring the needle all the way from the back of the first piece at the exact point where the first seam ended, through the bases of the three points, and out through the fourth piece. The needle should come up just above your thumbnail.
10. Nestle the needle next to the seam allowances and push it straight down. If you check the back, you will see once again that the needle comes out

Step 10. Nestle needle next to seam allowances and go straight down

On back, needle comes out right at end of seam line

Step 11. Sew to end, then open out

Step 12. Make sure that two points of middle pieces in each half meet exactly

Step 13. Insert pin, exiting at point of triangles facing you

Step 14. Pin, then begin sewing toward center points

right at the end of the previous seam line. Without bringing the thread through, bring the tip of the needle back up, taking a small stitch.

11. Continue sewing to the end of the seam and then open out the pieces. Check to make sure that the two points in the middle end at the exact same place and that there is ¼″ (0.75 cm) seam allowance above the two points.
12. Sew the remaining four pieces in the same manner so that you now have two halves. Finger press the seams on the two halves so they are going away from the points. Place the two halves together with right sides facing each other, making sure that the two points of the middle pieces in each half meet exactly. You should be able to feel the bulk of all the seams and then the sudden void where the points meet.
13. From the front of the work insert a pin below the point and into the back, extending the tip beyond the point. Gently pull the pin back until it snaps off the bulk of the seams and bring it to the front, so that the point comes out right at the point of the triangles facing you.
14. Pin the two ends together as well, then begin sewing towards the center points. Stitching should start right where the two seam allowances cross.

Step 15. *As you approach seams, pull seam allowances gently to left*

Step 16. *Push needle beyond ridge created by seams. . .*

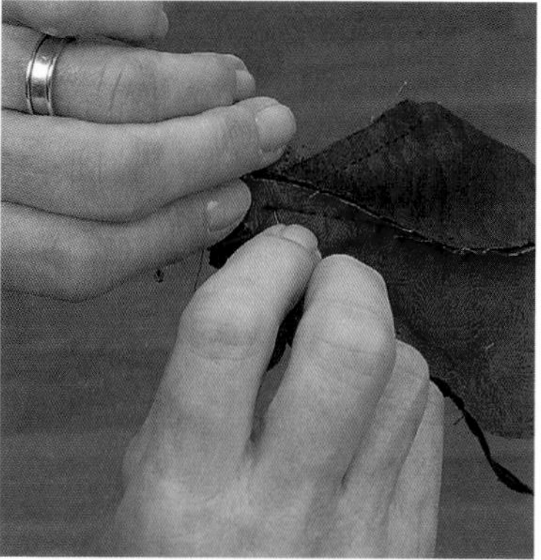

. . . let it snap off ridge and come out at base of seam line. Take back-stitch

On front, tip of needle will come out right at seam line

Step 17. *Remove pin; insert needle from right, directly through base of seams on top piece*

Step 18. *With seam allowances to right, nestle needle next to seam . . .*

. . . and go straight down back

Step 19. *Bring needle back up and continue sewing*

Step 20. *Complete*

15. As you approach the seams, pull the seam allowances gently to the left. This creates a bulky ridge that you can easily feel.
16. Put the needle in to take a stitch with the tip at the back of the work. Push the needle beyond the ridge created by the seams and then gently pull it back until the tip of the needle snaps off the ridge and comes out just at the base of the seam line. Take a small backstitch and repeat the process. On the front of the work, the tip of the needle will come out right at the seam line.
17. Carefully remove the pin and bring the seam allowances up. Push your left thumbnail firmly against the seams and insert the needle from the right directly through the base of the seams on the top piece, bringing it through just above your thumbnail. The needle does not go into the back piece at this time.
18. Now, gently pull the seam allowances to the *right.* The thumbnail of your left hand should still be pushing directly next to the bulk of the seams. Nestle the tip of the needle right next to the seam and your thumbnail and go straight down to the back. You are not going into the seam at all, just very tightly next to it into the piece on the back.
19. As soon as the tip of the needle goes down next to the ridge, bring it back up to make a small stitch and continue the running stitch to the end of the piece.
20. Open the pieces out and check to see that all of the points are secure. Check that there is no hole in the middle and that all the points are sharp and meet at the exact same place.

As you can see, joining eight points is really not that difficult as long as you follow these simple steps. And with the skills learned here, you have now practiced the most difficult part of hand piecing.

Next Steps in a Hand-Pieced Quilt

With the new techniques learned so far in this chapter, you are ready to continue the project you began at the end of Chapter Four–the next stages of either *Starflower* or *Columbia* shown in the pattern section. The *Flying Geese* quilt is another perfect pattern for practicing the techniques presented in this chapter. Cut some pieces, organize the units in plastic bags, put these in a larger bag, and add a spool of thread, along with some pins, needles, and small scissors. Keep all of this tucked away in your purse or tote bag, by the phone, or on an end table near the TV. This way, you'll be ready to sew a few pieces, here and there, in "found" moments. Before long, you will be amazed at how much sewing you have accomplished.

Antique ***Sunflower****, circa 1840. Maker unknown*

Piecing Mastery

Setting In Angles and Piecing Curves

"One lovely feature of this quilt show was the reverence with which men brought to us the quilts their mothers made. Plain farmers, busy workers, retired businessmen, came to us, their faces softened to tenderness, handed us, with mingled pride and devotion, their big bundle containing a contribution to the display, saying in softened accents 'My mother made it.'"

Marie D. Webster,
Quilts, Their Story & How to Make Them, 1915

EWING BY HAND CREATES MEMORIES—AND NOT JUST FOR the maker of the quilt, but for family members or friends who may have sat and chatted with the quilter while the work was being stitched. Loving memories are part of the hand-quilting tradition. I can look at each and every one of the quilts I have made and recall images of what was happening in my life and in the lives of those around me during the time a particular quilt was being stitched. Often, it is the quilts that have the most pieces and perhaps the more involved techniques that hold the strongest memories of all.

By now, you have mastered the sewing of straight seams and have the skills to make any design that is pieced with simple squares, triangles, or diamonds. You are now ready to learn two more techniques that will give you even greater freedom and allow you to choose from an ever-broader range of quilt designs. These two skills are setting in angles and piecing curves. Often the bane of machine quilters, who find designs that incorporate set-in pieces or require curved-line stitching the most troublesome of all, both techniques are a delight to sew by hand. As you read this chapter, you will quickly find that designs like these are far easier to sew by hand than on the sewing machine. You will also build memories with each stitch.

World in Their Hands. *Jinny Beyer, 2003.* *See full quilt on page 30*

Setting In Single Pieces

Not all patchwork designs can be assembled with continuous straight seams. In all designs that contain hexagons and many designs that contain diamonds, for instance, there are pieces that need to be set in. Many *Mariners' Compass* patterns and quilts such as *Day Lilies*, *Windows*, *Starflower*, and *Columbia* all have portions of the design that require setting in. Do not let yourself be intimidated by these types of designs. The process of setting in pieces is very similar to the techniques you have already learned.

By now you will have realized that achieving sharp points in the various techniques described in the last two chapters involves pretty much the same steps. When sewing right handed, as you approach the points, the seam allowances are brought to the left. A tight backstitch is taken next to the seam, and the allowances are kept free as the needle passes through the base. They are then pulled to the right, another tight stitch is taken on the left side of the seam, and the running stitch continues. The process is similar for setting in pieces.

Any time the joining of two pieces results in an *inward* angle, another piece must be *set in* to fit inside that angle. Because of the inward angle, the stitching cannot go all the way to the end of the pieces being sewn but must stop at the point where the two seam allowances cross. (Seams can be sewn all the way to the edges of the pieces if an *outward* angle will be the result, but not if it will be an *inward* angle.)

The same diamond shape that was used on page 89 to illustrate sewing diamonds in rows and on page 96 for sewing six points can also be used for forming a *Tumbling Blocks* cube. This is a good example to demonstrate setting a piece into an inward angle. Begin by arranging three diamonds (one light, one medium, and one dark) on a table, then follow these steps.

1. Pick up two of the diamonds and, with right sides together, line them up exactly, matching the angles and cut edges. Pin in place and begin stitching at the point where the seam allowances cross. Continue to the pin.
2. Remove the pin, open out the two diamonds, and, right side facing up, finger press the seam on the back to the left. You will be able to feel a bulky ridge created by the seam allowances.
3. Place the diamond to be set in on top of the diamond on the right, making sure to match the cut edges and angles and making sure that the seam on the bottom diamond is still pulled to the left. If you need a guide for the place where the seam allowances cross, put the template over the wrong side of the diamond at this time. Mark small dots through the template holes at the intersection. (Speed this process by using *Jinny Beyer Perfect Piecer*, described on page 56.)
4. Put a pin through the diamonds below where the seam allowances cross, push the tip beyond the bulk of the ridge from the seam allowance, and gently pull it back until the tip of the pin bounces off that ridge. This should

Quick Tip

I'm often asked whether it's best to begin stitching at the edge of the pieces or at the seam allowances. The answer is that sometimes you can begin at the edges and sometimes you must begin at the place where the seam allowances cross. Whenever the stitching results in an *inward* angle, the stitching *must* begin at the place where the seam allowances cross. Where the stitching results in an *outward* angle, the stitching can begin at the edges, perhaps lending a little more stability. For straight line sewing where no angles are involved, I usually stitch all the way to the end.

Setting In Single Pieces

Lay out pieces

Step 1. Align, then pin in place and begin stitching . . .

. . . up to point where seam allowances cross

Step 2. Open out, with seam allowance finger-pressed to left

Step 3. Position diamond to be set in on top of diamond on right, pulling seams to left

Steps 4 and 5. Sew to pin and take a backstitch

Step 6. Pivot the piece and line up unsewn edges

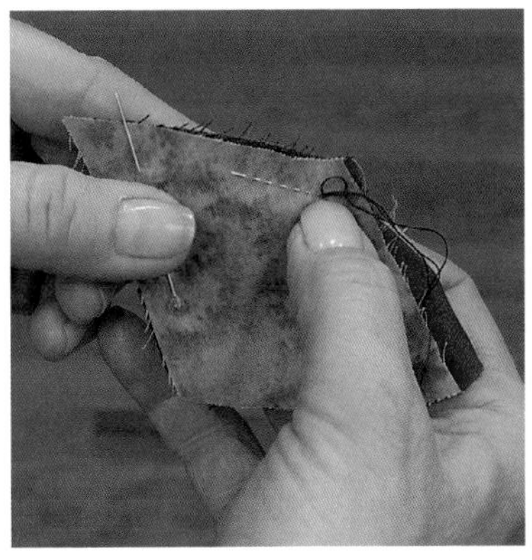

Step 7. Continue sewing to end

Complete

Tumbling Blocks charm quilt, circa 1870. Maker unknown

be precisely at the point where the seam allowances cross. Bring the tip of the pin out right at the crossing of the seam allowances.

5. Begin sewing from the right hand edge toward the set-in corner. As you approach the angle, pull the seam allowances to the left and stitch just to the corner dot. Gently remove the pin. To ensure a tight intersection, take a backstitch, pushing the needle beyond the ridge created by the seam allowances and then gently pulling it back until it snaps off the seam and comes up right at the dot. Do not cut the thread.
6. Pivot the piece being set in. Line up the unsewn edge with the unsewn edge of the diamond on the left and pin in place.
7. Finger press the sewn seams to the right and push the thumbnail of your left hand right next to the ridge. Using the same method as before, insert the needle straight down between the thumbnail and the ridge of the seam, being careful not to stitch into the ridge. Bring the tip of the needle back up in a small stitch and continue the seam to the end. When the pieces are opened out, you will see the diamond has been set in with a nice clean angle.

"The invention of the sewing-machine has, undoubtedly, made a great difference in our habits, and a knowledge of its management and working is considered by many people as an equivalent to skill in hand-sewing. Very little thought on the subject will show how great a mistake this is; for though the machine causes a great saving of time in long seams and close stitching, there must be knowledge sufficient to make up the materials; and the mending, altering, darning, and general repairing—the most essential part of the business in a large family—can only be done by clever hands. To the true woman the influence of the needle, at once soothing and giving an excuse for quiet thought, is well-nigh indispensable."

S. C. A. Caulfield and Blanche C. Saward,
The Dictionary of Needlework, 1882

Setting In Consecutive Pieces

No matter what shapes you are setting in, you will use the same process described so far in this chapter. However, if you are setting in several pieces consecutively around a block, as necessary when making a six- or eight-pointed star block, for instance, you must also keep in mind the piecing process learned in Chapter Five when joining three points (see page 90).

To set in the pieces around an eight-pointed star, begin by laying the pieces out on a table with the squares and triangles arranged in the way they will be sewn. Then follow these steps.

*Antique **Lone Star**, circa 1850. Maker unknown*

1. Pick up the first square and lay it on top of the side of one of the diamonds. Mark dots at the places where the seam allowances will cross on both the diamond and square, then match the dots (see page 56). Note that because the square and the diamonds between which it is being set do not have the same angles, the tip of the diamond will extend beyond the right angle of the square on the right. Likewise, if we could see through the fabric on the left side, we would also see that the right angle of that corner of the square would extend a little beyond the wider angle of the diamond. (See page 86 on joining unmatched points.) Pin the pieces in place, with the tip of the pin coming out right at the dot. Before inserting the pin on the left, pull the seam allowance to the left side of the pieces. Insert the pin below the dot, and, with the tip at the back of the work, extend it beyond the seam and gently pull it back until it "snaps" off the seam. Bring it back up right at the dot. Careful pinning like this will help ensure a tight joining of the pieces.

Lay out pieces

Step 1. *Pick up first piece. Align edges and pin in place exactly where seam allowances cross*

Step 2. *Pull seam allowance to left and sew all way to pin*

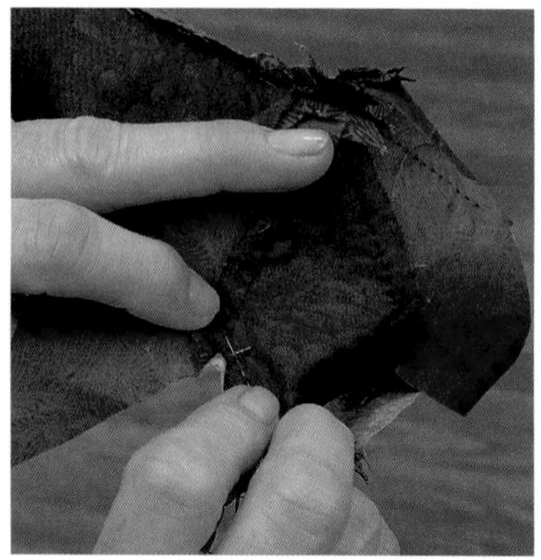

Take backstitch, pushing needle beyond ridge created by seam allowance

Gently pull needle back so tip snaps off ridge and . . .

. . . bring it up so that it exits right at pin. Do not cut thread

Setting In Consecutive Pieces

2. Begin sewing ¼″ (0.75 cm) from the edge of the square towards the dot on the left. As you approach the seam, pull the seam allowance on the back to the left. Insert the needle to the back and extend it beyond the seam, and then gently pull it back until it snaps off the seam. Bring it to the front, right at the dot. Do not cut the thread.
3. Remove the pin, pivot the square, and line it up with the next diamond, making sure to match the points where the seam allowances cross. Pin in place. Once again, the tip of the diamond will extend beyond the right angle of the square.
4. Pull the seam allowances to the right, then nestle the needle right next to the ridge created by the seam allowance.
5. Bring the needle back up and continue sewing to ¼″ (0.75 cm) from the edge on the left hand side of the square. Do not cut the thread. Open out.
6. Pick up the triangle that will be going in next. Hold it so that the right angle is positioned as shown. The short side on the right of this triangle is to be sewn next. With right sides together, lay it down on the remaining side of the diamond that was just stitched. This time, the diamond and sharp point of the triangle have the same angles. Line these angles up on the right, and

Step 3. Pivot set-in piece and align edges with next piece. Pin at left, exactly where seam allowances cross

Setting In Consecutive Pieces *continued*

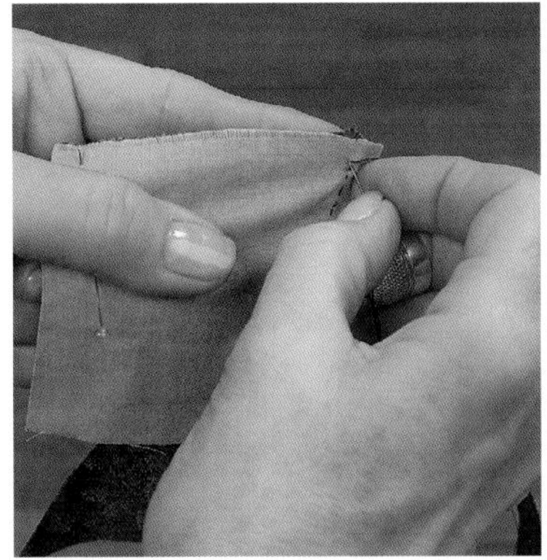

Step 4. Seams to right, insert needle straight down next to ridge. Bring tip back up in small stitch

Step 5. Sew to end. Open out. Do not cut thread

Step 6. Position, align, and pin next triangle

Step 7. Seams to right, push needle into stitch just sewn . . .

. . . and bring back up onto triangle on top of thumbnail

Step 8. With thumbnail still in place, push needle straight down and bring up in small stitch

Step 9. Complete

on the left side, match the dots where the seam allowances cross. Pin in place by pulling the seam allowances to the left and, from the front, inserting a pin just below the seam allowance. Extend it on the back side beyond the seam and then gently pull it back until it snaps off the seam allowance. Do not place a pin on the right, but just make sure the angles of the two pieces are lined up.

7. Finger press the seam just sewn to the right. Push your thumbnail next to the base of the ridge of that seam, then, from the back of the work, insert the needle into the last stitch of the seam just sewn and bring it out onto the triangle on top of your thumbnail.
8. With the thumbnail still in place, insert the needle straight down between the ridge and your nail. Go through to the back of the work and then straight up again in a small stitch.
9. Continue sewing to the next seam and keep repeating the process until all pieces have been set in.

Tumbling Blocks

A quilt where every piece is cut from a different fabric is called a *charm quilt*. Charm quilts are usually made with pieces cut from a single shape, such as a square, diamond, triangle, or hexagons. *Tumbling Blocks* (see page 110) is one of my favorite designs for a charm qult and is a great hand-piecing project.

Tumbling Blocks, or *Baby Blocks* as it is also known, is one of my all-time favorite patterns. I think it is an especially good design to teach beginning quilters basic hand-piecing skills. It also helps with color and value placement. While there are many variations of this design, if you want the blocks to show up as three dimensional cubes, care must be taken in terms of the placement of light, medium, and dark values. To achieve the cube effect, the darks must always be on one side, the mediums on another, and the lights on the third side.

To make a *Tumbling Blocks* quilt, I recommend that rather than sewing individual blocks made up of three diamonds each, it's easier to make larger units composed of 12 diamonds. The unit is laid out as shown here. The piecing sequence is as follows.

1. Treat the six diamonds in the middle of the unit as a six-pointed star and sew the star together as explained on page 96.
2. Set in the six diamonds around the outside edges of the star, following the same instructions used for setting squares and triangles into an eight-pointed star, as explained on page 111. The process is exactly the same. The pieces are sewn in a continuous line without breaking the thread and each piece is added just as though you were joining three points, as explained on page 90.

Don't stitch any sewn units together until all are complete. You will then have the fun of arranging and rearranging them to your satisfaction. Lay out several units at a time, put them in a bag with basic supplies, and keep them at hand as a hand-piecing project. It is a good idea to keep a sketch of the unit in the bag, with the values shaded in, so that, as the units are sewn, you can check that the values are correct.

Step 1. *Lay out pieces*

Step 2. *Complete*

Tumbling Blocks

If you would like to try making your own *Tumbling Blocks* quilt, just begin sewing units together in the manner explained above. This is a great carry-with-you project. All you have to think about is having fabrics in colors you like. Periodically, you can simply sort them into units made up of light, medium, and dark values. Put the arranged units in a plastic bag and have them ready to stitch at any "found" moments. Just keep making units until you have enough for the size quilt you might like to make. The same diamond template used for *Shamrock* or *Boxed Blocks* can be used for *Tumbling Blocks* as well (see template section).

"There are many things to induce women to piece quilts. The desire for a handsome bed furnishing, or the wish to make a gift of one to a dear friend, have inspired some women to make quilts. With others, quiltmaking is a recreation, a diversion, a means of occupying restless fingers. However, the real inducement is love of the work; because the desire to make a quilt exceeds all other desires. In such a case it is worked on persistently, laid aside reluctantly, and taken up each time with renewed interest and pleasure. It is this intense interest in the work which produces the most beautiful quilts."

Marie D. Webster,
Quilts: Their Story & How to Make Them, 1915

Working with Curves

Several quilts featured in *Quiltmaking by Hand*, including *Love Ring*, *Starflower*, *Day Lilies*, and *Windows*, have some curved piecing as part of the design. While working with curves is intimidating to a lot of people, it is really not a difficult process and by following the guidelines here, you should soon feel at ease.

The technique for sewing curved pieces together is basically the same, no matter how concave or convex the curve is or how complex the piecing. The mid-points of the two pieces to be sewn are pinned together, then the ends. Next, the mid-points of the sections between the pins are found and pinned. The pinning continues in this manner until the edges have been eased together.

English Paper Piecing

ONE REASON MANY PEOPLE shy away from doing patchwork by hand is that they have the mistaken notion that all patchwork is done in the cumbersome method known as *English paper piecing.* With this method, many pieces of sturdy paper are cut the exact size of the finished piece. The fabric is cut about ¼″ (0.75 cm) larger than the paper all the way around. The extra ¼″ (0.75 cm) is then folded over the paper and basted in place. After many pieces are prepared in this way, they are arranged as desired, placed with right sides facing, and whip stitched together.

English paper piecing was often used with scraps of silk and other fine material, but I have also seen many quilts made in this manner with cotton fabrics. While the method produces very accurate shapes and offers stability for pieces sewn with silk and other delicate fabrics, it is extremely time consuming and—in my opinion—it is rather a waste of time when sewing with cotton fabrics. You not only have to cut out the fabric pieces, but the paper ones as well. Furthermore, by the time one piece of fabric is basted around one paper, you could have sewn several pieces together. In addition, the whip stitching takes a lot longer than sewing a simple running stitch. Then there is additional time involved in removing the bastings and the paper before beginning the quilting.

There are many explanations of how the English piecing method is done. One of the earliest written sources is one I found in Caulfield and Saward's *Dictionary of Needlework,* written in 1882.

> "This needlework which consists in sewing pieces of material together to form a flat, unbroken surface, possesses many advantages, as it is not only useful and ornamental, but forms out of odds and ends of silk, satin, or chintz, which would otherwise be thrown away, a handsome piece of work. . . . The great essential is that every piece should be cut with perfect uniformity, and the use of a thin plate of tin, cut to the size required, is therefore recommended; the other requisites are old envelopes and letters, or other stiff pieces of writing paper, the patches, and sewing silk or cotton matching the patches in colour, with which to sew them together.
>
> "The manner of working is as follows: Select the design to be copied and the shades of material, have a piece of tin cut out to correspond with each shape to be used, and lay this upon the silks or satins, and outline round with a pencil. Cut out the shapes larger than the outline, to allow of [*sic*] turning in the raw edges, and divide off the various pieces, keeping together all of one shade and all of one form. Then cut out upon the paper the exact outline of the tin plate, leaving nothing for turnings. TACK

the paper and the silk piece together, turning the raw edge of the silk over the paper, and tacking it down so as to keep it from fraying out while working. Arrange the patches thus made on a table, according to the design and the position each is to occupy as to colour; take up two that are to be close together, turn the silk sides inwards, so as to stitch them together on the wrong side, and then carefully stitch them together so that they accurately join point to point, angle to angle. Continue to sew the pieces together until the size required is obtained, then tear the paper away from the silk, and iron the work upon the wrong side."

The photo shown here is of a quilt top made of cotton fabrics and done in the English paper piecing method. The quilt dates back to about 1850. The papers, which were never removed, were cut from old periodicals and letters. Both the basting threads and fine whip stitching can be seen.

***Around the World**, circa 1930. Maker unknown*

***Love Ring**. See full quilt in pattern section*

Sewing Two Simple Curved Pieces Together

The popular traditional quilt design known as *Drunkards' Path* involves sewing a quarter circle to another curved piece to form a square block. The squares are then arranged in a variety of ways to create many different variations on a similar theme, such as *Love Ring* and *Around the World*, shown here. Begin by laying out the pieces to be sewn. It may appear as though the pieces will never fit together perfectly, but follow the directions below and they will. When joining curved pieces, it is best to sew with the concave piece on top. The reason for this is that the concave piece has more fabric that has to be eased in. If that piece is on the bottom, small puckers may occur during the sewing process. When it is on top, any extra fullness can be more easily eased in.

1. Mark dots through the template at the points where the seam allowances cross at the ends of each piece (see pages 55 to 56). Folding from dot to dot, find the midpoint of the edge to be sewn on each of the two pieces. Crease that exact midpoint with your fingers and then insert a pin to mark the spot. Alternatively, put additional holes in each of the two templates to indicate where the midpoints are and mark these dots with a pencil.
2. With the quarter circle underneath and the concave piece on top, and with right sides facing each other, place the two pieces together, with the crease lines (or mid-point dots) exactly matching. Carefully remove the pins and put one of them back in through both pieces right along the crease. Next, on each end, match the dots where the seam allowances cross on the two pieces and pin at that spot.
3. It is going to seem like the piece on top is too big, but that is just an illusion and if you follow these next steps, the two will fit together perfectly. Use the same folding method to find the midpoints on each of the pieces between the pins. Finger crease, then match the creases and pin again at the crease. Make sure at all times that the cut edges on the two pieces are exactly lined up. Continue pinning in this manner until the fullness in the piece on the top is eased in.
4. Begin stitching, easing in any fullness. When the seam is complete and the pieces unfolded, you will see that it makes a nice smooth curve. Finger press toward the concave piece.

Sewing Two Simple Curved Pieces Together

Lay out pieces

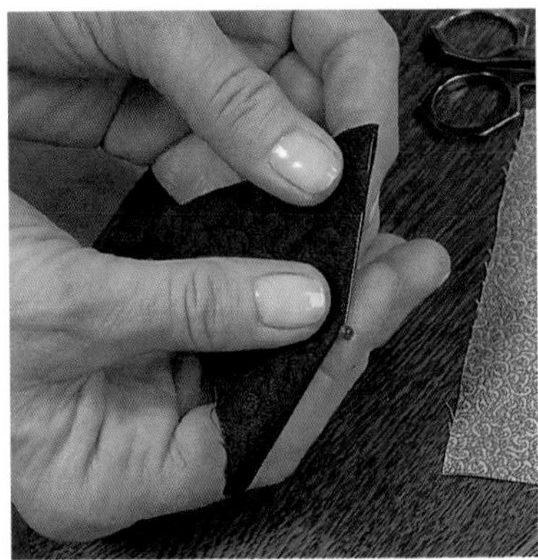

Step 1. *Crease at midpoint and insert pin to mark spot*

Step 2. *Align, with concave piece on top. Pin at either end where seam allowances cross*

. . . and along crease

Step 3. *Fold to find midpoints between pins. Pin at midpoints*

Finger crease, then pin

Continue pinning until all fullness is eased in

Step 4. *Sew together, easing in fullness*

Complete

MANY PEOPLE LOOK AT my quilt *Day Lilies* and wonder how the pieces could ever be sewn together. But sewing those pieces requires no skills other than some illustrated here and in earlier sections—straight line sewing, joining six points, setting in, and sewing curves. The quilt is made up of individual units. Each unit has seven pieces, and all seven can be sewn together with a straight line of stitching. The main considerations when sewing those pieces are to make sure that the dots where the seam allowances cross on each piece are lined up and that the sewing line stops at the seam allowance at any places where there will be inward angles.

Once the individual units have been made, six of those units are sewn together to create a flower. Since six points meet at the center of each flower, the units are sewn together in two halves, with each half containing three units. Then the two halves are sewn together.

Notice that the units have a gentle curve. Those curves are sewn in the manner described on the preceding pages. First, find the

At inward angle, do not sew past seam allowance

Lay out units

Three flowers come together

Sew–pivot . . .

. . . sew–pivot . . .

. . . sew–pivot, without breaking thread

midpoints of each piece. When you *fold* the piece to find the midpoint, do not fold the entire piece all the way to the ends of the cut angles, but find the places where the seam allowances cross and mark those dots, then fold dot to dot. This is important, since because of the odd shapes of the pieces, some of the points extend further than others, making it difficult to find a true midpoint. Alternatively, you may want to mark "matching" dots on each of the two templates of the pieces that will be sewn together and then transfer those dots to the fabric pieces.

Once the individual flowers are sewn, they are joined together using the same consecutive setting-in process described on page 111. Notice how the three different-colored flowers come together. There are some sharper angles here and there, but the process is exactly the same and no more difficult. The setting-in sequence when joining the flower units together is a simple rhythm of sew-pivot, sew-pivot, sew-pivot, without breaking the thread.

Columbia. *See full quilt in pattern section*

Simple Steps to a *Mariners' Compass*

Mariners' Compass is one of the most beautiful quilt blocks used for patchwork, but sadly it is often considered too difficult a pattern to tackle. Yet sewing a *Mariners' Compass* block requires no additional skills to those that have already been presented in this book. All that is necessary is to know how to sew a straight line, how to join three points, and then, depending on how the center of the design is laid out, it might be necessary to join eight points. Next, you need to know how to set in an angle, and finally how to sew two curved pieces together. Here, you will see just how easy a block like this is to construct using skills you have already mastered.

1. Begin by making the center star. (If you wish, use the templates for *Columbia* provided in the template section, work from another pattern, or create your own.) Look at the center block for *Columbia*, shown here. Because of the way the border print is used, eight pieces (four mirror-imaged pairs) come together to create the star at the very center. Those star points will be sewn first. If a border print is not used, each point can be cut from a single piece of fabric so that there will be just four points coming together. If your compass design is similar to this, follow the same steps as for sewing either four or eight points together (see page 77 or 100).
2. Once the star is complete, begin constructing the rest of the compass. From this point on, you will be working from the outside of the block inwards, following these steps. When working with blocks made up of many pieces, if an exact ¼″ (0.75 cm) seam is not maintained, there is a risk of the block not finishing to size and perhaps not laying flat. I recommend making what I call *checking templates.* A checking template is made from a line drawing of the block and incorporates several of the pieces. Seam allowance is added on all sides. The first photograph opposite shows a line drawing for *Columbia*, which outlines in red and green the two different wedge-shaped units that make up the remaining points of the design. Make plastic templates for each of these "wedges". You will use the ones shown here to check the finished sizes of the wedge units that will be sewn in steps 3 and 4. Checking templates for *Columbia* are provided in the template section.
3. Make the small wedges. Sew a light background piece to either side of the smallest point. With the pointed piece facing you, carefully pin a light background piece to the right hand side; match the places on each piece where the seam allowances cross, pin carefully and begin sewing towards the tip of the point. When the point tip is reached, do not cut the thread, but following the directions for joining three points on page 90, pick up the next piece, pin it in place, and sew it on. Open out the pieces and finger press the seams. Eight of these small wedges are needed for the block. When

Step 2. *Make checking templates for small and large wedges*

Step 3. *Lay out pieces.*

Use small checking template to check size of small wedge

Step 4. *Use large checking template to check size of large wedge*

Step 5. *Lay out star and four large wedges*

each wedge is complete, place the smaller of the two checking templates on top to make sure that the wedge is the exact size. If it is not, adjust the seams until it is correct.

4. Using the same technique as step 3, sew one small wedge to either side of the next larger point to make the large wedge unit. Now you will need the large checking template made in step 2 that incorporates the larger point and the two pieced wedges on either side. After making each of four large wedges, place the checking template on top to be sure they are each the correct size. If not, make adjustments to the seams.
5. Lay out the four large wedges and the final corner pieces next to the center star as shown. To complete the circle, the larger wedges are first set into the center star. Follow the directions on setting in on page 111. With the exception of these set-in wedges, all sewing up to this point is done in straight lines.

As you can see, in designs based on *Mariners' Compass*, a complete circle is stitched into a background piece. It is easiest, when sewing circular

Step 6. *Pin snaps off ridge at back of work . . .*

. . . and exits at front, right at compass point

Step 7. *Open out and check that you have not cut off any points*

Step 8. *Stitch small seams to join four quarter sections*

designs such as this, to break down the background into four separate pieces. Each piece is sewn to a quarter section of the circle, and the quarter sections are then connected by seams. (The process of sewing the circle into these four quarter sections is exactly the same as that described in joining two curved pieces on page 118, except now you have to take care that the compass points are not cut off.)

6. Mark with pins a quarter circle section of the compass block. For most compass designs there will be a point going to each quarter section. Find the middle of this section. There will most likely be another compass point at this spot. Finger press all seams towards the background pieces and away from the point. Find the middle of the corner background piece and place that on the compass point at the middle of the quarter section of the compass block. Line up the cut edges exactly and hold them securely with the fingers of your left hand. Insert a pin below the seam line and towards the raw edges. Extend the pin beyond the bulk of the seams of the point and then gently pull it back until it snaps off the seams right at the tip of the compass point. Bring the pin to the front of the work. The pin has come

out right at the point, so if you aim any stitching to the place where the pin came out, you should avoid cutting off any of the tips of the points.

Continue pinning the quarter corner piece to the quarter section of the block in the same way as described above, making sure that you have a pin securing each of the compass points to the top piece and that the pin has come up right at the tip of each compass point.

7. To begin stitching, pull the seam allowances of the first compass point all the way to the right. (Since the concave piece is on top, the compass points will be at the back of the work.) With your thumbnail, you will be able to feel the ridge created by the bulk of the seam. Push the nail directly next to this ridge. Keeping your left thumb tight against the ridge, let the bottom seams go and then insert the needle from the back of the work to the right of the point and bring it out right where the pin came out of the cloth and on top of your thumbnail. Gently remove the pin. Begin stitching around the curve, aiming for precise places where the pins exit the fabric. If you need extra help on sewing a curve, refer back to the sequence of photographs on page 119. Take special care when approaching the compass points. It is important that these remain sharp and that the tips are not cut off. Refer back to page 92 for help on sewing a plain piece of fabric to a piece with three points. As the seams are approached, make a little backstitch to secure the stitching tightly on either side of the point. When finished, open out the piece and check to make sure that you have not cut off any points with the stitching. Continue adding the other three corner pieces in the same manner.
8. Stitch up the small seams that connect the four quarter sections to complete the block.

Many compass designs contain even more points than *Columbia*, but this does not make these designs any more difficult. They simply require additional wedges. As long as they are stitched as described above, there should be no problems.

Next Steps in a Hand-Pieced Quilt

You have now learned all the hand sewing skills that are necessary for creating a pieced quilt top. If you have been following along through each chapter, working on one of the two quilts, *Starflower* or *Columbia*, that require each of the piecing techniques discussed in this book, you are ready to proceed with the skills taught in this chapter. If you are working on *Columbia*, try your hand at the compass block in the center. If you are working on *Starflower*, join the border-print points to the curved pieces. As you work, practicing each of the techniques you have learned so far, you will come to appreciate the accuracy, speed, and portability of sewing by hand.

Enriching Patchwork Designs

Using Decorative Border Prints

"'Why spend so much time and labor making new quilts and worrying about designs when you already have a number which are never used?' Perhaps it is for the same reason which prompts the planting of flowers in the alley . . . or the landscaping of our gardens in places seen only by the few; because of our love for beauty and regard for order in everyday living. It is in us and must come forth and become a material artistic expression."

Carrie A. Hall and Rose G. Kretsinger,
The Romance of the Patchwork Quilt in America, 1935

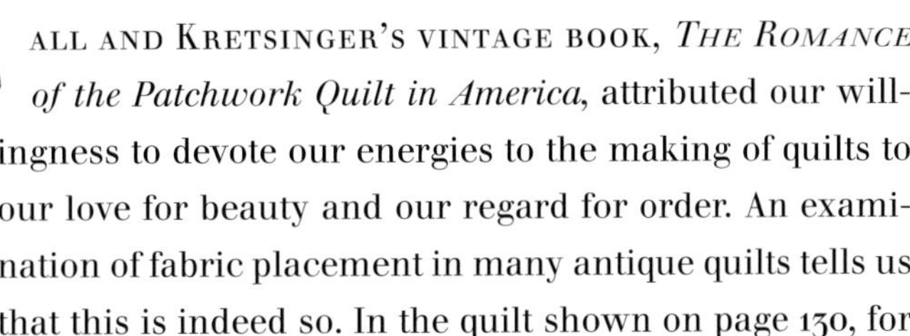

Hall and Kretsinger's vintage book, *The Romance of the Patchwork Quilt in America*, attributed our willingness to devote our energies to the making of quilts to our love for beauty and our regard for order. An examination of fabric placement in many antique quilts tells us that this is indeed so. In the quilt shown on page 130, for instance, through careful cutting, a flower has been precisely–and very prettily–positioned at the center of each hexagon. The quilt might lose some of its appeal without this delicate touch.

By taking similar time and care to cut our fabrics in such a way that they enhance our quilts, we, too, can satisfy our passion for beauty and order. For most blocks, we tend to cut fabrics quickly by layering them to cut up to four patchwork pieces at one time. Yet this type of speed cutting does not pay any regard to how the designs that make each fabric so appealing fall within the piece. If we take a little extra time on certain portions of the block to center motifs from fabric within the individual shapes, the rewards are well worth the effort. Using the motifs in individual fabrics to enhance the overall look of a block or as part of the body of the quilt adds a wonderful new dimension to quiltmaking.

Many of the quilts I have made involve a technique of using decorative border prints–the kind that are usually intended as borders to frame the outside

A Fascination for Border Prints

When I first became interested in quilt-making, I was living in India with my husband and three young children. I had fallen in love with Indian textiles and would make frequent trips to the small villages where craftsmen would carve intricate designs into wood blocks. They would mix up dyes from a variety of natural ingredients and then use those blocks to hand-print designs on cotton cloth. The decorated textiles were then used for bed covers, table cloths, garments, and myriad other purposes. Rather than being printed "by the yard" as are the textiles we purchase today, they were carefully printed by the piece. And in most, a border motif framing the outer edge made up part of the design.

My fascination with these richly colored, hand-printed textiles led to quite an accumulation of fabric. At first, I used them for clothes and other projects. When I began to quilt, I used them in all my patchwork. It seemed a shame not to use the ones that had framing around the outside edges. I found ways to use them around the outside edges of my quilts, similar to the way in which they had framed Indian textiles. Eventually, I began to experiment with using these border motifs within patchwork blocks as well. That led me to a whole new way of looking at patchwork patterns, and I have been using border fabrics in my designs ever since.

Indian textiles and a wood block carved with an intricate border design

Sunflower. *Designed, hand-pieced, and hand-quilted by Jinny Beyer, 1974. This quilt incorporates Indian block prints*

Two textile designs with mirror images (top), and two without (bottom)

Upon returning to the United States, I eventually began running out of the Indian fabrics and started looking for American fabrics with border motifs. These fabrics, then called "stripes," were very hard to find and, when I did find one, I was usually disappointed in the layout of the cloth. One decorative border would be right next to another so that by the time I had added seam allowances and cut out a single stripe, the stripe next to it couldn't be used because it had already been cut into.

Furthermore, many of the borders I found did not contain mirror-imaged motifs—portions of the design that are reversed. When using a border-print fabric to frame a quilt, if the border print does not contain a mirror-imaged motif, then it is not possible to obtain perfectly mitered corners. As you will see, without mirror-imaged motifs, working with borders in the manner explained in this chapter is impossible.

After a few years I began designing fabrics and, because printed fabric borders had now become an integral part of my patchwork, each collection contained what I called a *border print*. In this chapter, you will discover myriad ways to use border prints for stunning effects *inside* your quilts.

In this antique quilt, a flower motif is centered on each hexagon. Circa 1840, maker unknown

edge of the quilt—within the body of the quilt top as well. Border prints are some of the most exquisite of designs available today, often incorporating beautiful motifs. I see no reason to limit their use to borders when they can be used to striking effect within blocks or as part of the central design. It is my hope that this chapter will open your eyes to the wonders and the endless potential I have discovered in decorative border-print fabrics.

What Is a Border Print?

Almost ever since I began quiltmaking, I have incorporated *border prints* into my designs. Usually there are two different stripes—one narrow and one wider—and each is repeated at least four times across the width of the fabric. I still include a border print in each of my fabric collections. These are fabrics made up of repeat stripes with mirror-imaged designs. Each stripe is separated by at least ½″ (1.5 cm) so the stripes can be cut apart while still allowing a standard ¼″ (0.75 cm) seam allowance on each one.

There are different types of mirror-imaged designs that I use in border-print fabrics. Some are vertically mirrored motifs, some are both vertically and horizontally mirrored, and others are "flipped" motifs. The flipped motifs are more difficult to work with, and, for the most part, I design borders that are either vertically mirrored or both vertically and horizontally mirrored.

Finding motifs in border-print fabrics

Fabric designs with mirror-image motifs

Using Border Prints within Patchwork Shapes

One dimension of creating a new quilt that I especially enjoy is the challenge of looking at a patchwork block and figuring out where in that block a border print might be used to enhance the design. Border prints can add a unique look to a square, triangle, hexagon, octagon, diamond, or any other geometric shape. Rather than cutting these types of shapes individually from a single piece of fabric, the shapes can be divided into smaller triangles and identical individual pieces can be cut from mirror-imaged portions of a border print.

One of the aspects of working with border-print fabrics that I particularly like is the fact that the various shapes can be outlined using a small stripe from the print. Therefore, when cutting out the pieces, I like to place the template on the fabric so the portion of the template that will form the *outside* of the shape will fall along one of the straight line edges of the border print. I make sure that this line falls just within the sewing line so that it will still be visible when all the pieces of the shape are sewn together. This technique is described below.

Block without border print

Block with border print

Quilt design alternating first block with plain square

Quilt design alternating second block with square pieced from border print

Using Border Prints with Patchwork Shapes

Once the individual pieces have been cut from the border print, they can then be sewn together again to reform the shape and produce amazing kaleidoscopic images. These enhanced shapes can be used within a patchwork design, or large versions of them can be used for quick pillows, potholders, place mats, or other projects. Large squares created from four triangles cut from a border print can also make excellent alternating blocks for a patchwork design. Once you understand how to create interesting effects with border prints within individual shapes, you will begin looking at patchwork designs in a completely new light.

Border-Print Squares

The simplest and most common shape to work with when experimenting with border prints is the square. Many patchwork blocks have squares as part of the design. Often, the entire quilt top is made up of pieced blocks that alternate with plain, unpieced squares of cloth. The use of a border print in place of these unpieced squares can greatly enhance the overall design of a quilt. Compare the quilt block shown above, with and without the use of the border print in the center square. In the second pair of designs, blocks alternate with a square–

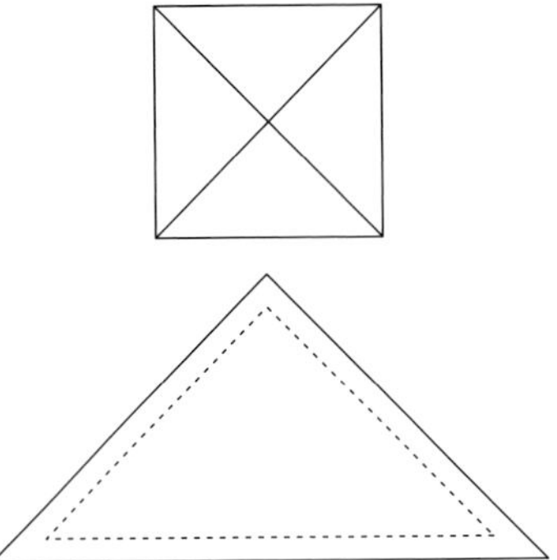

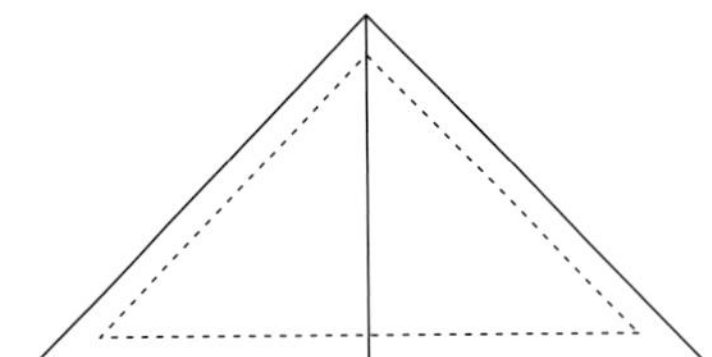

Steps 1 and 2. *Divide square to create four triangles. Make template that includes seam allowance*

Step 3. *Draw line through middle of template*

Step 4. *Center template on fabric . . .*

. . . and cut four identical triangles

Step 5. *Complete*

Border-Print Squares

on the left, the square is a plain fabric; on the right, the square is made up of four triangles cut from a border print.

To change a portion of a quilt design to use a border print in a square, you must go back to the original line drawing of the block or work with a template of the square in your pattern. If you are working from a template given in a pattern, do not use the seam allowance at this time–only the *finished* size of the square. To use a border print for an alternate block, draw a square the *finished* size of the patchwork block. Then follow these steps.

1. Divide the square diagonally from corner to corner to create four triangles.
2. Using semi-transparent template material, make a template from one of the triangles, adding a ¼″ (0.75 cm) seam allowance around all sides. (For help on making templates, see page 51.)
3. Draw a line down through the middle of the template. This line will be used as a guide for centering the motifs of the fabric. To draw an accurate line, place one of the short sides of a right angle triangle ruler along the *long* edge of the triangle template and bring the other short edge to the right angle on the template. Draw the line.

Previewing the Finished Shape

If you want to see what the finished shape will look like before actually cutting into the fabric, place the template on to the fabric in the place where you think you want to cut. Then carefully place two square mirrors on to the seam allowance of the template. Place these mirrors on the two sides that will be sewn to reform the shape. Gently remove the template, and the image in the mirror will show you how the finished piece will look once it is sewn together.

Create different effects by repositioning the template

4. With the line marked in step 3 as a guide, center the template on one of the mirror-imaged motifs in the border-print fabric, making sure that a stripe or straight line from the border print falls just inside the sewing line on the long side of the triangle template. This ensures that you will have a nice line or frame around the outside of the finished square. With the template in place on the fabric, trace some portion of the design directly onto the template. As you move the template to cut the other pieces, this mark can be used as a guide for lining up the template in the exact place as the first triangle. Carefully draw around the template and cut the piece out. Then cut three more triangles identical to the first one.
5. Sew the four triangles together, carefully matching the design.

It is amazing how many different squares you can cut from the same border strip by simply placing the template on a slightly different portion of the fabric. The squares shown here illustrate just a few possibilities from the same border print used in the example above.

Border-Print Octagons, Hexagons, and Triangles

Other geometric shapes can be made with a border print in exactly the same way as the square. Simply divide the shapes down into smaller triangles, as shown in step 1 on the previous page, then cut from the fabric however many triangles are needed to reform the shape. Just as with the triangle template for creating a square, mark a line down the center of the template and then center that line on a mirror-imaged portion of the fabric. Make sure that all triangles are cut in exactly the same way.

Border-Print Octagons

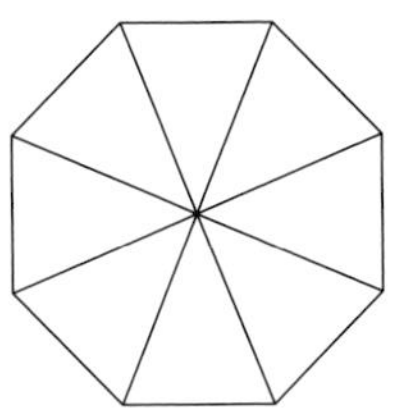

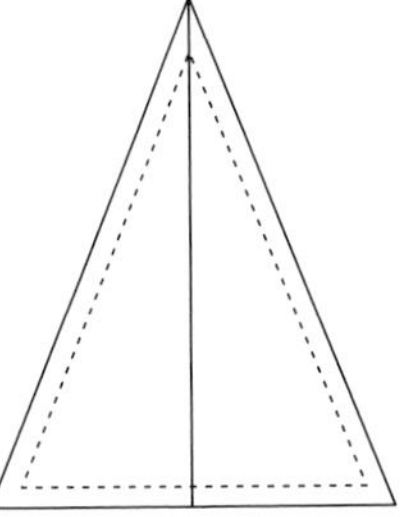

Steps 1, 2 and 3. *Draw octagon. Make template that includes seam allowance; mark center*

Step 4. *Center template on fabric*

Step 5. *Complete*

Border-Print Hexagons

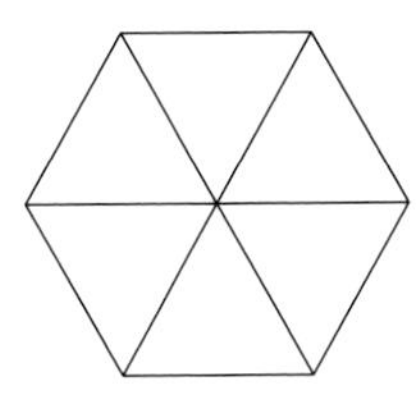

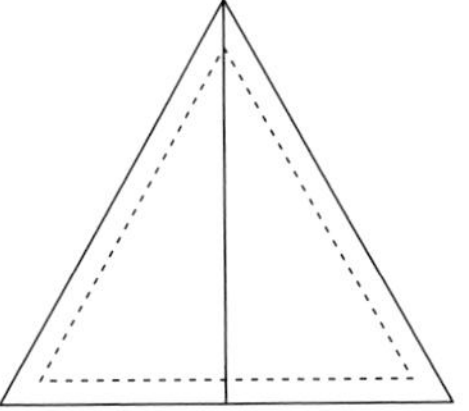

Steps 1, 2 and 3. *Draw hexagon. Make template that includes seam allowance; mark center*

Step 4. *Center template on fabric*

Step 5. *Complete*

Border-Print Triangles

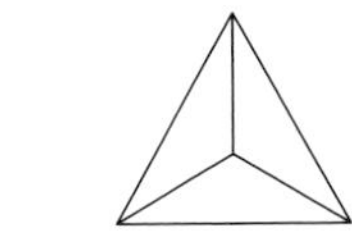

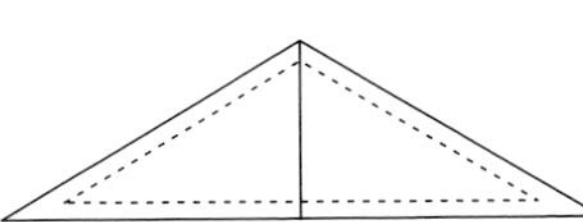

Steps 1, 2 and 3. *Draw a triangle. Make template that includes seam allowance; mark center*

Step 4. *Center template on fabric*

Step 5. *Complete*

Border-Print Diamonds

Creating a diamond with a border-print fabric is a little different from the examples covered so far, but it can give a spectacular effect. *Triple Play* is an example of a quilt where diamonds made from border prints have been used as part of the design. Four separate pieces make up the completed diamonds, and three diamonds–light, medium, and dark–join together to create a cube in the center of each block. *Columbia* has two separate pieces cut from border prints which form *half diamonds* as part of the design element.

To create a border-print diamond, four triangles must be cut. Two are exactly the same, and the other two are the exact mirror image of the first two. This time, do not try to center a mirror-imaged portion of the border print in the middle of the template. The reason for this is that the triangle shape used to create the diamond is not symmetrical, therefore it would be impossible to center a motif in the middle of the template. What is important is that two of the pieces are the exact mirror image of the other two and that a line from the border print falls along the *long* side of the triangle to act as a frame around the completed shape.

Triple Play. *See full quilt in pattern section*

Columbia. *See full quilt in pattern section*

To create a border-print diamond, follow these steps:

1. Divide the diamond in half lengthwise and sideways.
2. Make a template from one of the four resulting triangles. Mark the grain line arrow on the template along the *long* side of the triangle. This is very important, as the arrow indicates the straight grain of fabric. The template must be placed on the border- print fabric so that a line from the fabric will fall just inside the sewing line. The arrow will help you to place the template correctly.
3. After positioning the template on the border print, draw some portion of the design from the fabric on the template. This will act as a guide for cutting the remaining pieces.
4. Cut the first piece and then, using the marked design on the template as a guide, cut a second one exactly the same.
5. Carefully flip the template horizontally and, once again using the marked design on the template as a guide, find the exact mirror image of the first piece. Cut two diamonds that are the exact mirror image of the first two.
6. Position the triangles as shown, then sew together.

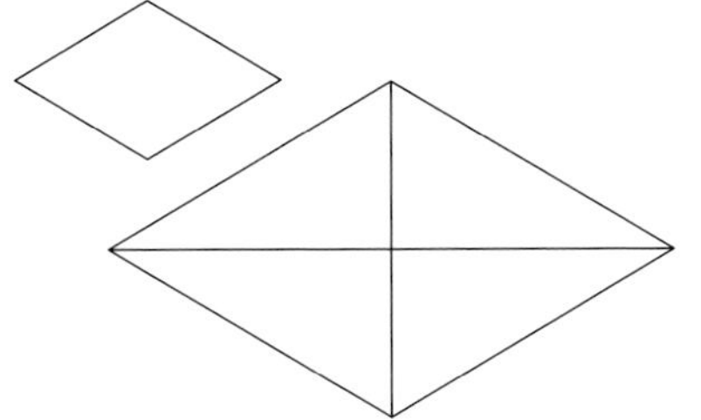

Step 1. Draw diamond and divide in quarters

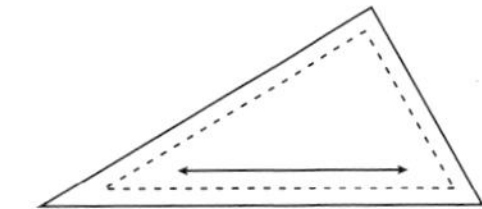

Step 2. Make template that includes seam allowance, mark grain line

Steps 3 to 5. Flip template horizontally to find exact mirror image

Step 6. Two pairs of diamonds, each pair the exact mirror image the other

Complete

Border-Print Diamonds

"The arranging of patterns to make a good and well-balanced design calls for much ingenuity on the part of the worker. A few designs carefully arranged are much more effective than a mass of different ones showing no forethought."

Beatrice Scott,
The Craft of Quilting, 1935

Using Border Prints to Frame Shapes

Sometimes, for design impact, it is nice to have a small border-print stripe frame a particular shape. *Shamrock* has border-print stripes around the set-in triangles. Borders used in this way can enhance the overall design of the quilt.

To find the correct templates for creating such effects, you must work from the original *finished* size of the shape being framed. Measure the width of the *finished* size of the border print and mark that same distance in from all sides of the shape. Make two templates, one for the smaller resulting shape and another for the portions to be used for the border print. Be sure to add seam allowances around all sides of the templates.

When cutting the pieces from the border print to frame a shape, the pieces *must* be centered on a mirror-imaged portion of the border print, and all framing pieces must be cut exactly the same or else the corners will not match.

Shamrock. See full quilt in pattern section

Using Border Prints to Frame Squares

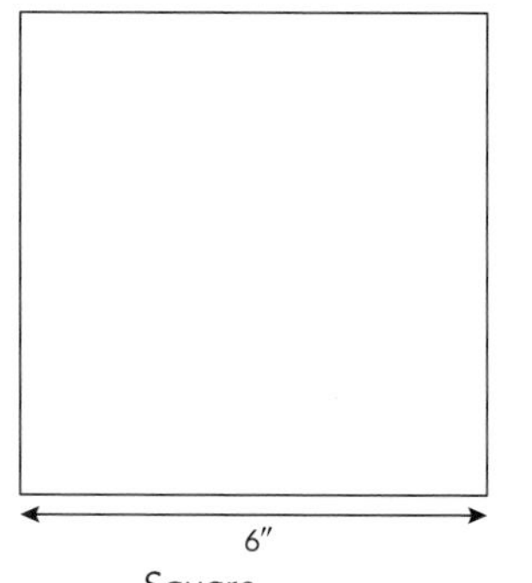

Square

7/8"
7/8"
7/8"
7/8"
7/8"

Step 1. Make measurement

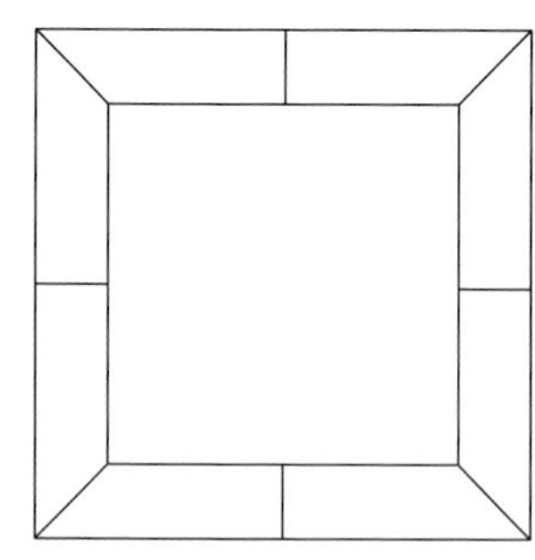

Step 2. Mark measurement

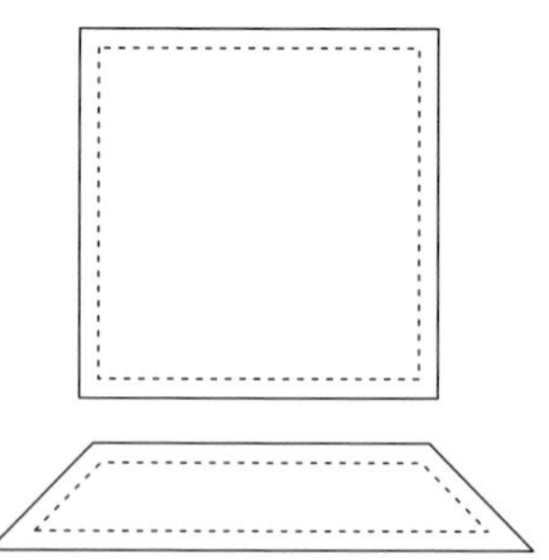

Step 3. Complete templates

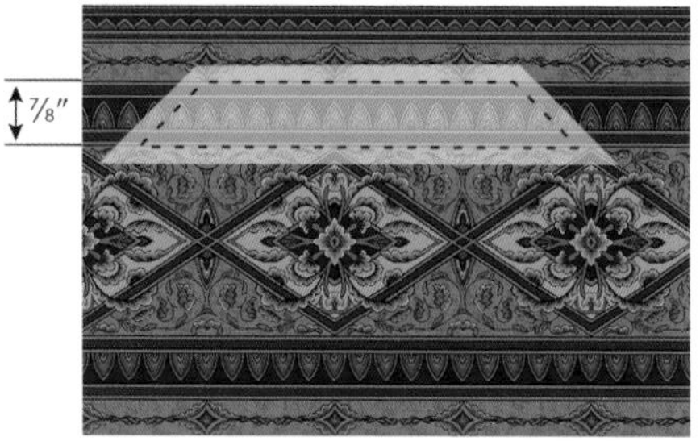

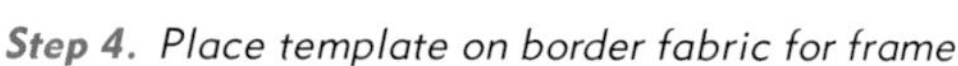

Step 4. Place template on border fabric for frame

Step 5. Cut pieces

Step 6. Complete

Using Border Prints to Frame Triangles

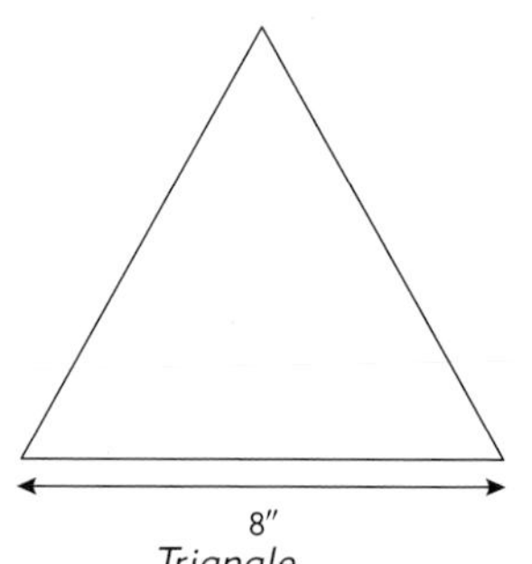

Triangle

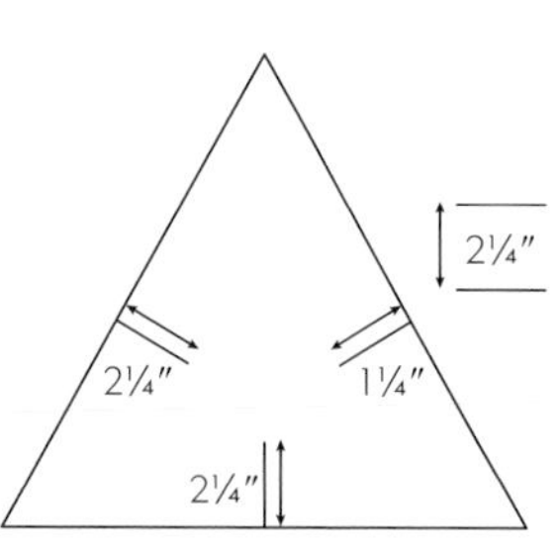

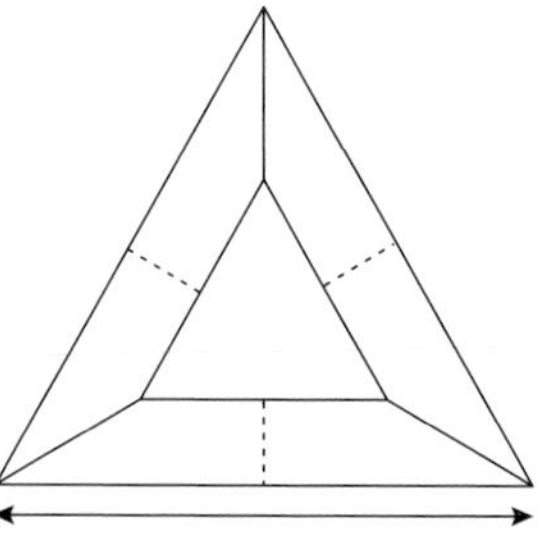

Step 2. Mark measurement

Step 3. Complete templates

Step 4. Place template on border fabric for frame

Step 5. Cut pieces

Step 6. Complete

The examples illustrated here of how to use border prints within various shapes are just a few of the many possibilities. Once you understand how to create interesting effects with border prints in individual shapes, you will begin looking at the shapes in patchwork designs in a completely new light. Have fun experimenting!

Liberty's Crown, *detail from smaller circles in* ***Windows***

Detail from larger circles in ***Windows***

Creating "Curved" Borders from Border Prints

One of the questions that is often asked about my quilt *Windows* is, "How did you ever find circular border-print fabrics to frame the circles?" In actual fact, the border prints are not curved at all. I used straight strips cut from border-print fabrics and manipulated them to look as though they were curved. In fact, all of the curved areas are made up of "wedges" that have been cut from border-print fabrics. These wedges are shorter on the inside and wider on the outside, and they must be individually drafted to fit each curved design. Some of the stripes are simply straight bands of color, but the ones that contain designs must have the same mirror-imaged motif from the border print centered in the middle of each of the wedge pieces.

Refer to the full-size image of *Windows* on the cover of this book. Beginning at the center of the quilt, the first fabric piece is framed by 16 wedges, the central block, *Liberty's Crown*, is framed by 32 small, wedge-shaped pieces. The next, wider curved border is also made up of 32 wedges, and the last curved border is made up of 128 wedges. Even though each of these wedges has straight tops and bottoms, when they are sewn together, because the *sides* are angled, the illusion is that of a circle. In general, keep in mind that the larger the circle, the more wedges are required to maintain the image of a curve.

Liberty's Crown is used here to illustrate how to create a circular border print going around the outside of the block.

1. Divide the circle to be framed into a certain number of equal "spokes" or divisions radiating from the center outwards. In the case of *Liberty's Crown*, these spokes are extensions of the star points in the block.
2. Draw straight lines between each of the divisions. In effect, you will be cutting off the curved edge of the circle and creating a multisided polygon.
3. Now measure the *finished* width of the border print to be used. Then measure this exact same distance in two or three places from one of the straight lines just drawn, between the extended spokes. Mark with dots.

Liberty's Crown

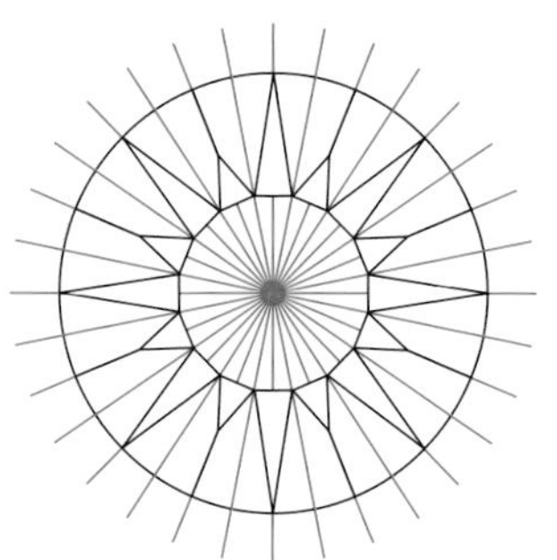
Step 1. *Draw spokes extending from center*

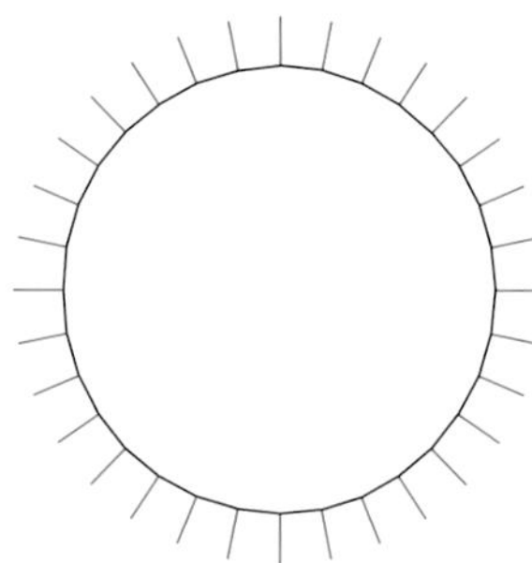
Step 2. *Cut off edges of circle*

Step 3. *Measure finished width of border print*

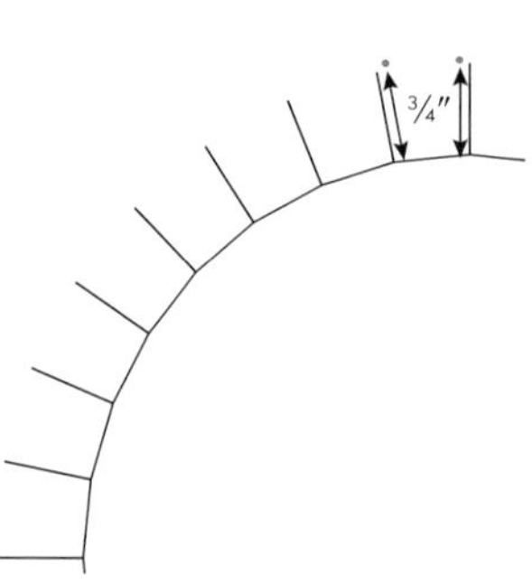

Find same measurement within block

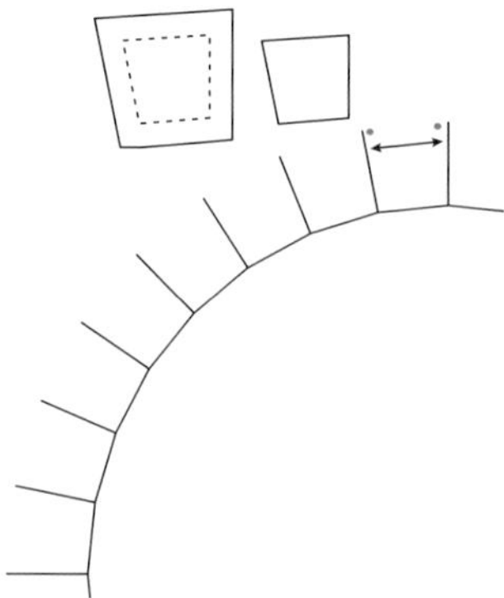
Step 4. *Find size of wedge needed*

Step 5. *Use template, with added seam allowance, to cut pieces*

4. Draw a straight line between the spokes at these dots, parallel to the first straight line between the spokes. This will give you the size of the wedge-shaped template needed for creating the circular border. Remember to add 1/4″ (0.75 cm) seam allowance around all sides of this wedge.
5. Use this template to cut identical pieces for the circular border of the quilt. In *Windows*, there were 16 wedges for the innermost circle; 32 wedges for the next two circles; and 128 wedges for the outer circle.

Since the overall design of *Windows* was based on a circle divided into multiples of eight, the spokes that radiated outwards to create the borders were also based on multiples of eight. More spokes were added as the circles increased in size. In that way, I could ensure that the seams of the wedges of the circular border would also match up with the seams of the overall patchwork design.

Sewing Pieces Cut from Border Prints

When sewing most patchwork pieces by hand, cut edges are lined up, pinned, and an exact 1/4″ (0.75 cm) seam allowance is taken to sew those pieces together. When working with shapes cut from border-print fabrics, you need to work a little differently. There may be a slight distortion in the fabric, or the pieces may not have been cut exactly the same. This means that, if the cut edges are merely lined up and stitched together, the printed design on the border print may not match exactly at the seams. It is far more important in this instance to carefully match the border-print design on the two pieces being sewn rather than to line up the cut edges. After carefully matching the design on the pieces, pin them together in several places so the design does not shift. This may mean that the seam allowance on one of the pieces being sewn ends up being a little less than 1/4" (0.75 cm), and the seam allowance on the other is a little more. But it will balance out in the end, and the *design* of the border print will match up.

When sewing border-print pieces together, follow the same guidelines as sewing any other pieces. Try to have straight line sewing wherever possible. For example, when sewing four triangles together to make a border-print square, first join two pieces, then the other two, and finally sew the two halves together in one straight line.

If a shape is to be framed with a border print, such as the triangles in *Shamrock* (see pattern section), sew the borders onto the shape first, then carefully match the design on the borders at the miter points and sew those seams last.

Enhancing a Hand-Pieced Quilt with Border Prints

I love teaching classes on working with border prints, because it is almost instantly gratifying when so little effort produces such amazing results. As students realize how easy it is and see such spectacular changes in simple shapes, it is as though one light bulb after another goes on. I urge you to give border prints a try. As mentioned previously, two of the quilt patterns in this book, *Starflower* and *Columbia*, were specifically designed to incorporate all of the techniques of hand piecing. Experiment with the half diamond points or center motif of *Columbia* or with the star points of *Starflower*. If you want to see the result before cutting into the fabric, photocopy the fabric and cut from paper, as explained on this page. No matter what shape you try, you will be amazed at how the simple techniques of incorporating border prints into your designs can so dramatically change the look of patchwork.

Quick Tip

If you are afraid to cut up your border-print fabric until you know exactly what you want to do with it, make a trip to the copy machine with both your fabric and design in hand. Most copy machines do a good job of photocopying fabric. Reduce the image to the maximum amount available on the copy machine, then make several copies of the fabric. Reduce your design by the same amount as well and make a couple of copies. Then make templates from the shapes in the reduced design and begin working with paper copies of the border print to see what border-print effects you can achieve. Because both the fabric and design have been reduced by the same amount, the proportions will be the same as when you cut from the actual fabric.

Borders for Quilts

Using Border Prints

"The borders of quilts are seldom given the prominence that they deserve. Too often we say, 'I want my quilt about 72 inches wide by 84 long so I'll use blocks 12 inches square, that's 6 × 7—42 blocks. All right, that's that;' and the quilt may be ever so much work, beautifully done, and yet look disappointingly ordinary when finished. Personally I'd as soon hang my pictures unframed, as to finish my quilts unbordered."

Ruby Short McKim,
101 Patchwork Patterns, 1931

Like Ruby Short McKim, I have seldom seen a quilt that would look better without a border than with one. The border for a quilt top is its finishing touch. It is the final frame that sets off the inside. As such, adding a border should not be considered a task that is tacked on at the end of a project. When deciding the blocks and central design of a quilt, I think part of that planning should be to reserve room for a border. As much thought should go into the border as goes into the rest of the quilt. That said, I should point out that while I know my quilt will have a border, and I have a general idea of its approximate size, I never know exactly what the border will be until the main part of the quilt is finished. Just as with a picture, it is impossible to know what the frame should be without first seeing what goes inside.

Types of Borders

There are many types of borders to consider. Some quilts simply have a wide strip of fabric for the final frame. Others, such as the antique *Tumbling Blocks* shown on page 110, have two or more strips of plain fabric as the border. Many quilts have pieced or appliqued borders; others have been specifically designed to allow for a finely quilted border. Often a combination of two or more different border types will form the frame for a quilt. *Windows* and *Columbia* combine pieced borders with unpieced fabric borders made from decorative border-print fabrics. The antique *Mariners' Compass* on page 180 has a pieced border framing the blocks, and then a much wider border with an elaborate quilting pattern as the final frame. Flip through the pages of this book and notice the border of each quilt photographed. This will help you understand how borders can add to the overall design of a quilt.

"The border should be considered from the beginning as part of the design not added as a makeshift use for the pieces that are left over . . . If the center pattern and the border have one distinctive thing in common, such as repeats of a motif or a definite combination of color, the design is united."

Averil Colby,
Patchwork Quilts, 1965

Border Design

The border for a quilt is as integral a part of the overall design as the center of the quilt top. Think of it as the frame that finishes off the picture. Just as you would not select a frame before you have a picture to go inside of it, likewise I think it is best to decide the border for a quilt *after* the inside is complete. With this in mind, you need to leave room for a little flexibility as to the finished size of the quilt. Sometimes wider borders look better and sometimes narrow borders are the obvious best choice.

It is impossible to know ahead of time what colors, designs, or patterns are going to look best as the final frame. The main concern should always be that the border enhances the rest of the quilt. It should never look as though it was added as an afterthought, just to make the quilt larger. Another important consideration is that the border should reflect an element already contained within the quilt rather than introduce something completely new. A printed-fabric border might, for example, pick up the colors used at the center of the quilt top, or a pieced border may adapt a shape or element of design from another portion of the quilt.

Unless you are making a small wall hanging, a single border print strip will rarely suffice as a border. Just as a picture framer will include several mattes before the outer frame, quilts, too, need more than a single strip surround. One of my favorite choices is a border made up of two strips of border-print fabric, with a contrasting fabric set in between them. The borders of *Shamrock*, *Starflower*, *Boxed Blocks*, and *Triple Play* in the pattern section are all constructed in this way. In each example, the border print and contrasting strips were selected to enhance the colors inside the quilt. The color of the contrasting strip can drastically alter the overall color effect of the quilt. Look at the three designs shown here. The first quilt is framed only by a single border-print strip. The others have two border-print strips with a coordinating fabric in between. See how different each of the quilts looks, depending both on the width of the border and the color of the middle strip.

Quick Tip

In general, for a full- or queen-size quilt, I usually plan a border that is at least 10" (25 cm) wide, often more. For instance, the border for *Triple Play* (see pattern section) measures 10½" (26.5 cm), while the border for the quilt on the cover, *Windows*, is 12½" (32 cm) wide.

Serendipity. *Single border-print strip*

Contrasting fabric at center

Alternate contrasting fabric at center

In general, the design and proportions of the border are individual to each quilt, and it just takes some experimentation to find which arrangement is best. When building borders, I usually like to position a narrow stripe, cut from a border-print fabric, closest to the quilt top, then a coordinating fabric that is also used inside the quilt. I typically cut this fabric wider than the first border strip. The final piece is a wider border-print strip. The width of the coordinating fabric between the inner and outer strips is arbitrary. Lay out all of the pieces next to the quilt and experiment with different widths until the proportions are found that seem right for that particular quilt. For instance, in *Triple Play* that width is 2½″ (6.5 cm), in *Boxed Blocks* it is 2″ (5 cm), and in *Shamrock* it is only 1¼″ (3 cm). When I had to decide upon the design for the pieced circular border that surrounds the central medallion in *Windows*, I had a terrible time finding just the right one. In fact, I pieced sections of six different borders before I found the one that worked the best. I often find it helpful to invite a friend over during the border planning stage. Sometimes an extra pair of eyes is all that is needed to help with making the final decision.

Measuring for Borders

When cutting borders for a quilt, it is very important how the measurements are taken. Too often, I've noticed quilts–even some that are on display at quilt shows–that have a wavy or ruffled effect along the outside edges. They do not lie smoothly against the wall because the outer edges are distorted. This problem is usually a clear sign that the border pieces were cut too long for the quilt. Let me explain. An all-too-common mistake is to lay out the quilt top on the floor or a table and then to measure around the *edges* in order to determine the length of the borders. The problem here is that the outer edges of the quilt usually have quite a bit of stretch in them. Even though you may have made every effort to cut all your pieces so that only the straight of the grain lies along the outside edges, it is possible that there still may be some bias pieces to contend with when adding your border. Further, sometimes the quilt stretches at the seams. If you cut the borders to the measurement along the edges, you will not

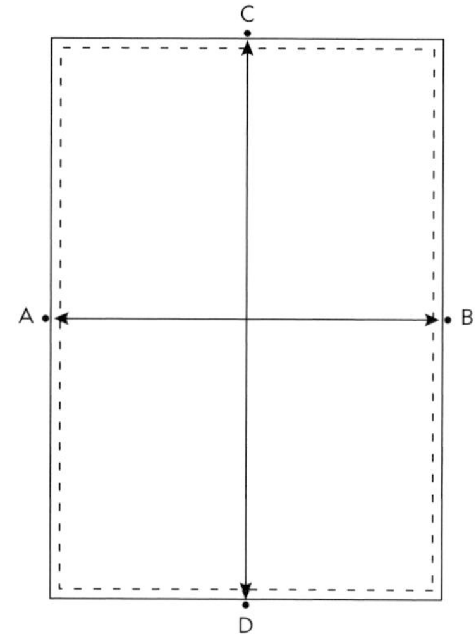

Measure through middle *of quilt for borders, all way to edge*

have allowed for stretch and you, too, may end up with a quilt that has a ruffled edge that will not lie flat.

For a true, accurate measurement, always measure your quilt top horizontally and vertically across the *middle.* Do not measure along the outer edges. When I see a quilt with ruffled edges, I fold the top edge down to the center, then compare the measurement of the top edge with the measurement across the middle of the quilt. I have seen quilts where the edge is as much as 6″ (15 cm) longer than the measurement across the middle of the quilt. When measuring a quilt, I find it easiest to lay the quilt out on a carpet rather than on a wooden floor or table. The fabric grips the carpet, and the quilt can be smoothed out evenly and won't slip during the measuring process. For the horizontal borders, refer to the diagram shown here and measure from point A to point B; for the vertical borders measure from point C to point D.

Plain Fabric Borders with Mitered Corners

Unless there is some patchwork design in the corners, I recommend mitering the corners of all borders. It is not difficult and results in a more finished look. All the patterns provided in *Quiltmaking by Hand* are mitered in this way. While some quilters sew the borders on and cut the miters later, I prefer to measure and cut the borders and the miters all at the same time. The reason for this is that if the strips are sewn first, before cutting the miters, you will have to cut across the stitching lines–adding the extra step of re-stitching the seams at the edges to reinforce them. When you cut each piece individually, as I do, there is no need to re-stitch. After I cut the borders and the miters, I sew the four borders on to the quilt and stitch the miters last.

If the border is to be simply a single piece of fabric with no particular patterns or motifs that need to match at the corners, prepare the border as follows.

Cutting miters

1. Cut a strip the *width* of the finished size plus ¼″ (0.75 cm) seam allowance on either side. The *length* of this strip should be the measurement across the middle of the quilt, plus two times the width of the strip, which you will use for the miters. In addition, just to be safe, I like to add an extra 4″ (10 cm).
2. Center the strip across the *middle* of the quilt, smooth it out until it comes beyond the edges, then cut the miters. To do so, align one of the short sides of a right-angle, 45° degree triangle along the bottom of the border strip, moving the triangle until the diagonal edge falls right at the edge of the quilt (see arrows). Mark the line and cut the miter. Move the triangle to the other edge of the quilt and cut the second miter. Since the quilt has the seam allowance at the edge, as long as the triangle comes to the edge, there is no need to add additional seam allowance to the border strip along the miter.
3. If your quilt is square, use this first cut border strip as a "pattern" and cut three more strips exactly the same size. If the quilt is rectangular, meas-

Step 1. Center mirror-image in middle of quilt

Step 2. Position triangle on fabric and quilt

ure the short sides of the quilt in the same way and cut two identical strips, then measure the long sides and cut two more strips. See page 156 for directions on sewing border strips on to the quilt.

Borders Made from Decorative Border-Print Fabrics

The steps involved in cutting and mitering borders cut from border-print fabrics are identical to the process of adding plain fabric borders to a quilt, with two exceptions. First, extreme care must be taken to ensure each of the border strips is cut exactly the same and that the design from the fabric matches perfectly at the mitered corners. Second, to achieve a perfect match, it is necessary to add to the cut length of the border strips. Only by doing so will you have enough fabric to allow for the proper positioning of the border-print design when mitering the corners. When working with borders that are 3″ (7.5 cm) wide or less, I typically add 9″ (23 cm) of fabric–rather than the usual 4″ (10 cm)–to the cut length of each border strip. On border-print strips that are wider than 3″ (7.5 cm), I add an extra 18″ (45 cm) to the length.

Note that the measurements for borders given in the patterns at the back of this book have allowed for extra length. This is to accommodate any variation in size of the overall quilt as well as to make it possible to manipulate the fabric in order for a mirror-imaged motif to be centered in the middle of the quilt. Sometimes the "repeat" of a design on a border print may be as much as 12″ (30 cm), and, depending on where the mirror-imaged design was when cut off the bolt, that extra length may be needed.

Quick Tip

Once the miters are cut, save the leftover border-print pieces and add them to your fabric stash. You can use them to make diamonds for a quilt such as *Triple Play*!

Framing Square Quilts with Border-Print Fabric

If the quilt is square, it is quite easy to cut the strips and have perfectly mitered corners. Follow these steps.

1. Smooth the quilt out on a carpet, then place a strip of the border print across the *middle* of the quilt, centering the mirror-imaged motif from the border-print strip at the exact center of the piece. This ensures that the

Step 3. *Cut second miter*

Step 4. *Four identical strips*

Complete

design on the border print, where it comes to either edge of the quilt, will be exactly the same.

2. Use a right-angle, 45° triangle to mark the miter along one of the edges. Position the triangle so that one of the short sides of the triangle runs along the bottom edge of the border print. Then, carefully move the triangle until the angled portion touches the place where the top edge of the border print meets the edge of the quilt (see arrow). Mark, then cut the miter. Since you have cut the miter right at the edge of the quilt, the seam allowance will already be included.
3. Carefully pick up the mitered edge of the border strip and bring it over to the other end of the border strip at the opposite side of the quilt. Position it at the precise point where the miter will be, making sure that the design on the fabric matches. (If you correctly centered the motif in the middle of the quilt in step 1, the designs should match perfectly at the edges.) Cut the second miter.
4. Using this first mitered piece as a pattern, place it on additional strips of border-print fabric, matching the design exactly. Cut three more identical pieces, making sure that the design on the border print is exactly the same on all four pieces. See page 156 for directions on sewing border strips on to the quilt.

Framing Rectangular Quilts with Border-Print Fabric

Not all quilts are as easy to border as those that are square. Yet it is still a relatively simple process to ensure that the miters will match perfectly on quilts that are longer than they are wide. There is just one extra step involved. First, you will need to measure and cut two of the sides exactly as before. The other two sides are cut differently. Each side is, in fact, made up of *two* mirror-imaged pieces, each one with a mitered edge. The miters are cut to match

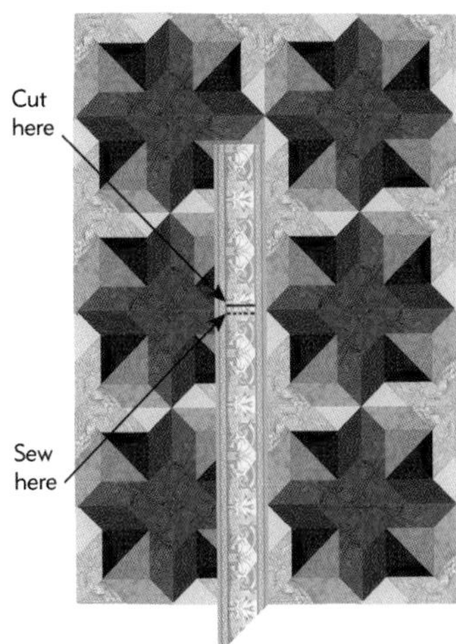

Step 2. *Position of mitered edge*

Step 3. *Two strips and two mirror-image strips*

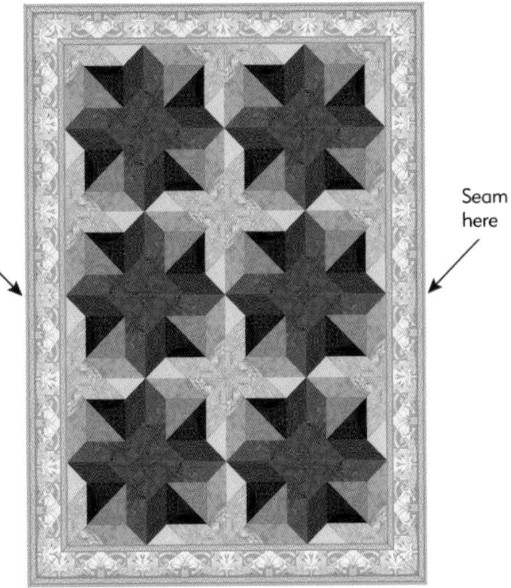

Step 4. *Rectangular quilt with perfectly mitered corners*

the miters of the first two previously cut sides, then the two mirrored pieces meet at the middle of the quilt to form their own mirror-imaged motifs. First look at the full quilts, *Shamrock*, *Triple Play*, *Boxed Blocks*, and *Day Lilies* in the pattern section, to see if you can find the seams where two border-strip pieces were joined in. The seams are all-but invisible.

Cut the border-print pieces for a rectangular quilt as follows.

1. First, follow steps 1 to 3 in the previous section, and cut two identical strips for the short sides of the quilt.
2. To match the design, place one of the cut strips on top of a length of the border-print fabric that has already been cut to the correct width. Cut one miter to match the miter on the already-cut strip. Place the newly cut strip along the length of the quilt (through the middle, not at the edge). The mitered edge is positioned as shown here. Bring the strip to the exact center of the quilt and cut it off ¼″ (0.75 cm) beyond the center. This will allow for seam allowance when the two mirror-imaged strips are sewn together.
3. Using this cut strip as a guide, cut one more piece identical to it and two strips that are the exact mirror images of the first piece.
4. Sew pairs of mirror-image strips together to make two long border strips. The mirror-image motif at the center of each will disguise the seam. See page 156 for directions on sewing border strips on to the quilt.

When adding border-print borders to a rectangular quilt in which two of the sides need a seam in order to get the corners to miter perfectly, should that seam be on the short sides or the long sides of the quilt? I usually choose the longer sides. If the quilt is to hang in a show, the short sides are likely to be parallel to the floor; I find that the seam is less visible on the *sides* than on the top and bottom. If the quilt will hang with the *long* sides parallel to the floor, then I put the seam on the shorter sides.

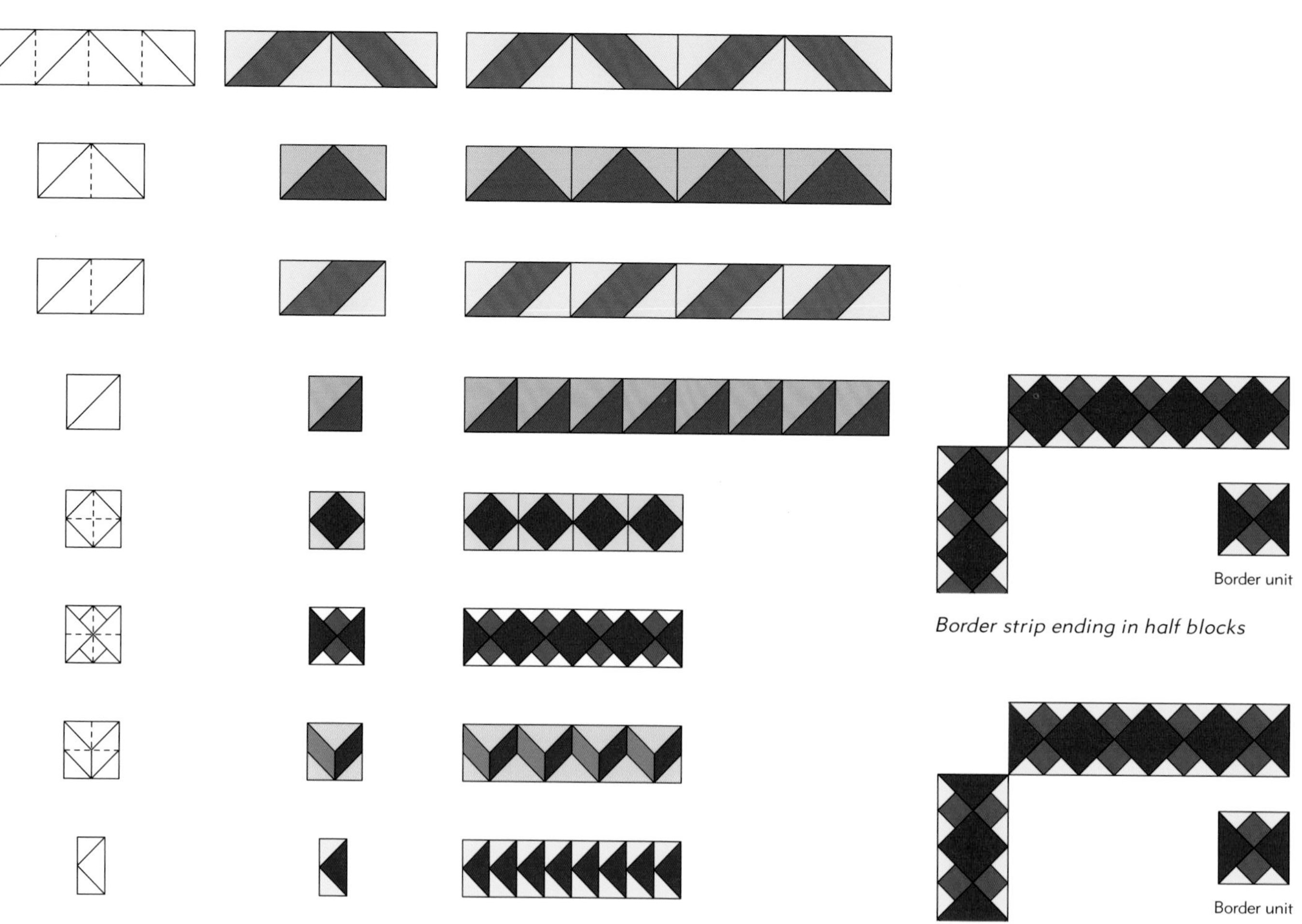

Pieced border units on a grid

Border strip ending in half blocks

Border strip ending in full blocks

PIECED BORDER UNITS

"Turning the corners of any border pattern may be a difficult matter without careful measurement and calculation. . . . Patterns which present difficulties at the corners sometimes are worked from a planned corner towards the middle of each side and the resulting hiatus, if any, is filled with the date of making and the name or initials of the worker."

AVERIL COLBY,
Patchwork Quilts, 1965

Designing Pieced Borders

There is a wide variety of traditional designs for pieced borders, and it is fun to design your own, working with shapes from inside the body of the quilt. A pieced border can add a beautiful new dimension to a quilt design. Planning pieced borders is relatively easy for square quilts, and a little more involved for rectangular quilts. For either one, the measurement is taken edge to edge.

Pieced Border Units

Pieced borders are comprised of *units* that repeat to fill the length of the space. Just as explained in drafting geometric block designs (see Chapter Two), these

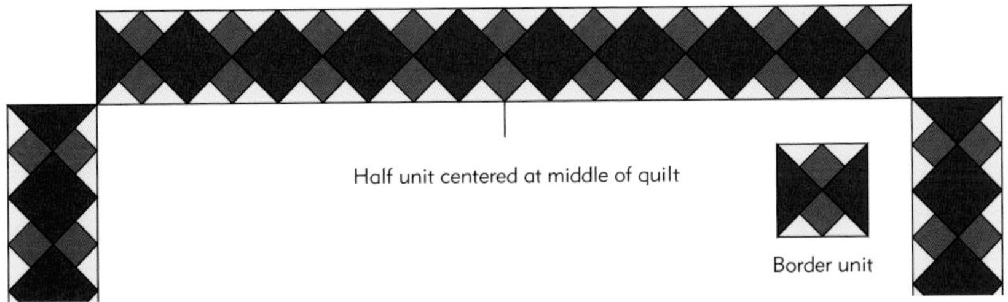

Half-block corner design, this time with design mirrored at center and with corner turn

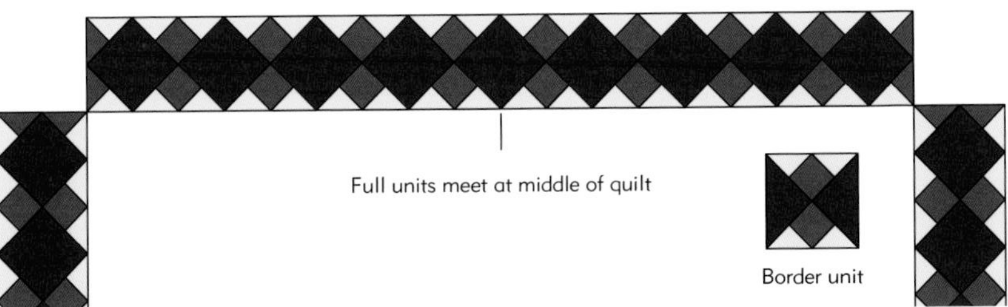

Full-block corner design, this time with design mirrored at center and with corner turn

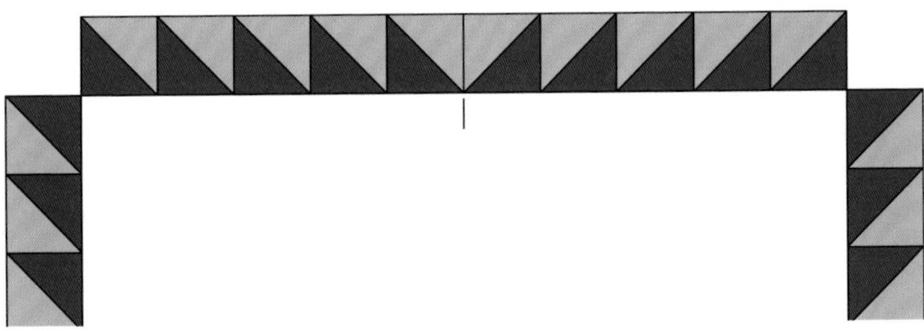

Non-symmetrical border, mirrored at center

Pieced Border Units *continued*

units are based on a grid made up of a certain number of squares. Some borders are comprised of units that are non-directional, and others are made up of units that are directional. A few such borders are shown here. These show the design when several units are put together, as well as showing the individual unit and the grid.

The biggest challenge in planning a pieced border is making sure that the same portion of the design falls in exactly the same place at each of the corners of the quilt. (To allow for a good corner design, it is usually best to plan for a full or half-unit to fall at each corner.) The key is accurate measurement. First, a measurement is taken edge to edge, and then a *corner unit* is planned that will connect the strips.

In order for all corners of the quilt to be identical, a mirror-imaged portion of the pieced design must fall at the *center* of the quilt. For non-directional symmetrical borders, the edge of a full unit or the center of a unit could fall in the middle. For directional borders, however, the design must actually be *reversed* or *mirrored* at the center in order for the motif to be the same at the two edges.

Quick Tip

If you plan to design and sew a pieced border, it is important to take extreme care when cutting the pieces. Make absolutely sure that no bias edges fall on the edges of the border, or there will be a tremendous amount of stretching all along the border edge, making it extremely difficult to sew on to the quilt with accuracy.

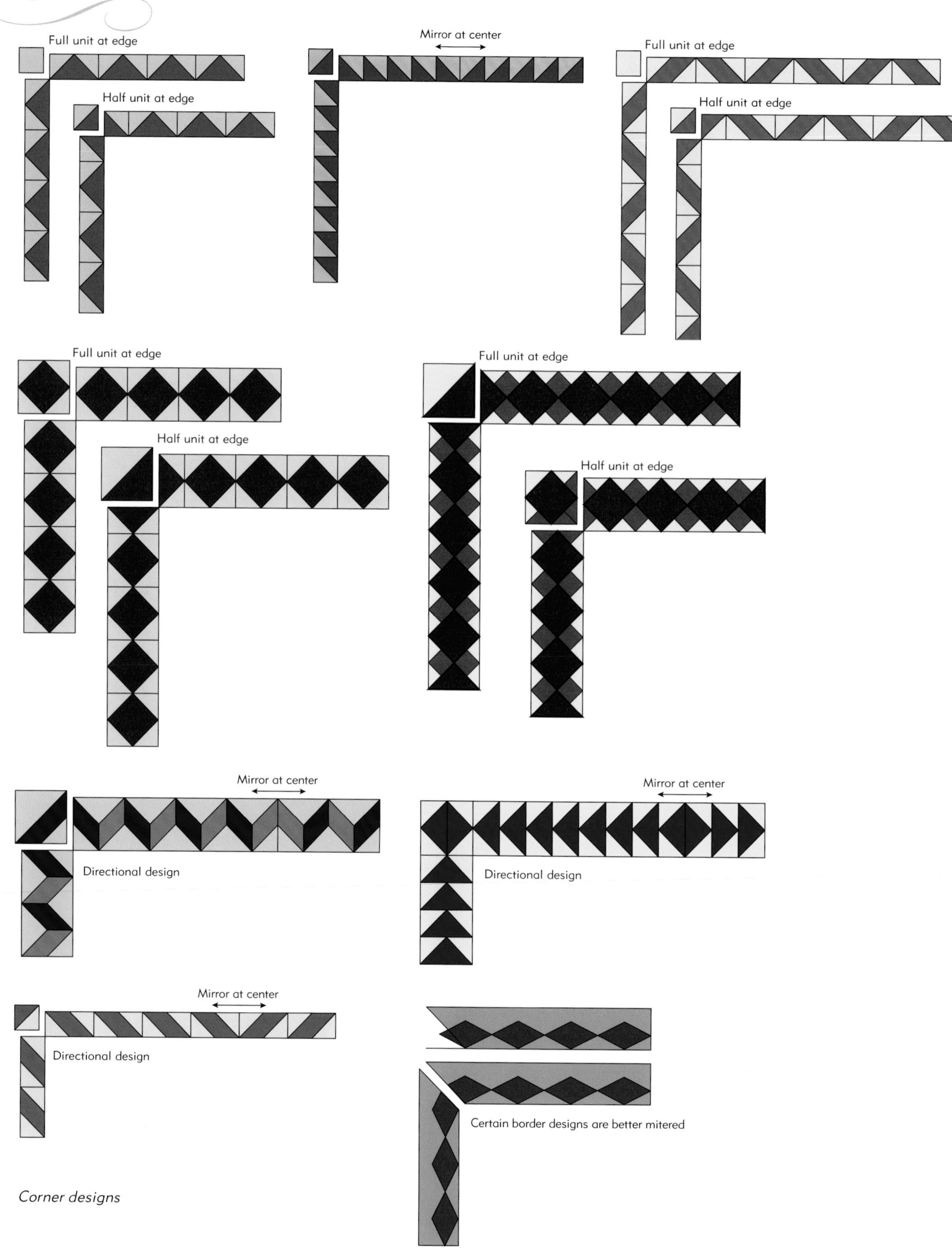

Corner designs

Corner Units

Once the design of the pieced border strips has been planned, then a *corner unit* must be designed to fill in the corners. The easiest way to plan the corner unit motif is to put two border strips together at right angles, as if they were meeting at the corner of the quilt, as was done above. If the border is directional, make sure that one of the strips is the reverse of the other. After this is done, it is usually quite obvious what should be used to fill in the corner. If the pieced strips end with a *full unit*, often another full border unit, exactly the same as the units that make up the rest of the pieced border, will look the best. When the strips end with a half unit, two halves can often be completed to fill in the corner. For more complex borders, an entirely different corner motif might be used. For instance, the original pieced border could be divided diagonally; then two mirrored diagonals could be pieced together for a mitered-corner effect.

Planning Pieced Borders to Fit a Square Quilt

It is one thing to have the *design* of the pieced border figured out, but how do you get it to *fit*? All too often, quilters will piece a beautiful border, only to find once they try to sew it onto the quilt that it does not fit! Most often, the corner motifs do not fall, as planned, exactly at the corners of the quilt. Careful planning and measurement will ensure this does not happen to you.

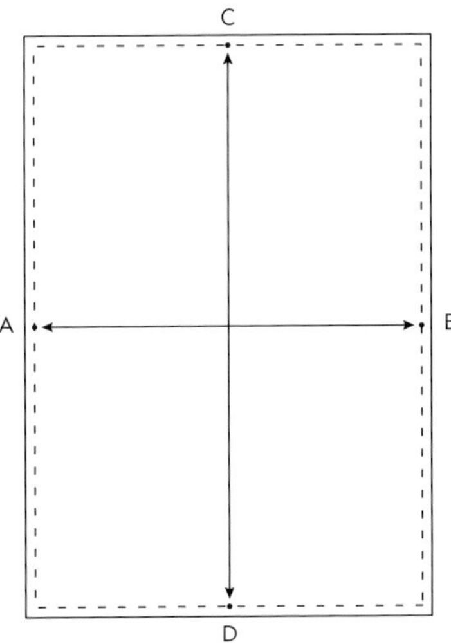

Measuring through middle of quilt for pieced border, stopping at seam allowance

When working with a square quilt, all that is necessary is to plan one side, make the other three sides identical to it, and then fill in with the corner units. The very first step is to take an accurate measurement of the portion of the quilt that is to be bordered. Just as when measuring for fabric borders, this measurement must be taken across the *middle* of the quilt. This time, however, do not measure all the way to the *edge* of the quilt. Stop the measurement at the *stitching line*. Seam allowances will be added later, once the size of the border unit is determined.

Once the correct measurement is taken, it is necessary to determine how many border units will fit into that measurement. Let's say that the measurement for the quilt is 55½″ (141 cm). Now, decide the approximate size you want the border unit to be. If the border unit is square, then the width and height will be the same. This means that the size of the unit will also determine the overall *width* of the pieced border strip. Say, for instance, that you want the pieced border unit to be approximately 3″ (7.5 cm) square. This means the border strip would also be 3″ (7.5 cm) wide. Next, to find out how many units are needed to fill the length of the border, simply divide the border length by the unit size. In this example, divide 55½″ by 3″ (141 cm by 7.5 cm). The calculation shows that 18½ units are needed to fill the border measurement.

Planning Pieced Borders for Windows

Curved border unit

Straight border unit

FOR *WINDOWS*, THE QUILT featured on the cover, a similar process to the method explained on page 139 was used for determining the design of the outer pieced border and of the matching border that curves around the central medallion of the quilt. The size of the curved border was determined by the 32 spokes that divided the center circle (see page 139). The border unit is shown here. It is 4¾" (12 cm) wide. The unit was drafted as though it were a square, but the inner and outer triangles were "skewed" to fit the wedge-shaped piece that was necessary for the curve. Thirty-two wedge-shaped units make up the curved border.

I wanted the outer pieced border to look like a straightened version of the inner curved border, but realized that it couldn't be *exactly* the same size. The size of the border unit for that outer pieced border was determined by first measuring across the middle of the quilt. It was 73" × 73" (185 cm × 185 cm).

Since I wanted the border to be as close to 4¾" (12 cm) wide as possible, I divided 73" by 4.75", which is 15.36. The closest whole number is 15, so I rounded down to 15 and divided 73" by 15, which is 4.86. Therefore the border unit was drafted into a 4.86" square. This was easy to do on the computer because it is possible to get a square exactly that size. (In metrics, 185 cm ÷ 12 cm = 15.4; closest whole number is 15; 185 cm ÷ 15 = 12.3. The border unit would be drafted into a 12.3 cm square.) No one can tell that the width of the outer border is 0.11" (0.3 cm) wider than the inner

Quick Tip

When designing a quilt with a pieced border, it is necessary to remain flexible as to the final border *width*. The *width* of the border strip will be determined by the *size* of the individual border unit. The size of the individual border unit is determined by the measurement of the area to be bordered.

Obviously, there's a problem here. If 18½ units are sewn together, there will not be either a full unit or a half unit at the edge. To make sure the corner falls properly, there must be either an odd or even number of *complete* units in the border. This means that 18½ units must be either rounded down to 18 or rounded up to 19 full units. To end up with an even number, it is therefore necessary to adjust the size of the original 3" (7.5 cm) size of the border unit. In this example, to approximate a 3" (7.5 cm) width, there could either be 18 or 19 units in the border. For an even number of 18 units, the pieced unit will need to be redrafted into a 3.08" square (55½" ÷ 18); for 19 units, redraft to a 2.92" square (55½" ÷ 19). (In metrics, divide 141 by 18 for a 7.8 cm square; divide 141 by 19 for a 7.4 cm square.) Now draft the border-unit design into a square this size, then make templates for each piece by adding ¼" (0.75 cm) seam allowances around all sides. The result is a pieced border that will exactly fit the space.

Pieced Borders for Rectangular Quilts

So far, we have only looked at adding pieced borders to square quilts, where all the borders are cut to the same length. What happens if the quilt is rectangular? For rectangular quilts, it is necessary to find a size for the border unit that will fit as closely as possible into both the width and length of the quilt. It may happen that there will be no unit size that will exactly fit both. In these cases, the best option is to find a unit size that fits one of the dimensions exactly

circular border. But had the border been pieced with the original unit size of 4¾″ (12 cm), that 0.11″ (0.3 cm) spread over 15 units would have produced a border strip that was almost 2″ (5 cm) too short.

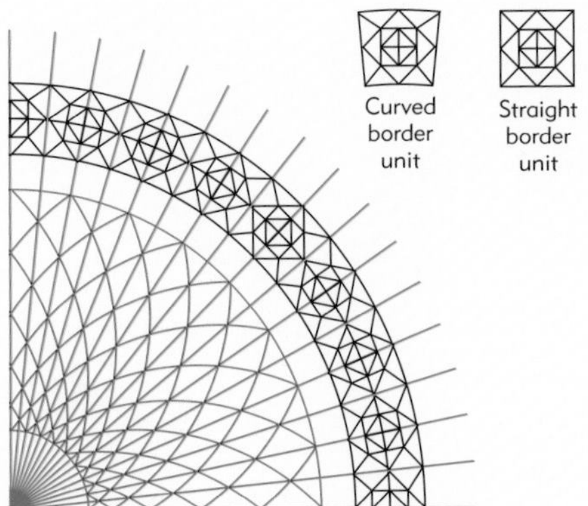

Wedge units in curved border of ***Windows***

and then fudge a little on the other by either stretching the border or shortening it. This is done by sewing a few seams a little thinner to stretch the border, or a little wider to shorten it.

Let's say that the quilt in the example above is not a square and now measures 55½″ × 67″ (141 cm × 170 cm). We have already determined that, on the short sides, if the border has 19 units, the size of each unit would be 2.92″ (7.4 cm). If there are 18 units, the size would be 3.08″ (7.8 cm). Divide each of those numbers into 67 to determine which one results in a number that will come as close as possible to a whole number. In the first scenario, 67″ ÷ 2.92″ is 22.94. If that unit size is used, there would be 23 units along the long side. (It is necessary to round up to the next nearest number from 22.94″.) This means the borders along the long sides would be .06 of a unit too long. That is only 0.175″—just a little more than ⅛″ (0.4 cm) over the entire border length (unit size 2.92″ × 0.06 = 0.175″ or 7.4 cm × 0.06 = 0.4 cm). This amount is so small that the border will probably just about fit, especially if one or two seams could be made just a little wider than the others.

In the second scenario, 67″ ÷ 3.08″ (170 cm ÷ 7.8 cm) is 21.75. That number, rounded up to 22 units, would mean that the border would be 0.25 of a unit too long. That number multiplied by the unit size of 3.08″ (7.8 cm) shows that the border would be a little over ¾″ (1.6 cm) too long. Clearly, it would be better to use the 2.92″ (7.4 cm) unit which, as we saw, is only 1/8″ (0.4 cm) too long.

One last consideration is whether or not the pieced border is directional. If so, since the border design must reverse at the center of the quilt, then both sides must have either an odd number of units (the design of all strips will end with half units at the corner) or an even number of units (the design of all strips will end with whole units at the corner).

As you can see, planning pieced borders is individual and unique to each quilt. With the aid of a calculator and some trial and error, the correct measurements can eventually be worked out, and the results are well worth the effort.

"An enclosure around angular or erratic forms, such as pieced blocks often are, sustains the whole. I well remember a testy old art teacher's example of that; the question was on rug design, as to what relation the border should bear to the pattern. We students must have all looked blank because he immediately hammered a desk with his cane and queried, "Well, well, if you had a bull in a pasture, should the bull or the fence be stronger?""

Ruby Short McKim,
101 Patchwork Patterns, 1931

Sewing Borders On to the Quilt

As noted earlier, due to bias-stretch, the edges of a quilt top are often longer than the measurements through the middle of the quilt (see page 145). Since borders are correctly cut to middle-of-quilt measurements, you will usually end up with border strips that are slightly shorter than the quilt edge. This means that when you sew the borders on, the quilt edges will have to be eased back to their proper size.

Sewing on borders

Begin by pinning the mid-point of one of the border pieces to the middle of one of the edges of the quilt. Pin the corners next, carefully matching the places where the seam allowances cross on both the quilt and the border strips. Now, by folding, find the mid-point of the quilt and the border strip between each of the two halves and pin those together. Continue finding the mid-points and pinning. Then ease in any fullness, pinning carefully all along the edge. If the border is pieced, make sure there is a pin at each seam. The point of the pin should come out right at the seam allowances on both the border and the quilt. Carefully sew the seam, easing in any extra fullness. Sew each of the border strips in this manner.

When sewing borders on to a quilt, there is often the question of whether the border or the quilt should be on top as you sew. Actually it all depends on what you are sewing. In general if there is a lot to "ease in," then it is better to have the piece with the fullness on top. This way, there are less likely to be puckers as the excess is eased in. However, if a border-print fabric is being used as a border, I *always* sew with the border print on top. This is because you will most likely be sewing along a *line* that is printed on the fabric, and the stitches should be exactly along that line throughout. If the border print is on the back it is more difficult and takes more time to sew directly on that line.

The next step is sewing the corners. For pieced borders, I usually sew two border strips so they are just the length of one of the sides of the quilt. These are sewn onto the quilt first. The next strips are sewn with the corner units included, and these are sewn on last.

When adding an unpieced fabric border on which the miters have already been cut, pin the miters carefully together, making sure not to stretch the bias edges. If the strips are border prints, make sure the design on the miters exactly matches and pin securely. Because of the length of bias miters, the pieces can become slightly distorted and stretched. I take one additional step that will remedy any distortion that may have occurred.

Once the miters are sewn, lay the corner, right side up, on the ironing board so that there is at least 12″ (30 cm) of border print on the ironing board on either side of the mitered corner. Reach underneath and gently push the seam allowances to one side or the other. Then softly run the iron over the seam, pushing in the direction *away* from the seam allowance. If there is any extra fullness in the miter, the iron will press it in place and make the corner perfectly square. Then re-stitch the portion of the miter along the crease left by the iron.

"If a border is included in the design it should harmonize in color and design with the body of the quilt."

Marie D. Webster,
Quilts: Their Story & How to Make Them, 1915

Add Borders to Your Hand-Pieced Quilt

If you have been practicing the sewing instructions presented in this book by making one of the quilts specifically designed to incorporate all of the techniques, now add a border. You will find that the sewing skills are no different than those already learned. Just reread the sections on measuring and cutting miters, and you should have no problems making a border that fits perfectly!

Olde World Star. *Designed, hand-pieced, and hand-quilted by Jinny Beyer, 1992*

Preparing to Quilt

"When the girl was promised, and the wedding day drew near, the patchwork top was sewn, or completed if it had been started earlier. It really looked lovely—not like everyday quilts at all, for a definite pattern had perhaps naturally followed on the definite color scheme. Well, then, the quilting must be worthy of such a fine top!"

Agnes M. Miall,
Patchwork Old and New, 1937

QUILTING SHOULD PLAY AS LARGE A PART IN THE creation of a beautiful quilt as the efforts that go into the workmanship, color, and design of the top. Originating as a simple way to hold layers of fabrics together and to keep cotton batting in place, quilting quickly evolved into an expression of the quiltmaker's expertise, design sense, and creativity. A carefully thought-out quilting pattern enhances the overall design by adding relief and texture to the quilt surface, sometimes emphasizing certain areas of the quilt top and sometimes acting as a background to others. And even though battings have been developed that advertise the need for less quilting, I still believe that more is better.

Planning the Quilting Design

One of the most common questions from new quilters, confused by the endless array of patterns and styles, is "How do I quilt my quilt?" There are so many answers, but in the end the type of quilting design selected is a matter of personal preference. It also depends on the look you are after and the amount of quilting you want to do. If you are willing to take a little extra time for the quilting, the result will be well worth the effort.

*Single, then double stitching on **Love Ring***

Planning the Quilting Design

"Circles and segments of circles can be marked on material by drawing or chalking round such articles as plates, saucers, coins."

Ann Heynes,
Quilting and Patchwork, 1925

All-Over Quilting

Sometimes, the quilting pattern is an all-over design that, rather than following the patchwork, perhaps echoes the style of the quilt. *Love Ring* (see full quilt in the pattern section) is a good example. While an all-over quilting pattern can be very effective, it does create a bit of a problem when quilting over seams. Stitches in those areas will tend to be larger because of the extra bulk. The maker of *Love Ring*, Carole Nicholas, started by making a large circle out of cardboard and drawing overlapping circles onto the quilt top. After stitching around each circle, she realized that the quilting could be enhanced by sewing another line around the petals, ¼″ (0.75 cm) in from the first line of stitching. The before-and-after details shown here illustrate the difference that the extra stitching makes in the overall look of the quilt. The final result was well worth the time spent.

Another type of all-over quilting is known as *saucer quilting*. In this method, a plate or saucer is used as the pattern. The quilting is begun in one corner of the quilt. The plate is placed on the corner and an arc is marked. After that line is quilted, another arc is marked and these overlapping arcs continue over the entire quilt top. The antique quilt *Sunflower*, shown on page 106, was quilted in this way. Because of the intricacy of the fabric and design, the quilting does not

*Saucer quilting on back of **Sunflower***

*Outline quilting in **Windows***

*Stitching in the ditch along the border of **Windows***

show up so much on the front, but a detailed photo of the back of the quilt reveals the pattern.

Outline Quilting

A popular quilting style known as *outline quilting* is often used for quilts that are made up of multiple pieces of patchwork. This type of quilting emphasizes the shapes of the pieces. I tend to be very traditional in my approach to quilting and, for the most part, this is the method I prefer. I usually quilt about ¼″ (0.75 cm) from the seams around each of the pieces. When quilting in this manner, make sure to sew just beyond the seam allowance, so you don't have the extra thickness of seams to sew through. I eyeball the ¼″ (0.75 cm) line, but if you prefer more of a guide, lay a strip of masking tape along the seam line and quilt next to the tape.

Quilting in the Ditch

Quilting in the ditch is another method of quilting that follows the design of the patchwork. With this method, the line of quilting runs right next to the seam. To avoid having to quilt through the bulk of the seam, extreme care must be taken to press the top properly prior to basting the quilt layers together. First, decide which side of the seam you will quilt next to, then always press the seam *away* from that side. If the seam is pressed sometimes to one side and sometimes to the other, there is the chance that you will have to stitch on the seam allowance now and then.

The only time I quilt in the ditch is when I have incorporated very narrow strips—½″ (1.5 cm) wide or less—of border-print fabrics into my quilts.

Quick Tip

When quilting straight lines, such as those in *Columbia*, I gauge the lines by placing masking tape along the areas to be quilted. I often plan the width of the spaces between the lines to be the width of the masking tape.

Stitch in a straight line, right next to the masking tape

Quilting decorative fabric in **Windows**

Border-print diamonds in **Triple Play**

Planning the Quilting Design *continued*

I press all the seams to the *middle* of the strip and quilt in the ditch on each side. This method gives additional relief to the strip and holds it securely in place. The narrow border strip in *Windows* is actually made up of three different pieces–two narrow strips sewn to either side of a wider strip. Since there needed to be stitching along the edges, I quilted in the ditch on either side of the narrow border pieces. This type of stitching gets lost in the seams on the front of the quilt, but it is visible on the back and is a necessary part of the overall design. The border pieces would have been too puffy without the extra quilting.

Quick Tip

When planning the quilting, you may want to consider whether the design is going to run across the straight or bias grain of the fabric. Curved and bias designs were used on old quilts so that the stitching did not run along the grain line. Some of the homespun fabrics were fairly coarse and, if the quilting ran along the grain of the fabric, the stitches could become lost in the weave. Most fabrics used for quilting today are more closely woven, so this is not such a problem.

Following Fabric Designs

For border prints and other areas that are filled with large-scale fabrics, quilting can be done following the design on the fabric. This type of quilting emphasizes the printed design and enhances the look of the quilt. It is easy to get carried away with the quilting inside decorative borders–and it's often difficult to know where to stop!

As noted in Chapter Seven, one of my favorite piecing techniques is to divide a square or other shape into triangles, then use a border-print fabric to recreate the original shape. When quilting these types of shapes, rather than emphasize the individual triangles, I prefer to highlight the design that is formed when all of those triangles are sewn together to reform the shape. In other words, instead of quilting around individual shapes, I quilt along the motifs formed when those shapes are combined. There is a lot of variety in the quilting design in the many border-print diamonds in *Triple Play*. It was fun to see how the quilting enhanced each one.

Quilting motifs in ***Olde World Star***

Single, then double stitching on ***Columbia***

Quilting Unpieced Spaces

Over the years many beautiful scrolls, feathers, wreaths, fans, and other decorative motifs have been designed for use as quilting patterns in open, unpieced areas of the quilt and in borders. These are most effective when quilted on solid colors or on simple printed fabrics, as the designs show up much better than they would on multicolored, larger-scale fabrics. While there are many commercially available patterns for quilting designs, it is often difficult to find one just the right size. Usually, I draft my own motifs. As you will see later in this chapter, this is not at all difficult to do. The motif should be designed to fill the area as much as possible, with just a little space around the edges. A detail of the quilting motif that I used for *Olde World Star* is shown here.

Since delicate quilting designs will not show well on large-scale prints, what are our options for those areas? Some people painstakingly quilt around the motifs in the fabric. Although this can be beautiful, it may be more work than you want to do. Instead, a simple geometric design that is repeated in all open areas can be very effective. Perhaps one of the designs suggested later as background quilting would work. You will be surprised at how pleasing the regular repeat of a geometric design can be, even on a very patterned fabric. Look, for instance, at the detail of the quilting in the large triangle section of *Columbia.* Concentric triangles were quilted inside the larger triangle. Note, too, the before-and-after photos showing the difference in how those triangles look with a single layer of stitching or with a double line of stitching–the second line quilted ¼″ (0.75 cm) away from each original line. As we saw with *Love Ring* earlier, the small amount of extra time spent makes a very big difference in the overall design.

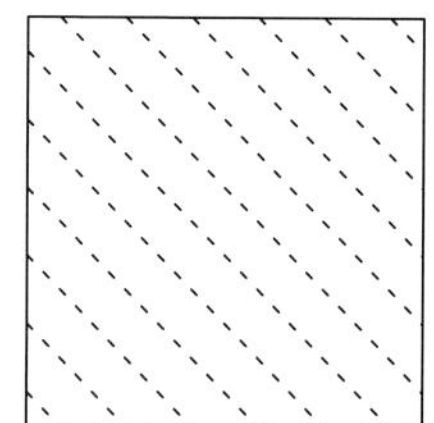

Diagonal lines

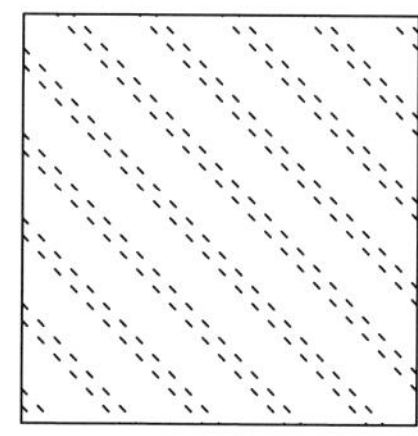

Double diagonal lines

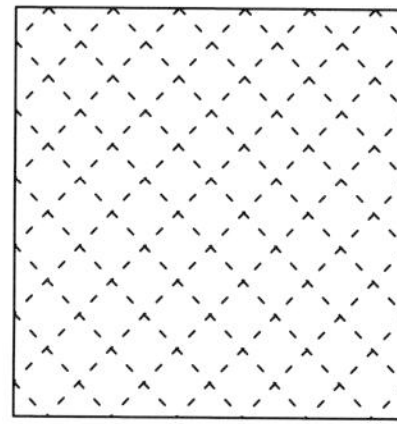

Cross-hatching

Double cross-hatching

Clamshell

Echo quilting

Background Quilting

If you plan to use a decorative quilting design, such as scrolls, wreaths, or feathers, you must also pay attention to the background space *behind* the motif. If you concentrate only on the decorative portion, the design will not show up well. The quilting must be planned to fill the entire space–not just the motif, but the background as well.

There are various ways to treat the background, depending on the look you want and the amount of quilting you want to do. Diagonal lines, double diagonal lines, cross-hatching, double cross-hatching, and clamshell are some traditional background patterns.

Echo quilting is another option, using concentric curves, squares, or triangles or by otherwise outlining the main motif. This type of quilting was traditionally used in Hawaiian quilts. For echo quilting, the lines are usually ½″ (1.5 cm) apart.

Stippling on **Ray of Light**. Designed, hand-pieced, and hand-quilted by Jinny Beyer, 1977

Stippling

Stippling, also known as *meander quilting*, is an older style of background quilting that has gained new popularity in recent years. It was common on 18th and early 19th century *white work* or applique quilts. At first glance, one might think that the stitches are taken at random, going this way then that way to produce the stippled effect. In fact, the quilting is done in waves. It is similar to echo quilting, but the rows are now only 1/16″ (0.2 cm) apart. After a few rows of tiny stitches are complete, the rows disappear, and the stippled effect appears. If you try this type of quilting and find that you still see the rows and are not getting a stippled effect, check to make sure that the quilting thread is pulled tight enough. If it is pulled too tight, the work will pucker; if it is not pulled tight enough the thread will just lie on the fabric without creating any relief. (For help on maintaining proper tension, see page 189.)

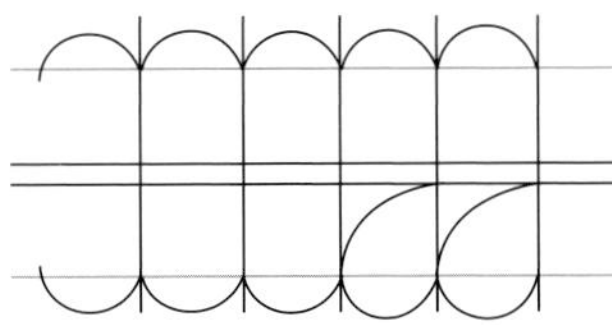

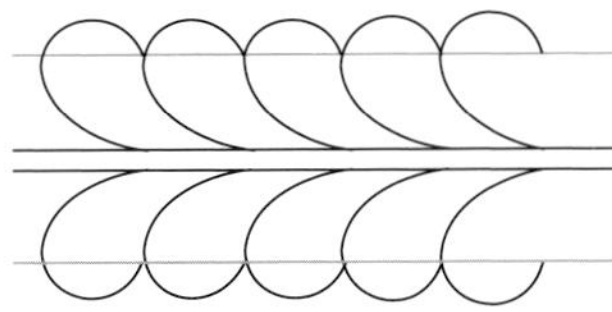

Draw spine, add half-circles, connect half-circles to spine

Feathers and Some Variations

"Drawing round familiar objects secures many a wanted shape. For instance, pencil round plates, saucers, cups, egg-cups or coins for circles. For the slightly elongated diamond and for the heart—the latter wanted for Flirtation and often for quilting—buy a set of bridge sandwich cutters at the sixpenny stores and mark round the shapes required."

Agnes M. Miall,
Patchwork Old and New, 1937

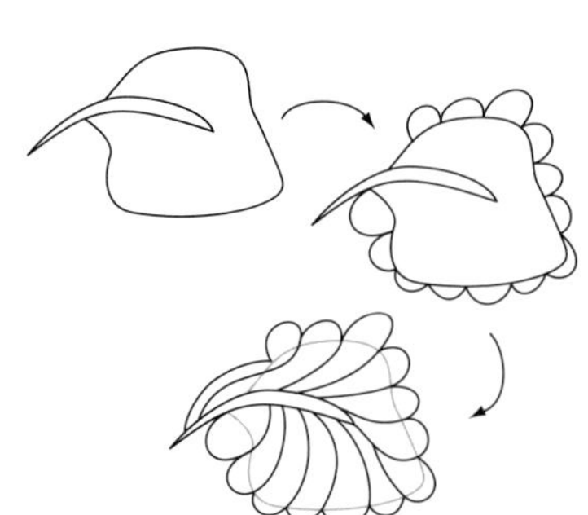

Drafting Quilting Designs

Just as important as knowing how to draft your own patchwork blocks is knowing how to draft your own decorative quilting patterns. A quilting design should fill the space, with not more than 1″ (2.5 cm) between the outer portions of the design and the edges of the shape being filled. A motif that is too small will look lost, while one too large will look crowded. Begin with the shape to be filled and draft the design to fill that space. A few techniques will be given here to let you see that drafting quilting designs is a relatively simple process.

Feathers

Feathers, one of the more common quilting motifs, can be used to embellish hearts, wreathes, scrolls, or any other shape you can imagine. To create a feather, first draw the *spine*. This looks best if it is a double line of stitching about ¼″ (0.75 cm) apart. Then draw lines on either side of the spine that will be the guide for the feather fronds. For a perfectly symmetrical design, these lines should be spaced equally on either side of the central spine. For other designs, where the feathers may be thinner on one side and thicker on the other, or where they might graduate, going from small to large, the lines should vary in their relationship to the central spine.

Next, using a small round object (a button, coin, or spool of thread all work well, depending on the size feather desired), draw half-circles, side by side along the line. Once again, if the design is not going to be completely even

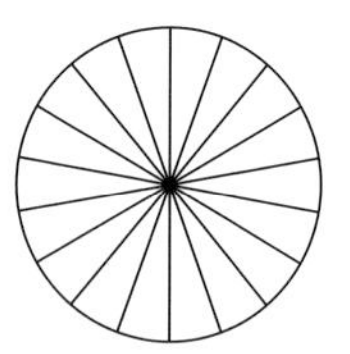

Divide circle with spokes, add scallops on outer circle

Variations of circle designs with feathers

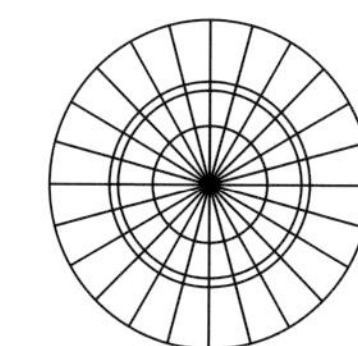

Divide circles with spokes, add scallops on inner and outer circles; draw lines

Finished wreath

throughout, it is probably best to graduate the size of the circles. (Start with a small button, graduate to a dime, and then go to a penny, nickel, quarter, and a small spool of thread.)

Finally, a curved line will connect the half-circles to the central spine. For perfectly symmetrical designs, once one design is drawn that is pleasing, a template can be made for that shape, and then that template can be used as a guide to draw all of the others. A few feather designs and their basic underlying structure are shown on the previous page. Experiment with shapes of your own and have fun creating your own feathers.

Circles

Many feather-like quilting designs are based on circles. These work well to fill alternate squares of a patchwork design. Draw a circle and divide it into a certain number of equal divisions, radiating from the center outward. Then, with a small, curved object, draw scallops between each of the spokes. Some variations on this simple technique are shown here.

Circles can also be used to create various types of feathered wreaths. This time, four circles are needed–two that are about ¼″ (0.75 cm) apart for the spine, one outside the spine, and one inside. I usually like to make the distance between the spine and the inner circle about 60 percent of the distance between the spine and the outer circle. Once again, the circle must be divided into spokes radiating from the center. A half-circle is drawn between each of those spokes around the outside, but the half-circles are drawn between every *two* spokes on the inside. To finish, the feather connects the half-circles to the central spine. It is best to make a template for this line, so that all the fronds will be identical.

Feathers can be added to any shape. Draw around an oval, a heart, a leaf, or any other shape that is pleasing to you, then add scallops outside or inside the line. It is fun to experiment. You'll quickly discover that any decorative motif at all can be used for a quilting pattern. Quilting patterns do not have to be feathers. Birds, grapes, flowers, and scrolls all make great designs. Sometimes, copying a design from a large print fabric that was used in the top makes a nice quilting pattern. Look at your quilt top and select a design that will enhance the work that you have already done.

Step 1. Draw length and width of unit

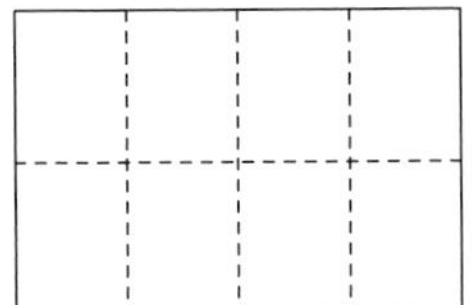

Step 2. Divide length by two and width by four

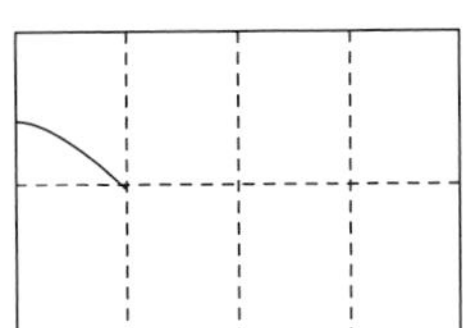

Step 3. Draw curved line

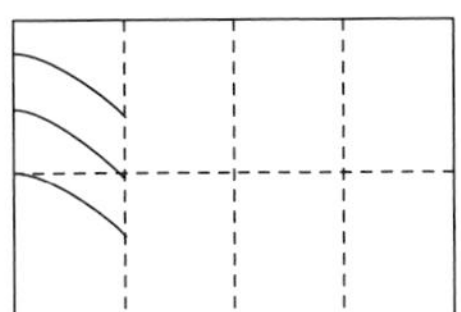

Step 4. Copy line equidistant on each side

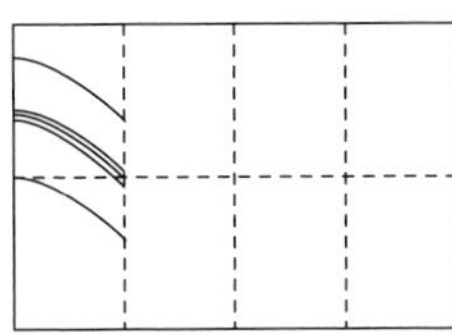

Step 5. Draw lines on either side of first line

"The continuance of a border pattern on the corners without a break is a test of skill, as the tidy manoeuvering of a pattern, such as a twist or running feather, is not easy."

AVERIL COLBY,
Quilting, 1971

Quilted Borders

Decorative quilting makes a lovely finish to plain fabric borders. In this case, planning the quilting design is very similar to planning pieced borders for quilts (see page 150). First, I plan a *unit* that begins and ends at the same place, then I put multiples of those units together to fill the space. There is usually a separate corner design that connects the border units. Sometimes the corner is a continuation of the unit pattern, where the two edges meet in a miter. Keep in mind that just as some pieced borders are directional, so too are some designs for quilted borders. With directional quilted motifs, the border should reverse direction at the center of the quilt, so that the two units coming to the corners will end at the same place.

It is much easier to plan quilted border motifs to fit than it is to plan pieced borders. For square quilts, simply plan the length of the border unit to be a number that will divide easily into the length of the quilt. For example, for a 40″ quilt, the unit could be 5″, 8″, or 10″. (For a 100 cm quilt, the unit could be 10 cm, 20 cm, or 25 cm.) For rectangular quilts, if a size for a unit cannot be found that will evenly divide into both sides, just slightly "stretch" or "shorten" the unit on one of the sides. Draft the unit separately for the short and the long side of the quilt. No one is going to notice a slight variance of ½″ (1.5 cm) or less in the length of a unit, but they would notice if the design did not flow smoothly around the corner.

Most border units are drafted in very much the same manner. Follow these steps for drafting a feathered motif. This will help you to understand how to draft other, similar types of border units.

1. Draw the size of the unit (length and width).
2. Divide the length of the unit in half and the width into fourths.
3. Draw a slightly curved line in the upper left section, as shown.
4. Copy the line at equal distances on either side.
5. To create the spine, draw lines ⅛″ (0.4 cm) from the first line on either side.

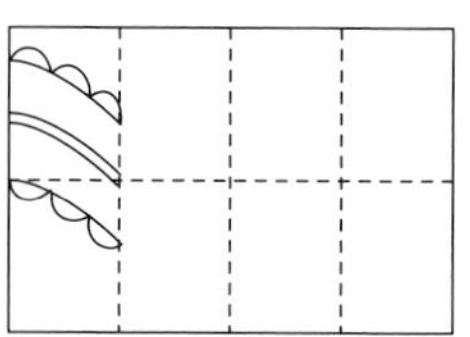

Step 6. Erase first line; add half circles

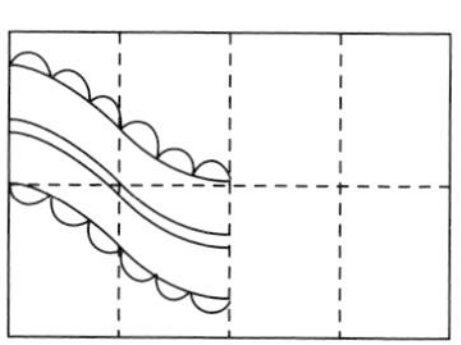

Step 7. Trace all lines, rotate 180°, and retrace

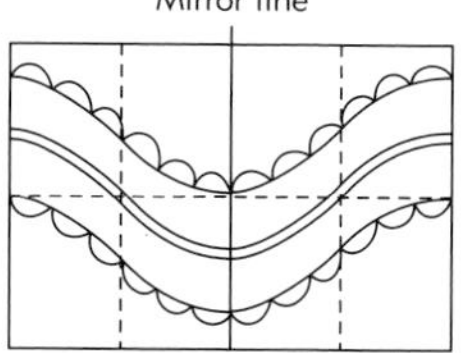

Step 8. Mirror all drawn lines

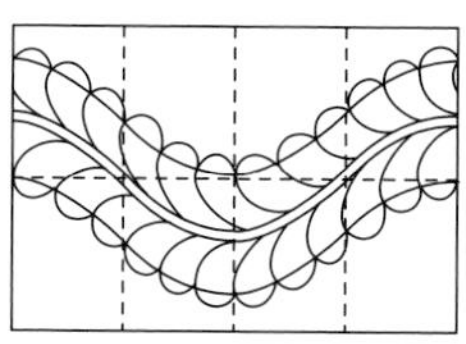

Step 9. Connect half-circles to central spine

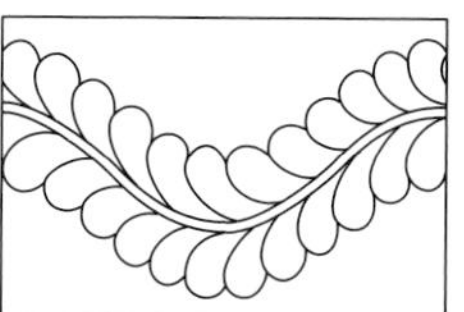

Complete

6. Erase the first line, then add half-circles to the outer edges, as shown. Note that the half-circles on the inward slope of the line will be slightly narrower than the half-circles on the outward slope.
7. Using tracing paper, copy all of the lines, rotate them 180°, and retrace them next to the first set of lines.
8. Mirror all of the drawn lines to get the shape of the complete unit.
9. Complete the feathers by connecting the half-circles to the center spine. Note that on either edge, part of the last feather will fall into the next unit. These will need to be drawn so that the units fit together smoothly.

One possibility for the corner is to extend the design and miter the corner. Mirror this miter to complete the other half. If the corner seems too empty, draw another line towards the corner and add more scallops to create feathers. Reverse this for the complete corner.

There is a wide variety of designs to use for quilted borders. A few of them are illustrated on page 169.

"To mark the pattern on the material for quilting, use faint pencil lines, or chalked lines. For the latter cover a thread or string with white or coloured chalk, stretch it tightly across the desired place, pull the string upward and let fly back. This will leave a straight line of chalk. For more elaborate forms, paper patterns may be cut . . . and chalked or run round."

ANN HEYNES,
Quilting and Patchwork, 1925

Marking the Quilting Design

It is best to plan the quilting design prior to basting the layers of a quilt together, as you may want to mark some of the designs on the quilt top before it goes into the frame. In most cases, I mark once the quilt is in the frame, a little at a time. I like to use markers that will disappear by the time the motif has been quilted. Usually I quilt by eyeballing ¼″ (0.75 cm) lines around the

Designing for a Mitered Corner

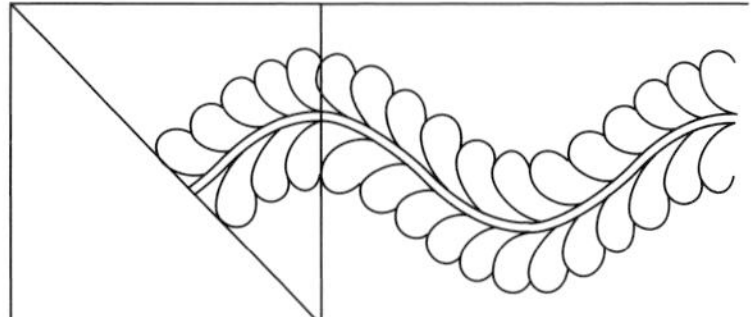

Step 1. Extend border design, miter corner

Step 2. Mirror miter to complete other half

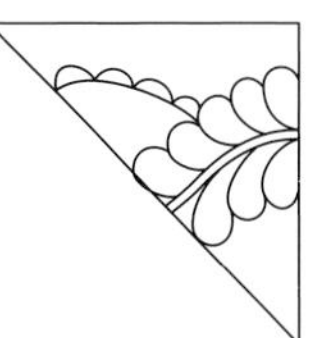

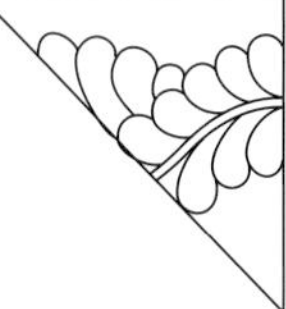

Step 3. To fill empty corner space, draw another line and add more scallops to create feathers. Mirror for complete corner

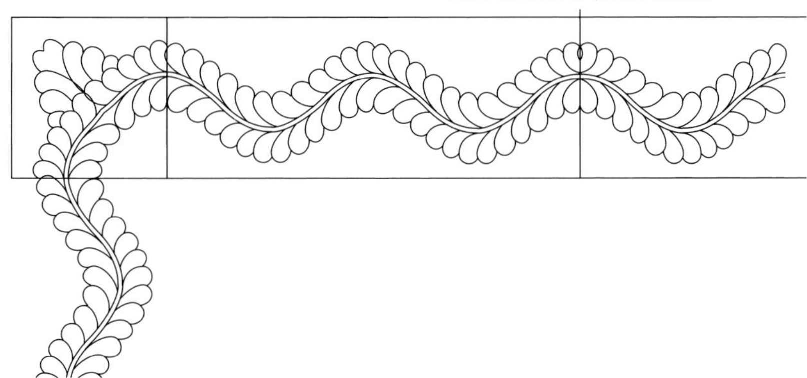

Sample Designs for Quilted Borders

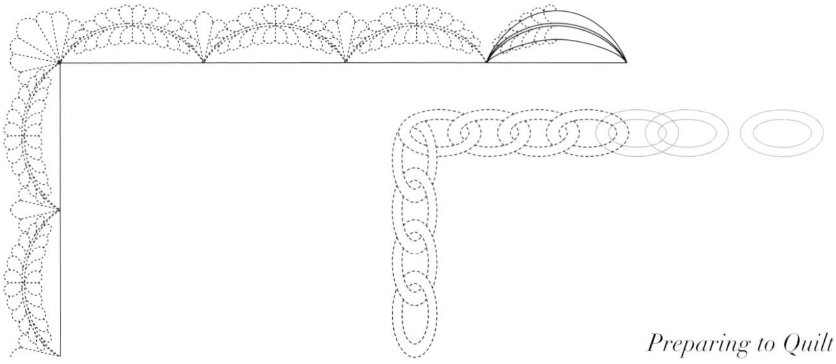

Patterns Galore

EARLY IN THE 20TH CENTURY, a revival of interest in patchwork and quilting led to the publishing of many commercial patterns not only for block designs but for quilting designs, too. Quilting patterns were made from cardboard or tin, which was then perforated with the design. Here is how quilting writer Ruby Short McKim describes them in *101 Patchwork Patterns,* 1931.

> "Marking a quilt for quilting is more nearly like an artist's job than any step in the making of a quilt. On pieced blocks straight lines, which follow the seams of the patchwork or cross into checkerboard to diamond effects, are usually best. On the alternate plain blocks or strips and on borders the quilting may be as ornate as desired.
>
> Manufacturers have adapted some of the old-time favorite designs in addition to originating new patterns, to fit other space plans. These come on a special tough but transparent paper, the design perforated so that it may be used over and over with stamping paste."

A pamphlet from *Aunt Martha,* released at the Chicago World's Fair in 1932, invites quilters to try out her stamping wax and stamping paste:

> "For stamping wax, moisten a piece of cotton in gasoline or benzine, and rub over the stamping wax, then over your pattern. You are offered your choice of stamping wax in black (No. 423), Blue (No. 424), or Rose (No. 425). A large cake, good for many, many stampings, 25¢.

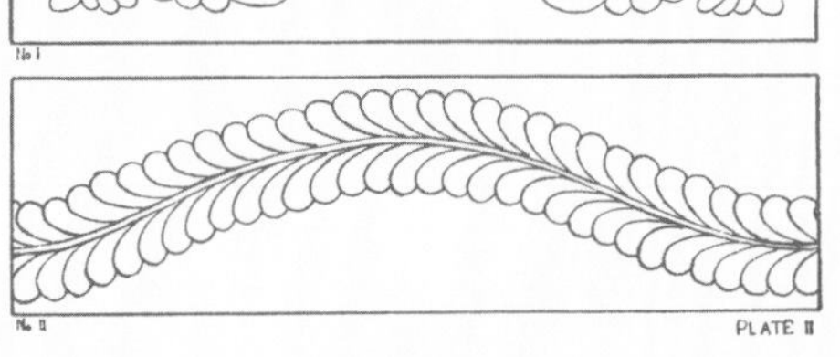

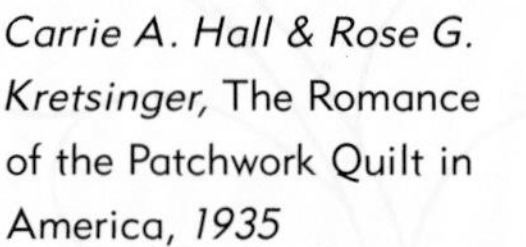

Carrie A. Hall & Rose G. Kretsinger, The Romance of the Patchwork Quilt in America, *1935*

"If you wish to remove your stamping design after you have completed your quilting, you will be delighted with our stamping powder. This gives you a clean distinct line, but may be brushed off, leaving no trace of color. Your choice of Rose (No. 426) or Blue (No. 427), per package, 25¢."

Aunt Martha,
The Quilt Fair Comes to You,
1932

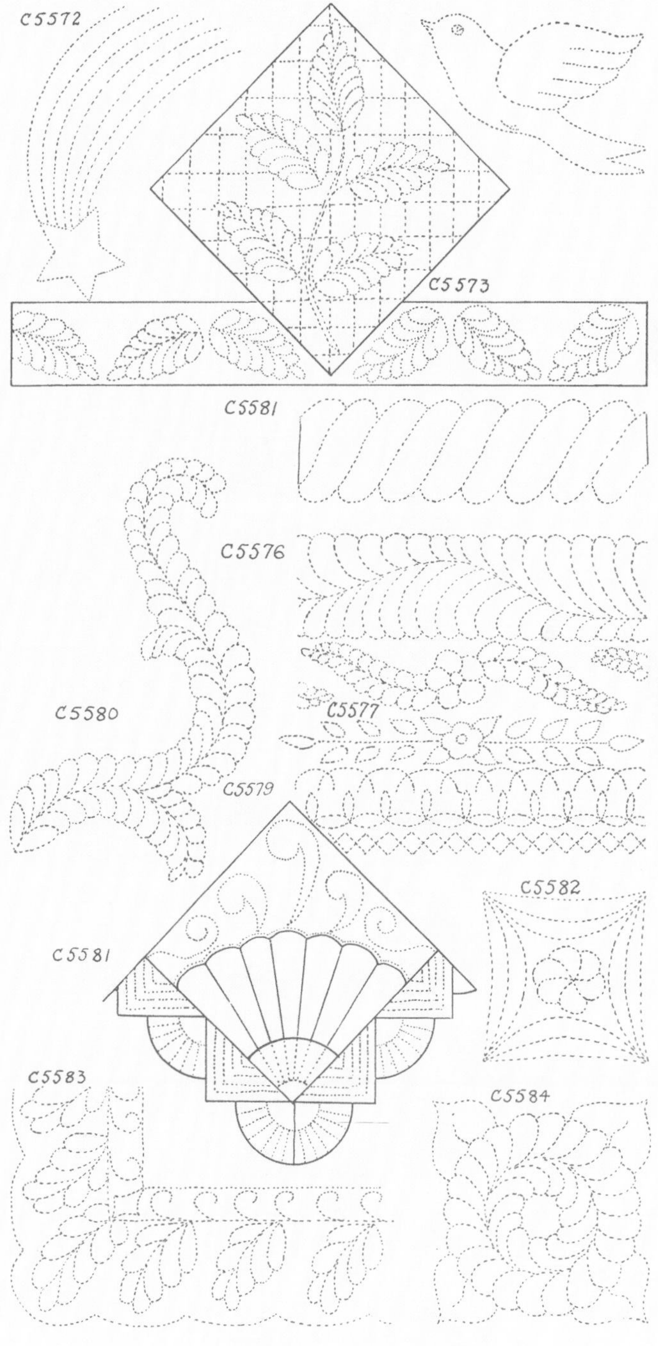

Stamping Powder

Of all the patterns that came to market during the quilting revival of the 1920s and '30s, the most popular by far were those with feather motifs. In *The Romance of the Patchwork Quilt in America,* Carrie A. Hall and Rose G. Kretsinger reflect on the motif's enduring popularity.

"Perhaps the one ornamental motif most familiar to us in America and especially adaptable to quilting is the Ostrich Feather or Plume. It has always furnished inexhausible [sic] ideas for motif design and bandings. The long slender center rib, bordered by segments of fronds, lends grace and beauty to mass arrangement or bandings. Variations of the feather have been used in wreath, scroll, band, wave, and medallions, large and small. Aside from its slender beauty, it offers less constructive difficulty than does the floral motif. After marking out the center rib it is a simple matter to draw in the segments of fronds which make up the body of the plume."

Quick Tip

Some quilters use water-soluble markers to mark designs on their quilt tops. A damp cloth rubbed over the mark or a light spray makes the line disappear. I do not recommend these markers. I have seen instances where the line returns a few years after it is marked and cannot be washed out.

patchwork pieces or by placing ¼″ or ½″ (0.75 cm or 1.5 cm) masking tape in straight lines along the areas to be quilted (see page 161). When there is a decorative motif, I usually mark it after the quilt is basted and put in the frame. I make plastic templates of the quilting design, lay them on top of the quilt, and draw around them. Tailors' chalk, a chalk pencil, or a hard sliver of soap are all good for temporary marking. A tapestry needle also works well. Put the point into a cork. The cork serves as a good handle, and the eye end of the needle will mark a temporary line.

There are times, however, with fairly elaborate designs, that it might be better to mark the quilt top prior to basting the layers of the quilt together. In these cases, you will need a marking device that will stay on the fabric long enough for you to quilt it. When marking on a light-colored fabric, mark very lightly with a sharp, hard lead #3 pencil. On dark-colored fabrics use a sharp Berol verithin pencil in yellow or white. Do a test prior to marking the fabric by drawing on a scrap of the same fabric and then washing it to be sure the pencil line will wash out.

A light table is useful for transferring the design to the quilt top prior to basting the layers and putting the quilt in the frame. If you do not have a light table, create your own by purchasing a heavy piece of glass. Pull apart a table that has leaves and set the glass over the opening in the table. Put a light on the floor underneath the glass. Using a bold line, draw the quilting design onto a piece of white paper and tape the paper directly onto the glass. Place the portion of the top to be marked over the design and transfer the pattern. Unless a very dark fabric is used, the design should be visible through the fabric.

Preparing the Quilt Top

After the quilt top has been completely stitched and borders added, it must be carefully prepared for the basting process. Reread the section on pressing on page 61 to carefully "set" any long seams. Iron press the entire quilt top. Make sure all the seams of any borders are pressed in the same direction. If there are any very light-colored fabrics next to very dark ones, make sure to iron the darks away from the lights.

Cut off any threads that may be hanging on the wrong side of the quilt top. If the quilt is basted with threads inside, they are apt to show through the light-colored fabrics. Nothing is worse than to be quilting along and suddenly discover a dark thread showing through the quilt top.

Clip the ends off any long points and, if there are any areas in the quilt top where several points come together, clip the excess off the points so they do not form a lump. Do not cut all the points the same, but taper each differently to ease out the bulk.

Backing

There are many considerations when selecting a fabric for the back of the quilt. Decide what color thread you are going to use for quilting. If you want the stitches to be prominent, use a backing that is of a contrasting color. If you want them to blend in, use one that is similar in color to the quilting thread. A beautiful paisley or floral may be the perfect backing to complement the colors on the front. However, solid-color fabrics will show up the quilting pattern on the back more than a printed pattern. If the quilt top contains white or very light-color fabric, select a backing that is also light in color. Dark fabric on the back might show through to the front.

The type of fabric to choose for the backing is also a consideration. Extra-wide *quilt back fabrics* are now produced by several manufacturers. The extra-wide goods that are available for use in fabric printing are slightly heavier than the standard weight fabric that is used for quilting. While they are excellent for machine quilting, the slightly thicker thread in these fabrics may make them a little harder to hand quilt. For hand quilting, I like the fabric on the back to be of the same weight as the fabric on the front. If you find an extra-wide fabric you like, feel it to see if it seems heavier that the other prints you have used.

Make the backing big enough so that it is at least 3″ (7.5 cm) larger than the quilt top on all sides. If you are using a standard 45″ (114 cm) wide fabric, usually two widths of fabric pieced together are large enough for a backing. Rather than one seam straight down the middle, however, I will often have two seams. One width of the fabric goes down the center, and the other width is split, with the two halves going to either side of the center panel. When selecting a large print fabric design for the backing, I like to purchase extra so that when I sew the seams, I can match the design on the pieces. If this is done, once the quilting is complete it is almost impossible to even see the seam.

Prior to stitching the pieces of backing together, tear or cut off the selvage edges. These should not be included in the seam, as they are very difficult to stitch through. Sew the backing pieces together using a ½″ (1.5 cm) seam allowance. When finished, set the seam (see page 61) and then press it to one side. Do not press it open. This causes weakness in the seam and allows fibers from the batting to migrate through the seam.

Quick Tip

It is important to know that most batting, like fabric, has a *grain* and will stretch more in one direction than another. To test this, gently pull the batting first one way, then another. See if there is more give in one of the directions. If so, when preparing the layers for basting, make sure the straight grain of the backing fabric goes in the same direction as the straight grain of the batting. Think also of the end use of your quilt. If you plan to hang it on a wall, determine how the quilt will be oriented, and then have the straight grain of the batting and backing going in the vertical position. This will help to keep the quilt from sagging or stretching when hung.

Batting

There are a wide variety of different types and sizes of batting available. Polyester batting will give a puffier look, while cotton will give a flatter appearance. You should select the batting that will give you the effect you want. My preference is a fairly thin, 100 percent cotton batting. More about types of batting can be found on page 19.

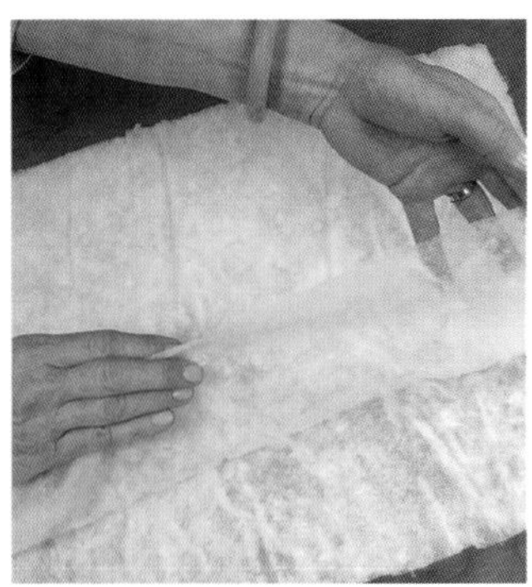
Separate both pieces by about 4″ (10 cm)

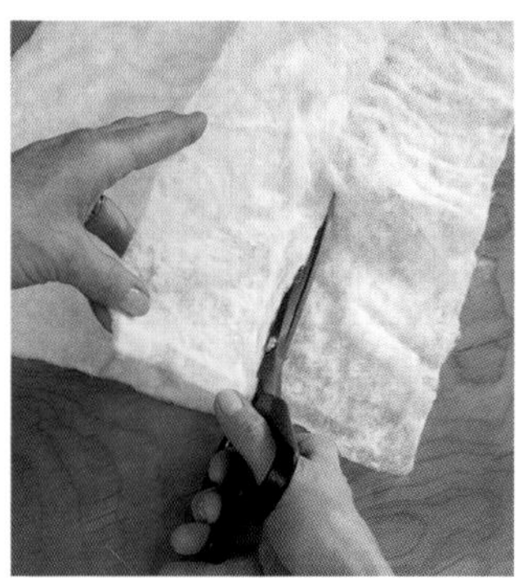
Cut top layer of one piece and bottom layer of other

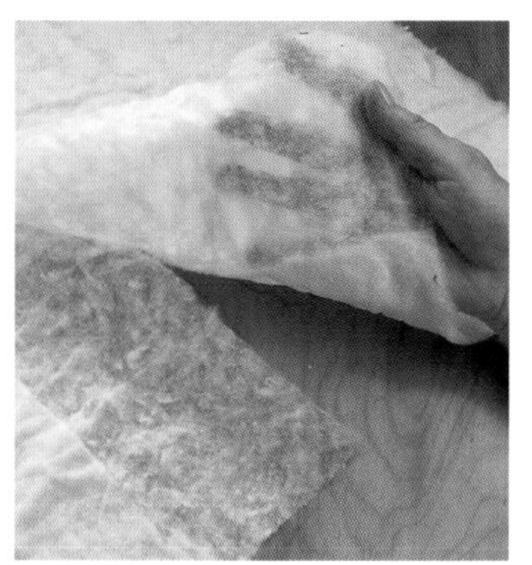
Overlap

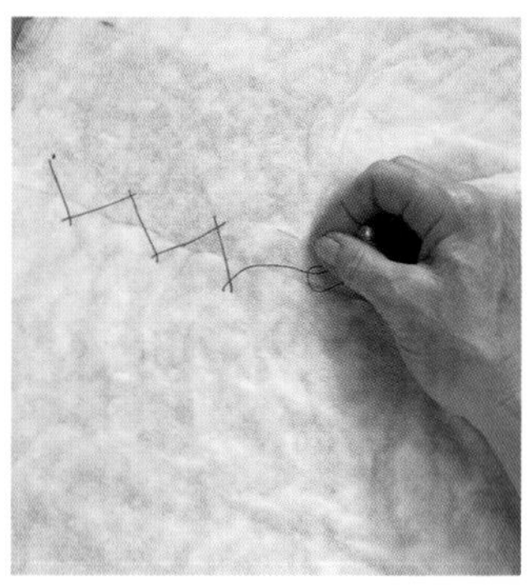
Stitch (use white thread to avoid show-through of stitches)

Splicing Batting

The batting should not be cut to the exact size of the quilt top. It is best to have at least 3″ (7.5 cm) extra all the way around. After all the quilting is complete, it will be trimmed. If you are unable to find a batting large enough for your quilt, you may have to splice two pieces together. To do this, use a type of batting that can be separated. Batting that is "needle-punched" cannot be separated, so check the label ahead of time. Orient the two pieces so that the straight grain, if there is one, is going the same direction on both pieces. Peel back about 4″ (10 cm) along the edge of each piece. Cut off the top of one piece and the bottom of the other and overlap them. Tack the two pieces together with large hem stitches. (For the photographs only, I used colored thread to make the stitches visible; I recommend using only white thread to hide these stitches.) Splicing the batting in this way eliminates the bulk caused if the two complete layers are simply overlapped. It also keeps the batting from separating, which would happen if the two pieces were simply butted next to each other.

Basting the Layers Together

Once the quilt top is complete and all preparations have been made, now is the time to layer the top with batting and backing. These three layers must be basted securely together so they do not slip during the quilting process. I have to admit that out of the entire process of making a quilt, this is my least favorite part. But I also have to say that once the three or four hours have been devoted to basting the layers, there is great satisfaction in seeing how different the top looks. Also, basting takes you one step closer to the most satisfying of all quiltmaking steps–taking the first quilting stitches.

Some people baste on a large table, moving the quilt layers as they get basted until the whole surface is complete. I find there is a tendency for the backing to bunch up because of the smooth table top, which also makes it difficult to square up the quilt. My preference is to baste on the floor on a carpet. You need a low-loft carpet (no shag), large enough to accommodate the size of the quilt. This is the procedure I use.

Quick Tip

It is worthwhile to enlist the help of a quilting friend when it is basting time. Not only will the time spent basting be cut in half, but two pairs of hands makes it easier to square up the top. Tell your friend that you will reciprocate when she is ready to baste her next quilt.

1. Lay the backing down onto the carpet with the wrong side facing up. Smooth it out very evenly. Go to the middle of one side of the backing and have a friend go to the opposite side. Each of you must take hold of the middle and stretch it slightly, then stick a pin at an angle directly into the carpet to secure the fabric in place. Insert two or three pins on either side of the first at about 4″ (10 cm) intervals. If you are alone, put the pins in one side and then go to the opposite side; stretch the backing slightly, and insert the pins on that side. Next, go to the other two sides of the backing and do the same. Then, working at opposite sides around the backing, slightly stretch and pin the entire backing to the carpet.
2. Carefully unfold the batting, checking to see if there is more stretch one way than another, and spread it out on top of the backing with the straight grain of the backing and batting matching. If the batting is larger than the backing, trim it down at this time to the size of the backing. Smooth out any wrinkles so that the batting lies perfectly flat.
3. Lay the quilt top onto the batting with the right side facing up. Carefully smooth it out. If the quilt has a border, have your friend go to one side, and you go to the opposite side and gently pull on the corners of the top, just at the point where the border begins. Pull slightly and insert a pin at that point. Do the same on all four corners. This is to help get the border straight. You may notice some slight fullness on the interior of the quilt top. Pat this down gently, evening out the fullness through the middle of the top. Put pins all along the inner part of the border in the same way as you prepared the backing. This time the pins can be about 8″ (20 cm) apart.
4. Next, working on opposite sides with your partner, pull slightly and pin the outer edge of the quilt top to the carpet. When this is all pinned, take a tape measure or yardstick and measure across the middle of the quilt in one direction. Move the tape or yardstick down, and make sure that the top is the same size all across. Next, do the measurements on the other side. If the quilt top is not evenly square or rectangular, adjust the pinning until it is.

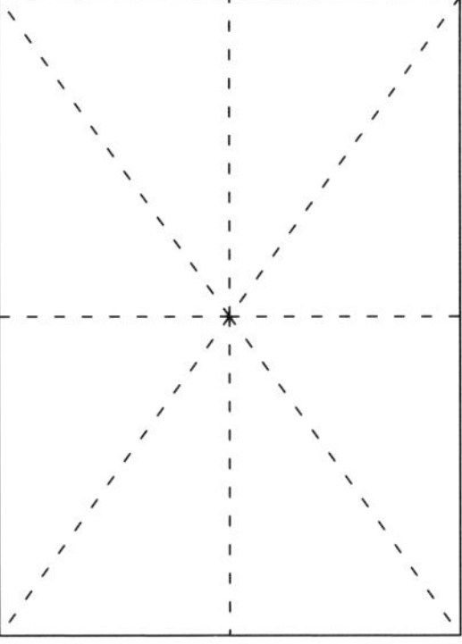

Preliminary basting

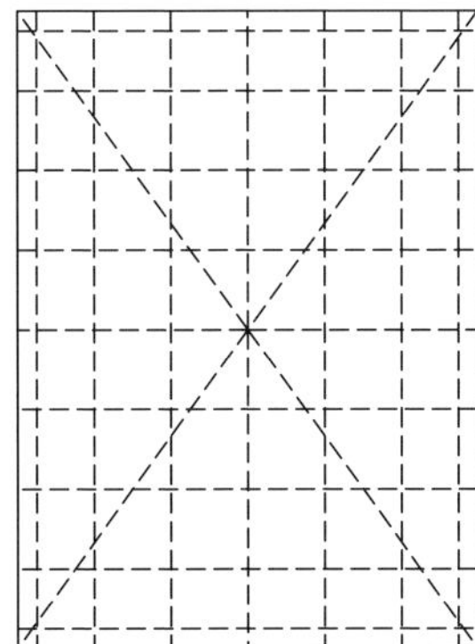

Basting grid

Finally, you are ready to begin basting. Fifty-weight sewing thread can be used, but basting thread is available for purchase–and it is less expensive than regular sewing thread. Select a light color. A dark thread may leave a dark fuzz on the surface.

Use a long, sturdy needle for basting (I like a milleners #3). Put a knot in the thread for the beginning stitches, but just leave the thread hang without a knot at the end of the row. This will make it easier to pull the basting stitches out when the quilting is complete. The stitches can be fairly large–up to 2″ (5 cm) long. To avoid sewing the quilt to the carpet, lift up slightly with each stitch to make sure you have not caught any of the carpet fibers with the needle. Begin at the center of the quilt and, working from the center each time, baste to the sides and then to the top and bottom. Again beginning at the center, make diagonal stitching lines to each of the corners. This is the preliminary basting.

Working from the middle of the quilt and in quarter sections, baste a grid over the entire surface. The lines of basting stitches should be no more than 6″ to 8″ (15 cm to 20 cm) apart.

"The authentic way to quilt is to have a large frame into which the whole coverlet is stretched. The frame itself is so simply constructed that every household used to have its own."

Ruby Short McKim,
101 Patchwork Patterns, 1931

Putting a Quilt in the Hoop or Frame

Some type of a frame is essential to get smooth even stitches. Whether it is a floor-standing frame or a hoop is a matter of personal preference and of available space in the home.

Hoop

If a hoop is to be used for quilting, it is advisable to bring the excess backing and batting over to the front of the quilt and baste it all around the edge of the quilt top. This will protect the batting as the quilt is moved in and out of the hoop and prevent it from getting torn and perhaps fraying into the actual quilt. Furthermore, cats and dogs seem to love to play with the fluffy batting. If you have an animal, this step may help avert a disaster.

The quilting hoop should be no smaller than 16″ (41 cm) across. If the hoop is any smaller, it will be difficult to get neat, even stitches. There will also be too much wear and tear on the quilt from taking it in and out of a hoop so many more times.

When using a hoop, it is best to begin at the center of the quilt and work outwards. Loosen the top ring of the hoop and separate the two pieces. Put the smaller ring under the quilt and, from the top, gently place the larger ring over the smaller one. Carefully pull the three layers all around the edge of the hoop until the portion inside is smooth and tight. Run your hand on the underneath side to make sure there are no puckers on the back side as well. When you are satisfied that there are no wrinkles on the top or bottom, and it is nice and tight, from underneath gently push up with your hand to loosen the quilt slightly. If the quilt is too tight in the hoop, it will be difficult to achieve small stitches.

Quilt as much as you can within the hoop. If you have not finished a line of stitching, but are at the edge of the frame, do not make a knot in the thread,

Install quilt in hoop and stretch tight

Push up from underneath

Secure edges

but just leave it hanging. Later you can rethread the needle and pick up where you left off.

When quilting the outer edges of the quilt, there will be portions that will not be fully enclosed by the hoop, yet it is important to continue to maintain the proper tension. Do this by lacing a strip of fabric around the hoop frame and pinning it to the quilt top as shown.

"Quite a simple frame may be made with four slats of wood, approximately 2½ in. wide, 1 in. thick and 9 in. to 12 in. longer than the quilt. These must be clamped together at the corners. To dress the frame cut four strips of calico or muslin about 12 in. wide and a little longer than the quilt. Attach these to the slats as follows: Fold one edge down for about 3½ in. fold. Place the slat near the other edge and fold the material over it for 1 in. Turn the slat and the material over and securely sew the edge to the double material of the 3½ in. fold. This will leave a loop for the quilt to be pinned to."

Ann Heynes,
Quilting and Patchwork, circa 1920

Frames

It seems that every early book on quilting had its own version of the typical quilting frame. All were quite similar. I by far prefer a traditional frame over a hoop for several reasons. First, when working on a large quilt there is so much bulk and weight to contend with all the time. In the summer, when it's hot, this makes quilting less pleasurable than it should be. Second, there is additional wear and tear on the quilt when it has to be moved in and out of the hoop. Third, I find I can get better stitches on a frame. I also find quilting on a frame more comfortable than quilting with a hoop. Both hands are free to work and it is not necessary to also contend with supporting the hoop. My last reason for preferring a frame may seem silly–I guess it is psychological–but I like the larger frame because you know always exactly how much quilting has been done and can gauge the time it will take to finish the quilt.

Pin to ticking all the way across

Begin rolling until quilt is fairly tight

Quilting in a Frame

There are a variety of full-size quilting frames available today. I use a fairly standard style that is similar to the original Stearns and Foster pattern from the 1930s. If you are handy, you may want to make the frame yourself, following that pattern, or simply put pieces of wood together as described in the quote on the previous page. If your frame is different than the one described there, follow the manufacturer's instructions as to how to put the quilt in the frame.

A traditional frame is made up of two "horses" and two long bars. The horses have notches to hold the bars in place. One of the bars has ratchets at both ends that match a piece on the horses. These ratchets tighten the quilt.

The bars have ticking or other sturdy fabric nailed along the edge. Begin by pinning or basting one edge of the quilt to the strip of fabric on the bar. If you are pinning, have the pins very close together. If you are basting, use a sturdy thread and take fairly small stitches with frequent backstitches. Make sure that the quilt is basted or pinned tight all the way across.

The opposite edge of the quilt is attached to the other bar in the same manner. Here, though, care must be taken to ensure that this edge is exactly opposite the edge that is pinned to the first bar. If the quilt goes into the frame crooked, it will be crooked when the quilting is finished. To avoid this, measure from the end of the first bar to the pinned edge of the quilt. Now measure this same distance from the edge of the opposite bar, and begin attaching the other edge of the quilt at this spot on the bar.

After two opposite edges of the quilt have been attached to the strips on the two bars, roll the bar without the ratchets until the center of the quilt is close to the bar. Carefully smooth the quilt towards the edges. When you reach the center of the quilt, insert the bar into the notches on the frame. Insert the bar with the ratchets into the other notches and begin rolling until the quilt is fairly tight.

Attach sides to narrow strips of fabric

Quilt installed in a frame

At this point, even though the quilt is going to appear tight in the frame, it is still fairly loose. Bring your arms and hands to chin level with your hands overlapped and your elbows out to the side, then lean over the portion of the quilt that is on top of the frame. Gently push down on the quilt all the way across. Your arms should be pushing about a 24″ (60 cm) section of the quilt at a time. This is going to slightly stretch the quilt and tighten it on the bars. Now tighten the quilt by rolling the ratchets one more time.

The sides of the quilt that are not attached to the bars must also be tightened. This is accomplished by lacing long, narrow strips of fabric around the horses and pinning them at intervals along each edge of the quilt. These will have to be unpinned and attached again each time the quilt is rolled.

Preparing Your Hand-Pieced Quilt for Quilting

If you have been working with one of the projects in this book, take whatever steps you need to finish the top and then *do not* set it aside. It is exciting to think about beginning another hand-piecing project, but if you put the newly finished top away, it can sometimes be a long time before you get back to it. Rather than let time pass, prepare the top for quilting and get it into a hoop or frame. If the quilt is sitting in sight, it will be easier to take a few stitches here and there. Only after it is all ready for quilting should you look to your next hand piecing project. In fact, I always like to have both a quilting and a piecing project going at all times. I keep my piecing project in a bag to carry with me when I am out of the house and the quilting project to work on in odd moments at home.

Quilting and Finishing

". . . for it was the quilting rather than the piecing—difficult and exacting as this was in many instances—that required the last degree of needlework attainment . . . Quilting was an accomplishment into which went not only technique but feeling."

Ruth E. Finley, *Old Patchwork Quilts and the Women Who Made Them*, 1929

"Quilting.—This term is employed to denote Runnings made in any materials threefold in thickness, i.e., the outer and right side textile, a soft one next under it, and a lining: Runnings being made diagonally, so as to form a pattern of diamonds, squares, or octagons, while serving to attach the three materials securely together."

S. F. A. Caulfield and Blanche C. Saward, *The Dictionary of Needlework*, 1882

Given its rather sterile definition of the quilting process, *The Dictionary of Needlework* does little to evoke the depth of feeling that Ruth Finley so aptly equates with hand quilting. There is a certain serenity and peace of mind that comes while quilting. At this point, all the decisions have been made and all that is required is to stitch according to a plan that you have already devised. Somehow, the simple repetitive action of taking the needle in and out offers a kind of meditation.

After I had been quilting for several years, a conversation with an old friend made me realize how true this is. My friend told me how she attended meditation classes twice a week, for two or three hours at a time. Knowing that I could never sit that long without doing something, I asked what happened during meditation. She explained it as a period of sitting in silence, during which you are able to come to grips with your inner self and reflect on what you feel. When the conversation was over, I remember thinking that is exactly what a quiet moment of quilting does for me!

Simple Preparations for Better Stitches

There are various considerations to keep in mind when the stitching is to commence. All contribute to a better quilting stitch. Once your quilt is in the frame, make sure that you consider each of these simple but important preparatory measures.

Light

Make sure the frame is situated where it will get good light. I like to quilt by a window to capture as much daylight as possible. *However, if your frame is next to a window, when not quilting, you should draw the curtains or cover the quilt with a sheet so that the sun does not fade the fabrics.* It is also important to have a good lamp that will direct the light right onto the area being quilted. I use a floor standing Ott Light, which has a moveable arm that can be twisted and turned to direct the light exactly where needed. I move this light up and down the frame as the quilting is done in different areas.

Sitting Position

When you first begin quilting with a frame you may experience all sorts of temporary discomforts. A lot of these discomforts may have to do with how high or low you are sitting in relation to the frame and how far into the quilt you are reaching. It may take a while to find the right chair and the right position to be comfortable, but you will be rewarded in the end with a much neater and smaller quilting stitch.

I recently taught a friend how to quilt using a frame. She had always done all of her quilting in her lap, without a frame or a hoop. I insisted that she should just try a frame and offered to lend her mine. First, she called to complain that her back was hurting. I told her that maybe it was the height of her chair. She was using an adjustable-height chair and tried several different heights. She called again to say her back was *still* hurting. I again asked about the chair. It was an office chair with a soft cushion. I realized the cushion was probably the problem, since I always use a straight-backed chair with a plain wooden seat. My friend switched to a plain kitchen chair, but called back a few days later–her back was better but now her *neck* was sore. I asked how far she was reaching into the center of the quilt while stitching. She replied that she was reaching across as far as she could go, probably 12″ to 18″ (30 cm to 45 cm). I told her to work all the way across the frame in only about a 5″ or 6″ (12 cm to 15 cm) section and to avoid reaching so far. She tried that and from there on had no problems. The quilting stitches in that quilt are far superior to the ones she had done without the use of a frame, and it only took her a short time to master the technique of quilting in a frame.

This story is related here to let you know to persevere. If you get a back ache or a neck ache, change the chair you are using, change the positioning of your body, or don't try to reach quite so far into the quilt to do the stitching. Keep the area being stitched a reasonable distance from you, then roll the frame and begin a new area.

The quilting process is exactly the same when a hoop is used. Yet I find that a hoop gets a little cumbersome because, while both hands are busy stitching, you also need to support the hoop. I rest the edge of the hoop on a table or the arm of a chair. The one advantage of a hoop over a large frame is that if you find it easier to quilt in one direction than any other, the hoop can be easily turned so that you are always able to quilt in that direction.

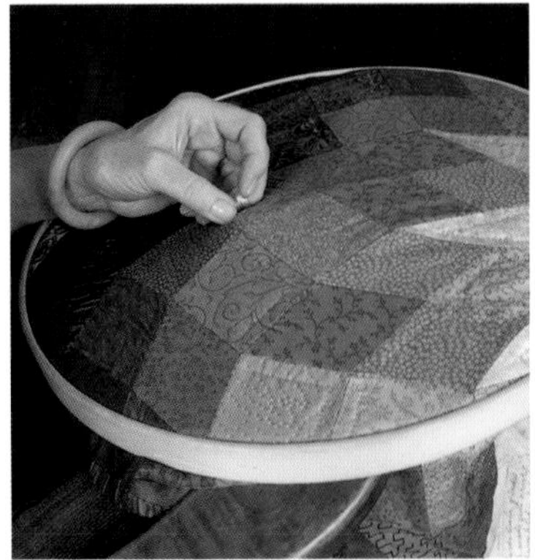

Rest hoop on the arm of a chair

"Telling you how to quilt is almost as impossible to write in words as to describe an accordion without moving your hands. One quilter says use a short needle, another holds out for a long needle, nicely curved! After trying it and observing experts it seems to me that the trick is in sewing clear around and back again like your hand could roll around the small curved units, sort of a standing on your head effect. Aye, this is the rub that may keep the quilts of today from really rivaling the ones of yester-year."

Ruby Short McKim,
101 Patchwork Patterns, 1931

The Quilting Stitch

Begin quilting at the *center* of the quilt and work your way out to the edges. When using a hoop, begin quilting at the center and keep working outwards in concentric circles towards the edge. When using a large frame, begin at the center and quilt from the center all the way to both edges. Then roll the quilt away from you and continue in this manner until you have quilted the first half. Roll the quilt to the center again and quilt the second half.

Quick Tip

Most people use a "Between" needle for quilting. These come in a variety of sizes. My preference is size 11. I find this needle strong enough so it does not readily bend, yet thin enough to glide easily through the fabric. It is difficult to get small stitches if the needle is too large. Begin with the smallest needle you feel comfortable with and, once accustomed to that, try the next size smaller. The larger the number of the needle, the smaller the size.

The Beginning Knot

Just as with piecing, the thread should be cut about 18" (45 cm) long, and you will need a knot to both begin and end the stitching. The knot for beginning is the same that you would make for piecing (see page 68). However, with piecing the knots will always be at the wrong side of the work. When quilting, all the wrong sides are now in the middle, between the layers, and the knot should not show on either the top or back of the quilt. It must be hidden between the layers.

To hide the knot, insert the needle into the quilt top about 1" (2.5 cm) away from where you will begin stitching. Make sure the needle does not go through to the back of the work, but just between the layers. Push it between the layers to the spot where you will begin to quilt. Bring the tip of the needle up at exactly that spot.

Exit exactly where you will start quilting

Gently tug thread . . .

. . . and knot will pop between layers

The Beginning Knot

Pull the thread through until the knot is lying on the quilt surface. Then, gently tug on the thread to pop the knot through the quilt top and bury it in the batting.

Every once in a while you may tug too hard, and the knot will pull right through. Other times it might be difficult to get the knot to pull through as far as the batting. In these cases, it might help to adjust the *size* of the knot. You will soon get a feel for what size knot works best.

An alternate method is to not make a beginning knot at all. Cut the thread 36″ (90 cm) long instead of 18″ (45 cm). When beginning the first stitch, pull the thread through half way. Begin stitching with a small backstitch which will secure the thread and quilt with the first half of the thread. When your thread runs out, go back and thread the needle with the remaining 18″ (45 cm) of thread and begin another line of stitching.

"As each stitch is made the left hand, below, feels where the needle will come through and helps it up again, whilst the right thumb presses down the material just ahead of where the needle will emerge . . . Take several stitches on the needle before pulling it through and try to work with a rhythmical movement, which helps to keep the stitches even. They should be the same size above and below, and the spaces should be the same length as the stitches."

Mavis FitzRandolph and Florence M. Fletcher,
Quilting: Traditional Methods and Design, 1955

Taking the First Stitches

Just as there is a lack of guidance on the techniques of hand piecing, a study of vintage quilting books also shows that very little was written about the actual process of the quilting stitch. The quote here is the most descriptive I have found.

The stitches used for quilting and piecing are both basically a running stitch. However, their execution is entirely different. Quilting is a completely new skill, and it takes some practice to get comfortable with the way it is done and to get small, even stitches. It can be very discouraging at first, and many people want to give up, believing they just can't do it. But have faith and a little perseverance and you will be rewarded. Like any other new skill, it just takes a little bit of practice.

Do not get discouraged if your stitches are large. It is more important to have even stitches than to have small stitches. Concentrate on having the same size stitches on both the front and the back of the work, which means getting the distance between the stitches to be the same length as the stitch. As you progress and become more comfortable with using a frame, you will find that your stitches will become smaller.

As you begin to quilt, you will soon find there will be a certain direction of stitching that is easiest for you. Most people find that quilting towards them is the easiest, but it is not always possible to stitch in that direction. Often the design may dictate that you quilt in a horizontal line or even away from you. It will take practice before you discover which direction feels right. When quilting in more than one direction, you may find that your hand position changes as well. I have a different position when quilting towards me than I do when quilting at a slight angle away from me or in a horizontal line. Everyone works a little differently, and what is comfortable for one person may not be right for another. There are no rigid rules–experiment until you find what works best for you. The photographs and explanations here of how I stitch in two different directions may help you to find the best position. No matter which direction I am quilting, the needle always rests against the *side*–never the tip–of the thimble, which is worn on the middle finger of the hand on top of the quilt.

"When the work is quite prepared for the quilting it should be started with the needle pointed towards the worker, and small, even stitches made, which pass through the three materials."

Ann Heynes,
Quilting and Patchwork, 1925

Quilting Towards the Body

Since most people seem more at ease quilting towards themselves, try this direction first. Follow these steps.

1. With the eye of the needle resting on the *side* of the thimble, insert the needle straight down into the quilt. The needle must be at a right angle to the quilt surface. Feel the tip of the needle with a finger of the underneath hand.
2. As that hand feels the needle, use the thimble to bring the needle down in an arc until it is parallel to the quilt. The thumb of the top hand immedi-

Step 1. *Insert needle straight down into quilt*

Feel tip of needle from underneath

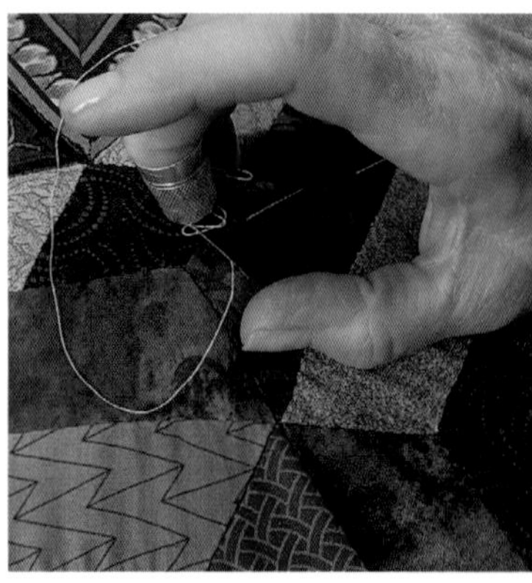

Step 2. *Bring needle down in an arc until it is parallel to quilt*

Step 3. *As soon as tip comes back up, bring needle perpendicular*

ately moves in front of the tip of the needle to help push the quilt down, so that the tip can come back up in as small a stitch as possible.

3. As soon as the tip of the needle comes back up, immediately bring the needle perpendicular again, then insert the tip into the quilt once more. The thimble all the time maintains a slight but even pressure on the needle so that it does not go in or come back up too far.
4. Continue this rocking back and forth of the needle until three or four stitches have been taken and then pull up the thread.

"The patience and skill of the quilter are especially taxed when, in following the vagaries of some design, she is forced to quilt lines that extend away from her instead of toward her."

MARIE D. WEBSTER,
Quilts: Their Story & How to Make Them, 1915

Quilting Horizontally or Away from the Body

When quilting horizontally or away from myself, my stitching technique is a little different. Working in this direction, it is very difficult to get the thumb of the top hand in front of the needle. Also, the thimble finger seems to need extra help to guide the needle up and down. I use the index finger and thumb to help

Step 1. *Guide needle through layers with index finger and thumb*

Step 2. *Push needle back up with underneath hand*

Step 3. *Guide needle back down . . .*

. . . and push it back up

Step 4. *Use thimble to push needle through . . .*

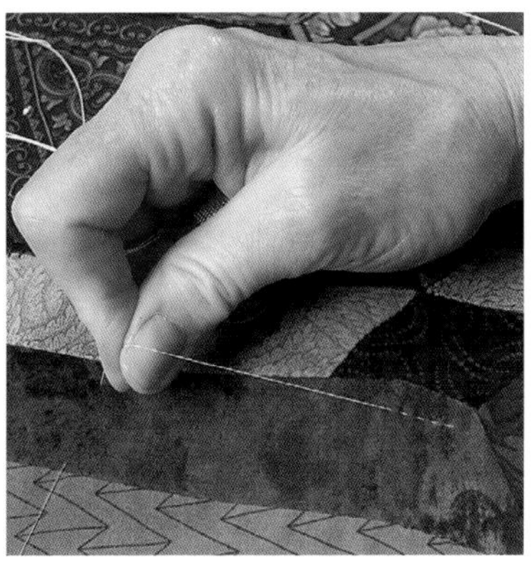

. . . Pull thread to create proper tension

guide the needle. Then, when I get several stitches on the needle, I move the thumb nearer to the front of the needle to help pull it through the cloth. These are the steps.

1. With the needle resting against the *side* of the thimble, guide it down through the layers with the index finger and thumb.
2. With the underneath finger, push the needle back up.
3. Immediately guide the needle back down again and push it back up.
4. Once there are several stitches on the needle, use the thumb to help push the fabric down, so the thimble can push the needle through. Pull the thread and give a slight tug to the stitches for the proper tension (see page 189).

"The stitching itself may be described as a running or darning stitch, not a stab stitch. The worker must keep her left hand under the work and must prick her finger every time the needle comes through the quilt, so as to ensure a perfect stitch on both sides of the work, and no one should be able to say on which side the quilting was done. It stands to reason that the thicker the quilt the coarser the stitching, but evenness counts for higher points than small stitches."

Beatrice Scott,
The Craft of Quilting, 1935

Time to end stitching

Take backstitch

Work needle through layers to seam . . .

. . . and pull thread up

Take another backstitch in the seam . . .

. . . and work through layers again, coming up ½" (1.5 cm) away from seam

Take backstitch and work through layers for about 1" (2.5 cm)

Pull on thread and cut close to quilt

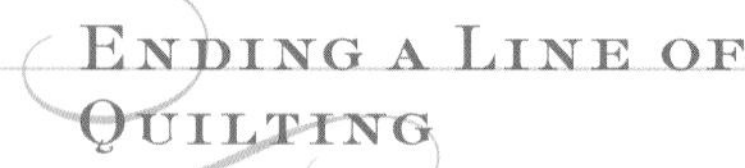

> *"When only a few inches of cotton are left in the needle, run it through the padding and bring it up, still on the line of the pattern; put it down again over only one thread of the material and repeat this until the cotton is finished. When a fresh needleful is started the new stitches will hold the end securely."*
>
> Mavis FitzRandolph and Florence M. Fletcher, *Quilting*, 1955

Ending a Line of Quilting

When you come to the end of a line of stitching, it is not necessary to end the thread and begin anew. As long as you still have thread, take a small backstitch to secure the line of stitching and then run the needle between the layers and come up in a new patch at the place where the stitching will start. Take another small backstitch and continue quilting.

When there is not enough thread to continue, it is time to end off. Some people make a knot at the end of the line of quilting and pop it through to the middle of the quilt. I prefer to take a small backstitch, work my needle through the layers to the seam and pull the thread up. I then take another backstitch in the seam and work the needle through the layers again, coming up about ½"

Insert needle straight down

Lower needle in an arc until it is parallel with quilt

Put thumb in front to help push fabric down

Once several stitches are on needle, pull thread up

(1.5 cm) away from the seam. If there is still thread left, I take another tiny backstitch and work the needle through the layers again for about 1″ (2.5 cm). I pull up slightly on the thread and cut close to the quilt so the thread end will be lost between the layers. *Caution, don't cut too close to the quilt, or you may snip the cloth by mistake!*

Quilting Left-Handed

The identical process described in the previous pages is also used when quilting left handed. With the right hand underneath, insert the needle straight down. Push the tip back up from underneath and at the same time bring the needle parallel to the quilt and the thumb of the left hand in front of the tip to help bring the needle out. Continue the process until there are several stitches on the needle. Then pull the needle through and give a slight tug to the stitches.

Maintaining Proper Tension

The main purpose of a frame or hoop is to maintain proper tension in the work, so that the stitches will be smooth and even. Embroiderers always use a hoop, since it helps them avoid pulling the thread too tight, causing puckering. It also prevents them from leaving the thread too loose, with the result that the stitches do not achieve a relief. The very same principles apply to quilting. Without a frame, the stitches might be too tight or too loose. Quilting stitches look best when the thread is pulled just the right amount to give relief to each stitch. The hoop or frame allows this to occur and gives the stitches a more finished look.

When quilting, three or four stitches are usually taken at a time, before the thread is drawn up. Each time I pull up the thread, I give a slight pull on the stitches. This "sets" the stitches and helps to create a nice evenness to the work.

Uneven Stitches

Many new quilters find, just as I did, that the first stitch they make is larger than the others. How is it possible to get even stitches when that first one is so big? First of all, you have to understand *why* it is difficult to make the first stitch smaller. The main reason is that the needle is being pushed in too far. Think

Quick Tip

It is easy to check to see if your stitches are too tight or too loose when the quilt is stretched in a frame. Insert the tip of a needle into one of the stitches and then try to pull up the thread a little. If you cannot even get the needle into a stitch, the tension is too tight. If you can pull up any excess thread, the stitches are too loose. Another way to check on the tension is to run a finger along a stitching line on the back side of the quilt. There is good tension if you can feel the ridge of the stitches. If you do not feel any stitches at all, then the thread has not been pulled tight enough.

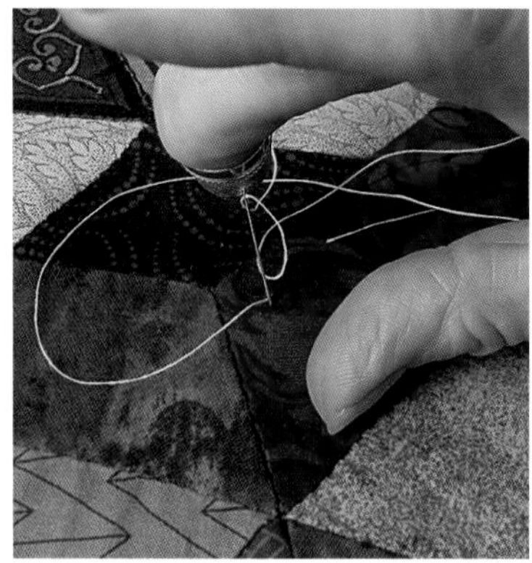

Make sure needle is perfectly perpendicular to the quilt

about it. There is a nice slick needle and three layers of cloth. It is difficult to push the needle in the first time by just the right amount because it is so slippery. If it is not pushed in far enough, the stitch won't show on the back; if it is pushed in too far, the stitch will be too big. As the second and third and fourth stitches are taken, there will be resistance on the needle because of the extra bulk of the fabric. This bulk makes it easier to get consistent stitches. A small pressure from the thimble will push the needle just the right amount, and it is not as easy for the needle to slip in too far.

The best way to ensure that the first stitch will be as small as possible is to make sure that the needle is perfectly perpendicular to the quilt and that it goes straight down into the cloth, as shown here.

"If you try quilting continuously for several hours your fingers are apt to become very sore. A remedy for this is to dip them in hot alum water which toughens the membrane."

Ruby Short McKim,
101 Patchwork Patterns, 1931

Spoon Quilting

It is common for the fingers on the hand underneath the quilt to get sore from constantly being pricked by the needle as it goes into the layers. If the finger isn't there to catch the tip of the needle and push it back up again, there is a risk that the stitch will not go all the way through to the back of the quilt. For years, I constantly had calluses on my fingers. When one finger got sore, I would switch to the next. Before long, since I quilt with both hands, all my fingers were sore.

Over the years, quilters have devised various ways to relieve this problem. Some people hammer the top of a thimble to flatten it into a ridge. Then this thimble is used underneath the quilt. The needle hits the ridge, and the thimble finger pushes the needle back up. There are now some thimbles made that already have a metal extension that serves this same purpose. Another device, Aunt Becky's Finger Protector, is just a flat piece of metal that has been bent into a tent shape. The "tent" fits over the underneath finger and does pretty much the same thing as a flattened thimble.

I saw a most ingenious method of protecting the finger during a trip through South Carolina. I happened upon a small quilt shop and went inside. I heard laughter coming from the back room and poked my head in. A group of ladies sat around a quilting frame, working away. One older lady was going to town! She had that needle going in and out faster than I had ever seen before. I commented that she must do a lot of quilting, and she replied "Oh, yes, I quilt every day for several hours a day." I asked her how she kept her fingers from getting sore. Well, she got a big smile on her face and whipped out that underneath hand and proudly held up her thumb. And there, securely taped to her

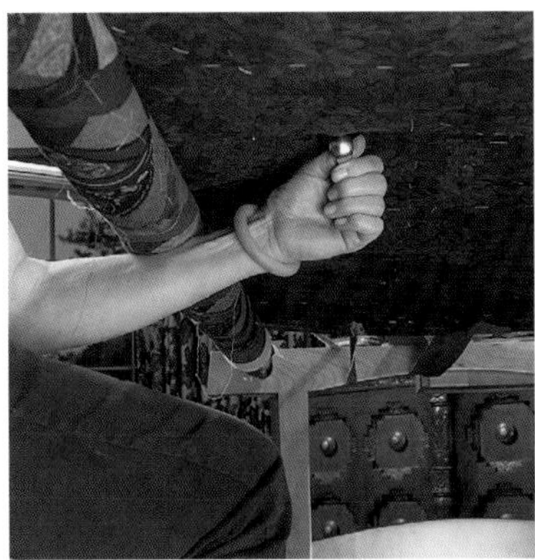

Step 1. *Hold spoon in underneath hand*

Step 2. *Position outside of bowl of spoon at spot where needle will come through*

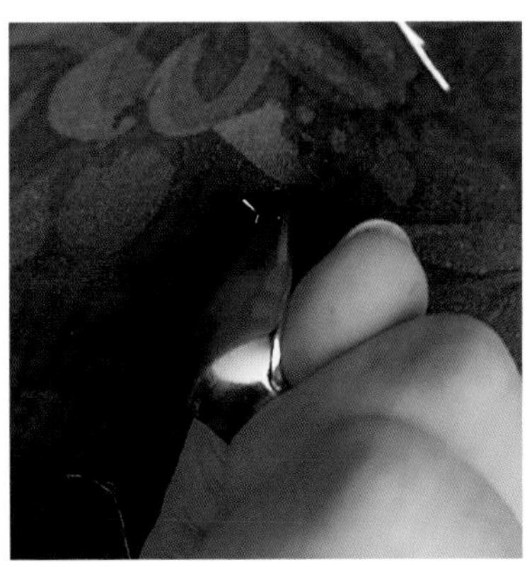

Step 4. *Needle deflects off spoon*

thumb, was a quarter! That quarter served the same purpose as a pounded thimble or a piece of metal placed over the finger.

I quilted for years without using anything to protect my fingers, but a friend, Gayle Ropp, kept talking about using a spoon on the underneath side. Finally, in desperation, I tried it. I got an old stainless steel spoon from the kitchen and, for a time, it worked. The problem was that the spoon became so scratched that it dulled the needle, and the needle kept catching in the grooves. Then Gayle showed me her spoon–TJ's Quick Quilter. Made specifically for quilters, it is nickel plated so that it does not get scratched–and it produces smooth even stitches. I now use it all the time. This is how it works.

1. Hold the spoon in the hand that goes underneath the quilt.
2. The outside of the bowl of the spoon faces the spot where the needle will come through to the back of the quilt.
3. The tip of the spoon pokes up into the quilt, just in front of where the needle is stitching. This pushing up from underneath with the edge of the spoon serves the same purpose as pushing down in front of the needle with the thumb of the hand on top. This is how I am able to quilt away from me and still get small stitches. The spoon takes over from the thumb that can't get into position.
4. As the needle comes down, it hits the bowl and, as it does, the spoon is rocked forward so that the needle slips up the bowl and slides off the tip of the spoon. The spoon is then rocked back so the bowl will catch the next stitch, and then pushed forward so that the needle deflects off the tip. Before long a smooth, rocking motion is developed.

Quilting with a spoon or other similar devise serves several purposes. As well as keeping fingers from getting callused and sore, it helps maintain uniformity of the stitches. It also helps ensure that the stitches on the back are just as good as the ones on the front.

"As the result of many years spent over the quilting frame, some quilters acquire an unusual dexterity in handling the needle, and occasionally one is encountered who can quilt as well with one hand as with the other."

Marie D. Webster,
Quilts: Their Story & How to Make Them, 1915

Quilting with Either Hand

No different from most new quilters, I enjoyed making my first quilt top and knew that I wanted to make many more quilts. But my first attempts at quilting that first top were extremely discouraging. I couldn't make small stitches. Furthermore, the first stitch always seemed larger than the rest. I couldn't get comfortable. Even though I had enjoyed making the top, it seemed that quilting just wasn't for me.

After a couple of weeks of struggling, a funny thing happened. I am ambidextrous and do some things with my left hand, others with my right, and still other things with either hand. Since I had been hand piecing with my right hand, I just figured that I would also quilt right-handed. One day, in the middle of my frustration, it seemed that the quilting was going better, that the stitches were smaller, and that I wasn't struggling so much. It suddenly hit me–I was quilting with my left hand on top! It felt natural and as though I had been doing it for a long time. I didn't even remember picking the needle up in that hand.

Eventually, I became comfortable quilting with either hand. It is very convenient being able to switch hands, especially when working on a large quilting frame. Now I urge everyone to try quilting with either hand. Since quilting is a completely new skill and something that must be learned anyway, why not see if quilting with the opposite hand will work for you?

Finding the Best Direction for Quilting

Quilting can be done with the needle and stitches coming towards you, away from you, at an angle, or in a horizontal line. Depending on what you are quilting, it will be necessary at one time or another to go all of those directions. You will most likely find that going one way is easier for you than another. All quilters have their own preferences.

Once you find a direction that is most comfortable for you, try to plan the quilting to take best advantage of it. For instance, I find quilting in a horizontal line, at a slight angle upwards, or towards me are the easiest directions for me to quilt. Therefore, when quilting a row of triangles, rather than try to quilt around a complete triangle and then go to the next one, (up one side, down the next, and then back to the beginning, where it would mean practically standing on my head), I quilt up one angle of the triangle, down the next, then put

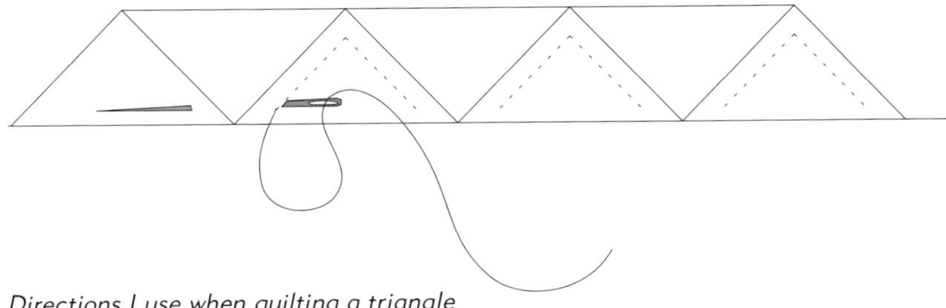

Directions I use when quilting a triangle

the needle between the layers and come into the next triangle. This up and down quilting pattern continues until the thread is finished. Then with a new thread, I go back to the first triangle and quilt across the base. I then pass the needle and thread through the layers to the next triangle, and continue quilting the bases of the triangles.

> *"Too much stress can hardly be placed on the quilting, for after all, this is what really 'makes' the quilt, and gives it its personality."*
>
> Aunt Martha,
> *The Quilt Fair Comes to You*, 1932

Finishing Touches

As the quilting is approaching the finishing stages, I find myself spending more time at the frame. It is very exciting when the last stitch is finally taken. From there, all you need do is remove the strips attached at the sides of the quilt, unroll the bars of the frame, and carefully remove the pins on the stretcher bars. Remove all basting stitches, then trim off the excess batting and backing just to the edge of the quilt top.

Binding the Quilt

There are various methods of finishing off the edges once the quilting is complete. In fact, entire books are devoted to the finishing process. The most popular method (and the one I prefer) is a cut binding that is added around the quilt to finish off the raw edges. Binding can be cut from straight pieces of fabric or it can be cut on the bias. I prefer binding cut on the bias for two reasons. First, I think it gives a smoother finish to the edges of the quilt and, second, I believe bias is more durable over time. The edges of the quilt are going to get the most wear. Straight grain binding is folded along one continuous thread, creating a weakness that can cause it to wear and fray much more quickly. With bias binding, if a thread gets frayed, it will only go at a diagonal a short distance. To make the binding even more durable, I usually cut it twice as wide as the finished width, plus seam allowance, then I double it over.

The Quilting Bee

THE QUILTING BEE WAS a social event in many communities. After the quilt top was made, friends would be gathered and the women would quilt while the men worked. Then, after a certain amount of quilting and work was done, everyone would come together for a party. Many times the quilting bee was an actual coming out party for a young woman. "The Quilting Party," written by T. S. Arthur for the September 1849 issue of *Godey's Lady's Book*, gives insight into a typical quilting bee that took place 20 years earlier.

> "Our young ladies of the present generation know little of the mysteries of 'Irish chain,' 'rising star,' 'block work,' or 'Job's trouble,' and would be as likely to mistake a set of quilting frames for clothes poles as for anything else. It was different in our younger days. Half a dozen handsome patchwork quilts were as indispensable then as a marriage portion; quite as much so as a piano or guitar is at present. And the quilting party was equally indicative of the coming-out and being 'in the market,' as the fashionable gatherings together of the times that be . . . we are not disposed to sigh over it as indicative of social deterioration . . . And yet . . . we have never enjoyed ourselves with the keen zest and heartiness, in any company, that we have experienced in the old-fashioned quilting party . . . but we were young then . . . of the world we knew nothing beyond the quiet village; and there we found enough to fill the measure of our capacity . . . .
>
> "There was one quilting party—can we ever forget it? Twenty years have passed since the time . . . In our village there dwelt a sweet young girl, who was the favorite of all. When invitations to a quilting party at Mrs. Willing's came, you may be sure there was a flutter of delight all around. The quilting was Amy's, of course, and Amy Willing was to be the bright, particular star in the social firmament. It was to be Amy's first quilting . . . and the sign that she was looking forward to the matrimonial goal, was hailed with a peculiar pleasure by more than one of the village swains. . . .
>
> "We had been to many quilting parties up to this time; but more as a boy than as a man . . . We could play at blind man's buff, hunt the slipper, and pawns, and not only clasp the little hands of our fair playfellows, but even touch their warm lips with our own, and not experience a heart-emotion deeper than the ripple made on the smoother water by a playful breeze . . . There was an uneasy fluttering of the heart as the time drew near, and a pressure upon the feelings that a deep, sighing breath failed to remove . . . At last the evening came . . . The sun still lingered above the

horizon when we came in sight of the cottage—fashionable hours were earlier then than now . . . The room was full of girls, who were busy in binding Amy's quilt, which was already out of the frame, and getting all ready for the evening's sport . . . It was not long before the old-fashioned parlor was filled, and the but half-bound quilt was forcibly taken from the hands of the laughing seamstresses, and put 'out of sight and out of mind.' The bright, particular star of that evening was gentle, quiet, loving Amy Willing. When the time for redeeming pawns came, and it was our turn to call out from the circle of beauty a fair partner, the name of Amy fell from our lips, which were soon pressed, glowing, upon those of the blushing maiden . . . Soon it became Amy's place to take the floor. She must 'kiss the one she loved best.' . . . her eyes wandered around the room . . . 'Kiss the one you love best,' was repeated by the holder of the pawns . . . Our name at length came, in an undertone, from her smiling lips. What a happy moment! The envied kiss was ours, and we led the maiden in triumph from the floor. . . ."

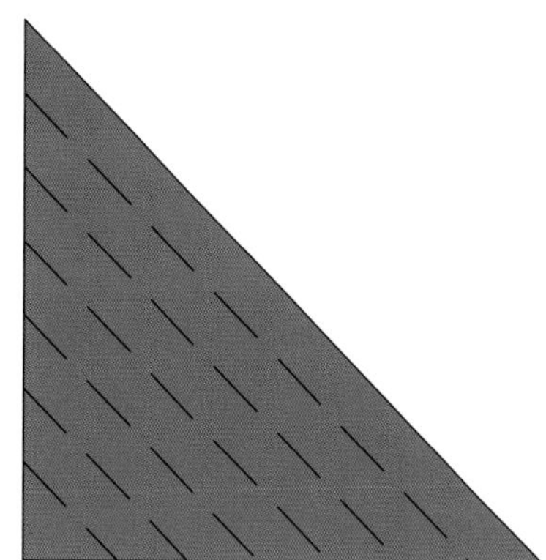

Step 2. Cut through both layers

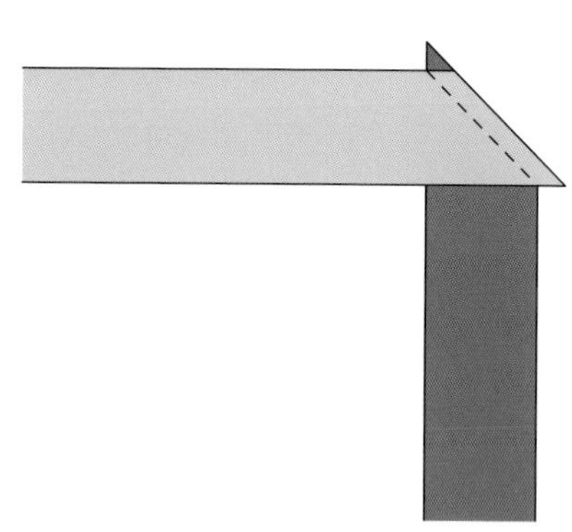

Step 3. Ends will be at correct angle for easy sewing

Cutting the Binding

For this double-fold bias binding, you will need to cut strips of fabric four times the desired finished width of the binding, plus the seam allowance. Most quilters cut their binding somewhere between 2″ and 2½″ (5 cm and 6.5 cm) wide.

1. Begin with at least ½ to 1 yard (0.5 m to 1 m) of fabric. Remove the selvages from both sides, fold the fabric in half on the diagonal, and press.
2. Cut along the fold, but leave the two pieces aligned. Using a see-through ruler and a piece of tailor's chalk, mark cutting lines the desired width, along the diagonal on the top piece of fabric. Cut through both layers.
3. With right sides facing, use a ¼″ (0.75 cm) seam allowance to sew the binding strips together at their ends. Since the strips have been cut all the way to the edge of the fabric, their ends should be at the correct angle.

Quick Tip

If you are adding a bias binding, *slightly* stretch the binding just a little as you pin. This will help to give a smooth edge to the quilt when the binding is finished. Do not stretch too much or the edge of the quilt will pucker. *Note: This stretching is only done when applying bias binding, not when working with straight binding.*

Attaching the Binding

The conventional way of adding binding is to sew it to the front of the quilt and then bring it to the back and stitch it down in an invisible hem stitch. When a border-print stripe is used as the final border around the outside of the quilt, I do the opposite. In order for the seam to look even, it is important to sew the binding directly to a line along the border print. Therefore, I pin the binding to the back of the quilt, sew the binding first to the back, and then bring it to the front. I use a small blind stitch and sew it alongside the edge of a line on the border print. For double-fold binding, follow these steps.

1. Fold the long binding strip in half lengthwise, wrong sides together, and gently press, making sure that the bias edges do not stretch.
2. Beginning along one side of the quilt, align the raw edges of the binding along the edge of the right side of the quilt. (If using a border print, align along *wrong* side.) Pin the binding to the quilt, leaving a 5″ (13 cm) tail. Pin small sections at a time.
3. Working with the front side of the quilt facing you, (if a border-print is used on the outside edge of the quilt, align the raw edges of the binding along

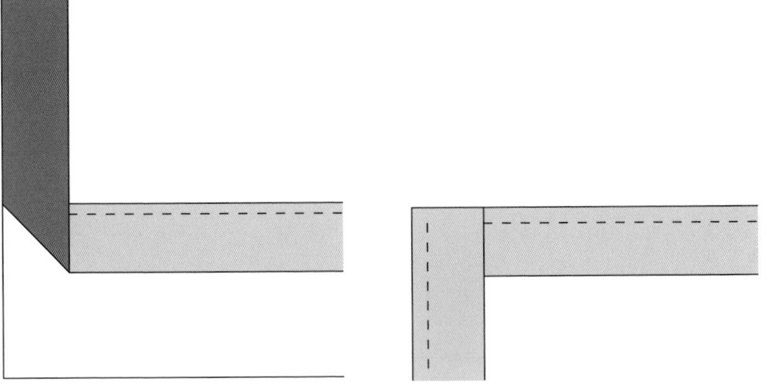

Step 4. Fold up at 45° angle

Fold strip back down

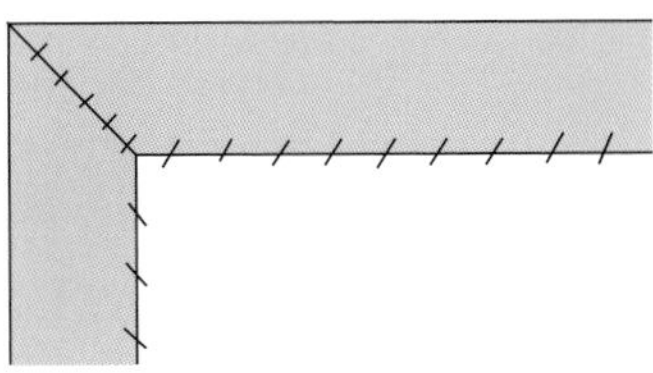

Step 7. At corner, fold adjacent sides to form miter

the *wrong* side of the quilt), sew ¼″ (0.75 cm) from the edge, stitching just outside a line on the border-print design, if there is one.

4. As you approach a corner, stop stitching ¼″ (0.75 cm) from the edge and take a backstitch. Fold the binding strip up at a 45° angle. Fold the strip back down so there is a crease at the upper edge. Insert the needle through the base of the fold and continue sewing down the next side.
5. When you are approximately 8″ (20 cm) from the original starting point, take the piece you are currently sewing and bring it over to meet the 5″ (13 cm) tail. Cut off the excess binding, allowing enough length to connect the two ends and have a 5″ (13 cm) overlap (it is better to cut it too long than too short). Cut the binding to match the angle of the original tail. Fold under ¼″ (0.75 cm) at the cut-off end and press. Slip the raw edges of the 5″ (13 cm) tail inside the folded edges. Blind stitch the ends together.
6. Carefully pin and sew this last bit of binding down.
7. Bring the binding over to the front of the quilt and blind stitch the folded edge in place along the line of the border print, covering the first set of stitches with the folded edge. At the corners fold in the adjacent sides to form a miter. Take several stitches in the miter on both sides of the quilt.

Signing and Dating the Quilt

Over the years I have accumulated a collection of antique quilts. Of all I have, there is only one that has initials and a date. How sad that we know so little about the people who stitched these wonderful heirlooms.

I urge you to sign and date your finished quilt. There are a variety of permanent markers available which you can use to sign and date the front or back of the quilt. You might prefer stitching the information directly into the quilt or sewing a label onto the back.

Whether the signature is simple or elaborate, it is so important to document your work as part of our quilt history and heritage and as a legacy to your family. Those simple stitches that have turned into an exquisite quilt will be a reminder to all who view it of your dedication and your love of the craft.

Patterns

Ten Hand-Pieced Quilts

"It will be a great pity if this lovely and traditional craft is allowed to die out, it is so typical of our country life. Of course, a large frame in a small house is very cumbersome, and it certainly is very trying to have to make the fingers so sore, but surely to create such lovely things it is worth while. In all the present-day hurry, it is restful to look back on the peaceful leisured workers who employed their spare time to such effort, and achieved such art, and who would be 'scumfished' [astonished] at the interest and wonder which their work arouses in the eyes of visitors."

BEATRICE SCOTT, *The Craft of Quilting*, 1935

THE PATTERNS ARE ARRANGED IN ORDER OF DIFFICULTY. They begin with a simple design made by joining rectangles—the first piecing technique you learned—and end with a *Mariners' Compass* and *Day Lilies*, two designs that too often may be considered beyond the abilities of beginners. Once you have practiced each technique covered in the piecing chapters, you will be able to make any of these quilts. All require the same piecing skills.

To demonstrate that this is the case, look at the patterns for *Columbia* and *Starflower* on pages 226 and 230. Many who see these quilts are surprised to hear that I use both for teaching *beginning* hand-piecing classes. Most students come to class without any hand-piecing skills—some have never even threaded a needle. I title the class "Mystery Quilt—Beginning Hand Piecing." The quilt is a mystery, because students do not see what the finished design looks like until the next-to-last class.

In the first of six classes on *Columbia*, we begin with fabric selection and learn how to make a simple running stitch. We then learn how to match four points. Students go home with the assignment of piecing individual sets of squares and triangles together. (These are the patches that eventually form the border strips of *Columbia*.) By next class, all are expert in joining four points. In the second session, students join three points. At home, they sew sets of squares and triangles into long strips. They also make the smallest wedges needed for the outer points of the compass at the center of *Columbia*. In the third class, we experiment with border prints and learn how to mirror-image designs. At home, everyone completes the large border-print points in *Columbia* and the background pieces that go on either side of the compass. They also sew the small wedges for the compass to either side of the next-largest set of points. This is more joining of three points. In the fourth class, we experiment further with border prints and cut the pieces for the central star. We then learn how to join eight points. The fifth class teaches curved piecing, as students add the corner pieces to the compass design. I show how all the disparate pieces come together for the main body of the quilt. During the last class, students learn how to add border prints to frame the quilt.

I cannot describe how much fun it is to teach a class in this way. By the last session, students are very excited that they have created such a complex-looking quilt with such simple skills. We always end up scheduling a reunion class so students can bring in their finished projects. The quilts all look different because of the wonderful variations among the fabrics selected.

The reason for explaining my mystery quilt method at such length is to persuade you that–once you have practiced the piecing techniques in *Quiltmaking by Hand*–none of these quilts is too difficult for you. All use the same simple skills, and all are within your reach.

Yardages for Borders and Backing

To make sure that you do not run short of fabric, all the yardages provided are generous. At first glance, it may seem that the recommended yardages for borders will give you more fabric than you need. Why not, for instance, save on fabric by cutting borders across the width of the bolt (selvage to selvage), rather than lengthwise? I advise against cutting across the width for three reasons. First, I don't like unnecessary seams in the borders, since I feel that they detract from the look of the quilt. Second, if there is any specific design or motif in the fabric, cutting cross-grain will distort it. The design will not run straight. Third, since there is more stretch across the width of the fabric, cutting the borders this way could cause the quilt to ruffle at the edges (see page 145).

For most patterns, the yardages provided assume that you will piece the backing widthwise to save on fabric. However, for rectangular quilts, I like to piece the backing lengthwise, depending on how the quilt will hang. I prefer the straight grain of the backing to be perpendicular to the floor. This lends more stability and helps to keep the quilt from sagging. Note how the yardages have been calculated for each of the patterns, and if you wish to piece your backing differently, make the adjustments.

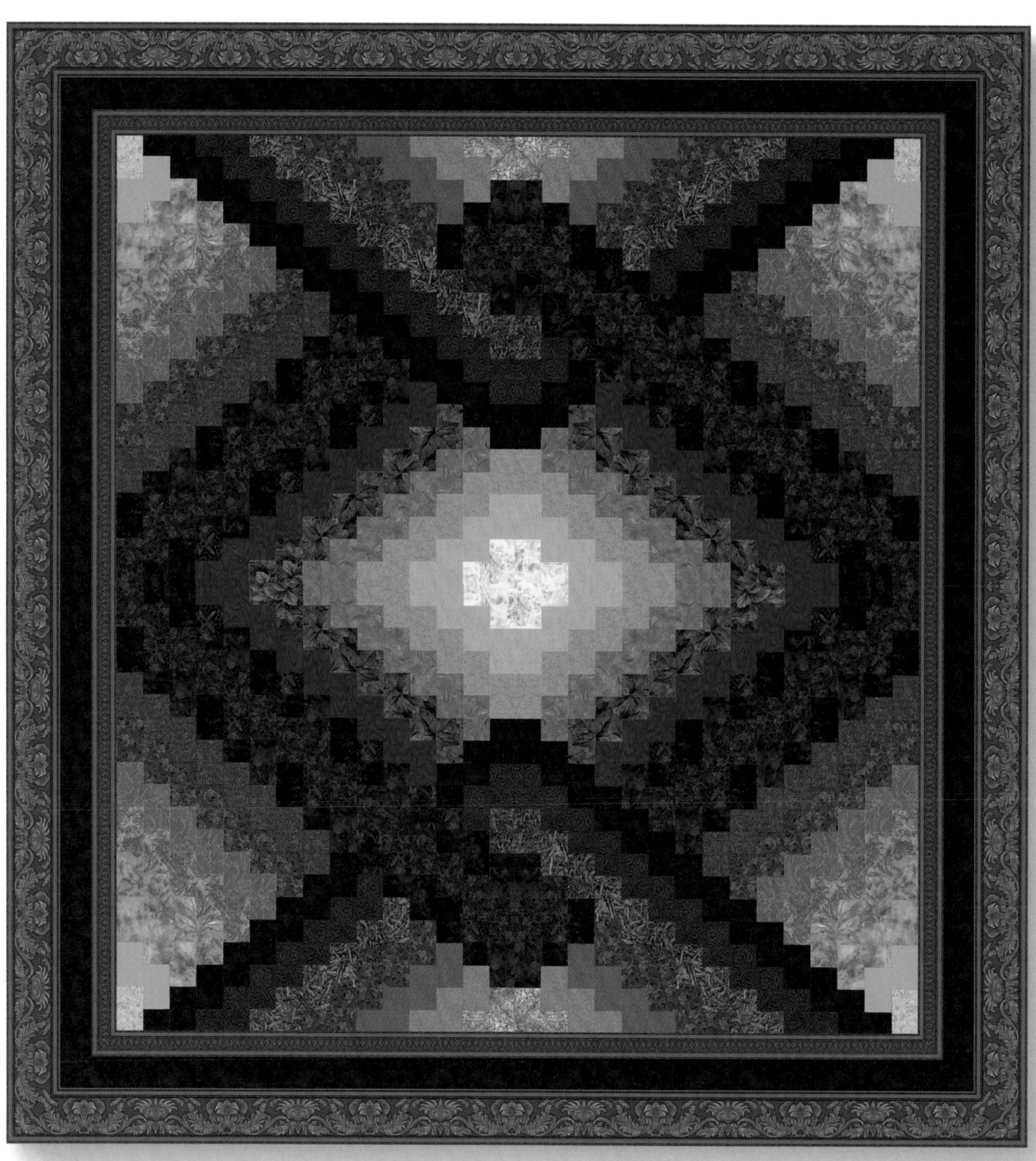

Golden Rectangle.
Designed by Jinny Beyer, 2003

Finished size: 89″ × 94½″ (226 cm × 240 cm)
Center quilt size (without borders): 69½″ × 75″ (176.5 cm × 190.5 cm)
Finished size varies according to width of selected borders

Golden Rectangle

See Templates on page 244

The design for *Golden Rectangle* was inspired by an antique quilt (see page 83). Two similar but different units make up the center design. You will need two of each unit. To make the rectangles pleasing to the eye, I derived the height/width proportion from the Golden Ratio–1:1.618. This is the same ratio that was used for the rectangles in the antique quilt.

The piecing required for this quilt is straightforward, making it an ideal project for beginners. At the same time, the fun of making *Golden Rectangle* lies in the challenge of successfully arranging a large selection of light, medium, and dark shades of fabrics to create an interlocking, geometric design. The design is framed with multiple borders–a print fabric with a border-print strip on either side.

Fabric Requirements

There are 22 different fabrics in the pieced center of *Golden Rectangle* (see piecing diagrams for fabric identification). Refer to the chart opposite for the yardages required from these fabrics. To match the geometric layout of this quilt, take care to identify and arrange your light, medium, and dark shades as I did. Be sure to label each of the 22 fabrics to keep them straight!

- 3¼ yd (3 m) of border print for inner and outer borders
- 2⅝ yd (2.5 m) of navy texture for middle border
- 8¼ yd (7.6 m) backing (piece widthwise)
- 1 yd (0.9 m) of fabric for binding

Fabric	Yardage	Number of Template A	Number of Template B
1	⅛ yd (0.15 m)	4	0
2	⅛ yd (0.15 m)	8	0
3	¼ yd (0.25 m)	12	0
4	¼ yd (0.25 m)	16	0
5	⅜ yd (0.4 m)	20	0
6	⅜ yd (0.4 m)	24	0
7	⅝ yd (0.6 m)	44	4
8	½ yd (0.5 m)	32	0
9	1¼ yd (1.2 m)	100	4
10	⅝ yd (0.6 m)	54	0
11	½ yd (0.5 m)	32	4
12	½ yd (0.5 m)	28	4
13	⅜ yd (0.4 m)	24	4
14	⅜ yd (0.4 m)	20	4
15	¼ yd (0.25 m)	12	4
16	⅛ yd (0.15 m)	4	4
17	⅝ yd (0.6 m)	46	4
18	⅝ yd (0.6 m)	38	4
19	½ yd (0.5 m)	30	4
20	¼ yd (0.25 m)	12	4
21	¼ yd (0.25 m)	8	4
22	⅛ yd (0.15 m)	4	4

Cutting

Cut the 22 quilt center fabrics in the quantities indicated in the chart. Feel free to deviate slightly from the border-print cutting widths presented on the next page if the stripes in your border print are different widths than those used for *Golden Rectangle.* Included in the inner and outer strips of border-print fabric is excess length, so you can successfully center and mirror motifs when cutting miters, as described in Chapter Eight.

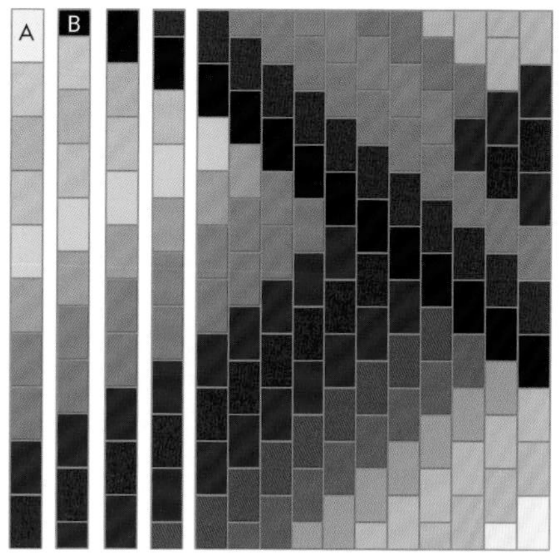

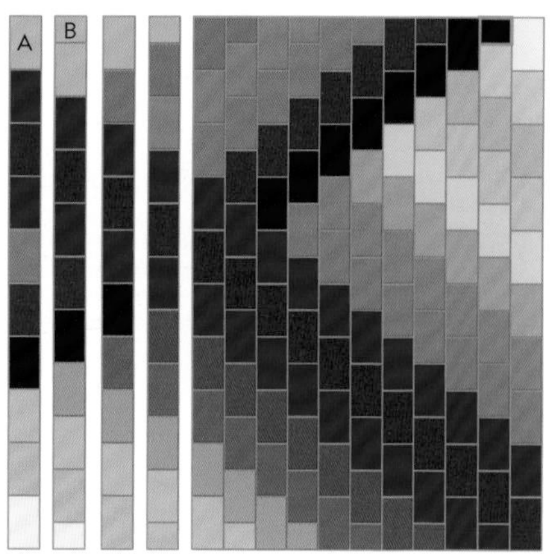

Step 1. *Arrange rows. Make two each of Units 1 (top) and 2 (bottom)*

Border print, inner border (top/bottom):
two strips measuring 2¾″ × 82″ (7 cm × 208 cm)

Border print, inner border (sides):
four strips measuring 2¾″ × 44″ (7 cm × 112 cm)

Navy texture, middle border (top/bottom):
two strips measuring 3¼″ × 84″ (8.3 cm × 214 cm)

Navy texture, middle border (sides):
two strips measuring 3¼″ × 90″ (8.3 cm × 229 cm)

Border print, outer border (top/bottom):
two strips measuring 5″ × 106″ (12.7 cm × 269 cm)

Border print, outer border (sides):
four strips measuring 5″ × 56″ (12.7 cm × 142 cm)

Piecing Four Center Units

1. Carefully arrange the rectangles in the correct color sequence, and stitch vertical rows using Template A and B fabrics, as shown. Sew rows together. Make two of each unit.

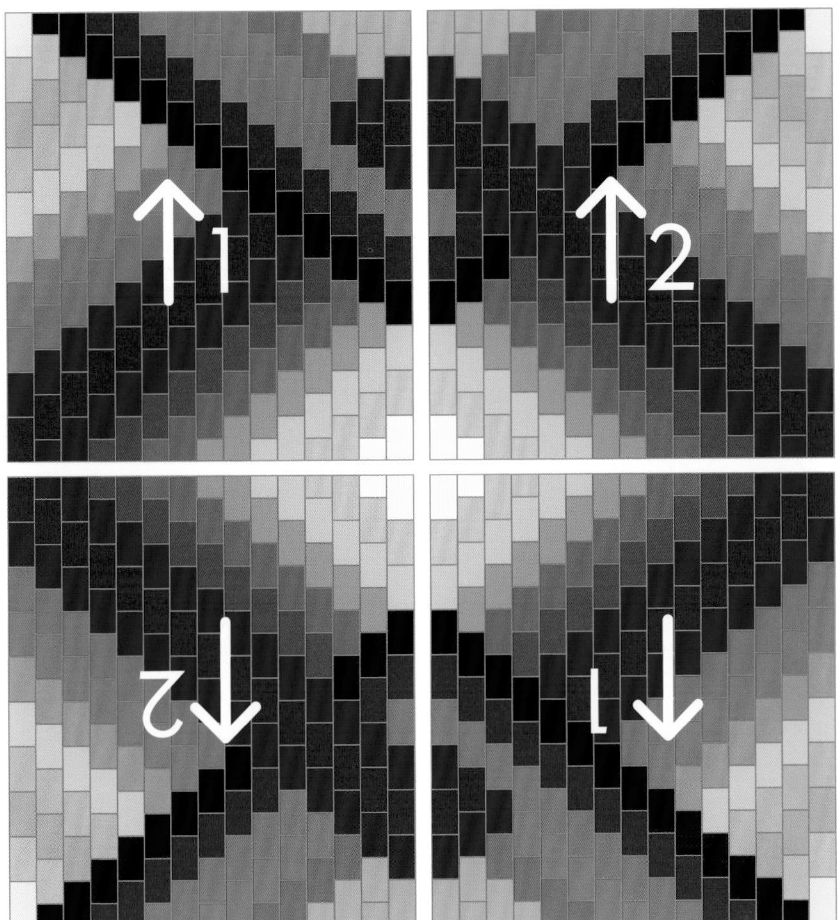

Step 2. *Arrange four units*

Assembling the Quilt Top

2. Arrange the four units as shown and sew together.
3. Follow the instructions on page 148 to frame a rectangular quilt with multiple border-print borders.

Finishing the Quilt

4. Refer to Chapter Nine to prepare your quilt for quilting. You may choose to use 1/4″ (0.75 cm) outline quilting around each rectangle. Or, to emphasize the interlocking, geometric design, you may wish to quilt a diagonal line through each color band. Quilt the border-print fabrics following the printed motifs, and 1/4″ (0.75 cm) outline the middle border.
5. Bind and label your quilt (see Chapter Ten).

Quick Tip

To increase accuracy when piecing, mark dots exactly where the seam allowances will cross, as explained on page 56.

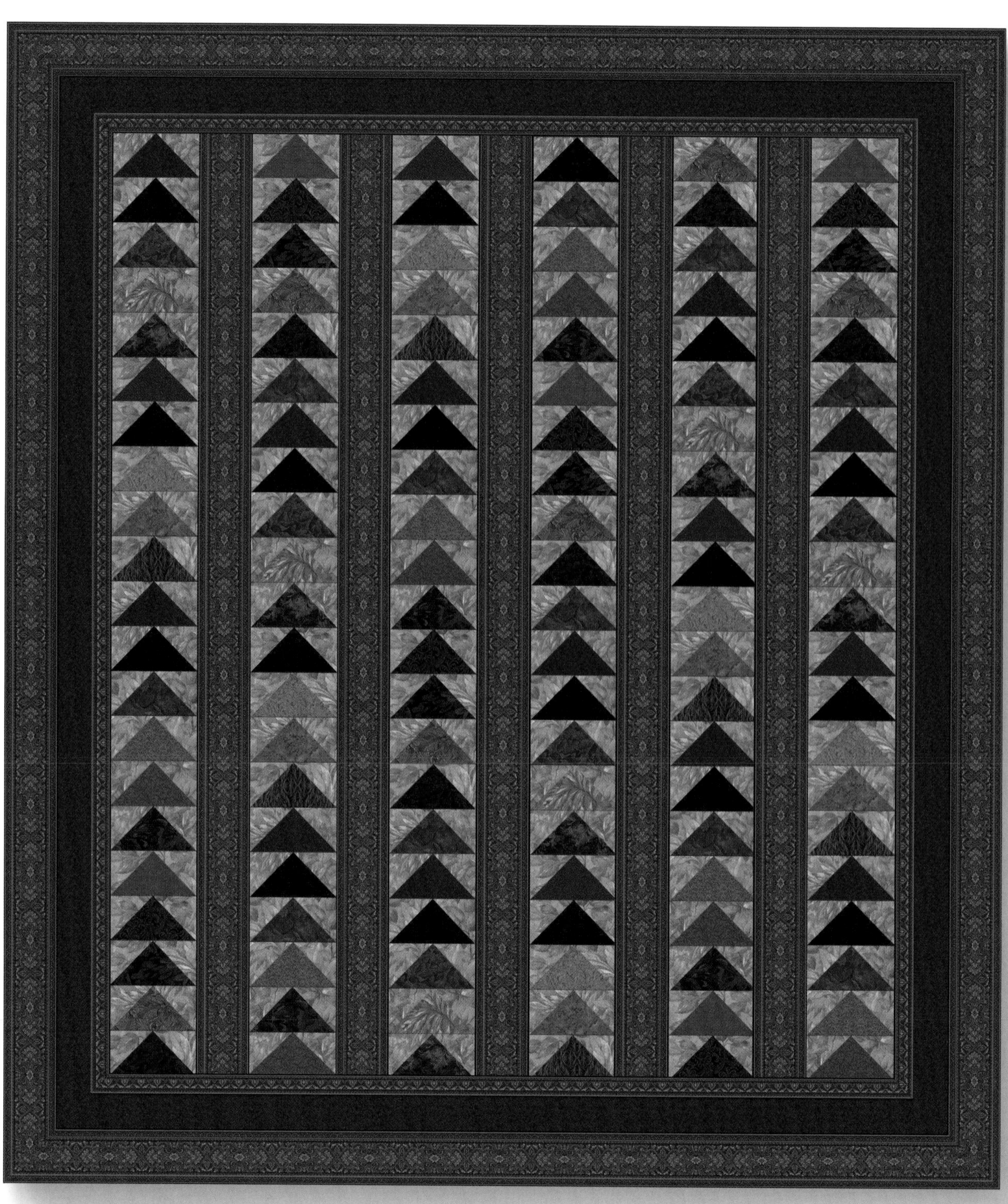

Flying Geese. *Designed by Jinny Beyer, 2003*

Finished size: 77″ × 86¼″ (196 cm × 219 cm)
Center quilt size (without borders): 60⅜″ × 69½″ (153.5 cm × 176.5 cm)
Finished size varies according to width of selected borders

Flying Geese

SEE TEMPLATES ON PAGE 244

Strippy quilts are a great way to incorporate and display your favorite border-print fabrics. In this design, I alternated *Flying Geese* strips with border-print strips. It can be difficult to decide how wide to make the border-print strips between the geese. I have found that it is most pleasing to the eye when the proportion between the geese and strips is equal to the Golden Ratio–1:1.618. The same ratio was used for the quilt on page 84.

This *Flying Geese* strippy pattern is ideal for beginners. Techniques involved include joining multiple points, cutting mirror-imaged border-print strips, and framing a rectangular quilt with multiple border-print borders. See pages 90 to 92 for extra help on joining three points.

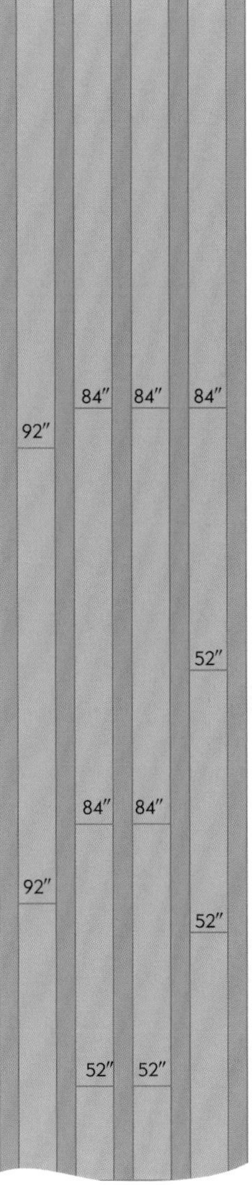

Cutting wide border print

Fabric Requirements

Use a large assortment of scraps for the geese, and arrange them randomly in the strips. I recommend selecting the border-print fabric first, then heading to your quilt shop or stash to find fabrics that coordinate with the border-print color family. You'll need a piece that's approximately 4½″ × 8″ (12 cm × 20 cm) for each Template B triangle.

2 yd (1.9 m) of beige print (geese background)
2 to 3 yd (1.9 m to 2.8 m) total of assorted prints/textures
6⅜ yd (5.9 m) of border print for strips between the geese and for inner and outer borders
2½ yd (2.3 m) of magenta texture for middle border
5¼ yd (4.8 m) backing (piece lengthwise)
⅞ yd (0.8 m) of fabric for binding

Cutting

Cut fabrics in the quantities indicated on the templates. Refer to the diagram to plan the cutting of the 4⅝″ (11.8 cm) width strips in the lengths listed on the next page. If the stripes in your border print are different widths from those used for this design, it may be necessary to deviate slightly from the border-print cutting widths presented here. However, for the most pleasing design (based upon the Golden Ratio mentioned above), I recommend that you match the widths given here. Included in all of the border-print strips is excess length, so you can successfully center and mirror motifs.

Border print, alternate strips:

five strips measuring 4⅝″ × 84″ (11.8 cm × 214 cm)

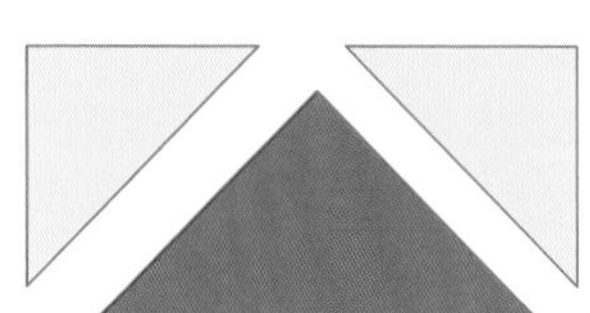

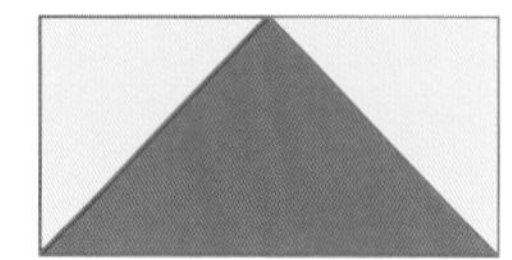

Step 1. *Make 126 flying geese rectangles*

Step 2. *Make 6 flying geese strips*

FLYING GEESE

Border print, inner border (top/bottom):
two strips measuring 2″ × 72″ (5 cm × 183 cm)
Border print, inner border (sides):
four strips measuring 2″ × 42″ (5 cm × 107 cm)
Magenta texture, middle border (top/bottom):
two strips measuring 3″ × 76″ (7.5 cm × 193 cm)
Magenta texture, middle border (sides):
two strips measuring 3″ × 85″ (7.5 cm × 216 cm)
Border print, outer border (top/bottom):
two strips measuring 4⅝″ × 92″ (11.8 cm × 234 cm)
Border print, outer border (sides):
four strips measuring 4⅝″ × 52″ (11.8 cm × 132 cm)

QUICK TIP

To increase accuracy when piecing, mark dots exactly where the seam allowances will cross, as explained on page 56.

Piecing the Geese Strips

1. Sew two beige Template A fabrics to an assorted print Template B fabric. Make 126 flying geese rectangles.
2. To make one flying geese strip, stitch together 21 geese as shown. Make six.

Step 3. Assemble the flying geese strips

Assembling the Quilt Top

3. Measure exact length of geese strips. Trim the five border-print strips measuring 4⅝″ × 84″ (11.8 cm × 214 cm) to exact geese strip length in the following manner. Select a mirror-imaged motif near the midpoint of a 84″ (214 cm) border-print strip. Centering the selected motif in the middle of one of the strips, measure and cut the strip to exact geese-strip length. Cut four additional strips that are identical to the first. Alternately stitch geese strips together with trimmed border-print strips.
4. Follow the instructions on page 148 to frame a rectangular quilt with multiple border-print borders.

Finishing the Quilt

5. Refer to Chapter Nine to prepare your quilt for quilting. I recommend ¼″ (0.75 cm) outline quilting for the flying geese triangles. Quilt the border-print fabrics following the printed motifs, and ¼″ (0.75 cm) outline the middle border.
6. Bind and label your quilt (see Chapter Ten).

Boxed Blocks. *Designed, hand-pieced, and hand-quilted by Tanis Rovner, 2003*

Finished size: 83½″ × 97½″ (216 cm × 248 cm)
Center quilt size (without borders): 65″ × 79″ (169 cm × 201 cm)
Finished size varies according to width of selected borders

Boxed Blocks

SEE TEMPLATES ON PAGE 245

Boxed Blocks is the first quilt made by Tanis Rovner, and is an excellent example of the complex-looking, intriguing designs you can create using simple 60° diamonds. The primary unit is a pieced diamond made up of nine smaller diamonds. In each pieced diamond, the arrangement of light, medium, and dark fabrics is consistent. The pieced-diamond units are stitched together and set with side, top/bottom, and corner triangles to square off the quilt edges.

While the simplicity of the piecing in *Boxed Blocks* makes it an ideal beginner quilt, the intrigue of the color and shading possibilities makes it a fun and satisfying project for experienced quiltmakers as well. Specific techniques involved in its construction include joining odd angles, joining multiple points, setting in pieces, and framing a rectangular quilt with multiple border-print borders.

Fabric Requirements

Tanis used a wonderful selection of scrap fabrics for the diamonds. She selected them from a controlled, earth-toned palette of greens, olives, browns, golds, beiges, and grays. Take care to select distinct lights, mediums, and darks so your design will glow, as Tanis's does.

2 to 3 yd (1.9 m to 2.8 m) *total* of assorted light prints and textures
2½ to 3½ yd (2.3 m to 3.2 m) *total* of assorted medium prints and textures
3 to 4 yd (2.8 m to 3.7 m) *total* of assorted dark prints and textures
3½ yd (3.2 m) of border print
2½ yd (2.3 m) of dark green texture for middle border
7¾ yd (7.1 m) backing (piece widthwise)
1 yd (0.9 m) of fabric for binding

Cutting

Cut all fabrics in the quantities indicated on the templates. Feel free to deviate slightly from the border-print cutting widths presented on the next page if the stripes in your border prints are different widths from those used for *Boxed Blocks.* Included in the inner and outer strips of border-print fabric is excess length, so you can successfully center and mirror motifs when cutting miters, as described in Chapter Eight.

Border print, inner border (top/bottom):
two strips measuring 2″ × 76″ (5 cm × 193 cm)

Border print, inner border (sides):
four strips measuring 2″ × 48″ (5 cm × 122 cm)

Step 1. *Make 97 diamond units*

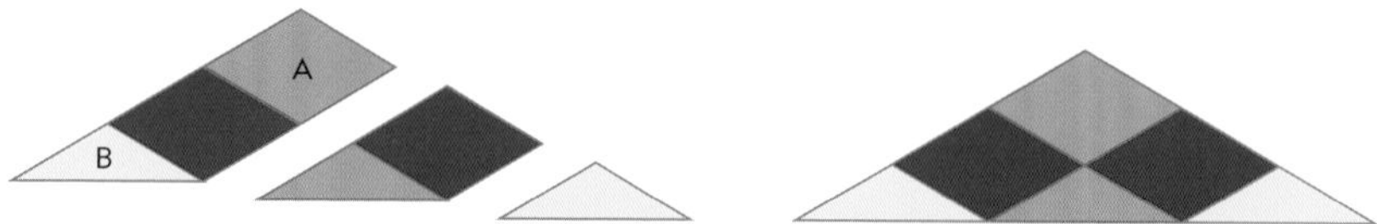

Step 2. *Make nine triangles for edges*

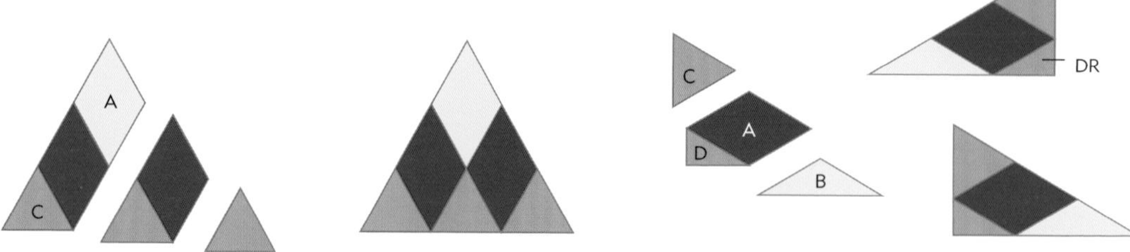

Step 3. *Make six side-setting triangles*

Step 4. *Make one of each corner triangle*

Dark green texture, middle border (top/bottom):
two strips measuring 2½″ × 76″ (6.5 cm × 193 cm)

Dark green texture, middle border (sides):
two strips measuring 2½″ × 90″ (6.5 cm × 229 cm)

Border print, outer border (top/bottom):
two strips measuring 6¼″ × 100″ (16 cm × 254 cm)

Border print, outer border (sides):
four strips measuring 6¼″ × 60″ (16 cm × 152 cm)

Piecing the Diamonds and Setting Triangles

1. Carefully arrange and stitch together nine Template A fabrics as shown, using two lights, three mediums, and four darks. Make 97 diamond units.
2. Arranging lights, mediums, and darks as illustrated, use Template A and B fabrics to make nine triangles for top and bottom edges.
3. Arrange and stitch Template A and C fabrics together to make a side setting triangle. Make six.
4. Using A, B, C, and D fabrics, make one corner triangle, plus one reversed.

Quick Tip

To increase accuracy when piecing, mark dots exactly where the seam allowances will cross, as explained on page 56.

Step 5. Construct quilt

Assembling the Quilt Top

5. Carefully arrange diamond units and stitch together with top/bottom triangles, side triangles, and corner triangles.
6. Follow the instructions on page 148 to frame a rectangle with multiple border-print borders.

Finishing the Quilt

7. Refer to Chapter Nine to prepare your quilt for quilting. The patchwork fabrics are ¼″ (0.75 cm) outlined, and the border-print fabrics are quilted following the printed motifs.
8. Bind and label your quilt (see Chapter Ten).

Shamrock. *Designed, hand-pieced, and hand-quilted by Jill Amos Gibbons, 2003*

FINISHED SIZE: 86½″ × 92″ (220 cm × 234 cm)
HEXAGONAL BLOCK SIZE: 18″ × 15½″ (45 cm × 39.4 cm)–18 blocks total
CENTER QUILT SIZE (WITHOUT BORDERS): 72½″ × 78″ (182 cm × 196 cm)
Finished size varies according to width of selected borders

Shamrock

SEE TEMPLATES ON PAGE 246

Shamrock, made by Jill Amos Gibbons, is her first hand-pieced quilt. Like *Boxed Blocks*, *Shamrock* is a very achievable pattern based upon simple 60° diamonds. The primary unit is a pieced diamond made up of four smaller diamonds. Six medium/dark diamond units are stitched together to make a six-pointed star. Then six light/medium diamond units are added between the points, creating a hexagonal star block. Triangles framed with border-print fabric are set between the hexagonal blocks, and they add a touch of elegance to the design. *Shamrock* is an ideal pattern for beginning hand piecers. It is also a pleasing project for experienced quilters.

Techniques used in making *Shamrock* include joining odd angles, joining multiple points, setting in pieces, framing triangles with a border print, and framing a rectangular quilt with multiple border-print borders.

Fabric Requirements

The scrappiness of *Shamrock* may inspire you to dig into your stash for piecing fabrics! Jill used a variety of greens, teals, olives, and browns in her quilt. For a successful design, be sure to use distinct lights, mediums, and darks.

The border-print yardage depends upon the number of stripe repeats across the width of the fabric (from selvage to selvage). Because the setting triangles are framed with the narrow border-print stripe, lots of narrow stripe is required. If there are six narrow stripes across the width of your border stripe fabric, you will need 6½ yards (6 m). If there are only four narrow stripes, you will need a full 12 yards (11 m).

1¼ to 2¼ yd (1.2 m to 2.1 m) *total* of assorted light prints and textures
2 to 3 yd (1.9 m to 2.8 m) *total* of assorted medium prints and textures
1¼ to 2¼ yd (1.2 m to 2.1 m) *total* of assorted dark prints and textures
6½ yd (6 m) of border print (see explanation above)
2½ yd (2.3 m) of dark green print for triangles and middle border
1 yd (0.9 m) of fabric for binding
8 yd (7.5 m) backing (piece widthwise)

NOTE: Templates for the triangles framed with border-print fabric are presented with a single outline representing the finished sizes of the setting triangles. To use these templates, follow the special instructions, *How to Make Setting Triangle Templates* on the following page.

How to Make Setting-Triangle Templates

REFER TO PAGE 138 for detailed instructions on how to frame a triangle with a border-print fabric.

1. Begin with the finished size outline of Template C & D on page 246. Measure the finished width of the narrow stripe in your border print. Mark this width onto the C & D triangle, measuring in from each side. Draw lines and connect to make smaller triangle inside the large triangle outline.
2. Draw the miters. On a piece of see-through template plastic, trace a center (smaller) triangle line using a *dashed line*. Add a solid line ¼″ (0.75 cm) around all sides for seam allowance.
3. Repeat, this time tracing the Template D shape using a *dashed line,* then adding ¼″ (0.75 cm) seam allowance beyond the dashed line to make Template D.
4. Following the same procedure, make Templates E/ER and F/FR.

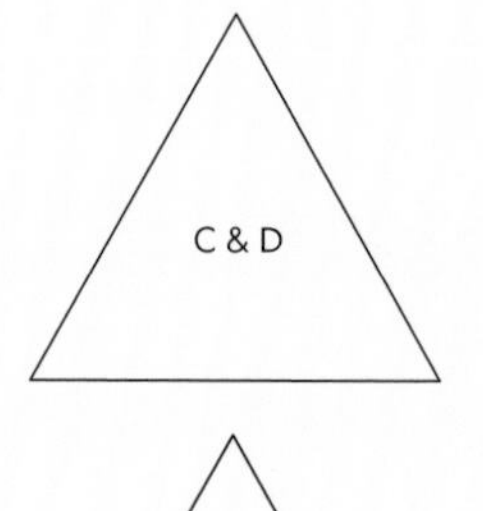

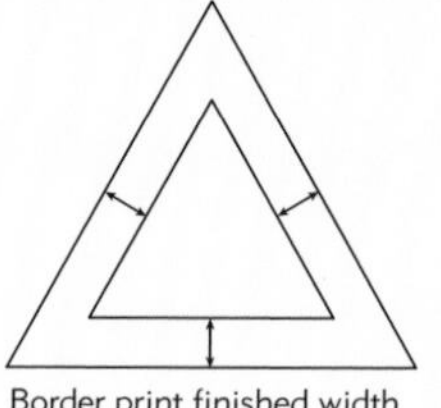

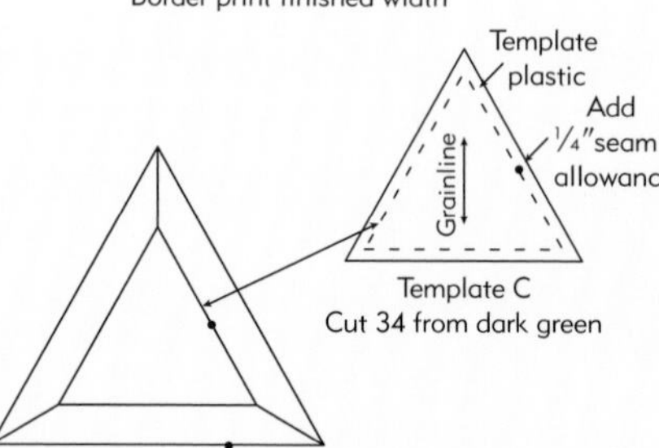

Step 1. Use finished width of border print to draw inner triangle. Add miters. Trace inner triangle

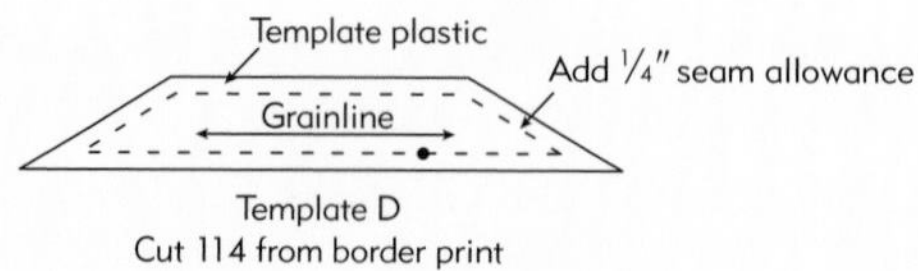

Step 3. Repeat with template D

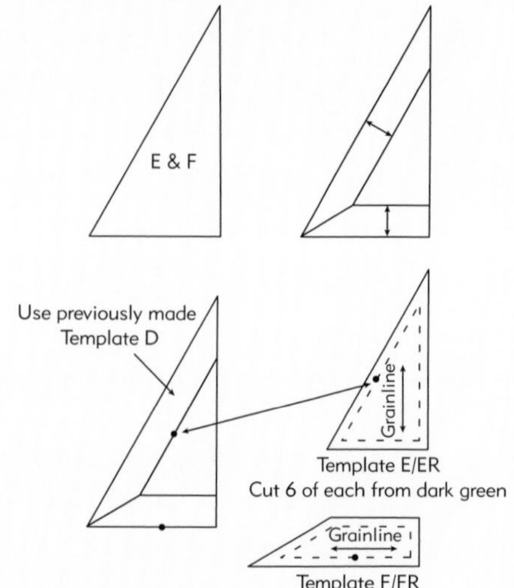

Step 4. Repeat with Templates E/ER and F/FR

Cutting

Cut all fabrics in the quantities indicated on the templates. The cutting quantities for the setting triangle fabrics are presented with the special instructions for making the setting-triangle templates.

Feel free to deviate slightly from the border-print cutting widths presented here if the stripes in your border print are different widths than those used for *Shamrock.* Included in the border stripe inner and outer strips is excess length, so you can successfully center and mirror motifs when cutting miters, as described in Chapter Eight.

Border print, inner border (top/bottom):
two strips measuring 1¼″ × 82″ (3 cm × 208 cm)
Border print, inner border (sides):
four strips measuring 1¼″ × 44″ (3 cm × 112 cm)
Dark green print, middle border (top/bottom):
two strips measuring 1¾″ × 84″ (4.5 cm × 214 cm)

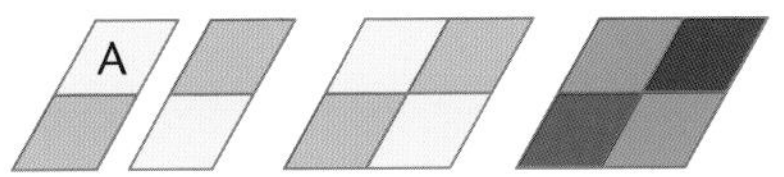

Step 1. Make 120 light/medium diamonds and 116 medium/dark diamonds

Step 2. Make eight half-diamonds

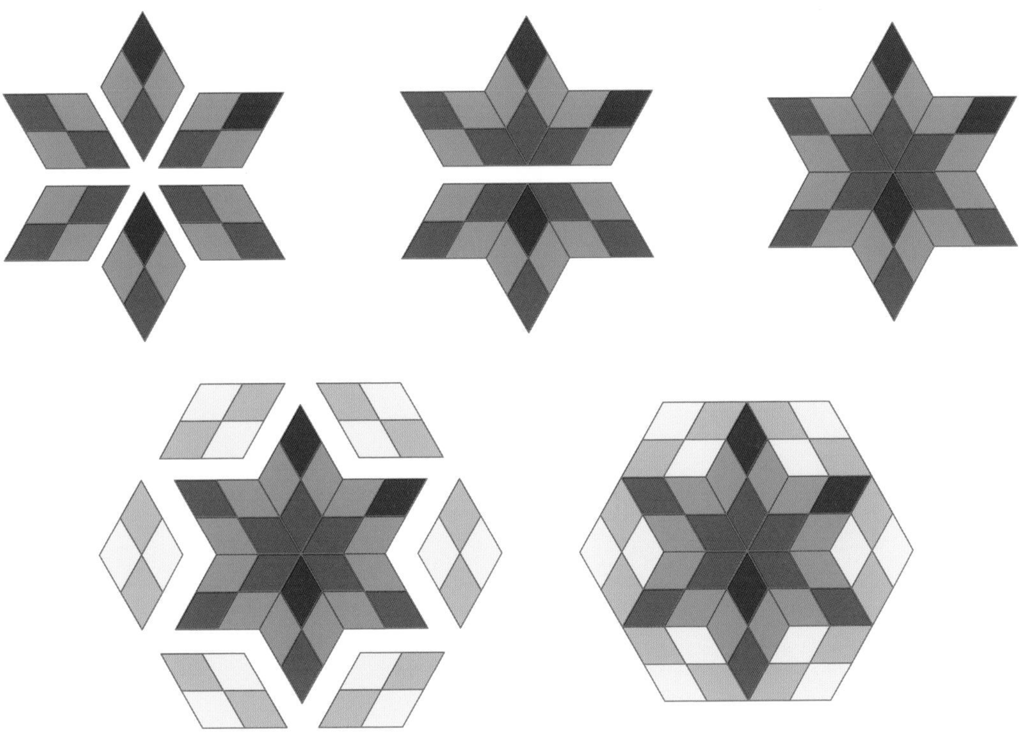

Step 3. Make six-pointed star then set in diamonds for hexagonal block. Make 18 blocks

Dark green print, middle border (sides):
two strips measuring 1¾″ × 90″ (4.5 cm × 229 cm)

Border print, outer border (top/bottom):
two strips measuring 5½″ × 104″ (14 cm × 264 cm)

Border print, outer border (sides):
four strips measuring 5½″ × 56″ (14 cm × 142 cm)

Piecing the Blocks and Setting Triangles

1. Stitch together Template A fabrics to make 120 light/medium diamond units and 116 medium/dark units, as shown.
2. Make eight half-diamond units using medium Template A fabric and two dark Template B fabrics each; set aside.
3. Stitch six medium/dark diamond units together to make a six-pointed star. Set in light/medium diamond units to make the block. Make 18.
4. Make four half-blocks, as shown.

QUICK TIP

To increase accuracy when piecing, mark dots exactly where the seam allowances will cross, as explained on page 56.

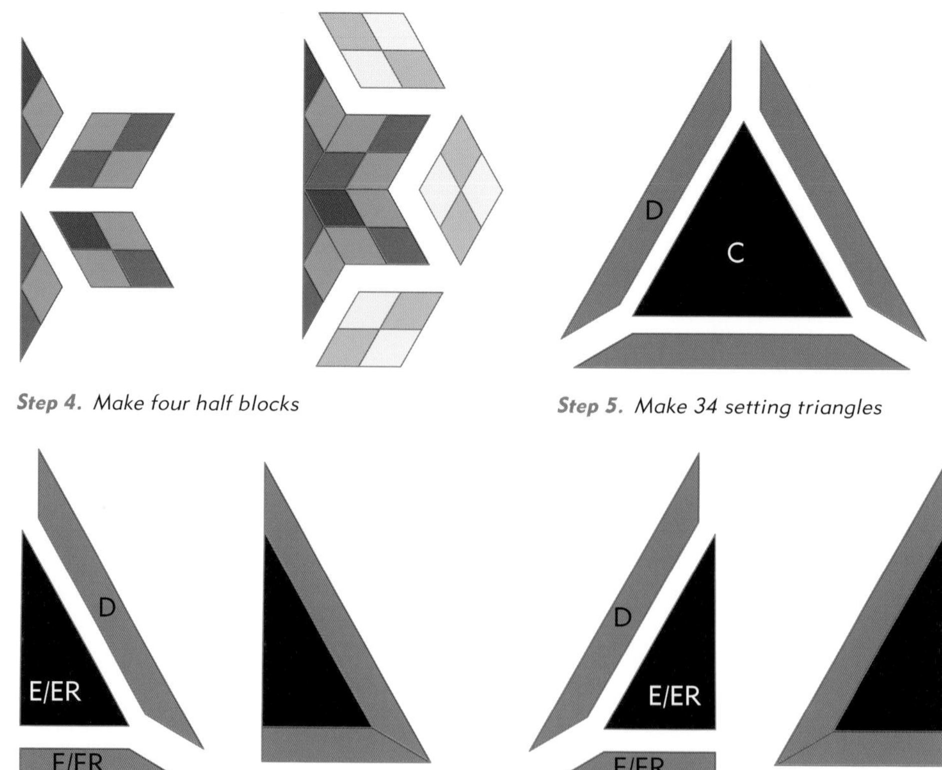

Step 4. Make four half blocks

Step 5. Make 34 setting triangles

Step 6. Make six of each half-setting triangle

5. Refer to *How to Make Setting Triangle Templates* on page 214 to prepare C, D, E/ER, and F/FR templates. Carefully cut D and F/FR fabrics from the narrow stripe of a border-print fabric. Stitch three D fabrics to C fabric to make a setting triangle. Make 34.
6. In the same manner, make six of each half-setting triangle illustrated.

Assembling the Quilt Top

7. Carefully arrange blocks, half blocks, setting triangles, and half-setting triangles into rows, as shown. Make three of top row and two of bottom row shown. Alternating rows, sew rows together.

Step 7. Arrange blocks in rows. Make three of top row and two of bottom row

8. Follow the instructions on page 148 to frame a rectangular quilt with multiple border print borders.

Finishing the Quilt

9. Refer to Chapter Nine to prepare your quilt for quilting. The patchwork fabrics are ¼″ (0.75 cm) outlined, and the border-print fabrics are quilted following the printed motifs.
10. Bind and label your quilt (see Chapter Ten).

Love Ring. *Designed, hand-pieced, and hand-quilted by Carole Nicholas, 2003*

Finished size: 62½″ × 62½″ (159 cm × 159 cm)
Size of blocks: 4″ × 4″ (10 cm × 10 cm)–total of 144 *Drunkard's Path* blocks
Center quilt size (without borders): 48″ × 48″ (122 cm × 122 cm)
Finished size of quilt varies according to width of selected borders. See below for border widths used in this quilt.

Love Ring

See Templates on page 247

Based on two positive/negative blocks, *Drunkards' Path*, with its endless variations, has long been popular with quilters. The antique quilt from the 1930s, shown on page 118, is just one example. You'll gain lots of experience sewing curves while making the variation shown here, *Love Ring* by Carole Nicholas.

In addition to providing practice in joining four points, piecing curves, and mitering corners, *Love Ring* also offers the opportunity to experiment with color arrangement. Multiple border-print frames complete the design.

Fabric Requirements

Carole worked with a collection of coordinating prints–half large scale and the other half small-scale "tonal" fabrics, in which the small-scale tonal prints are lighter (in shade) than the larger-scaled floral prints. To do likewise, select a large-scale print and a small-scale one from each of five color families, and number the colors from #1 (centermost color) to #5. You will have two fabrics for each color, a large-scale print (P) and a small-scaled, "textured" print (T). Carole used the following color families in her quilt: teal, taupe, blue, lavender, and yellow. Refer to the chart opposite for the piecing fabric yardages. She repeated the lavender print in the middle border. You may decide to select a different print for that border. You will need a 1¾ yard (1.6 m) length of the border fabric so the strips do not have to be pieced, but there will be sufficient left over for use in the top. The yardages are presented separately, so you can decide which of the piecing fabrics you wish to repeat for the middle border.

- 2¼ yd (2.1 m) of border print for inner and outer borders
- 1¾ (1.6 m) of lavender print for middle border (Note: after border strips are cut, there will be enough left to cut pieces for inside the quilt.)
- 4 yd (3.7 m) backing
- ⅝ yd (0.6 m) of fabric for binding

Fabric	Yardage	Number of Template A	Number of Template B
1T	⅜ yd (0.4 m)	8	8
1P	⅜ yd (0.4 m)	8	8
2T	½ yd (0.5 m)	8	12
2P	½ yd (0.5 m)	12	16
3T	⅝ yd (0.6 m)	16	20
3P	¾ yd (0.7 m)	20	24
4T	¾ yd (0.7 m)	24	20
4P	⅝ yd (0.6 m)	20	16
5T	⅝ yd (0.6 m)	16	12
5P	½ yd (0.5 m)	12	8

Fabrics are numbered #1 to #5, starting in quilt center (#1) and working outwards. T = small-scaled, textured print; P = large-scale print

Note: If the fabric for the middle border is the same as one of the fabrics in the design, 1¾ yd (1.6 m) will be plenty for both the border and the other pieces.

Cutting

Cut all piecing fabrics in the quantities indicated in the chart. Feel free to deviate slightly from the border-print cutting widths presented here if the stripes in your border print are different widths than those used

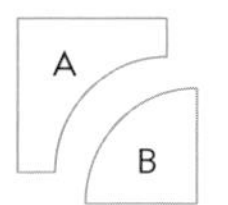

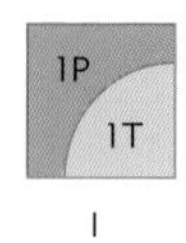

I
Make 8

2T 1P
II
Make 8

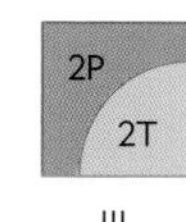

III
Make 12

3T 2P
IV
Make 16

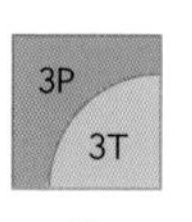

V
Make 20

4T 3P
VI
Make 24

4P 4T
VII
Make 20

5T 4P
VIII
Make 16

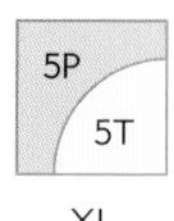

XI
Make 12

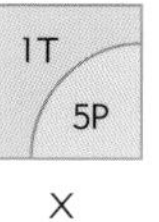

X
Make 8

Step 1. *Make blocks*

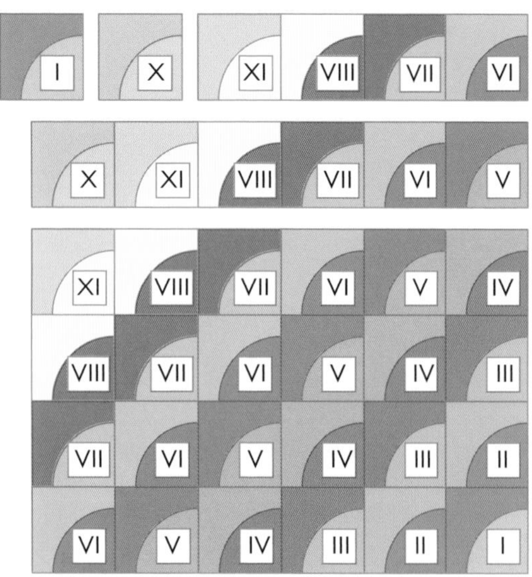

Step 2. *Arrange rows. Make four quarter-sections*

for *Love Ring*. Included in the border stripe inner and outer strips is excess length, so you can successfully center and mirror motifs when cutting miters, as described in Chapter Eight.

Border print, inner border:
four strips measuring 1½″ × 58″ (4 cm × 147 cm)
Lavender print, middle border:
four strips measuring 3″ × 60″ (7.5 cm × 152 cm)
Border print, outer border:
four strips measuring 4″ × 80″ (10 cm × 203 cm)

Piecing the Blocks

1. Refer to page 118 for detailed instructions on sewing curves. Stitch Template A and B fabrics together to make the *Drunkard's Path* squares in the color combinations shown. Make quantities indicated.
2. To make a quarter-section of quilt top, carefully arrange six rows of six squares each. Sew rows together. Make four.

Step 3. Join quarter sections

Assembling the Quilt Top

3. Refer to the diagram to arrange quarter sections. Sew together to complete pieced center.
4. Follow the instructions on page 147 to frame a square with a border print.

Finishing the Quilt

5. Refer to Chapter Nine to prepare your quilt for quilting. To emphasize the curves in *Love Ring*, Carole quilted large, overlapping circles over the entire quilt top (see quilting detail on page 160).
6. Bind and label your quilt (see Chapter Ten).

Quick Tip

To increase accuracy when piecing, mark dots exactly where the seam allowances will cross, as explained on page 56.

Triple Play. *Designed, hand-pieced, and hand-quilted by Jinny Beyer, 2003*

Finished size: 76½″ × 85″ (194 cm × 216 cm)
Finished block width: 13½″ (34 cm)
Center quilt size (without borders): 55½″ × 64″ (140 cm × 162 cm)

Triple Play

See Templates on page 248

Reminiscent of the traditional *Tumbling Blocks, Triple Play* adds unique twists to the three-dimensional block concept. Each block face is a diamond pieced from four matching border-print patches (two are identical and two are mirror images). As with any *Tumbling Blocks* quilt, the three-dimensional effect is achieved by using darks, mediums, and lights. Here, the design changes visually, depending on the orientation of the quilt. Turn this book sideways and upside down to see the differences–hence the name, *Triple Play*.

Triple Play incorporates many of the topics featured in this book, including bias edges, set-in seams, joining multiple points, working with border prints, and adding perfectly matched and mitered border-print borders.

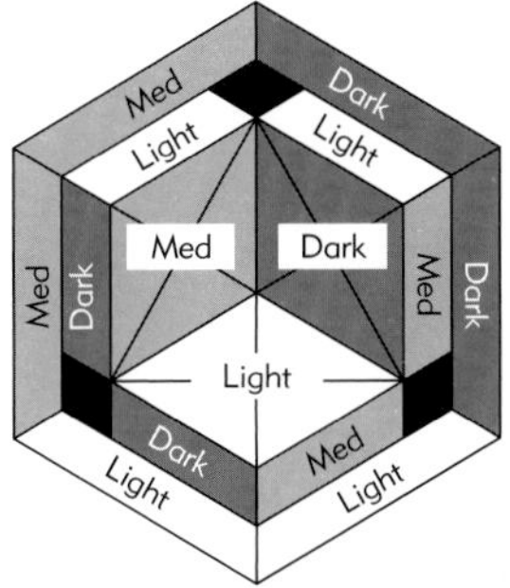

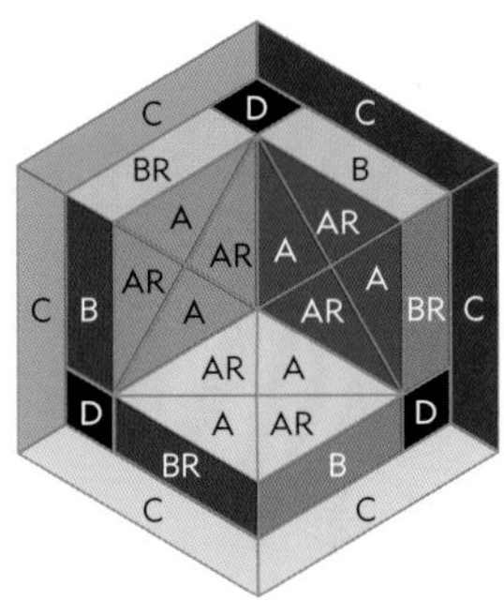

Fabric planning

Fabric Requirements

To match the *Triple Play* palette, use a variety of blues, browns, reds, and grays. The blues range from light blue to navy, the browns from tan to dark brown, the reds from pink to burgundy, and the grays from light gray to black. Use 18 fat quarters of assorted border prints for tumbling block faces (six lights, six mediums, and six darks).

- 1½ to 2 yd (1.4 m to 1.9 m) of assorted light prints and textures
- 1¼ to 2 yd (1.2 m to 1.9 m) of assorted medium prints and textures
- 1¼ to 2 yd (1.2 m to 1.9 m) of assorted dark prints and textures
- ⅜ yd (0.4 m) of black texture
- 3 yd (2.8 m) of border print for inner and outer borders
- 2¼ yd (2.1 m) of dark red texture for middle border
- 7⅛ yd (6.5 m) of backing (piece widthwise)
- ⅞ yd (0.8 m) of binding

Quick Tip

Refer to pages 136 to 137 for instructions on cutting mirror-image border print triangles for Template A and AR patches. Be sure to make whole Template F by mirroring on dotted line as instructed on the template. This will be used as a cutting guide to trim the partial blocks that complete the quilt's top and bottom edges. Use the alignment line (see corner) for guidance with placement on pieced units.

Cutting

Study the block diagrams and carefully plan the cutting for each block, taking care to ensure that lights, mediums, and darks are easily distinguishable. Also, notice the way matching pairs of fabrics are used for B, BR, and C. See pages 136 to 137 for help cutting center diamonds from border-print to border print.

Because stripe width varies from border print to border print, it may be necessary to deviate slightly from the border stripe cutting widths listed on the next page. The inner border strips may be cut 2½″ to 3″ (6.5 cm to 7.5 cm) wide. The outer border strips may be cut 5″ to 6″ (12.7 cm to 15 cm) wide. The measurements given also include excess length, so you can successfully center and mirror motifs when cutting miters, as described in Chapter Eight.

Border print, inner border (sides):

four strips measuring 30″ × 40″ (75 cm × 102 cm); two are mirror images

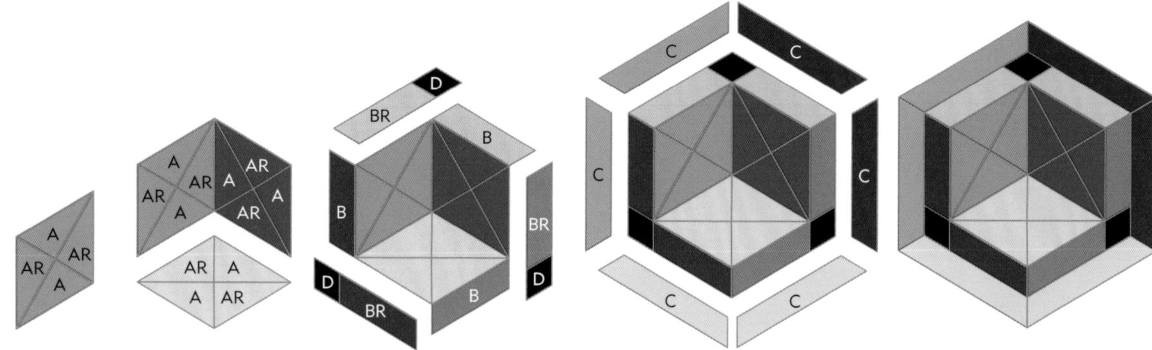

Step 1. Piece border-print diamonds

Step 2. Piece center block and add first set of surrounding pieces

Add second set of surrounding pieces. Make 17 full blocks

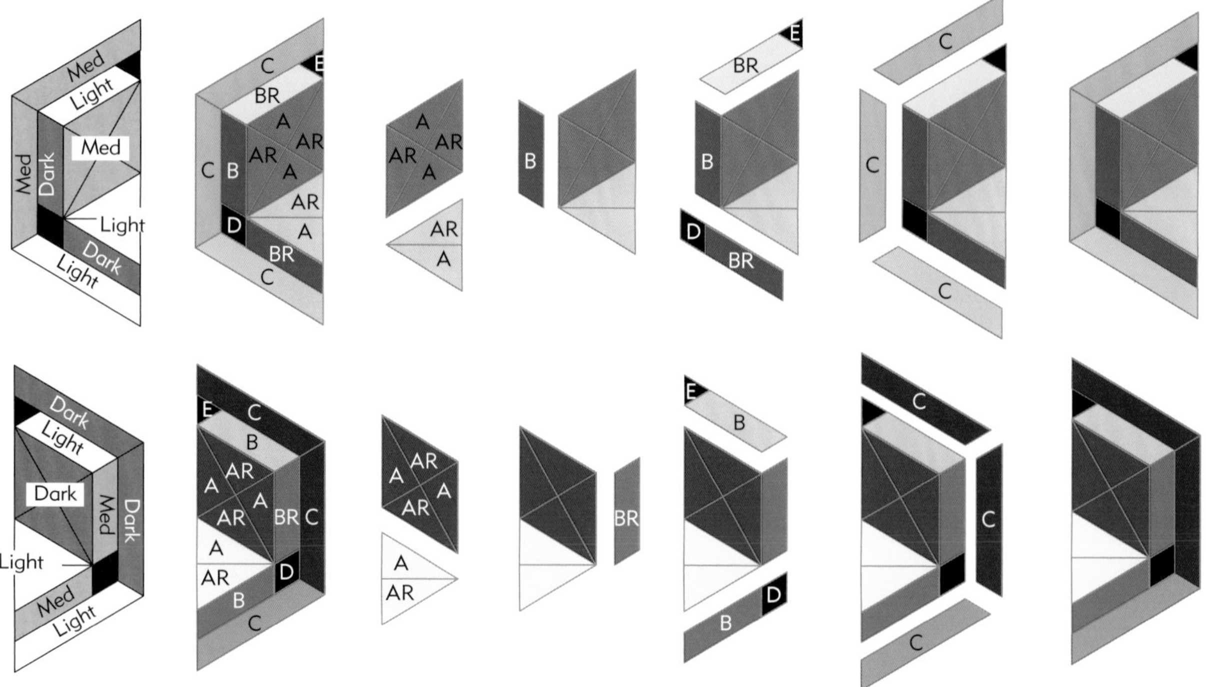

Step 3. Make three half blocks for both left and right sides of quilt

Triple Play

Border print, inner border (top and bottom):
two strips measuring 3″ × 68″ (7.5 cm × 173 cm)

Dark red texture, middle border:
four strips measuring 3″ × 78″ (7.5 cm × 198 cm)

Border print, outer border (sides):
four strips measuring 6″ × 52″ (15 cm × 132 cm); two are mirror images

Border print, outer border (top and bottom):
two strips measuring 6″ × 96″ (15 cm × 244 cm)

Quick Tip

Refer to the fabric planning diagrams to plan fabric/shading arrangement for each block. When piecing, mark dots on template fabrics as needed (see page 56).

Piecing the Blocks

1. Carefully matching the design on the fabric, piece light, medium, and dark border-print diamonds, using Template A and AR fabrics. Note that you are

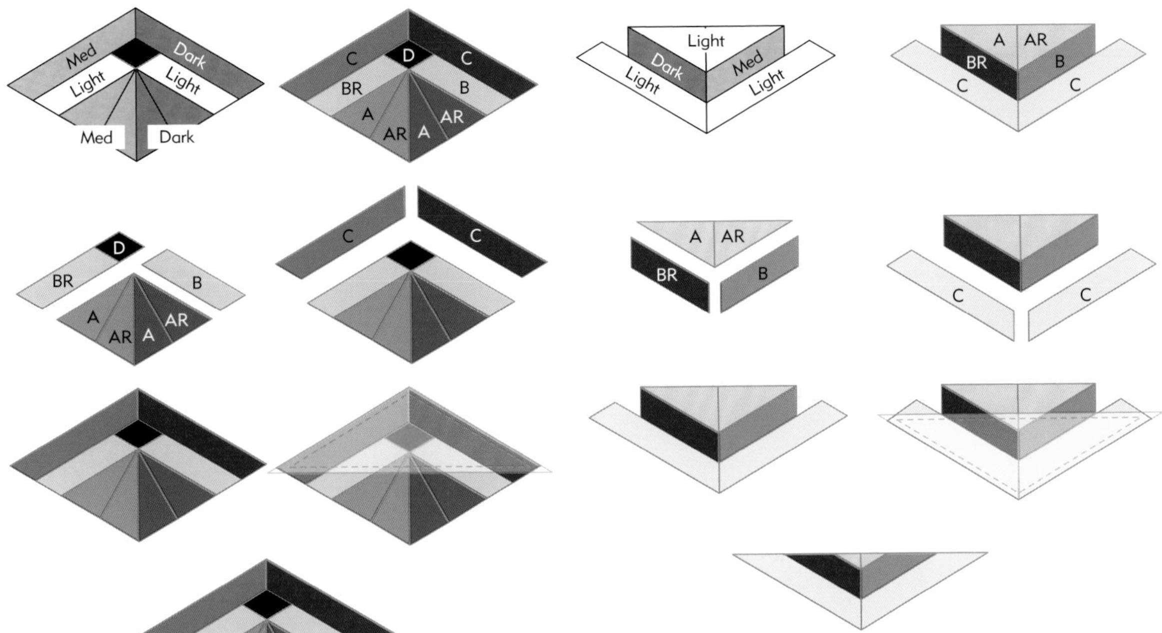

Step 4. *Make and trim four partial blocks for top and bottom edges*

stitching bias to bias–see page 85 for additional help. Make one light, medium, and dark for each of 17 blocks.

2. Piece 17 blocks, following the diagrams.
3. Make three half-blocks for left side and three half-blocks for right side.
4. Piece partial blocks for top and bottom edges as shown. Make four for the top edge of quilt and four for the bottom edge. Position Template F on the pieced units, aligning corner lines. Mark and trim away excess fabric. Take care to avoid stretching bias edge. Since trimming cuts some of the stitching lines, go back and reinforce each cut seam along the top and bottom edges of the quilt.

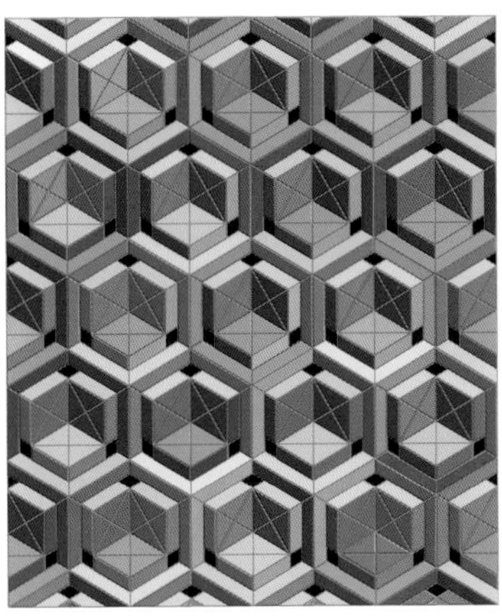

Assembling the Quilt Top

5. Referring to layout diagram, arrange and stitch full blocks, half blocks (sides), and partial blocks (top/bottom). Keep light/medium/dark orientation consistent.
6. Follow the instructions on pages 148 to frame your rectangular quilt with multiple border-print borders.

Finishing the Quilt

7. Refer to Chapter Nine to prepare your quilt for quilting. The B, C, D, and E patches are ¼″ (0.75 cm) outlined. The border-print diamonds and the outer border are quilted following the printed motifs.
8. Bind and label your quilt (see Chapter Ten).

Columbia. *Designed, hand-pieced, and hand-quilted by Jinny Beyer, 2003*

Finished size: 56″ × 56″ (142 cm × 142 cm)
Center block size (without borders): 36½″ × 36½″ (92 cm × 92 cm)
Finished size varies according to width of selected borders

Columbia

I use *Columbia* for my beginning hand-piecing classes, as described on page 198. The design is far less difficult than it seems, perhaps due to the pieced center, which resembles a traditional *Mariners' Compass.* Here, the four central points of the compass are created from mirror-imaged border-print fabrics. The compass is echoed with large mirror-imaged border-print points just outside the on-point center medallion. Framing the design is a pieced border set between narrow and wide border stripes.

Once you are familiar with some key skills, namely joining multiple points, setting in pieces, using border-print fabrics, sewing curves, and mitering corners, this quilt will come together for you beautifully. For extra help read pages 122 to 125.

Fabric Requirements

Select the border-print fabric first, then coordinate the remaining fabrics with it. Choose a border print with a stripe approximately 6″ (15 cm) wide to allow for a well-proportioned outer border and to have flexibility when cutting the large, mirror-imaged star points. The fabric you choose should also have a narrow stripe that can be cut to a finished size of 2⅛″ (5.4 cm).

1¼ yd (1.2 m) of ivory texture for medallion and pieced border backgrounds
¾ yd (0.7 m) of beige print for remaining background
¼ yd (0.25 m) *each* of five assorted textures, shaded from bright to dark
3¾ yd (3.5 m) of border print
3¾ yd (3.5 m) of backing
⅝ yd (0.6 m) of fabric for binding

Cutting

Label five assorted texture fabrics from #1 to #5, with #1 being the brightest and #5 being the darkest. Cut all fabrics in the quantities indicated on the templates. See page 136 for help on cutting mirror-image, border-print triangles for Templates D, DR, F, and FR. Template H and I fabrics may be rotary cut:

H–cut squares measuring 2″ × 2″
I–cut 56 squares measuring 3⅜″ × 3⅜″ then cut twice diagonally

In order to ensure that the pieced borders properly fit the quilt top, it is necessary to cut the narrow border-print strips the exact width given below. The outer border strips may be cut 5″ to 6″ (12.7 cm to 15 cm) wide, depending on the width of your stripe. Included in the inner and outer strips of border-print fabric is excess length, so you can successfully center and mirror motifs when cutting miters, as described in Chapter Eight.

Border print, center medallion border:
four strips measuring 2⅝″ × 34″ (7 cm × 87 cm)

SEE TEMPLATES ON PAGES 249 TO 252

If you are making *Columbia* as you work through *Quiltmaking by Hand,* follow this sequence:

1. Sew strips of squares
2. Sew wedges for compass
3. Sew eight points of central star
4. Set in wedges to center star
5. Sew curved pieces to compass block
6. Create border-print points and add triangles to either side
7. Assemble pieces
8. Add final border

Cut strips for borders prior to cutting the mirror-imaged Template D, DR, F, and FR fabrics. Be sure to make whole Template E by mirroring on dotted line as instructed on template. Also, make sure to match the pieces of Templates F/FR and G/GR to make complete templates.

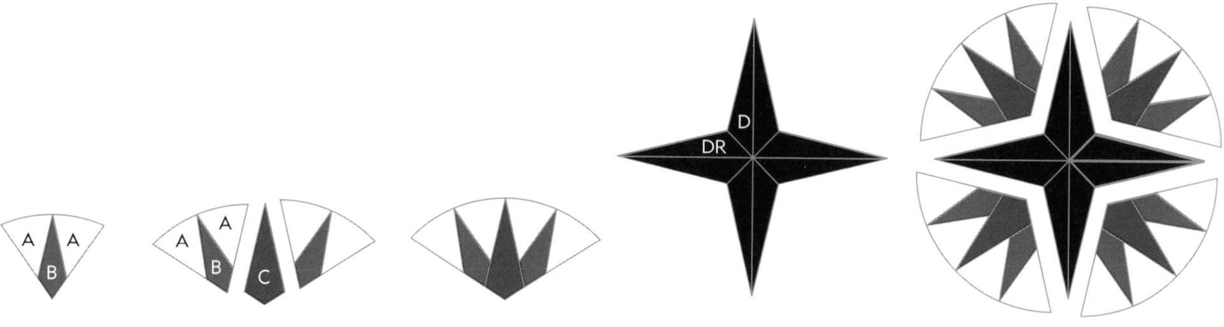

Step 1. Piece four wedge units

Step 2. Join D and DR to make star. Set in four wedge units

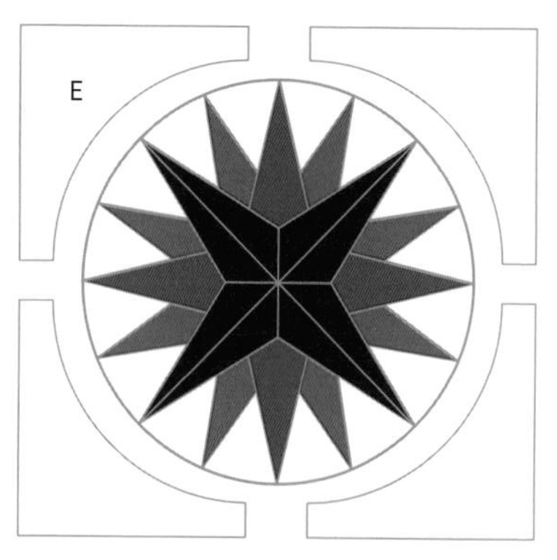

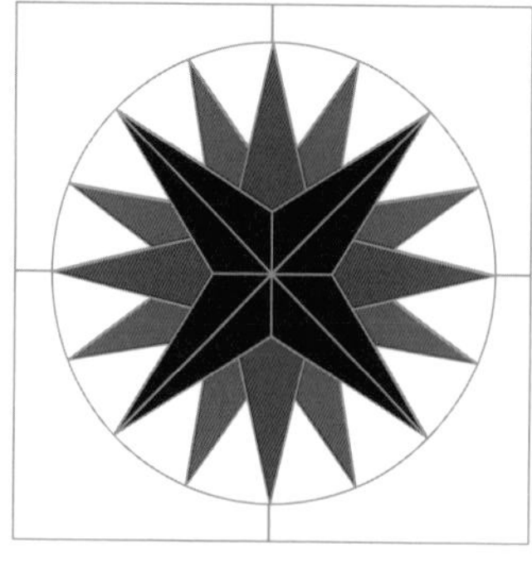

Step 3. Add curved Template E fabrics

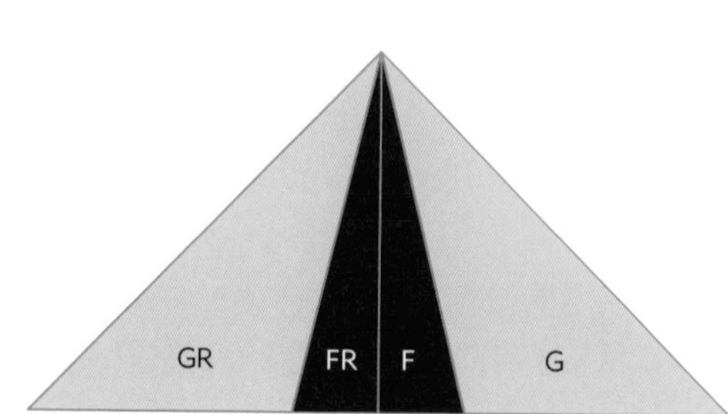

Step 4. Make four large pieced triangles

Border print, inner border:
four strips measuring 2⅝″ × 48″ (7 cm × 122 cm)

Border print, outer border:
four strips measuring 6″ × 74″ (15 cm × 188 cm)

Quick Tip

To increase accuracy when piecing, mark dots exactly where the seam allowances will cross, as explained on page 56.

Piecing the Center Elements

1. Piece four wedge units as shown. Make A/B wedges first, using Checking Template 1 in the template section to ensure accuracy. Then sew an A/B wedge to either side of C. Verify size with Checking Template 2.
2. Stitch together D and DR mirror-image, border-print fabrics to make star (see pages 100 and 122); set-in the wedge units (see page 108).
3. Add curved Template E fabrics (see Chapter Six for detailed instructions on sewing curves).
4. Make four large pieced triangles. Avoid stretching bias edges at base.

Making Pieced Borders

5. Follow the diagrams to make the pieced border strips in the fabric arrangements and quantities indicated. First, join I triangles to either side of the H squares. Then use a straight seam to join the three-piece units.

Assembling the Quilt Top

6. Sew shortest pieced-border strips (Step 5) to *Mariners' Compass* square (Step 3). Miter corners.

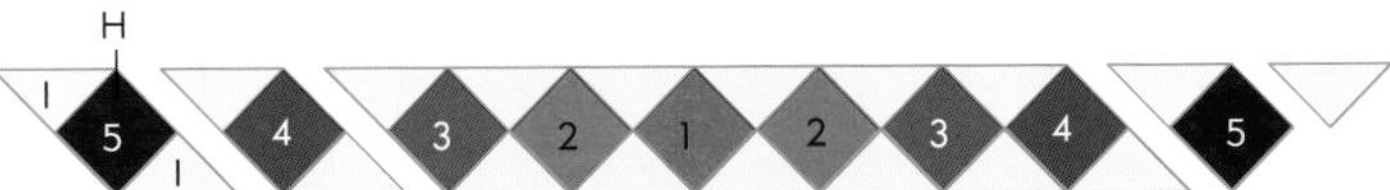

Join triangle I to either side of square H, then join these three-piece units. Make four strips

Short, pieced border strips (to surround center compass)

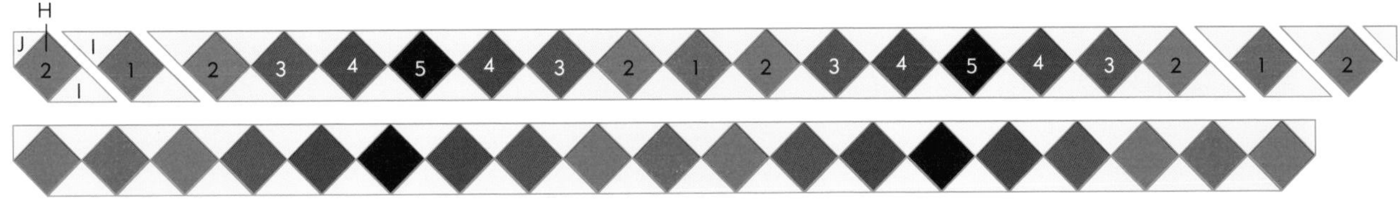

Side border strips for outer pieced border. Make two strips

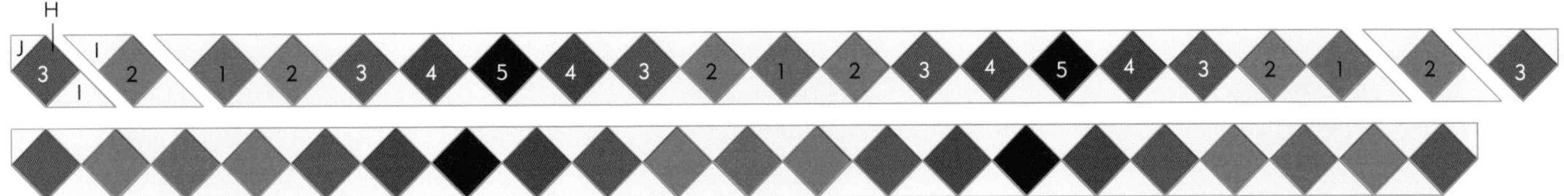

Top and bottom border strips for outer pieced border. Make two strips

Step 5. Making pieced borders

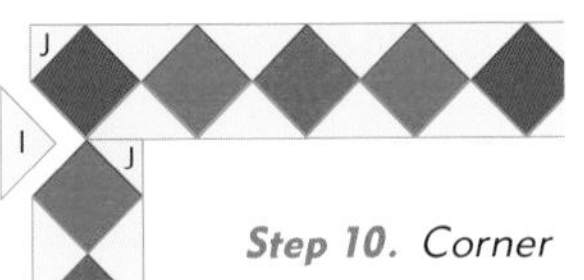

Step 10. Corner

7. Follow page 147 to frame a square with a border print. Add the border-print strips measuring 2⅝″ × 34″ (7 cm × 87 cm). Miter corners.
8. Sew the large pieced triangles from Step 4 to the sides to complete quilt center.
9. Again, following page 147, add the border-print strips measuring 2⅝″ × 48″ (7 cm × 122 cm). Sew miters.
10. Sew the pieced side border strips to the sides. Sew the pieced top/bottom strips to the top and bottom (see Step 5) Add extra I triangle, as shown. Note the position of the J triangles.
11. Frame the design with the border-print strips measuring 6″ × 74″ (15 cm × 188 cm). Sew miters.

Finishing the Quilt

12. Refer to Chapter Nine to prepare your quilt for quilting. All border print fabrics are quilted following the printed motifs. Remaining *Mariners' Compass* fabrics and pieced-border patches are ¼″ (0.75 cm) outlined. Echo quilting fills the ivory and beige backgrounds.
13. Bind and label your quilt (see Chapter Ten).

Starflower. *Designed by Jinny Beyer. Hand-pieced and hand-quilted by Paola Novara, 2002*

Finished size: 52″ × 52″ (132 cm × 132 cm)
Center block size (without borders): 36½″ × 36½″ (92 cm × 92 cm)
Finished size varies according to width of selected borders

Starflower

See Templates on pages 253 to 254

If you are making *Starflower* as you work through *Quiltmaking by Hand,* follow this sequence:

1. Sew four-patch squares
2. Sew four-patch squares to K triangles
3. Make pieced triangles
4. Sew center star block
5. Sew H, I/IR, and J/JR pieces
6. Create G triangles
7. Assemble top
8. Add borders

I have taught *Starflower* as a mystery quilt in my beginning hand-piecing classes, as mentioned on page 198. In fact, the quilter, Paola Novara, was a beginning hand piecer when she made this quilt in one of my classes. The quilt is fun to sew–the design grows outward from an eight-pointed center star–and it is not nearly as complex as it appears. In fact, *Starflower* will go together quickly once you are familiar with the key skills involved in its construction–joining multiple points (three, four, and eight), setting in, using border-print fabrics, sewing curves, and mitering corners.

A narrow border-print frame surrounds the central *Starflower* design. The mirror-imaged, border-print star points bring a touch of elegance, while the curved background pieces add a glow behind the star.

Fabric Requirements

Select the border-print fabric first, choosing one with both a wide and a narrow stripe. Coordinate the remaining fabrics with the border print.

3/8 yd (0.4 m) of navy texture (darkest fabric)
5/8 yd (0.6 m) of dark green texture (second darkest fabric)
1/8 yd (0.15 m) *each* of nine assorted textures, shaded bright to dark
1/4 yd (0.25 m) of ivory texture (lightest fabric)
7/8 yd (0.8 m) of beige print (second lightest fabric)
3/8 yd (0.4 m) of gray texture
2½ yd (2.3 m) of border print
3/8 yd (0.4 m) of black texture for middle border–use 44″-wide (112 cm) wide fabric to avoid piecing strips
3½ yd (3.2 m) of backing
5/8 yd (0.7 m) of fabric for binding

Feel free to deviate slightly from the border-print cutting widths listed below if the stripes in your border-print fabric are slightly different widths from those used in the quilt photographed. Included in the border-print measurements is enough excess length, so that when the final border pieces are cut you can successfully center and mirror motifs when cutting miters, as described in Chapter Eight.

Border print, inner border:
four strips measuring 2″ × 48″ (5 cm × 122 cm)
Black texture, middle border:
four strips measuring 1¼″ × 48″ (3 cm × 122 cm)
Border print, outer border:
four strips measuring 6″ × 70″ (15 cm × 178 cm)

Quick Tip

Cut strips for borders prior to cutting the mirror-imaged Template H, HR. in the quantities indicated on the templates. See page 135 for help on cutting mirror-image border-print pieces for Templates H, HR. Be sure to make whole Template J by mirroring on dotted line as instructed on template.

Making Template G

7½″
(19 cm)
Starflower
Template
G
Add ¼″ (0.75 cm)
seam allowance
15″ (38 cm)

USING THE DIMENSIONS given in the diagram, draw a 90° right-angle triangle on graph paper. Add seam allowance all around. Make the full size template from template plastic (see page 51).

Label your nine assorted texture fabrics from #1 to #9, with #1 being the brightest and #9 being the darkest. Cut all fabrics in the quantities indicated on the templates. Template B, C, E, F, K, and L fabrics may be rotary cut using the following dimensions.

B–cut 4 squares each from fabrics 1 to 9, measuring 2″ × 2″
C–cut 20 squares from navy and 16 from ivory, measuring 2⅜″ × 2⅜″, then cut once diagonally
E–cut 1 square measuring 7¼″ × 7¼″, then cut twice diagonally
F–cut 4 squares measuring 3½″ × 3½″
K–cut 12 squares from dark green and two from beige, measuring 5½″ × 5½″, then cut twice diagonally
L–cut four squares measuring 3″ × 3″, then cut once diagonally

To increase accuracy when piecing, mark dots exactly where the seam allowances will cross, as explained on page 56.

Piecing the Units

1. Piece an eight-pointed star from A/AR fabrics, as shown (see page 100).
2. Make four B/C units; add to the eight-pointed star, using the setting-in technique explained on page 108.
3. Sew together D, DR, and E fabrics. E will be set in to D/DR. Make four and add to the center star unit, using the setting-in technique.
4. Set in Template F fabrics to complete the center star block.
5. Refer to Chapter Seven on adding a border print to a square or triangle. This same process must be used for adding a border strip to a triangle to create completed triangle G. Look at *Making Template G* to prepare this template. Note that the dimensions given do not include seam allowances. The seam allowances will be added later, once the exact sizes of the two pieces that make up triangle G (a smaller triangle plus a border-print strip along one side) are determined. Measure the finished width of the narrow border strip on the fabric you have selected, then mark that distance in from one of the short sides of triangle G. Mark that distance across the entire short side. This will determine the size of the two templates that make up triangle G. Make a template for each, and add seam allowance on all sides.

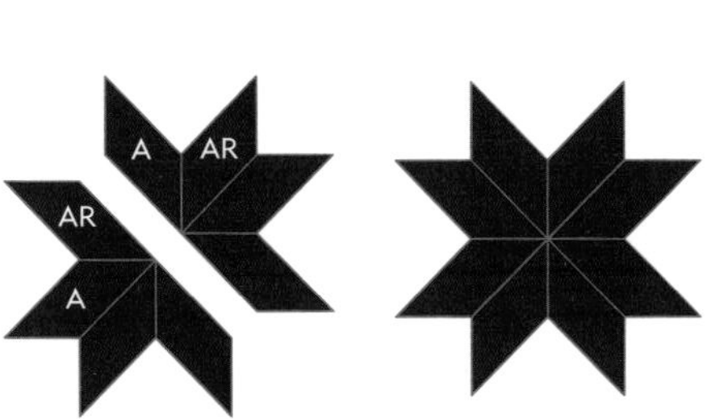

Step 1. *Piece eight-pointed star*

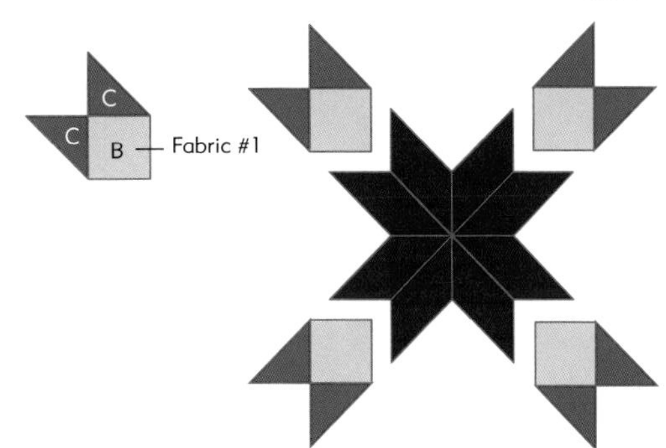

Step 2. *Add four B/C units*

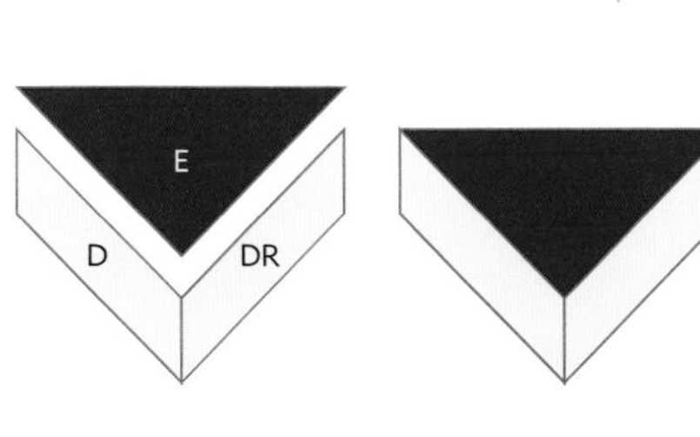

Step 3. *Add four D/DR/E units*

Step 4. *Complete center star block*

Step 5. *Border two large triangles, one the mirror image of the other. Make four and four reversed*

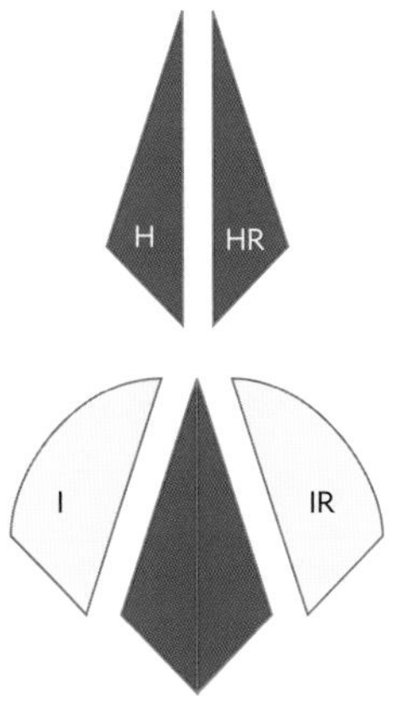

Step 6. *Piece curved unit*

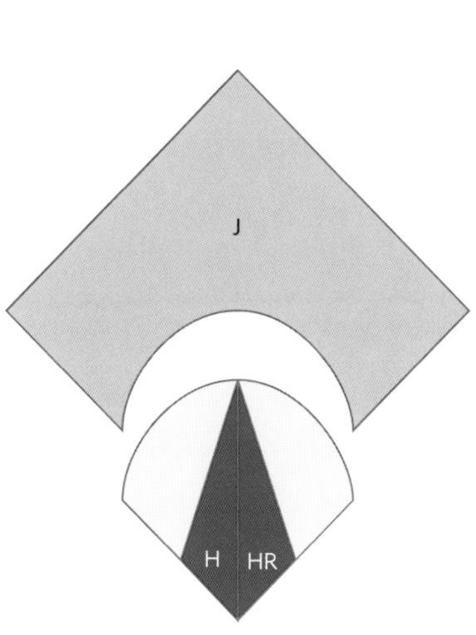

Step 7. *Make eight pieced triangles*

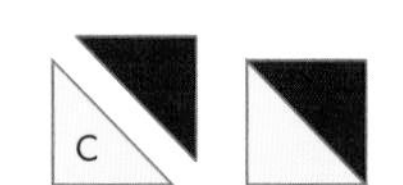

Step 8. *Make 32 pieced squares*

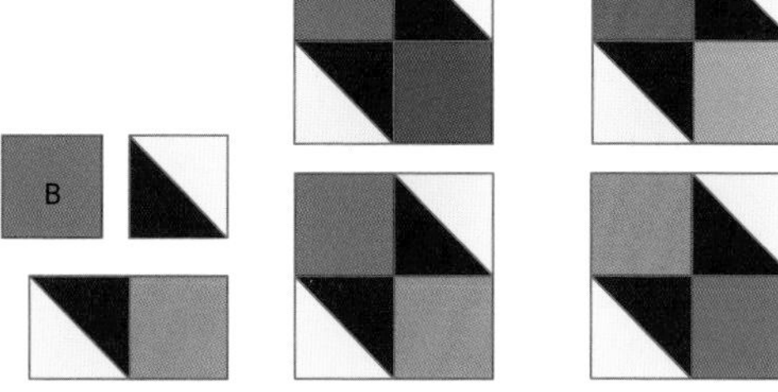

Step 9. *Piece four of each four-patch square*

Step 10. *Join K triangles to four-patch squares to piece diagonal units. Make four*

Step 11. *Add L triangles*

Complete quilt center

6. Stitch together H, HR, I and IR fabrics as shown, following the instructions for joining three points on page 90. Add Template J fabric (see Chapter Six for detailed instructions on sewing curves).
7. Again using the technique for joining three points, sew four K triangles together as shown to make pieced triangles. With the light beige triangle facing, right side up, pick up and sew each green triangle to it. Do this in continuous lines, without cutting the thread, joining the three points neatly at each intersection. Make eight. Set these units aside.
8. Using Template C fabrics, sew a navy triangle to an ivory one. Make 32.
9. Carefully following the fabric arrangements shown, stitch pieced squares together with Template B fabrics to make four-patch squares. Make four of each arrangement.
10. Join K triangles to four-patch squares as shown, taking care to achieve correct shading. Then use straight seams to sew the units together. Make four.

11. Piece four side units as shown, being sure to add the small L triangles to the bordered G triangles from step 5. Sew side units together with the center star block and four-patch strips to complete the quilt center.

Assembling the Quilt Top

12. Follow the instructions on page 147 to frame a square with a border-print fabric. After carefully measuring your finished quilt top, measure, cut, then add the narrow, inner border strips. Miter corners.
13. Re-measure, then cut and add the black texture strips for the middle border. Miter corners.
14. Once again, following the instructions on page 147, measure, cut, then add the outer border-print strips. Sew miters.

Finishing the Quilt

15. Refer to Chapter Nine to prepare your quilt for quilting. All border-print fabrics are quilted following the printed motifs. A variation of the border print motif fills the large background areas. The star fabrics are ¼″ (0.75 cm) outlined. A straight line is centered within each star "arm," extending to the quilt corners. Echo quilting fills the curved patches.
16. Bind and label your quilt (see Chapter Ten).

Compass Rose. *Designed by Jinny Beyer, 2003*

Finished size: 78″ × 96″ (198 cm × 244 cm)
Block size: 14″ × 14″ (35.5 cm × 35.5 cm)–12 total *Mariner's Compass* blocks
Center quilt size (without borders): 58″ × 76″ (147 cm × 193 cm)
Finished size varies according to width of selected borders

Compass Rose

See Templates on pages 255 to 256

With its *Mariner's Compass* blocks and sashed setting, the overall effect of *Compass Rose* is elegantly traditional. The blocks may appear intimidating, but with careful hand piecing, they are quite achievable.

Compass Rose incorporates many of the topics covered in this book, making it an excellent choice if you wish to practice the following techniques: joining multiple points, sewing curves, cutting identical border-print triangles and piecing them to make octagons and squares, framing a rectangle (on two sides) with a border print, set-in seams, and multiple border-print borders. Refer back to pages 122 to 125 for information on piecing a *Mariners' Compass* and for using checking templates.

Fabric Requirements

I recommend first selecting the border-print fabric, and using it to inspire a controlled selection of compass fabrics. To replicate the scrappy effect of my quilt, use a different set of fabrics for the compass points in each block.

The border-print yardage depends upon the number of stripe repeats across the width of the fabric (from selvage to selvage), as well as the way you choose to cut it for the Template A and G patches. If your border print contains only four narrow stripes and four wide stripes, you will need 9 to 9½ yards (8.3 m to 8.7 m). If your border fabric has five stripes of each, you may require as little as 7½ yards (6.9 m).

7½ yd to 9½ yd (6.9 m to 8.7 m) of border print for second and fourth borders, compass centers, sashing posts, and sashing frames
3¼ yd (3 m) of beige mottle for block background
⅛ yd (0.15 m) each of 12 assorted dark red textures for compass points
⅛ yd (0.15 m) each of 12 assorted rose textures for compass points
⅛ yd (0.15 m) each of 12 assorted teal textures for compass points
2½ yd (2.3 m) of dark red texture for first border
2⅝ yd (2.5 m) of teal texture for third border
7¼ yd (6.7 m) backing (piece widthwise)
⅞ yd (0.8 m) of fabric for binding

Cutting

Cut the template fabrics in the quantities indicated on the templates. See page 134 for help on cutting identical border-print patches for Templates A and G, and for the sashing rectangles. Notice that Template A triangles are cut from different portions of the border-print fabric. If you do likewise, be sure to cut sets of eight identical templates for each block. Feel free to deviate slightly from

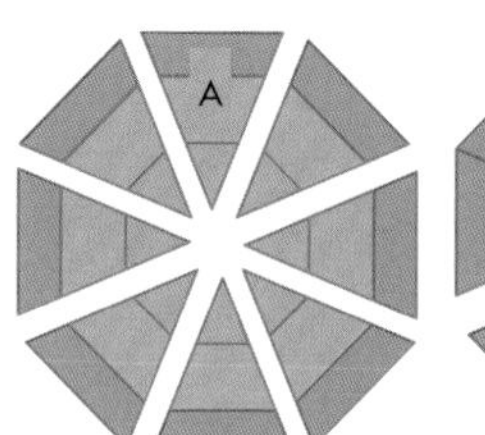

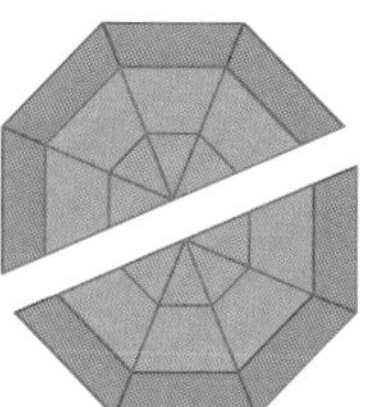
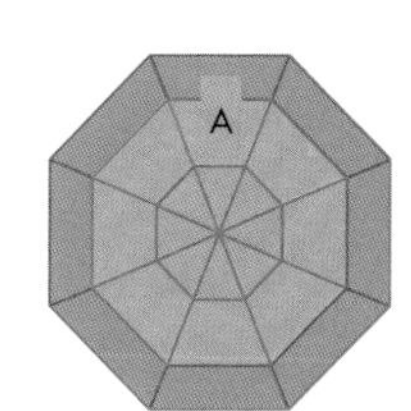

Step 1. Piece octagon. Make 12

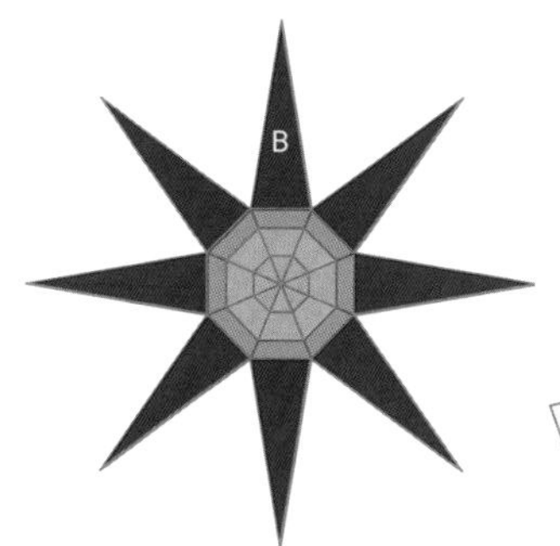

Step 2. Add large B points

C C D

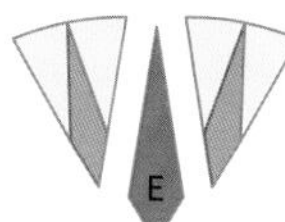

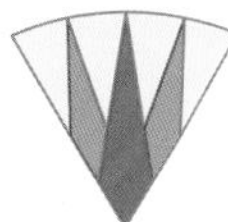

Step 3. Make 16 small C/D wedge units then add these to E to create 8 larger E/C/D units for each block

Step 5. Set in wedge pieces

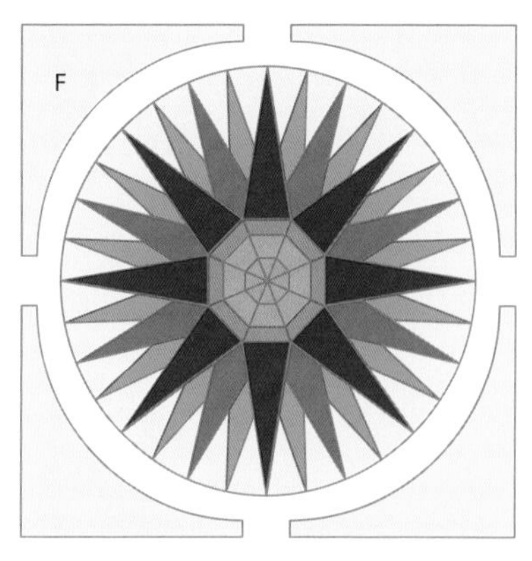

Step 6. Add curved pieces to complete block. Make 12

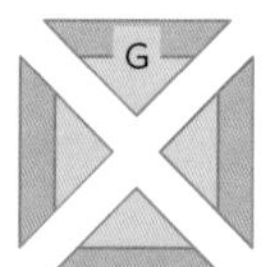

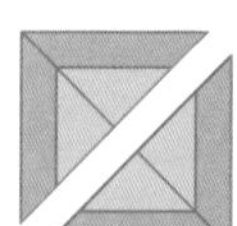
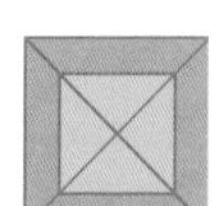

Step 7. Piece sashing post squares. Make 20

the border-print cutting widths presented here if the stripes in your border print are different widths than those used for *Compass Rose.* Included in the border stripe inner and outer strips is excess length, so you can successfully center and mirror motifs when cutting miters, as described in Chapter Eight.

QUICK TIP

Cut strips for borders prior to cutting fabric for Templates A and G or for the sashing rectangles, which will be used to make the octagonal compass centers, the sashing posts, and the sashing strips, respectively (see page 214).

Dark red texture, first border (top/bottom):
two strips measuring 3″ × 68″ (7.5 cm × 173 cm)
Dark red texture, first border (sides):
two strips measuring 3″ × 86″ (7.5 cm × 218.5 cm)
Border print, second border (top/bottom):
two strips measuring 1⅜″ × 72″ (3.5 cm × 183 cm)
Border print, second border (sides):
four strips measuring 1⅜″ × 46″ (3.5 cm × 117 cm)
Teal texture, third border (top/bottom):
two strips measuring 2¾″ × 74″ (7 cm × 188 cm)
Teal texture, third border (sides):
two strips measuring 2¾″ × 92″ (7 cm × 234 cm)
Border print, fourth border (top/bottom):
two strips measuring 4⅝″ × 94″ (11.8 cm × 239 cm)
Border print, fourth border (sides):
four strips measuring 4⅝″ × 56″ (11.8 cm × 142 cm)

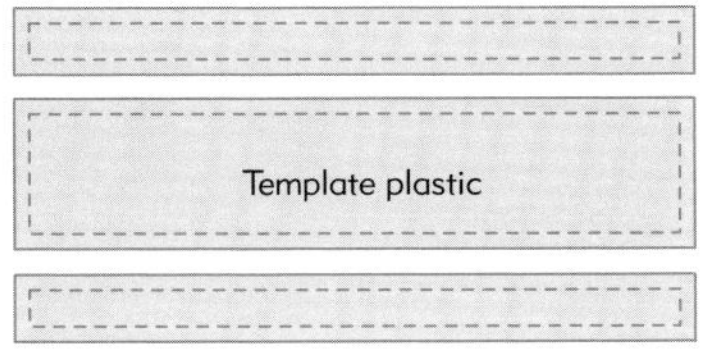

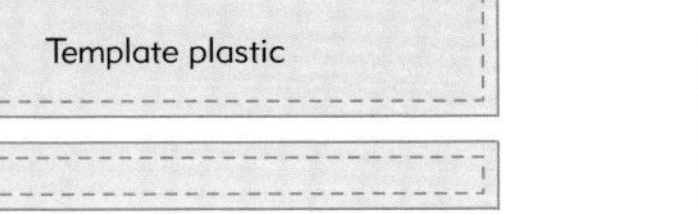

Step 8. Add border strip to rectangle

Step 9. Piece sashing rectangles. Make 31

Piecing the Blocks

1. Piece octagon using matching set of eight identically cut triangles from Template A (see page 140). Make 12.
2. Add matching set of eight dark red Template B fabrics.
3. Piece 16 C/D wedges for each block (see joining three points on page 90). As each wedge is sewn, use Checking Template 1 to ensure accuracy (see page 122). Piece 8 E/CD wedges for each block and use Checking Template 2 to check for accuracy.
4. Using set-in seams, add wedge units to Template A/B star.
5. Add curved Template F fabrics (see page 124). Make 12 blocks.

Making the Sashing Posts and Sashing Strips

6. Piece 20 sashing post squares, using four identically cut Template G triangles for each square. (See page 132.)
7. Reread pages 137 to 138, then add border strips to a rectangle as explained here. The finished rectangle will be 4″ × 14″ (10 cm × 35.5 cm), without seam allowance. To begin, make a rectangle template in this finished size from template plastic. Seam allowances will be added later, once the exact sizes of the three pieces of fabric that make up the rectangle are known. Measure the finished width of the narrow border strip and mark that distance along each long side of the rectangle template. This will determine the size of the templates that make up the sashing rectangle. Make a template for each, and add seam allowance around all sides. Cut the fabrics.
8. Piece 31 sashing rectangles as shown.

Step 9. Piece sashing rows and block rows

Assembling the Quilt Top

9. Piece four sashing rows and three block rows, as shown. Alternately sew together sashing rows and block rows.
10. Follow the instructions on page 148 to frame a rectangular quilt with multiple border print borders.

Finishing the Quilt

11. Refer to Chapter Nine to prepare for quilting. The compass fabrics and the sashing and border strips are ¼″ (0.75 cm) outline quilted. The beige F fabrics are echo quilted. The outer border follows the printed fabric design.
12. Bind and label your quilt (see Chapter Ten).

To increase accuracy when piecing, mark dots exactly where the seam allowances will cross, as explained on page 56.

Day Lilies. *Designed, hand-pieced, and hand-quilted by Jinny Beyer, 1998*

Finished size: 79″ × 88″ (200.5 cm × 223.5 cm)
Center quilt size (without borders): 59″ × 68″ (149.5 cm × 172.5 cm)
Finished size varies according to width of selected borders

Day Lilies

See Templates on pages 257 to 258

The pattern for *Day Lilies* is a *tessellation*–a shape that repeats itself and fits together without any gaps or overlaps. Six tessellating flower-petal units make up each flower. Seven templates (A through G) make up each petal unit.

Day Lilies involves joining multiple points, piecing curves, and framing a rectangular quilt with multiple border-print borders.

Fabric Requirements

Day Lilies was pieced using a large assortment of scraps from three different color families–red, purple, and brown. Select lights, mediums, and darks from each. If you're working from scraps, you'll need scraps that measure approximately 2″ × 8″ to 3″ × 11″ (5 cm × 20 cm to 7.5 cm × 28 cm) for each piece.

4½ to 6 yards *total* (4.2 m to 5.5 m) of assorted reds
4½ to 6 yards *total* (4.2 m to 5.5 m) of assorted purples
4½ to 6 yards *total* (4.2 m to 5.5 m) of assorted browns
3 yd (2.8 m) of border print for inner and outer borders
2½ (2.3 m) of red print for middle border
7⅜ yd (6.8 m) backing (piece widthwise)
⅞ yd (0.8 m) of fabric for binding

Cutting

For each flower petal unit, select seven different fabrics from a single family, ranging from light to dark. Cut fabrics in the quantities indicated on the templates. Feel free to deviate slightly from the border-print cutting widths presented here if the stripes in your border print are different widths than those used for *Day Lilies.* Included in the border print inner and outer strips is excess length, so you can successfully center and mirror motifs when cutting miters.

Border print, inner border (top/bottom):
two strips measuring 3¼″ × 72″ (8.3 cm × 183 cm)
Border print, inner border (sides):
four strips measuring 3¼″ × 42″ (8.3 cm × 107 cm)
Red print, middle border (top/bottom):
two strips measuring 2¼″ × 72″ (5.8 cm × 183 cm)
Red print, middle border (sides):
two strips measuring 2¼″ × 85″ (5.8 cm × 216 cm)
Border print, outer border (top/bottom):
two strips measuring 6″ × 96″ (15 cm × 244 cm)
Border print, outer border (sides):
four strips measuring 6″ × 52″ (15 cm × 132 cm)

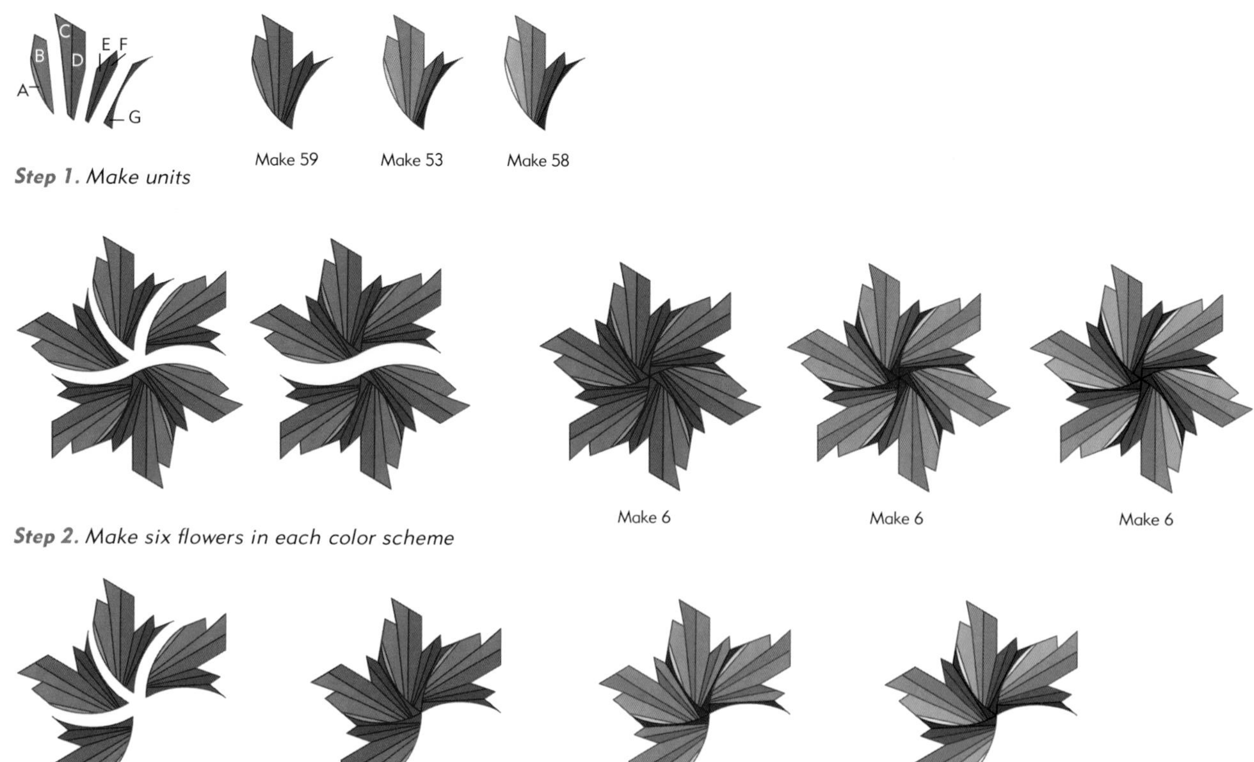

Step 1. *Make units*

Step 2. *Make six flowers in each color scheme*

Step 3. *Make side units*

Day Lilies

Piecing the Blocks

1. Select a set of A to G fabrics from one color family, ranging from light A to dark G. Stitch Template A through G fabrics together as shown to make a flower-petal unit. Make quantities indicated for each color family.
2. To make a full flower, arrange and stitch together six petal units from the same color family. (See pages 118 to 119 on sewing curves.) Make six of each.
3. Sew together four petal units as shown to make quilt side unit. Make quantities indicated.
4. Use three red petal units to make the lower right corner of quilt.
5. Stitch together two brown petal units for the top right corner of the quilt.

Assembling the Quilt Top

6. Carefully arrange and stitch together blocks, side units, and corner units as shown. Add remaining purple petal units.

To increase accuracy when piecing, mark dots exactly where the seam allowances will cross, as explained on page 56.

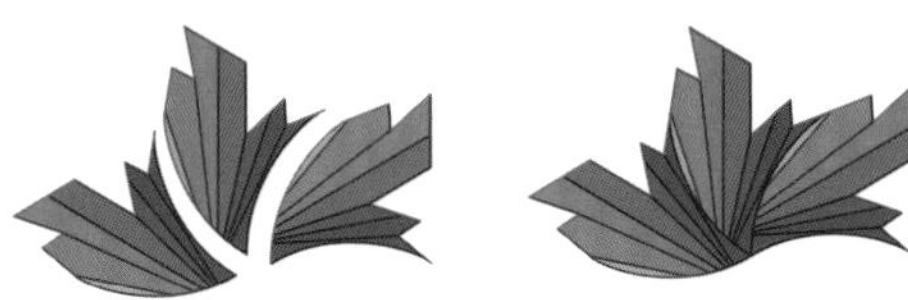
Step 4. Make lower right corner unit

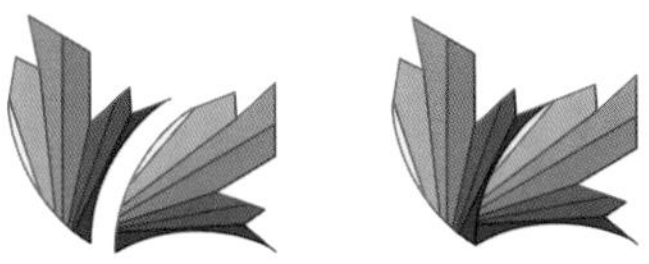
Step 5. Make top right corner unit

Step 6. Stitch blocks together, then trim edges

7. In preparation for trimming quilt edges even, using a yardstick and marking tool, mark a line connecting the block centers along each side (see dashed line in diagram). Trim quilt edge ¼″ (0.75 cm) *beyond* the dashed line, as indicated by the solid line on the diagram.
8. Since the trimming has caused some of the stitching lines to be cut, go back and reinforce each of the cut seams around the edges of the quilt.
9. Follow the instructions on page 148 to frame a rectangular quilt with multiple border-print borders.

Finishing the Quilt

10. Refer to Chapter Nine to prepare your quilt for quilting. The flower petals are stitched down the middle of each piece, ¼″ (0.75 cm) in from the edge. The border-print fabrics are quilted following the printed motifs, and the middle border is ¼″ (0.75 cm) outlined.
11. Bind and label your quilt (see Chapter Ten).

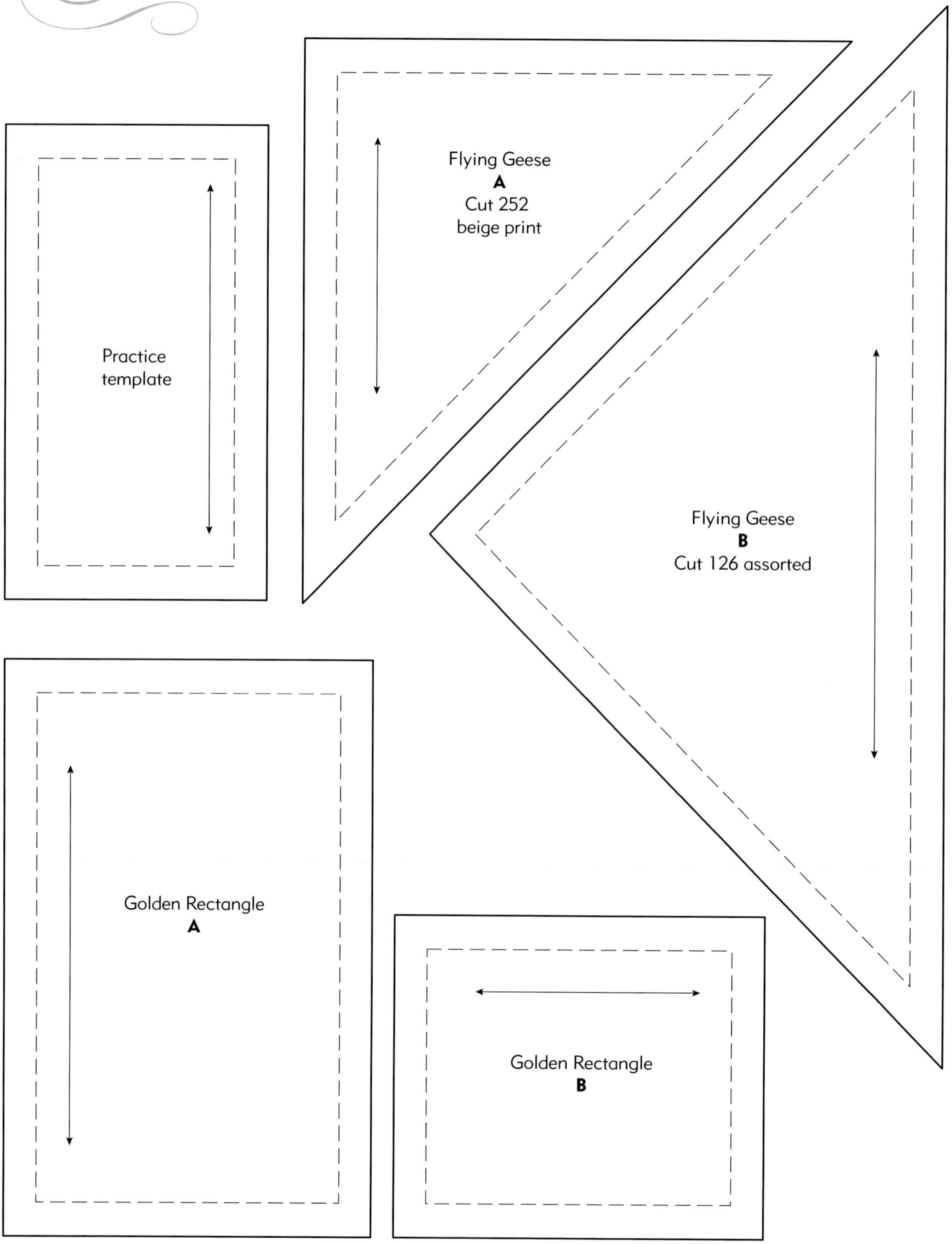

Practice template

Flying Geese
A
Cut 252
beige print

Flying Geese
B
Cut 126 assorted

Golden Rectangle
A

Golden Rectangle
B

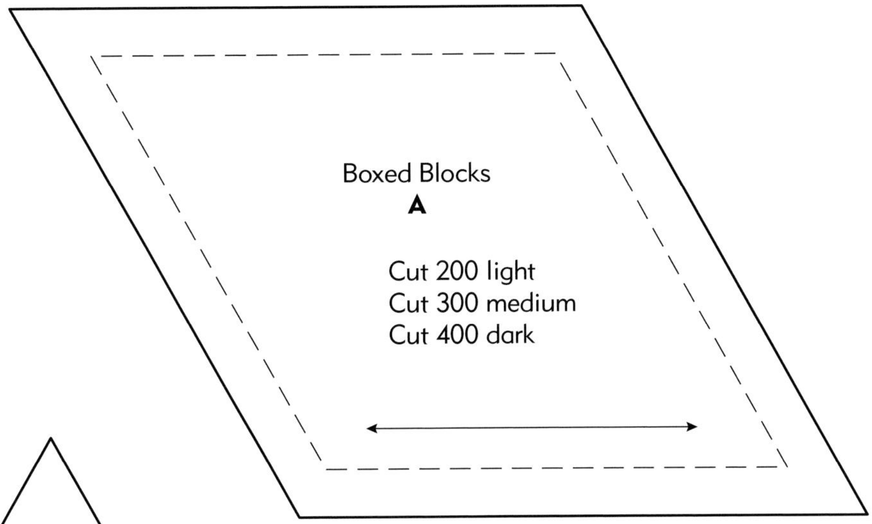

Boxed Blocks
A
Cut 200 light
Cut 300 medium
Cut 400 dark

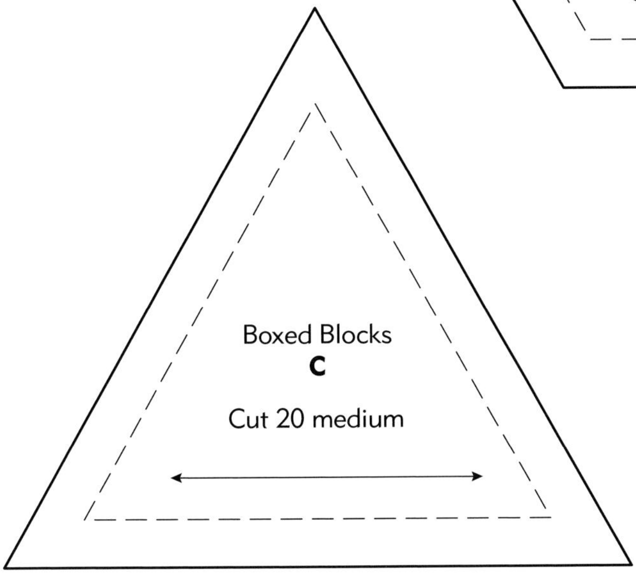

Boxed Blocks
C
Cut 20 medium

D/DR
Cut 1 of each
from medium

Boxed Blocks
B
Cut 20 light
Cut 9 medium

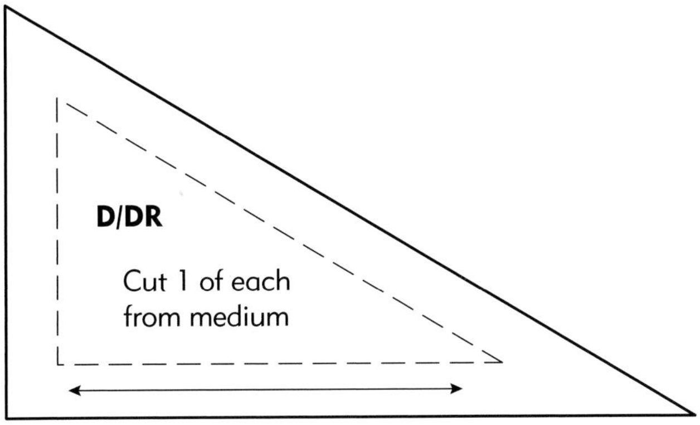

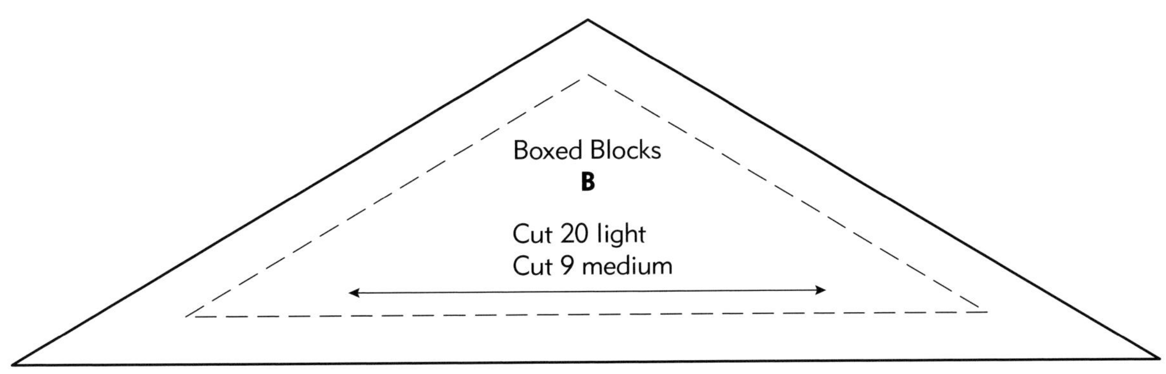

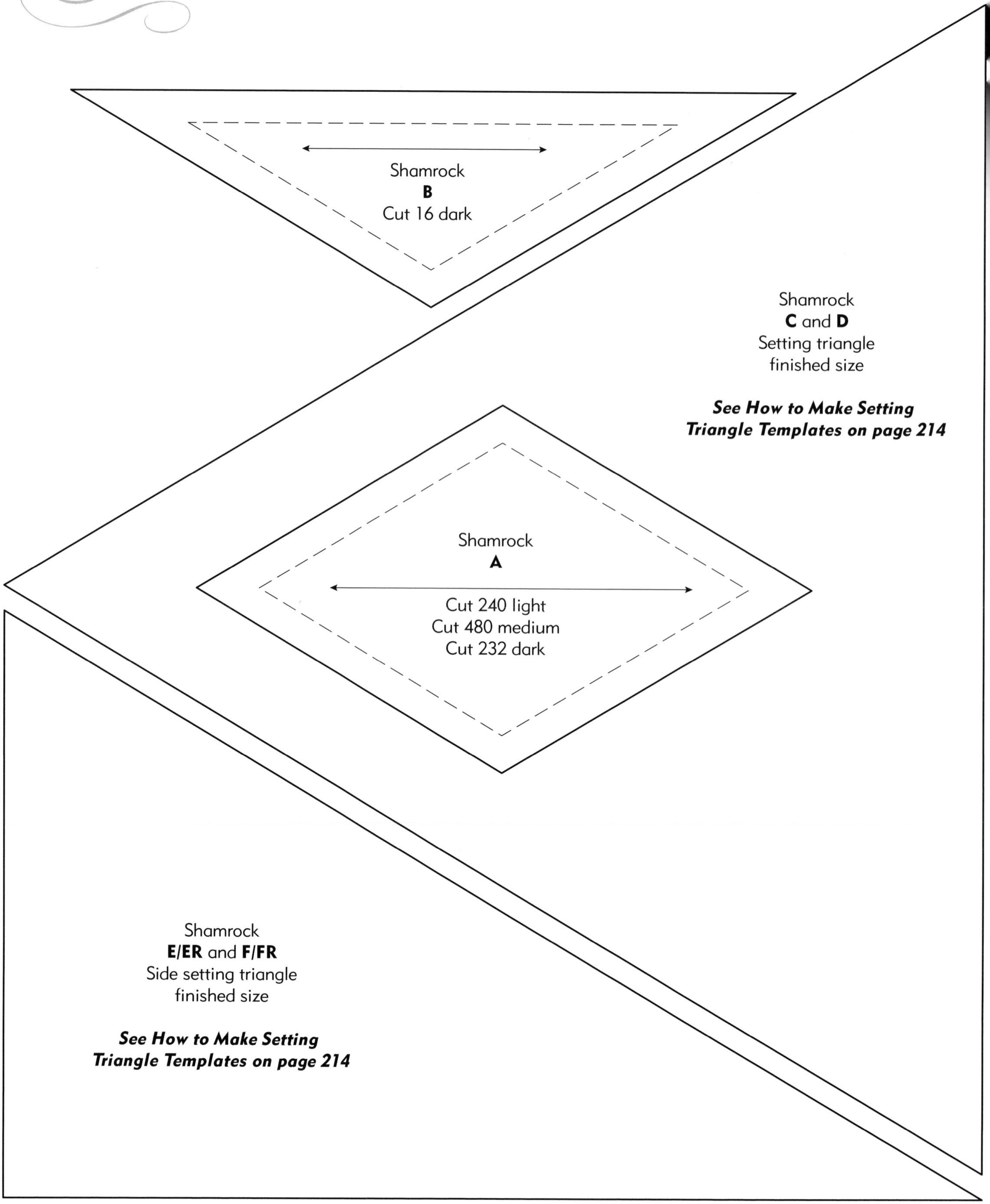

Shamrock
B
Cut 16 dark

Shamrock
C and **D**
Setting triangle
finished size

See How to Make Setting Triangle Templates on page 214

Shamrock
A
Cut 240 light
Cut 480 medium
Cut 232 dark

Shamrock
E/ER and **F/FR**
Side setting triangle
finished size

See How to Make Setting Triangle Templates on page 214

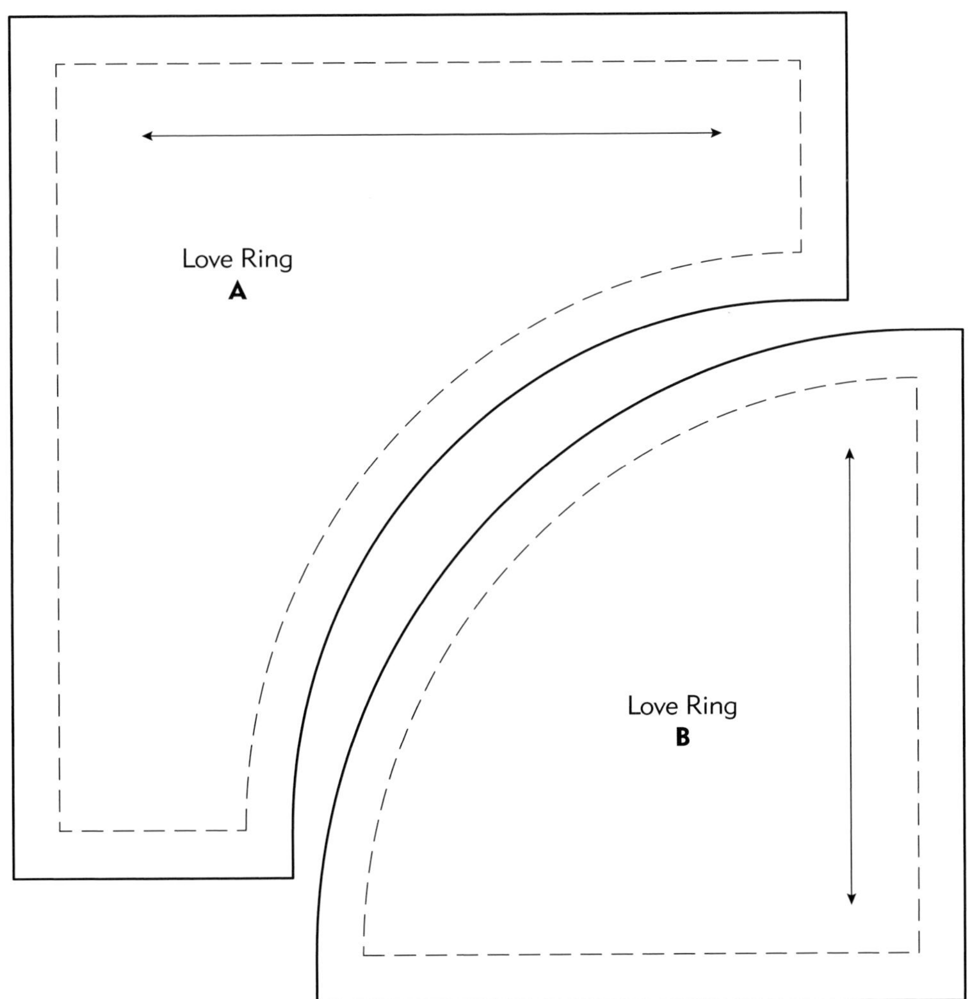
Love Ring
A
Love Ring
B

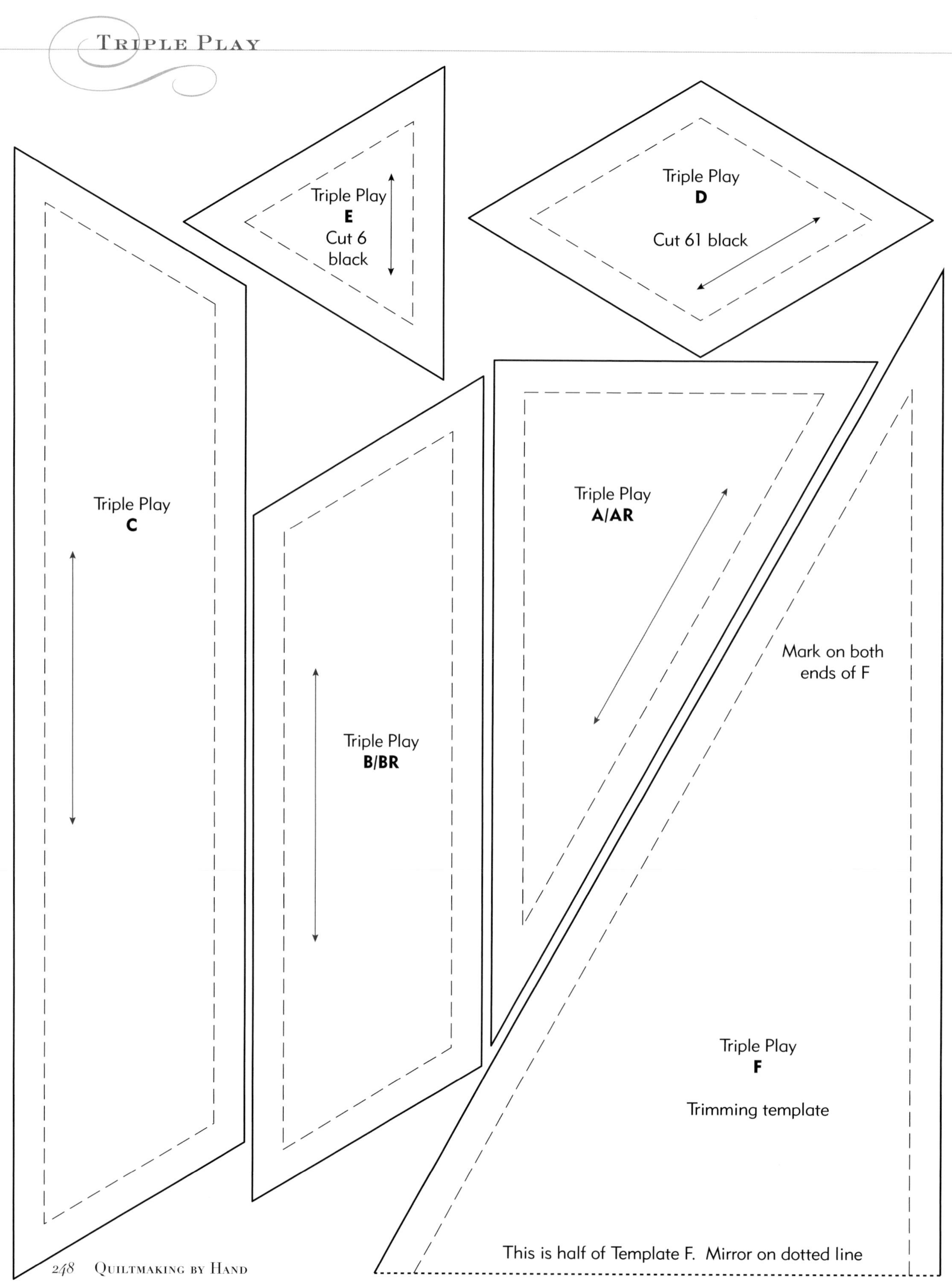
Triple Play
E
Cut 6
black
Triple Play
D
Cut 61 black
Triple Play
C
Triple Play
B/BR
Triple Play
A/AR
Mark on both
ends of F
Triple Play
F
Trimming template
This is half of Template F. Mirror on dotted line

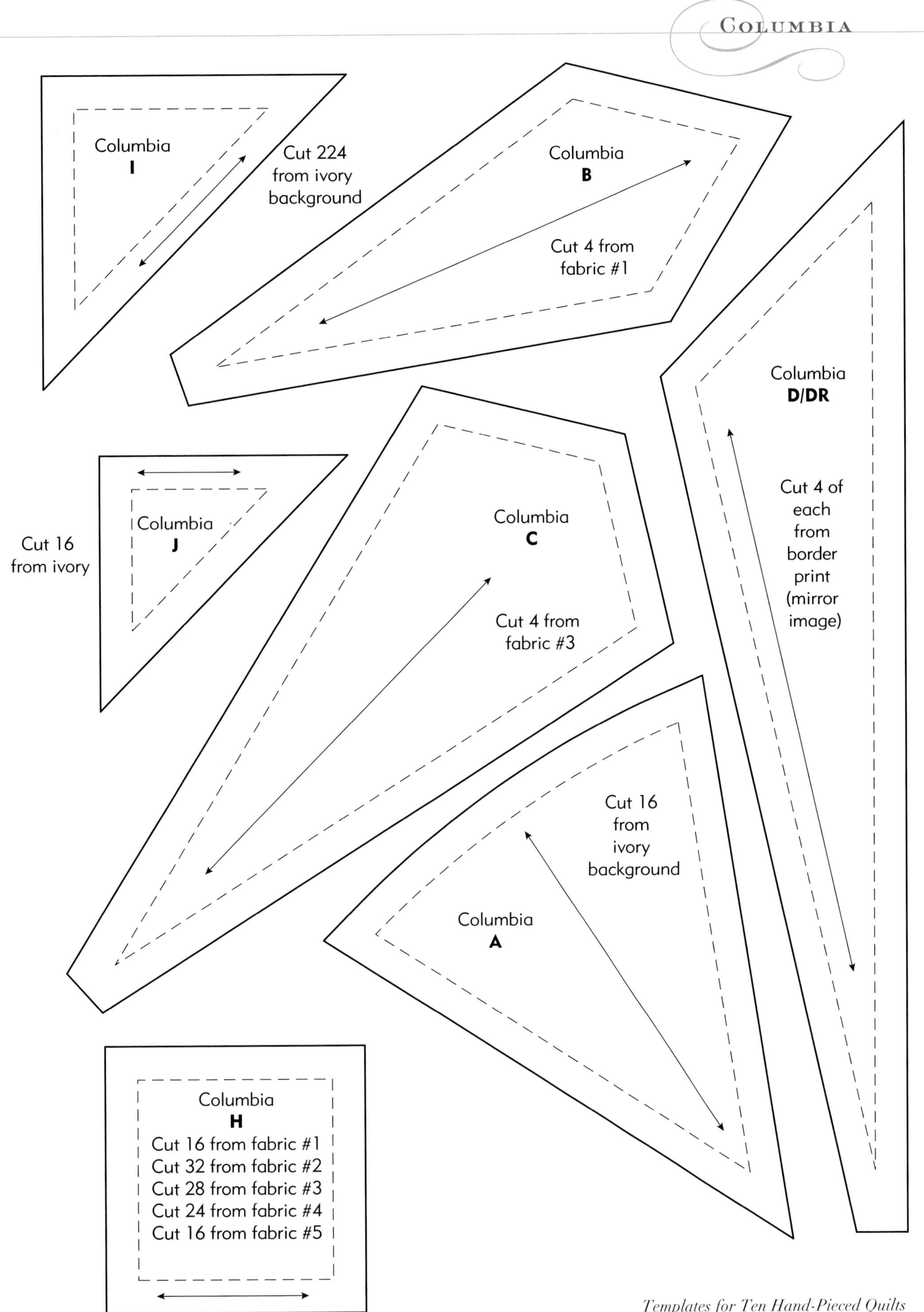
Columbia
I
Cut 224
from ivory
background
Columbia
B
Cut 4 from
fabric #1
Columbia
D/DR
Cut 4 of
each
from
border
print
(mirror
image)
Columbia
J
Cut 16
from ivory
Columbia
C
Cut 4 from
fabric #3
Cut 16
from
ivory
background
Columbia
A
Columbia
H
Cut 16 from fabric #1
Cut 32 from fabric #2
Cut 28 from fabric #3
Cut 24 from fabric #4
Cut 16 from fabric #5

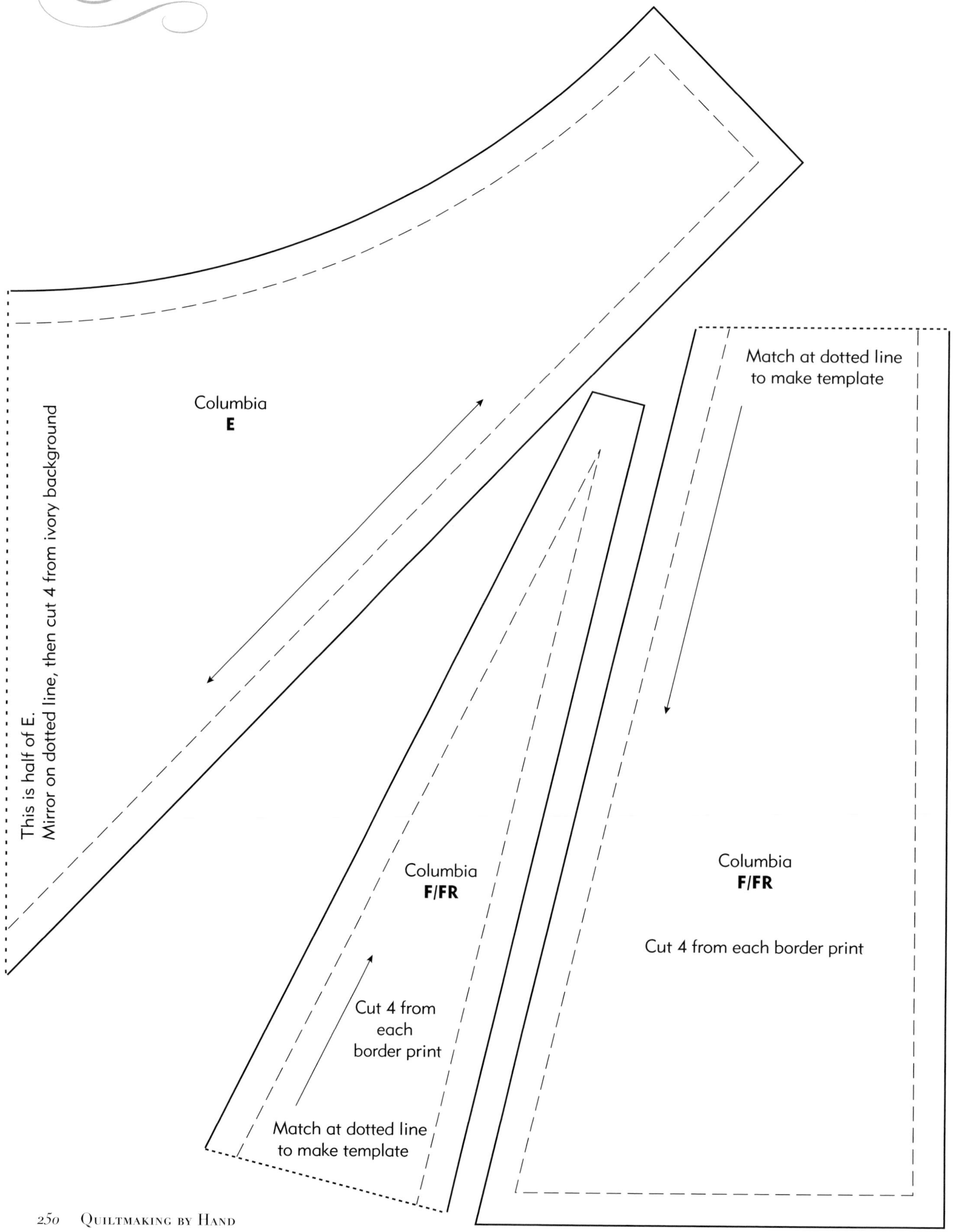

Columbia
E

This is half of E.
Mirror on dotted line, then cut 4 from ivory background

Columbia
F/FR

Cut 4 from
each
border print

Match at dotted line
to make template

Match at dotted line
to make template

Columbia
F/FR

Cut 4 from each border print

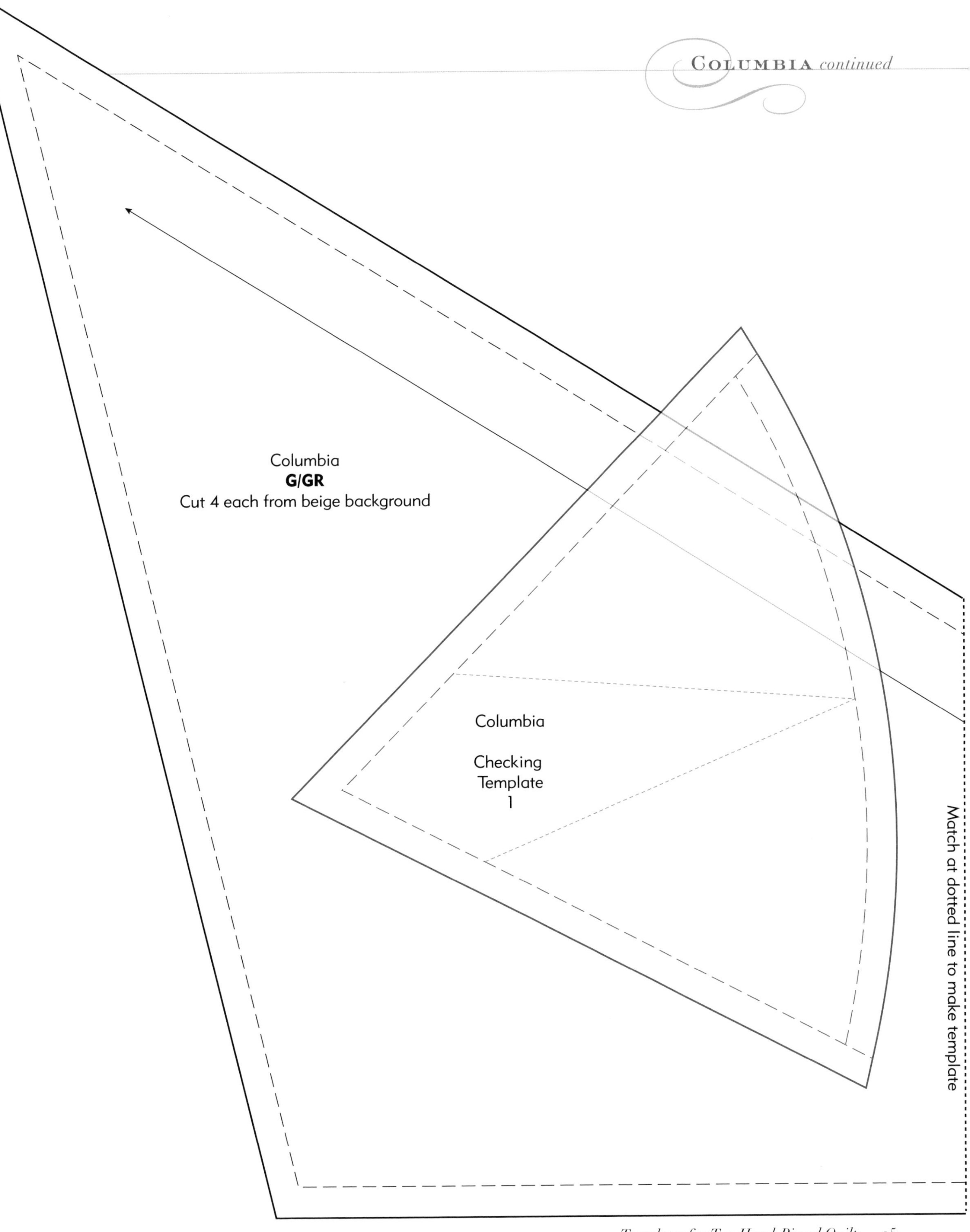
Columbia
G/GR
Cut 4 each from beige background
Columbia
Checking
Template
1
Match at dotted line to make template

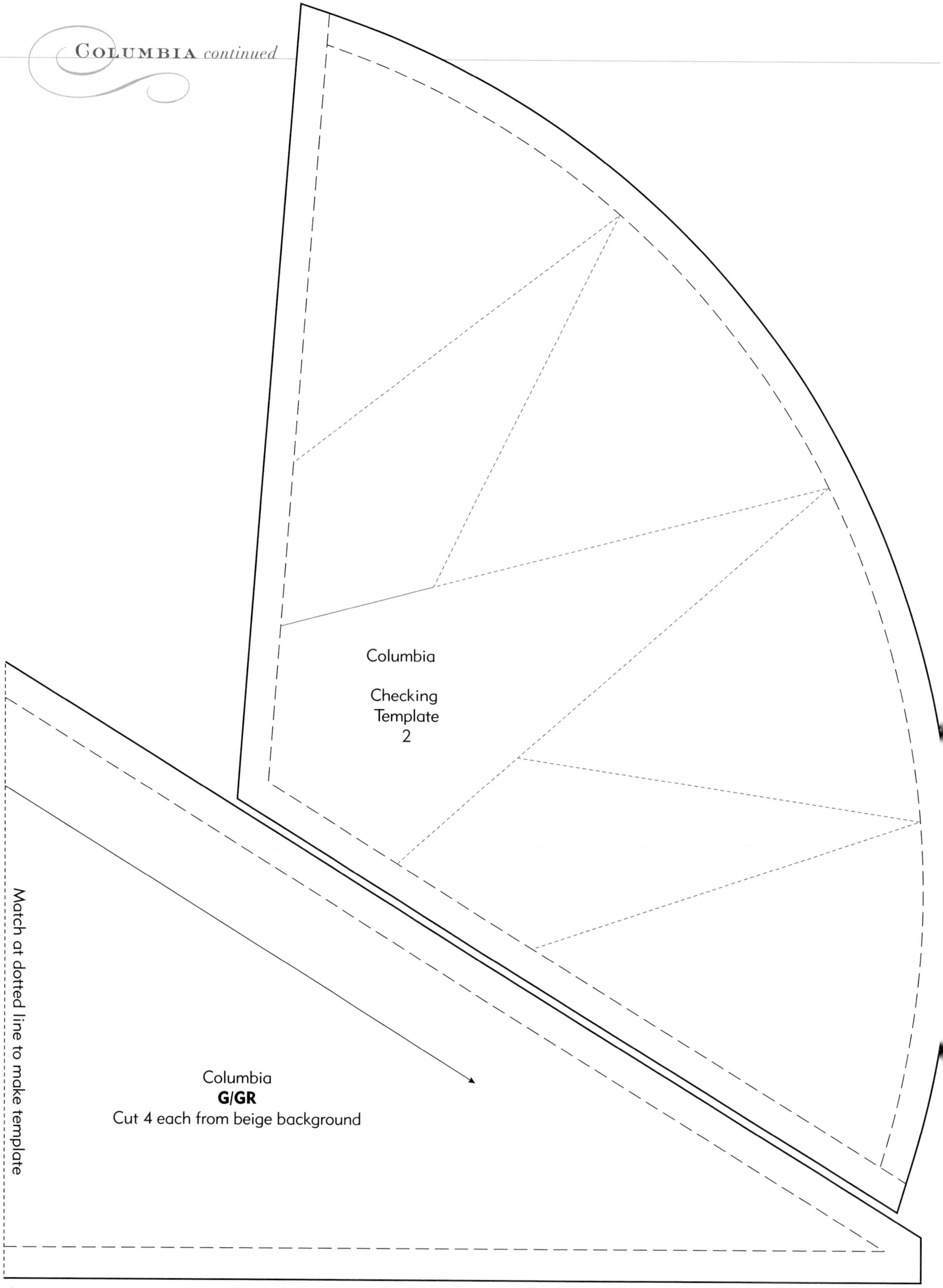

Columbia

Checking
Template
2

Match at dotted line to make template

Columbia
G/GR
Cut 4 each from beige background

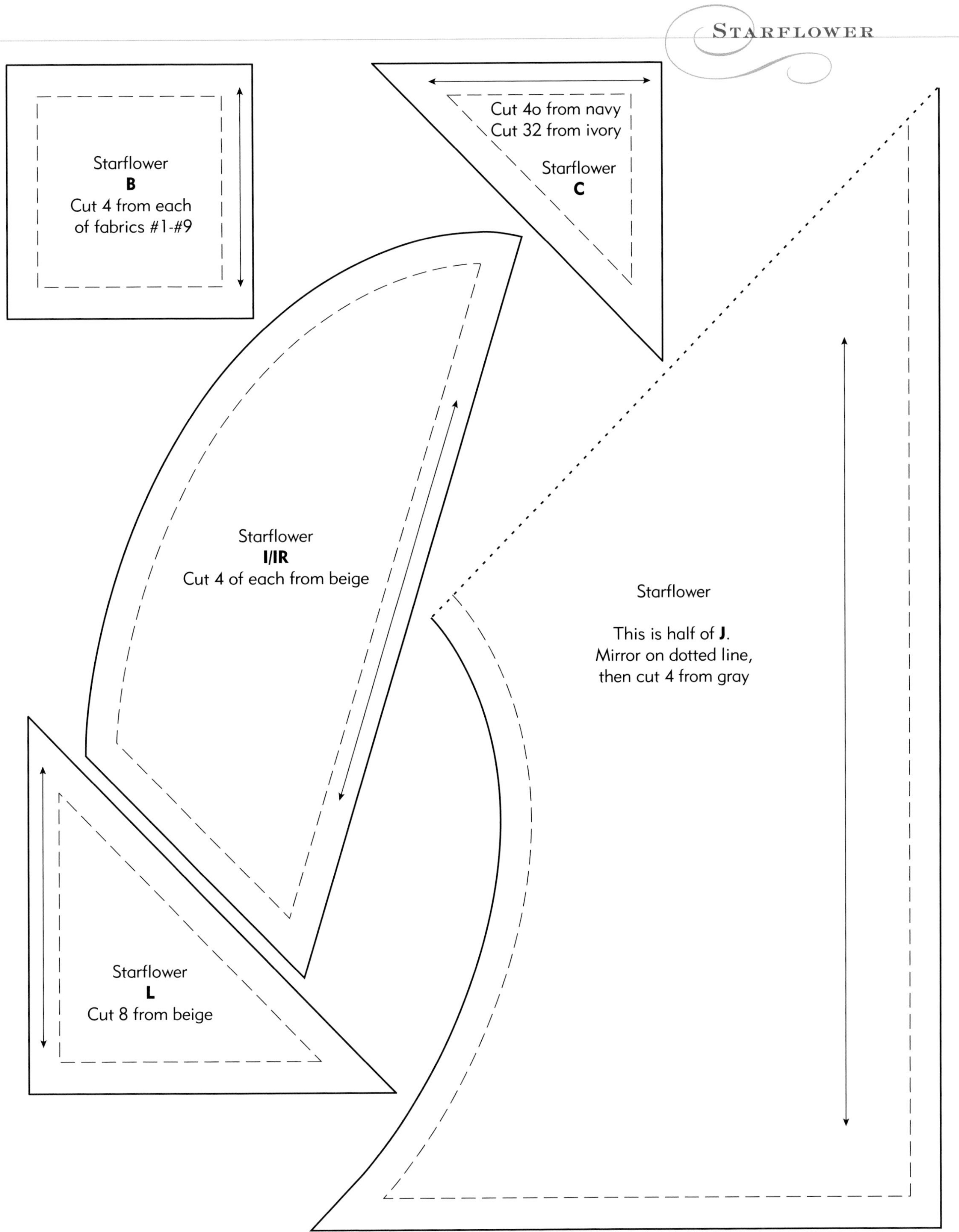
Starflower
B
Cut 4 from each
of fabrics #1-#9
Cut 4o from navy
Cut 32 from ivory
Starflower
C
Starflower
I/IR
Cut 4 of each from beige
Starflower
This is half of J.
Mirror on dotted line,
then cut 4 from gray
Starflower
L
Cut 8 from beige

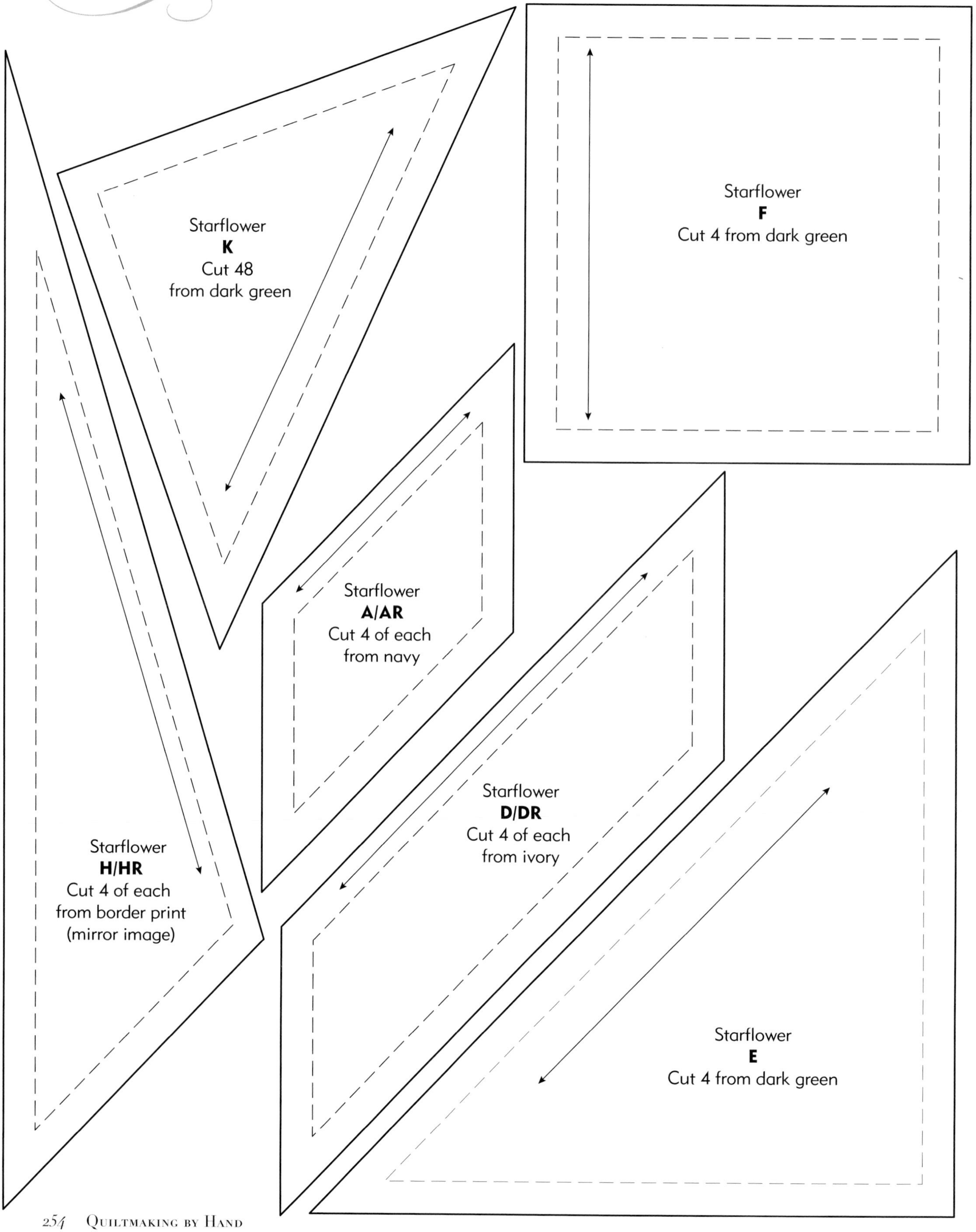

Starflower
K
Cut 48
from dark green

Starflower
F
Cut 4 from dark green

Starflower
A/AR
Cut 4 of each
from navy

Starflower
D/DR
Cut 4 of each
from ivory

Starflower
H/HR
Cut 4 of each
from border print
(mirror image)

Starflower
E
Cut 4 from dark green

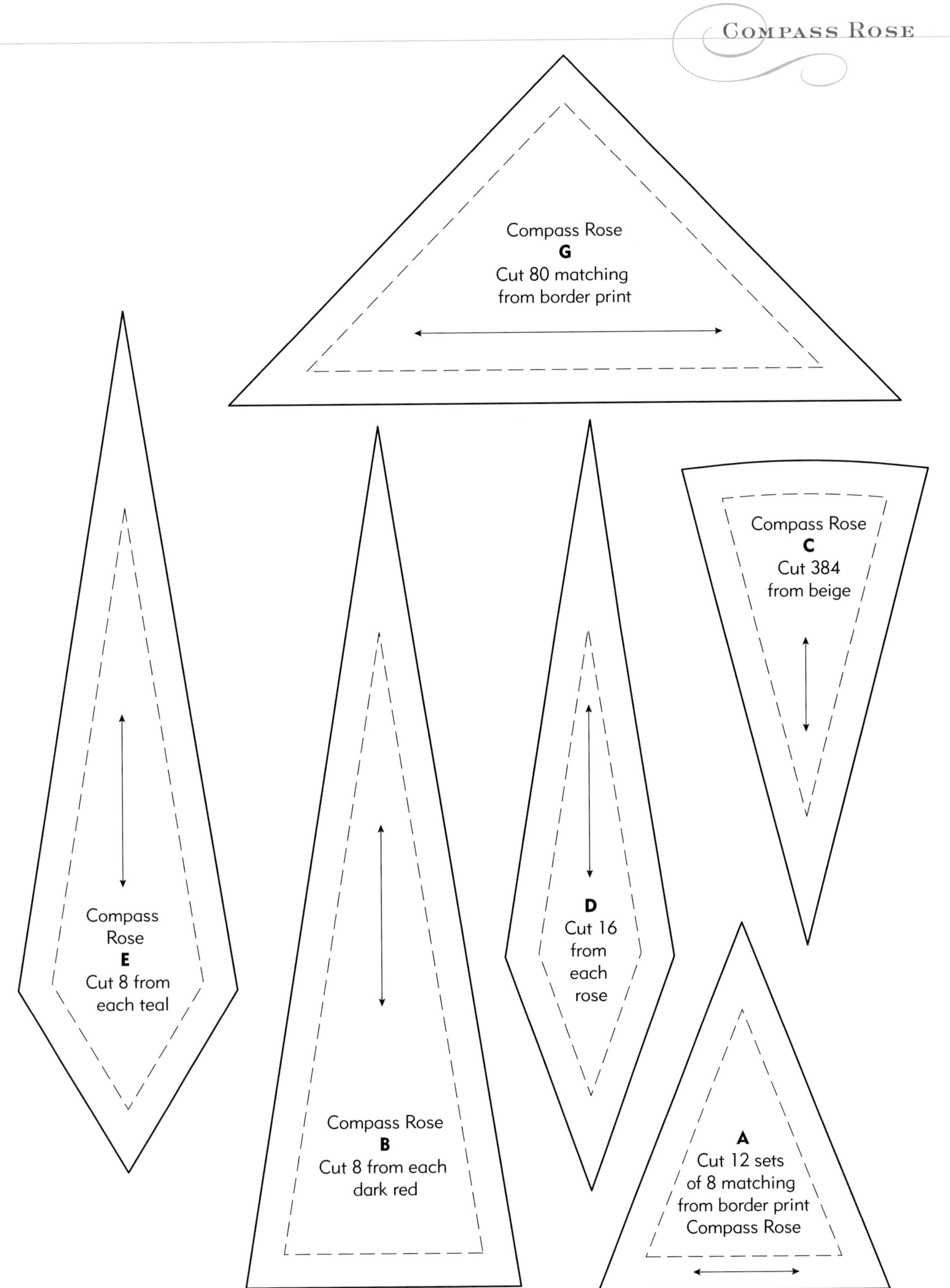
Compass Rose
G
Cut 80 matching
from border print
Compass Rose
E
Cut 8 from
each teal
Compass Rose
B
Cut 8 from each
dark red
D
Cut 16
from
each
rose
Compass Rose
C
Cut 384
from beige
A
Cut 12 sets
of 8 matching
from border print
Compass Rose

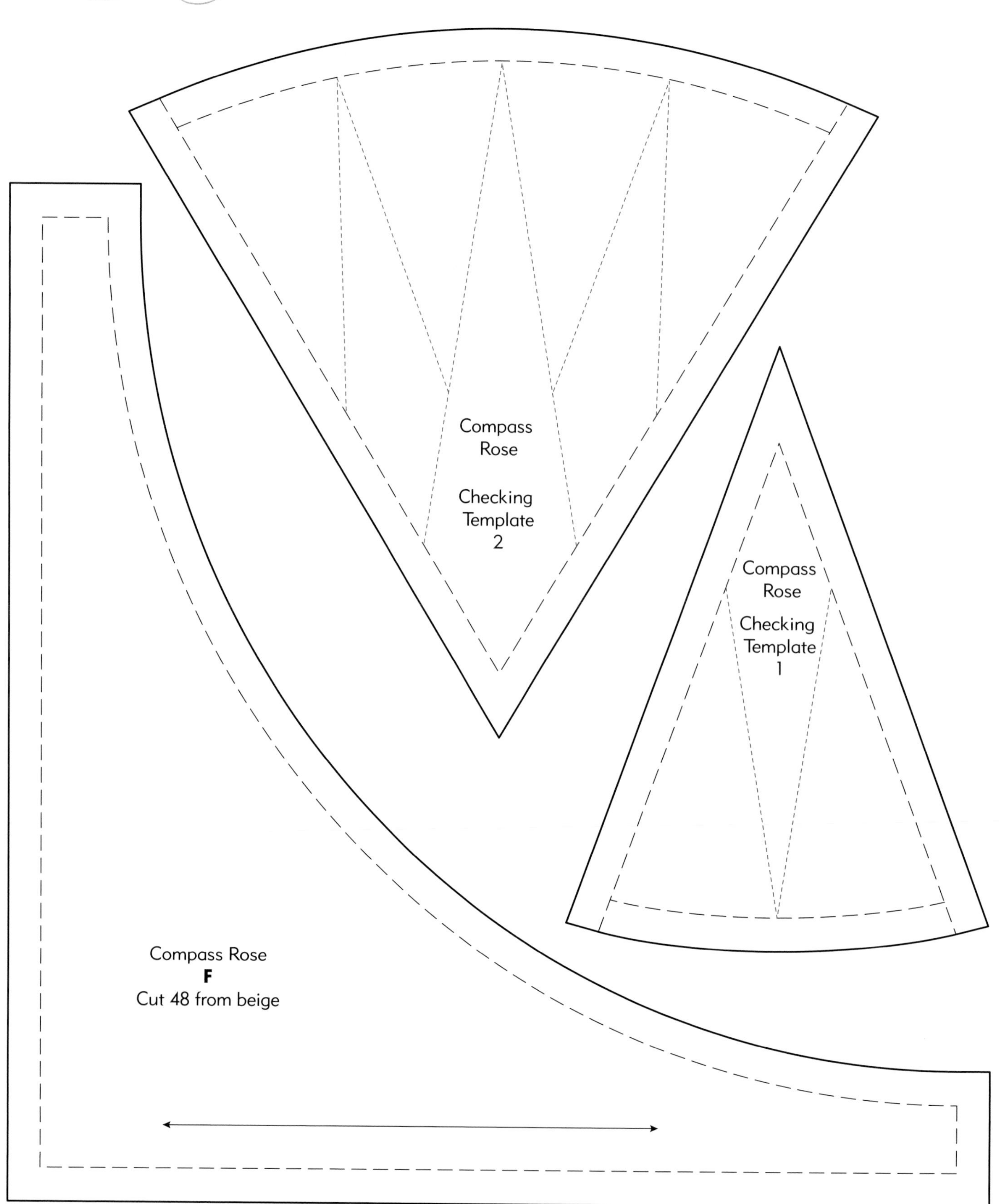
Compass
Rose
Checking
Template
2
Compass
Rose
Checking
Template
1
Compass Rose
F
Cut 48 from beige

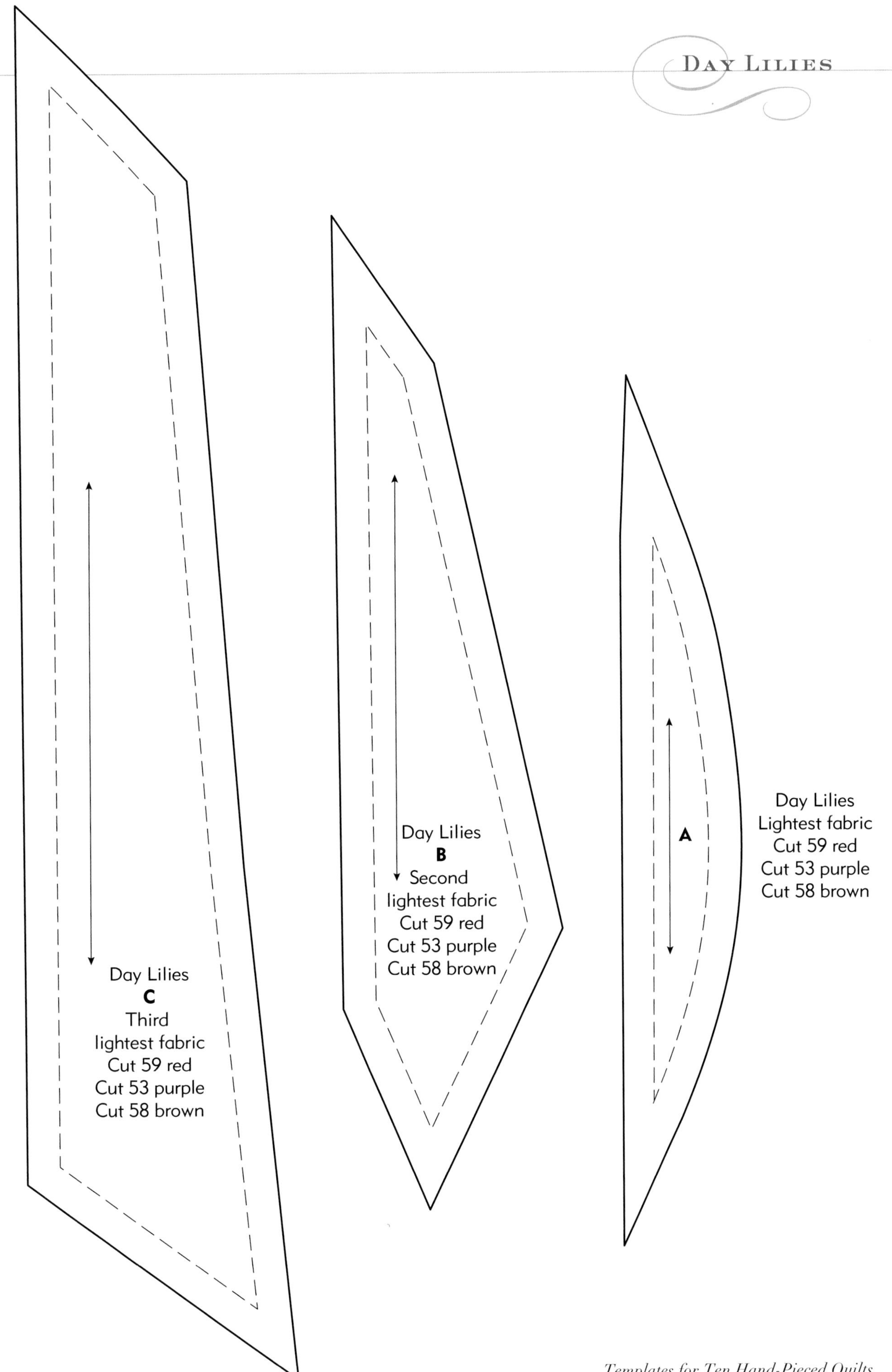
Day Lilies
C
Third
lightest fabric
Cut 59 red
Cut 53 purple
Cut 58 brown
Day Lilies
B
Second
lightest fabric
Cut 59 red
Cut 53 purple
Cut 58 brown
A
Day Lilies
Lightest fabric
Cut 59 red
Cut 53 purple
Cut 58 brown

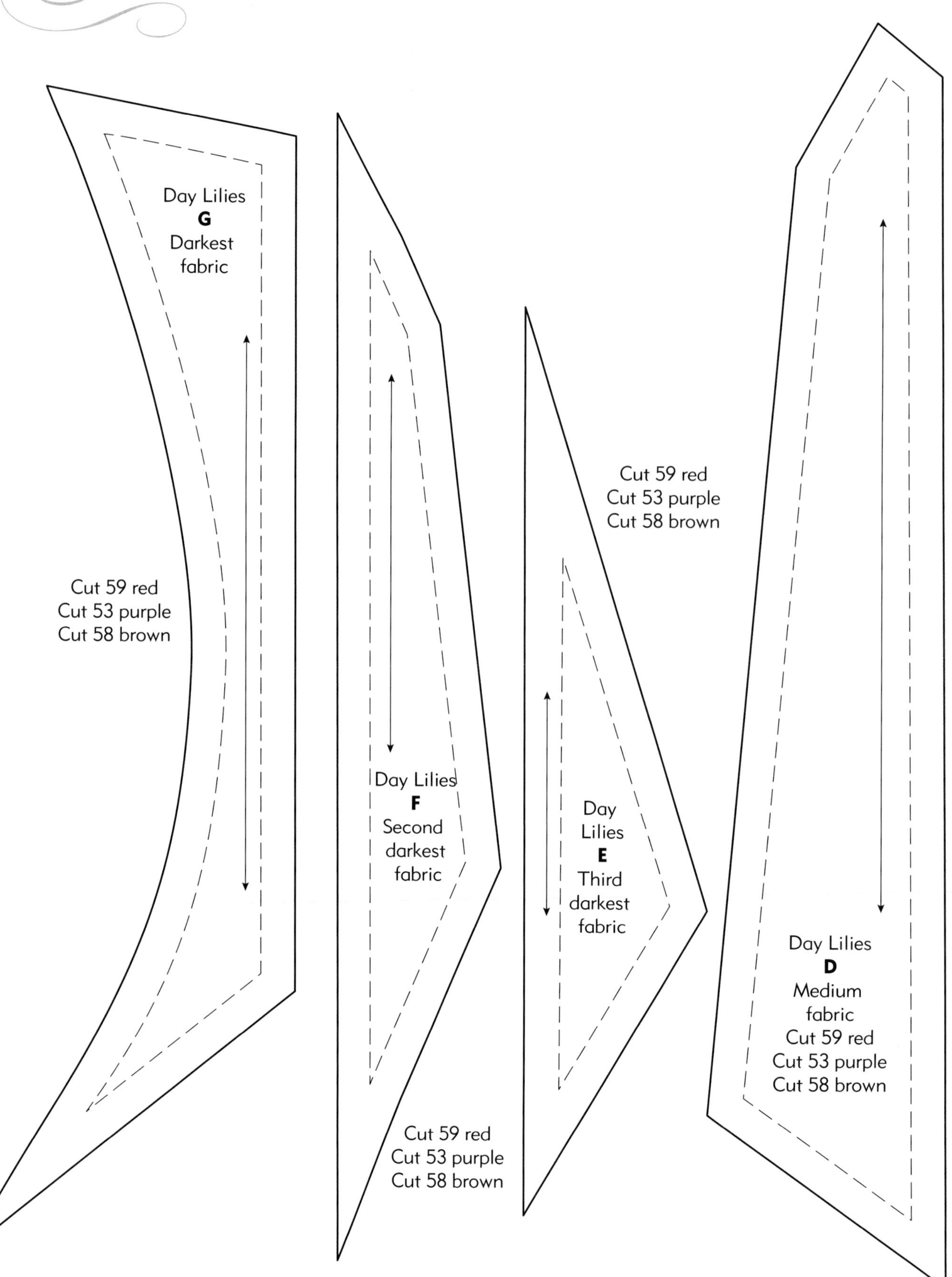
Day Lilies
G
Darkest
fabric
Cut 59 red
Cut 53 purple
Cut 58 brown
Day Lilies
F
Second
darkest
fabric
Cut 59 red
Cut 53 purple
Cut 58 brown
Cut 59 red
Cut 53 purple
Cut 58 brown
Day
Lilies
E
Third
darkest
fabric
Day Lilies
D
Medium
fabric
Cut 59 red
Cut 53 purple
Cut 58 brown

Bibliography

Aunt Martha, *The Quilt Fair Comes to You,* Colonial Patterns, Inc, Kansas City, 1932

Barbara Brackman, *Encyclopedia of Pieced Quilt Patterns,* American Quilter's Society, Paducah, KY, 1992

Cassell's Household Guide to Every Department of Practical Life: Being a Complete Encyclopaedia of Domestic and Social Economy, Volumes I–IV, Cassell & Company, London, circa 1875

S. F. A. Caulfield and Blanche C. Saward, *The Dictionary of Needlework,* A. W. Cowan, London, 1882. Reprinted as *Encyclopedia of Victorian Needlework,* Dover Publications, New York, 1972

Averil Colby, *Patchwork Quilts,* Charles Scribner's Sons, Copenhagen, 1965

Averil Colby, *Quilting,* Charles Scribner's Sons, New York, 1971

Genevieve E. Cummins and Nerylla D. Taunton, *Chatelaines: Utility to Glorious Extravagance,* Antique Collectors' Club, Woodbridge, Surrey (UK), 1994

Henri René d'Allemagne, *Les Accessoires du Costume et du Mobilier,* Schemit Libraire, Paris, 1928

Therese de Dillmont, *Encyclopedia of Needlework,* Dolluf-MIEG & C, Mulhouse, Alsace, 1884. (Reprinted by Running Press, Philadelphia, 1996)

The Englishwoman's Domestic Magazine, O. Beeton, London, 1873 (periodical)

Ruth E. Finley, *Old Patchwork Quilts and the Women Who Made Them,* J. B. Lippincott Company, Philadelphia, 1929

Mavis FitzRandolph and Florence M. Fletcher, *Quilting: Traditional Methods & Design,* Dryad Press Leicester, 1955

Mavis FitzRandolph, *Traditional Patchwork,* B. T. Batsford Ltd, London, 1954

Mavis FitzRandolph, *Traditional Quilting: Its Story and Its Practice,* B. T. Batsford Ltd, London, 1954

Jane Eayre Fryer, *The Mary Frances Sewing Book, Adventures Among the Thimble People,* The John C. Winston Co. Philadelphia, 1913

Godey's Lady's Book, Philadelphia, September 1849 (periodical)

Carrie A. Hall and Rose G. Kretsinger, *The Romance of the Patchwork Quilt in America,* Caxton Printers, Caldwell, Idaho, 1935

Adelaide Hechtlinger, *American Quilts, Quilting, and Patchwork,* Stackpole Books, Harrisburg, PA, 1974

Ann Heynes, *Quilting and Patchwork,* Dryad Handicrafts, Leicester, England, 1925

Rose Wilder Lane, *The Woman's Day Book of American Needlework,* Simon & Schuster, New York, 1963

Myrtle Lundquist, *The Book of a Thousand Thimbles,* Wallace-Homestead Co., Des Moines, Iowa, 1970

Ruby Short McKim, *101 Patchwork Patterns* (1931), reprinted by Dover Publications, New York, 1962. Compiled from patterns produced by McKim Studios, Independence, MO, and related syndicated columns and booklets from the late 1920s and 1930s.

Agnes M. Miall, *Patchwork Old and New,* The Woman's Magazine Office, London, 1937

Sydney Morse, *Household Discoveries,* NY Success Company, New York, 1890

Gay Ann Rogers, *American Silver Thimbles,* Haggerston Press, London, 1989

Beatrice Scott, *The Craft of Quilting,* The Dryad Press, Leicester, England, 1935

Mary Kay Waldvogel and Barbara Brackman, *Patchwork Souvenirs of the 1933 World's Fair,* Rutledge Hill Press, Nashville, TN, 1993

Marie D. Webster, *Quilts: Their Story & How to Make Them,* Tudor Publishing Company, New York, 1915

Estelle Zalkin, *Zalkin's Handbook of Thimbles and Sewing Implements,* Wallace-Homestead Book Company, Radnor, PA, 1988

Index

Accessoires du Costume et du Mobilier, Les, 23
all-over quilting, 160–61
angles, 56, 86–90, 108, 120
Aunt Becky's Finger Protector, 28, 180, 190

Baby Blocks, see Tumbling Blocks
backing, 173, 199
backstitch, 75, 79
ballpoint pen, 20, 55, 57
basting, 25, 117, 174–176
batting, 19, 173–174, 184
bearding, 19
Benartex, 8
Between needle, 25, 65, 73, 183
bias, 58, 85–86, 90, 162, 193
binding, 193, 196–197
bleeding, 12, 16
border,
  adding to quilt, 147–49
  curved, 139, 154
  measuring for, 144–145, 153
  pieced, 144, 150–156, 157
  quilting the, 167–168, 169
  sewing on to quilt, 156–157
  unit, 151, 155, 167
border print, 11, 15, 127, 130–141
  borders made from, 147–149
  shapes made from, 131–139
  to frame shapes, 137–138
  quilting on, 162
  sewing pieces cut from, 140–141
Boxed Blocks, 60, 89, 115, 144, 145, 148, 208–211, 213, 245

Cassell's Household Guide to Every Department of Practical Life, 11, 17, 45, 61, 85
chalk, 20, 57
charm quilt, 48, 96, 110, 114
chatelaine, 7, 22–23
Chatelaines: Utility to Glorious Extravagance, 22
checking template, 122–123, 228, 237, 239, 252, 256
clamshell, 164
Clover, 20, 21, 25
Colonial, 25
color, 8–10
  palette, 11
  shading, 8, 15, 50
  thread, 18
Columbia, 3, 60, 61, 64, 83, 90, 96, 100, 105, 108, 122, 125, 136, 141, 143, 161, 163, 198–199, 226–229, 249–252
Compass Rose, 51, 236–239, 255–256
computer, 40–41, 43–45, 50, 134
Conso Heavy Duty thread, 17, 18, 29
corner unit, 151, 153
Craft of Quilting, The, 44, 187, 198
crocking, 12, 14
cross hatch, 164
curve, *see* piecing curves
cutting, 52
  binding, 196
  diamonds, 59, 136–137
  line, 52

dating, 197
Day Lilies, 32, 50, 51, 96, 108, 115, 120–121, 148, 198, 240–243, 257–258
diamond,
  border-print, 136–137
Dictionary of Needlework, The, 19, 25, 27, 70, 111, 116, 181
Dovo, 21
drafting, 31–47, 168
Drunkard's Path, 118, 219

echo quilting, 164
eight-pointed star, 100–105, 111
eight-pointed star grid, 33, 35, 42–43
Encyclopedia of Needlework, 65, 67, 70, 77
English paper piecing, 116–117
Englishwoman's Domestic Magazine, The, 22

fabric, 7–16
  border-print, *see* border print
  care of, 12
  colorfast, 12
  Indian, 128
  manufacturers, 8, 12, 13
  motifs in, 127, 129
  placement, 49–50
  pre-washing, 12, 13, 16
  shrinkage, 16
Fairfield, 19
feather, 165–166
finger pinning, 72–73
finger position, *see* hand position
finger protector, 28
Flying Geese, 90, 105, 204–207, 244
  unit, 93, 94
Four Patch, 71
frame, 28–29, 177–179, 182

Gibbons, Jill Amos, 212, 213
Godey's Ladies Book, 194
Golden Ratio, 201, 205
Golden Rectangle, 63, 200–203, 244
grain, 52, 58, 173

grid, 32–33
for borders, 150–151
draw a, 36
recognize a, 34–36
Guterman, 18

hand piecing, *see* piecing
hand position, 70, 73
Hemming, 25
hexagon, 34, 127, 130, 134–135
Hobbs, 19
Hoffman California Fabrics, 8
hole punch, 20, 56
hoop, 28–29, 176–177, 183
Household Discoveries, 28

iron, 14, 16, 77, 172

Jinny Beyer Color Palette, 11
Jinny Beyer Perfect Piecer, 20, 56, 86, 108
John James, 25
J & P Coats, 18

knot, 17, 68–69, 76, 183–184

Lane, Tommie Jane, 21, 27
left-handed quilting, 188, 192
light, 182
light table, 172
Lone Star, 111
Love Ring, 115, 118, 160, 163, 218–221, 247

Mariners' Compass, 5, 59, 60, 100, 108, 144, 198, 227, 237
steps in making, 122–125
marker, 20, 54, 55, 57, 172
Mary Frances Sewing Book for Girls, The, 67, 68
masking tape, 20, 161, 172
meander quilting, 164
Metler, 18
mirror, 135
mirror image, 129, 130, 131
in pieced borders, 131, 151–152
miter, 20, 146, 149, 157, 169
Moda, 8
mystery quilt, 3, 5, 198–199, 231

nap, 64
needle, 25, 65, 175, 183
basting, 175
tapestry, 172
threader, 65, 68
threading, 64–65
Nicholas, Carole, 160, 218, 219
Novara, Paola, 230, 231

octagon, 35, 36
border-print, 134–135
Old Patchwork Quilts and the Women Who Made Them,, 31, 42, 181
Olde World Star, 158, 163
Olfa Touch Knife, 20
101 Patchwork Patterns, 53, 58, 59, 61, 96, 143, 156, 170, 176, 183, 190
outline quilting, 161

Palette collection by RJR Fabrics, 10
paper piecing, *see* English paper piecing
Patchwork Old and New, 53, 57, 70, 90, 159, 165
Patchwork Quilts
pattern,
Boxed Blocks, 208–211
Columbia, 226–229
Compass Rose, 236–239
Day Lilies, 240–243
drafting, *see* drafting
Flying Geese, 204–207
Golden Rectangle, 200–203
Love Ring, 218–221
Shamrock, 212–217
Starflower, 230–235
Triple Play, 222–225
piecing,
basics, 63–83
beginning, 3
border prints, 140–141
class, 3, 198–199
curves, 107, 115, 118–119, 120
four pieces with right angles, 77–80
eight points, 100–105, 122
pairs of three-point units, 94–95
rows of diamonds, 88–90
rows of triangles, 92
six points, 96–100, 120
straight line, 120, 122
three-point unit to another piece, 92–94
three points, 90–92, 122
two pieces, 71–77
two stitched pieces to a third piece, 81–82
unmatched angles, 86–89
pin, 25
pinning, 72
Portable Palette, 10
portable piecing kit, 29
practice template, 81, 244
press, *see* iron

quilt back fabric, 173
Quilt Fair Comes to You, The, 171, 193
quilt in-the-ditch, 61, 161

Quilter's Dream Cotton, 19
Quilting, 167, 188
Quilting and Patchwork, 160, 168, 177
quilting design, 159–164
background, 164
for borders, 166–167
drafting the, 165–168
following fabric design, 162
geometric, 163
marking, 168
meander, 164
in unpieced sections of quilt, 163
quilting spoon, 28, 190–191
quilting stitch, 182–193
beginning, 183–184
direction, 185, 192–93
ending, 188–189
uneven, 189
Quilting: Traditional Methods and Design, 184, 192
Quilts: Their Story and How to Make Them, 7, 8, 107, 115, 157, 186

Ray of Light, 164
RJR Fabrics, 8, 10, 11, 12
Romance of the Patchwork Quilt in America, The, 49, 54, 125, 170–171
Ropp, Gayle, 191
Roses, 62
rotary cutter, 20, 52, 53
Rovner, Tanis, 208, 209
ruler, 20
running stitch, 63, 70, 71–77

Sanford Verithin pencil, 20
saucer quilting, 160
scissors, 7, 21, 52
seam, 60
reinforcing, 146
set by pressing, 172
set-in, 61
seam allowance,
adding on computer, 54
marking, 56, 57
sewing through, 79, 82
stitching to end of, 108
selvage, 59
setting in, 61, 97, 107, 120
consecutive pieces, 114, 121
single pieces, 108–110
sewing bird, 66–67
sewing line, 52, 53, 72
Shamrock, 60, 61, 89, 96, 115, 137, 141, 144, 148, 212-217, 246
shrinkage, 16
signing, 197
sitting position, 182
six-pointed star, 96, 97, 114,
Snow Birds, 11
Social History of Flatbush, The, 7
spoon quilting, 28, 190–91
square, 34, 132–134, 138
Starflower, 3, 32, 64, 83, 100, 105, 108, 115, 125, 141, 144, 198, 230–235, 254 stash, 7, 10, 11, 147
Stearns and Foster, 19, 29, 177
stippling, 164
stitch, *see* running stitch *or* quilting stitch
stitch in the ditch, 61, 161
Sunflower, 129
supplies, 17–29

template (s), 244–258
checking, 122–123, 228, 237, 239, 251, 252, 256
making, 51–53
marking around, 57
material, 19, 51
plastic, 19
practice, 81, 244
tension, 63, 72–73, 77, 164, 189
tessellation, 241
thimble, 7, 21, 26–27, 190
cage, 21, 29
finger, 74
thread, 17
basting, 117, 175, 177
color, 18
cutter, 21
for hand piecing, 17
for hand quilting, 18
length of, 183
nap of, 64
untwisting, 76
ticking, 178
TJ's Quick Quilter, 28, 191
triangle, 92
border-print, 134–135
framing with border print, 138
Triple Play, 136, 144, 145, 147, 148, 162, 222–225, 248
Tumbling Blocks, 60, 108, 114–115, 143, 223

value placement, 49, 114

wadding, *see* batting
whip stitch, 116, 117
Windows, vi, 1, 4, 5, 77, 96, 108, 115, 139–140, 143, 145, 161, 162
Woman's Day Book of American Needlework, The, 1
World in Their Hands, 30, 108
wreath, 166

YLI, 18